T0140319

Variable Domain-specific Software Languages with DjDSL

Stefan Sobernig

Variable Domain-specific Software Languages with DjDSL

Design and Implementation

Springer

Stefan Sobernig
Institute for Information Systems and New Media
Vienna University of Economics and Business
Vienna, Austria

ISBN 978-3-030-42154-0   ISBN 978-3-030-42152-6   (eBook)
https://doi.org/10.1007/978-3-030-42152-6

This Springer imprint is published by the registered company Springer Nature Switzerland AG.
The registered company address is: Gewerbestrasse 11, 6330 Cham, Switzerland

Preface

In software development, ideas of incorporating newcomers to programming as well as business and industry experts without software-development background into analyzing, designing, implementing, deploying, and operating software systems have been gaining importance rapidly. This is because software development is more and more about gluing together software from existing code artifacts including, for better or worse, open-source application frameworks while adequately trained developer workforce is scarce [14]. An inclusive and participatory software development must go beyond mere interactions via a graphical user interface (GUI) and via spreadsheet programming [17].

Language-oriented software development advocates the idea that architecting, designing, and implementing a software system should be driven by developing software languages [30]. Key to these ideas are special-purpose software languages: *domain-specific software languages* (DSL). For long, DSL have been provided as an alternative programming interface targeting developers in the application domain wrapped around application frameworks to ease framework integration [7, 24]. In the same way, a DSL empowers non-developer experts in interacting with a domain-specific software system. Take as an example of such a software system a scheduling system in the services domain of energy trading [26]. Other examples from a manufacturing domain are device simulators for automobile testbeds and sensor arrays [28].

A DSL-based approach aims at developing the entire software system around a DSL. At the same time, the objective is to empower domain experts (i.e., energy traders, test engineers) as *co*-developers of their supporting software systems (i.e., scheduling system, device simulator). This is achieved by providing expressive means and tailored tooling to specify, to adapt, and to configure their software systems. To pick up the above examples: By providing a DSL, energy traders are enabled to implement new types of trading reports or trading messages autonomously, that is, without the need for in-house or external software developers. Device testers can create variants of a device simulator on their own. In addition, testers can structure a suite of test cases on a given device in previously unforeseen ways.

As a software language, a DSL is based on a well-defined but domain-specific vocabulary in addition to well-defined notations (textual, graphical, and beyond), semantics, and language-specific tooling. Expectations towards DSL compare with those on general-purpose software languages (GPL) such as Java or C# and their industry-grade tooling (integrated development environments, IDE). DSL and DSL-based tooling (e.g., editors) must not only be robust but also as sophisticated as development environments for GPL. At the same time, they must be highly specialized for a given task and domain of application. This double objective presents a considerable challenge to DSL development and its adoption [22].

A DSL itself is implemented using a *DSL development system* [6]. A DSL development system can be provided by a tool spectrum ranging from extensible general-purpose software languages as DSL host languages to dedicated language workbenches. A DSL is developed using processes and techniques of domain engineering, including domain analysis, domain modeling (including semi-formal and formal modeling techniques), and domain implementation. This is to guarantee that a DSL is realized according to the stakeholders' requirements. Hence, a DSL represents a complex software system in its own right [2, 6].

As a consequence, developing a DSL represents a heavy upfront investment. A DSL adds to the overall costs of the overarching software development project [10, 31]. This is because a DSL requires a thorough and systematic analysis of the application domain [33]. Moreover, the resulting DSL design and implementation as a software language plus tooling has a considerable complexity. To realize benefits of a DSL and its tooling over time, its reuse within the original application domain and for similar application domains becomes necessary. Research has found a considerable potential for reuse. For example, many engineering domains require variants of state machines as an abstraction [13, 34]. A recent review [27] identified groups of multiple DSL (10+) having been developed for business or technical domains with a clear overlap (e.g., for modeling service-oriented architectures and web services). Even within the boundaries of a single business organization, one finds multiple DSL-based solutions targeting one and the same domain [28].

Despite such reuse potential at different scales, DSL development presents many technical barriers to reuse. These barriers add to more general inhibitors of technology reuse within and between organizations (e.g., ownership). To begin with, a DSL is developed over multiple development phases and involves multiple interconnected definition artifacts [29]. Examples include abstract syntax definitions, concrete-syntax definitions, structural and behavioural context conditions, implementation, test cases, and documentation. At the same time, acceptance and quality-in-use of a DSL are determined by its tailored tooling (e.g., editors, debuggers, and code generators). The more tailored a DSL-based tool, the better its uptake by practitioners in the one targeted domain but the less its reusability for others [22].

Therefore, methods, techniques, and tools to develop a *DSL for reuse* systematically—as a DSL family—have attracted much attention. The methods, techniques, and tools are borrowed from *software product line engineering* [1] and combined with those of *software language engineering* [11]. Software product line engineering is inspired by the notion of mass customization based on composite products using product lines in business and manufacturing.[1] The ambition is to provide technical solutions to the following problems:

> **Problem Statements**
> *How can a DSL be developed in a way that fosters its reuse and, at the same time, that maintains the consistency of the various design and development artifacts? How can this be achieved without (a) incurring excessive pre-planning or (b) without requiring ad hoc intervention by specifically skilled software developers?*

A DSL, or DSL family more precisely, matching these expectations is said to have the *quality attribute of variability*, that is, the ability to derive different variants of a DSL systematically from a common set of implementation and configuration assets.

The main contributions documented in this book are the conceptual foundations, the design, and the implementation of the language-based DSL development system DjDSL. DjDSL facilitates design-decision making on and implementation of reusable DSL and DSL product lines. DjDSL embodies the state of the art in language-based and composition-based DSL development. DjDSL complements existing multi-DSL development approaches (e.g., Melange, MontiCore, Neverlang/ AiDE) by contributing the following:

- DjDSL as a DSL development system allows a DSL developer to develop families of different DSL types (internal, external, and mixed).
- DjDSL provides for a variable design and implementation of a DSL family across the different definition artifacts in an integrated manner (*collaboration-based designs*): abstract syntax, context conditions, and concrete syntaxes.
- DSL variability can be represented and analyzed as a first-class development artifact, by using the variability modeling language of DjDSL.
- Variable language models can be developed in a platform-independent manner (using DjDSL's UML extensions) or a platform-specific manner (using DjDSL directly).
- DjDSL supports different kinds of DSL composition for different scopes (i.e., artifact types). The supported composition kinds include, among others, DSL extension and DSL unification. These can be applied for the scopes of abstract syntax, with or without context conditions, with or without concrete syntaxes.

---

[1] A general background on the sources of inspiration for software product line engineering (e.g., assembly lines, automotive platforms) is provided by Czarnecki and Eisenecker [3] and by Apel et al. [1].

To realize a *multi-DSL* development system, DjDSL makes a number of original technical contributions regarding the composability of DSL development artifacts. As for language models, DjDSL allows a DSL developer to structure an abstract syntax definition into composable collaborations. A collaboration can directly represent optional features of a language-model family. Under composition, DjDSL guarantees important properties, for example, a collaboration-aware method-resolution order. DjDSL introduces novel techniques of contract composition to render context conditions composable (e.g., trimming). At the level of variable textual syntaxes, DjDSL offers a novel infrastructure for composing grammars. Most notably, grammar composition in DjDSL extends to support object grammars [32]. External-syntax definition and processing in DjDSL is based on an extended variant of parsing expression grammars (PEG): *object parsing-expression grammars* (OPEG).

This book concentrates, as its title indicates, on my work at the crossroads between software language engineering, model-driven software engineering, and feature-oriented software engineering. The book was prepared as part of my long-term habilitation project on designing and on implementing *variable* domain-specific software languages. This research effort was, however, not limited to the topics and to the content now presented in this book. Regarding domain-specific languages (DSL) and software language engineering, I have been active in empirical research on the external quality attributes of DSL-based software systems. In this context, over the last 2 years, I have been overseeing and contributing to industry projects with emphasis on usability and quality-in-use of DSL and DSL-based tooling (HybriDLUX, DLUX). As for software architecture, I work on architectural design decisions and reusable design rationale for UML-based DSL. As for variability and feature-oriented software development, I am involved in research on feature-oriented software composition, static analyses of feature-oriented programs, and the search-based analysis of variability models. Clearly, many of these works helped shape the contributions of this book.

Book Audience and Assumed Background

The book aims at readers interested in language-oriented as well as model-driven software development, in their roles as software-engineering researchers and software developers alike. For these readers, the book is primarily designed as an instructional text on how to design and to develop DSL families (a.k.a. DSL product lines) using the DSL development system DjDSL. In doing so, the book also serves those that aim at understanding, in more general, the systematic procedures, fundamental design decisions, and diverse implementation choices for variable DSL. Packed with textbook-level examples on standard problems for every elaborated concept, the book offers complementary materials such as tutorials for master's- and doctorate-level courses in Computer Science and Software Engineering with focus on software language engineering.

Readers should be familiar with the basics of object-oriented modeling (UML, MOF, Ecore) and programming (Java). The object-oriented programming language Next Scripting Language (NX), an extension to the Tool Command Language (Tcl), dominates the book, while mainstream software languages (Java, C, grammar languages) are additionally used for illustration. Therefore, readers may also need to consult background resources on Tcl [15]. An understanding of software-engineering basics (architecture, design, implementation, testing) and software patterns (e.g., the Gang-of-Four patterns [8]) is required.

Ideally, readers should have previously obtained a basic understanding of and experience in software language engineering as covered by Lämmel [11] and software product lines as covered by Apel et al. [1].

Book Overview

Chapter 1: DSL as Variable Software   The notion of a domain-specific language as variable software is presented in greater detail. In particular, this chapter introduces the reader to the idea of software product line engineering for DSL-based software systems (*DSL product lines*).

Chapter 2: Variability Support in DSL Development   This chapter sheds light on the different interrelated dimensions of DSL variability: variable development processes, variable design-decision, and variability implementation techniques for DSL. The three subsequent chapters are devoted to the key conceptual and technical contributions of this book: DjDSL.

Chapter 3: Variable Language Models   The reader is introduced to designing and to implementing the abstract syntax of a DSL in a variable manner (collaboration-based designs).

Chapter 4: Variable Context Conditions   The means to refine an abstract syntax (language model) by using composable context conditions (invariants) are provided.

Chapter 5: Variable Textual Syntaxes   Solutions to implement variable textual syntaxes for different DSL types (internal and external) are elaborated on. The theme common to all three chapters on DjDSL is to demonstrate the applicability of DjDSL to different types of DSL composition (e.g., extension and unification; [33]).

Chapter 6: A Story of a DSL Family   A story is told about developing a mixed DSL in a stepwise manner. The story cuts across the previous chapters. This is to exercise the previously introduced but complementing techniques (variable language models, variable context conditions, and variable textual syntaxes) on an advanced example of developing a DSL family.

On Supplemental Materials

All development and auxiliary artifacts (i.e., models, source code, build scripts, tutorials) are available from the author's public repository [23]. The code listings in this book are extracted from *executable* how-tos and tutorials maintained in this repository. All code by the author reproduced in this book is licensed under the MIT license, copyright held by Stefan Sobernig (2018–2020). When appropriate, the exact location of a how-to or tutorial in the repository is given in the text as a navigable link.

On Notation

The main body of the text does not feature peculiar uses of notation. Names of methods, techniques, and tools are written as-is, for example. There are two minor exceptions: Words in small caps indicate names of software patterns such as STRATEGY [8]. This corresponds to the notational convention as established in the pattern community. Words typeset using a monotype font, such as Class, refer to keywords or entities defined in diagrams, models, or source code which are then referenced from within the main narrative.

The diagrammatic notation used for UML diagrams at all levels (architecture, design, implementation) defaults to the one of UML 2.5 [20] and of MOF 2.5 [19], respectively. The diagrams and underlying models were created using Papyrus 3.3 (Eclipse Modeling Tools 4.7.3a, Oxygen 3a) and MagicDraw 18.5. Model-level constraint expressions are implemented using the Object Constraint Language (OCL; [18]). More precisely, the implementation uses the Eclipse OCL (i.e., its CompleteOCL variant) as a reference implementation of OMG OCL 2.4.

The diagrammatic notation to visualize feature models is the Czarnecki–Eisenecker notation, as defined and documented in Czarnecki and Eisenecker [3, Chapter 4].

If not indicated otherwise, the source-code listings exhibit code fragments in the syntax of the Tool Command Language (Tcl; [15, 21]) and the Next Scripting Language (NX; [16, 25]), or derivatives therefrom.

On Running Examples

Throughout the book, a number of running application examples[2] of variable DSL are provided and referred to. The aim was to select examples that clearly

---

[2]Note that the term "case study" is consciously avoided. This is because, despite the selected examples going beyond toy examples, they do not qualify as case studies by any definition.

demonstrate the challenges of developing variable DSL. The second objective was to adopt examples that represent—in one—*typical* examples from the perspective of readers having a background in research on software composition or software language engineering. The selected examples are:

- *Graph-Product Line* (GraphPL): Lopez-Herrejon and Batory [12] defined a library for graph representation and graph analysis with nontrivial variability as a standard problem for product-line and software-composition techniques. Graphs invite the use of DSL, e.g., for defining graph structures or for defining transformations on graphs.
- *State-Machine Definition Language* (SMDL): Both need and uses of domain-specific variants of state-machine modeling languages are omnipresent in research and practise. There are documented attempts to capture them as DSL families [4, 34]. Fowler [7] uses a state-machine example (Miss Grant's Controller) to contrast internal and external DSL techniques.
- *Expression Language* (a.k.a. Expression Product Line, EPL): This is the ubiquitous example of a small but immediately useful software language for defining and for evaluating expressions of all sorts. This small language family is ideal as a running example because it has already been used to highlight common software-composition problems (e.g., abstraction mismatches under separation and composition of concerns).

Chapter 6 presents an application example of DjDSL beyond that of a running example only. This application example (Pongo) has already served as a standard problem on advanced model-driven software development, in particular on co-evolution of model transformations [9].

Vienna, Austria   Stefan Sobernig
January 2020

References

1. Apel S, Batory D, Kästner C, Saake G (2013) Feature-oriented software product lines, 1st edn. Springer, Berlin. https://doi.org/10.1007/978-3-642-37521-7
2. Butting A, Eikermann R, Kautz O, Rumpe B, Wortmann A (2018) Controlled and extensible variability of concrete and abstract syntax with independent language features. In: Proceedings of the 12th International Workshop on Variability Modelling of Software-Intensive Systems (VAMOS'18). ACM, New York, pp 75–82. https://doi.org/10.1145/3168365.3168368
3. Czarnecki K, Eisenecker UW (2000) Generative programming — Methods, Tools, and Applications, 6th edn. Addison-Wesley, Boston
4. Degueule T, Combemale B, Blouin A, Barais O, Jézéquel JM (2015) Melange; a meta-language for modular and reusable development of DSLs. In: Proceedings of the 2015 ACM SIGPLAN International Conference on Software Language engineering (SLE'15). ACM, New York, pp 25–36. https://doi.org/10.1145/2814251.2814252

5. Erdweg S, Giarrusso PG, Rendel T (2012) Language composition untangled. In: Proceedings of the Twelfth Workshop on Language Descriptions, Tools, and Applications (LDTA'12). ACM, New York, pp 7:1–7:8. https://doi.org/10.1145/2427048.2427055
6. Erdweg S, van der Storm T, Völter M, Tratt L, Bosman R, Cook WR, Gerritsen A, Hulshout A, Kelly S, Loh A, Konat G, Molina PJ, Palatnik M, Pohjonen R, Schindler E, Schindler K, Solmi R, Vergu V, Visser E, van der Vlist K, Wachsmuth G, van der Woning J (2015) Evaluating and comparing language workbenches: existing results and benchmarks for the future. Comput Lang Syst Struct **44**(Part A), 24–47. https://doi.org/10.1016/j.cl.2015.08.007
7. Fowler M (2010) Domain specific languages, 1st edn. Addison-Wesley, Boston
8. Gamma E, Helm R, Johnson RE, Vlissides J (1995) Design Patterns - Elements of Reusable Object-Oriented Software. Addison Wesley Professional Computing Series. Addison-Wesley, Boston
9. Hoisl B, Sobernig S (2015) Towards benchmarking evolution support in model-to-text transformation systems. In: Proceedings of the 4th Workshop on the Analysis of Model Transformations (AMT@MoDELS 2015), CEUR-WS.org, CEUR Workshop Proceedings, vol 1500, pp 16–25. http://ceur-ws.org/Vol-1500/paper3.pdf
10. Krueger CW (1992) Software reuse. ACM Comput Surv 24(2):131–183. https://doi.org/10.1145/130844.130856
11. Lämmel R (2018) Software languages: Syntax, Semantics, and Metaprogramming, 1st edn. Springer, Berlin. https://doi.org/10.1007/978-3-319-90800-7
12. Lopez-Herrejon RE, Batory DS (2001) A standard problem for evaluating product-line methodologies. In: Proceedings of the 3rd International Conference on Generative and Component-based Software Engineering (GPCE'01). Springer, Berlin, pp 10–24
13. Méndez-Acuña D, Galindo JA, Combemale B, Blouin A, Baudry B (2017) Reverse engineering language product lines from existing DSL variants. J Syst Softw 133:145–158. https://doi.org/10.1016/j.jss.2017.05.042
14. Miller H (2019) The times they are a-changin'. https://speakerdeck.com/heathermiller/the-times-they-are-a-changin, talk given at the Scale By the Bay 2019 Conference. Accessed 4, Dec 2019
15. Nadkarni AP (2017) The Tcl programming language: A comprehensive guide. CreateSpace Independent Publishing Platform
16. Neumann G, Sobernig S (2009) XOTcl 2.0 – A ten-year retrospective and outlook. In: Flynt C, Fox R (eds) Proceedings of the Sixteenth Annual Tcl/Tk Conference. Tcl Association Publications, Portland, pp 179–204. http://nm.wu-wien.ac.at/research/publications/b806.pdf
17. Neumann G, Sobernig S, Aram M (2014) Evolutionary business information systems: Perspectives and challenges of an emerging class of information systems. Bus Inf Syst Eng 6(1):33–38. https://doi.org/10.1007/s12599-013-0305-1
18. Object Management Group (2014) Object Constraint Language specification, formal/14-02-03. http://www.omg.org/spec/OCL/2.4/
19. Object Management Group (2016) OMG Meta Object Facility (MOF) core specification. http://www.omg.org/spec/MOF, version 2.5.1, formal/16-11-01
20. Object Management Group (2017) OMG Unified Modeling Language (UML). http://www.omg.org/spec/UML, version 2.5.1, formal/17-12-05
21. Ousterhout JK, Jones K (2009) Tcl and the Tk toolkit, 2nd edn. Addison-Wesley, Boston
22. Selic B (2012) What will it take? A view on adoption of model-based methods in practice. Softw Syst Model 11(4):513–526. https://doi.org/10.1007/s10270-012-0261-0
23. Sobernig S (2019) DjDSL. https://github.com/mrcalvin/djdsl/
24. Sobernig S, Gaubatz P, Strembeck M, Zdun U (2011) Comparing complexity of API designs: An exploratory experiment on DSL-based framework integration. In: Proceedings of the 10th International Conference on Generative Programming and Component Engineering (GPCE'11). ACM, New York, pp 157–166. https://doi.org/10.1145/2047862.2047890

25. Sobernig S, Neumann G, Adelsberger S (2012) Supporting multiple feature binding strategies in NX. In: Proceedings of the 4th International Workshop on Feature-Oriented Software Development (FOSD'12). ACM, New York, pp 45–53. https://doi.org/10.1145/2377816.2377823

26. Sobernig S, Strembeck M, Beck A (2013) Developing a domain-specific language for scheduling in the European energy sector. In: Proceedings of the 6th International Language on Software Language Engineering (SLE'13). Lecture Notes in Computer Science, vol 8225. Springer, Berlin, pp 19–35. https://doi.org/10.1007/978-3-319-02654-1_2

27. Sobernig S, Hoisl B, Strembeck M (2016) Extracting reusable design decisions for UML-based domain-specific languages: A multi-method study. J Syst Softw **113**, 140–172. https://doi.org/10.1016/j.jss.2015.11.037

28. Stieglbauer G, Burghard C, Sobernig S, Korosec R (2018) A daily dose of DSL - MDE micro injections in practice. In: Proceedings of the 6th international conference on model-driven engineering and software development (MODELSWARD'18), SciTePress, pp 642–651. https://doi.org/10.5220/0006754406420651

29. Strembeck M, Zdun U (2009) An approach for the systematic development of domain-specific languages. Softw. Pract. Exp. 39(15):1253–1292

30. Şutîi AM, van den Brand M, Verhoeff T (2017) Exploration of modularity and reusability of domain-specific languages: An expression DSL in MetaMod. Comput Lang Syst Struct. https://doi.org/10.1016/j.cl.2017.07.004

31. Tambe S, White J, Gray J, Hill JH, Gokhale AS, Schmidt DC (2009) Improving domain-specific language reuse with software product line techniques. IEEE Softw 26:47–53. https://doi.org/10.1109/MS.2009.95

32. van der Storm T, Cook WR, Loh A (2014) The design and implementation of object grammars. Sci Comput Program 96:460–487. https://doi.org/10.1016/j.scico.2014.02.023

33. van Deursen A, Klint P (2002) Domain-specific language design requires feature descriptions. J Comput Inf Technol 10(1):1–17

34. Wille D, Schulze S, Schaefer I (2016) Variability mining of state charts. In: Proceedings of the 7th International Workshop on Feature-oriented Software Development (FOSD'16). ACM, New York, pp 63–73. https://doi.org/10.1145/3001867.3001875

Acknowledgments

Obviously, no long-term effort of this kind takes place in a vacuum. Most importantly, I am much indebted to my family, especially: my wife, Marlis, kept me loved; my daughter, Teresa, kept me cheerful; my son, Sebastian, kept me smiling; my brother, Georg, backed me up; my mother, Susi, hosted us; Martina and Joe, my parents-in-law, let us rest; Alois, my father, kept encouraging me.

Many people gave inspiration, advise, aid, and encouragement. Some people deserve, however, more than general mention: Gustaf Neumann gave me the room and his support to work on my habilitation project at the Institute for Information Systems and New Media, WU Vienna. Gustaf Neumann maintains much of the "languageware" (NSF/NX) allowing for the contributions in this book. He is also coauthor on a paper that forms the basis for Chap. 3. The earlier works on DSL development by Mark Strembeck and Uwe Zdun inspired many contributions in this book. Noteworthy are their ideas on DSL design decisions and Uwe's DSL toolkit Frag. Joint work with Mark Strembeck and Bernhard Hoisl on reusable design decisions for UML-based DSL entered Chap. 2. Moreover, I would like to thank Sven Apel whose contributions to feature orientation have influenced this work.

Vienna, Austria   Stefan Sobernig
January 2020

Contents

Acronyms

ADSL   Architecture domain-specific language
ANTLR   Another Tool for Language Recognition
API   Application programming interface
AST   Abstract syntax tree
BCEL   Boolean Comparison and Expression Language
BDD   Binary decision diagram
CFG   Context-free grammar
CNF   Conjunctive normal form
CP   Constraint programming
CRUD   Create, read, update, and delete
CSP   Constraint satisfaction problem
DAG   Directed acyclic graph
DNF   Disjunctive normal form
DR   Design rationale
DSL   Domain-specific (software) language
DSML   Domain-specific modeling language
E/BNF   Extended/Backus Naur Form
EMF   Eclipse Modeling Framework
E/MOF   Essential/Meta Object Facility
EPL   Expression Product Line
FFD   Free Feature Diagrams
FOP   Feature-oriented programming
GLL   Generalized left-to-right, leftmost
GLR   Generalized left-to-right, rightmost
GMF   Graphical Modeling Framework
GPL   General-purpose (software) language
GraphPL Graph-Product Line
GUI   Graphical user interface
IDE   Integrated development environment
INF   If-then-else normal form
JML   Java Modeling Language

LALR   Lookahead left-to-right, rightmost
LEA   Literal, Expression, Addition
LHS   Left-hand side
LL   Left-to-right, leftmost
LOP   Language-oriented programming
LR   Left-to-right, rightmost
MRO   Message-resolution order
MTD   Model-transformation diagram
NX   Next Scripting Language
OCL   Object Constraint Language
OMG   Object Management Group
ONM   Object-to-NoSQL mapper
OOP   Object-oriented programming
OPEG   Object parsing-expression grammar
PEG   Parsing expression grammar
QOC   Questions-Options-Criteria
RAC   Runtime assertion checking
RHS   Right-hand side
SAT   Satisfiability
SDF   Syntax Definition Formalism
SMDL   State-Machine Definition Language
Tcl   Tool Command Language
UML   Unified Modeling Language
VFD   Varied Feature Diagrams

Chapter 1
DSL as Variable Software

A software system is said to be *variable* when, first, there are stakeholders expressing the requirement to provide and to maintain different variants of a software system. Variants may be required over time or at a given point in time, in parallel. This has also been referred to as multi-system software development or software diversity [62].[1] Second, a software system and its implementation are deemed variable when they have the ability to derive different variants from a common set of implementation artifacts to meet the overall requirement on variability [1, p. 48]. Required and implemented variability of a software system can be a genuinely sought quality attribute of a software system [15] and, if realized, they contribute to reaching the overall goal of software reuse [39] in a systematic and efficient manner.

By *systematic*, approaches to variable software development refer to managing explicitly variability at all stages of a software system's life cycle: from requirements engineering to architecting, designing, implementing, testing, analyzing, and to deploying the variants of a software system.

By *efficient*, relevant approaches aim at facilitating systematic variation of a software system by building on proven development knowledge and development practice. This involves reuse of design and implementation rationale (reusable design decisions) as well as support of the automation of development tasks including embodiment in dedicated development tools.

Fostering reuse of domain-specific languages (DSL) and their tooling by rendering them variable is the underlying theme of this writing. This has been marked as general objective before [71]. Development of variable software systems, however, gives rise to particular challenges in all phases of a project, including operation, maintenance, and evolution [62]. These challenges must be tackled to render variable software development systematic and efficient.

---

[1]In Sect. 1.2, common drivers towards the requirement of a variable DSL are identified: domain interlock, language kernels, DSL-based modernization, and DSL evolution.

© Springer Nature Switzerland AG 2020
S. Sobernig, *Variable Domain-specific Software Languages with DjDSL*,
https://doi.org/10.1007/978-3-030-42152-6_1

1.1   Domain-Specific Languages

A domain-specific software language (DSL) is a software language that is tailored for describing, prescribing, or implementing software systems in a selected domain [25, 38, 74]. As a software language, a DSL comprises an abstract syntax, one or more concrete syntaxes, structural and behavioural context conditions, semantics definitions, and behavioral definitions based on a target platform. The concrete syntax refers to the well-defined representation of a DSL script (model) as text or visual. The abstract syntax means a well-defined representation of a DSL script (model) that abstracts from representation details as text or visual. This is to better serve a certain processing or tooling step on the DSL script (model). Behavioral definitions aim at a DSL's execution engine and other types of enactment (e.g., transformation, visualization, or analysis for a DSL for structural modeling; [70, 74]).

Semantics
Semantics are defined as the meaning (interpretation) of a DSL's syntax elements and their relationships in its domain of application [43]. A semantics definition (whether formal or informal, processable or opaque) contains a mapping of syntactic elements to elements of a semantic domain. The semantic domain itself is represented using natural or formal languages accepted among the practitioners of the domain [18]. What is commonly referred to as structural (or, static) semantics and behavioral (or, dynamic) semantics in modelware approaches, and in model-driven software development in general, is referred here as context conditions on structure and behaviour. This is to avoid any confusion with semantics and their definition (especially in Chap. 4).

These building blocks are manifest in terms of their corresponding development artifacts: e.g., syntax and semantics definitions, program or model transformations, interpreters. A *domain* is an area of practitioners' knowledge about solving certain types of technical or non-technical problems. A domain includes the following (see, e.g., [6, p. 34] and [17, p. 4]):

- a set of concepts and terminology understood by the practitioners to express themselves about the problems tackled (a.k.a. *problem domain*)
- the know-how to comprehend, to develop, to maintain, and to operate software systems in this area (a.k.a. *solution domain*)

A key characteristic of a DSL is that it contains an abstract syntax (including context conditions) and semantics (i.a., semantic mappings) defined at the level of the concepts and their relationships of the problem domain; as opposed to those of the solution domain. This is to hide details that are not relevant to solving the problems and tasks forming a domain (e.g., implementation-level concepts of the software system) and to attract non-developer practitioners as an audience [17, p. 11]. To the extent a DSL embodies concepts and terminology at the level of the problem domain in terms of its abstract and concrete syntax, the DSL becomes part of its targeted domain [51].[2] Depending on whether a DSL is used by the practitioners being software developers or non-developers to comprehend, to build, to maintain, and to operate software systems in the domain, DSL are sometimes labeled technical and non-technical DSL, respectively [74, p. 26]. Technical DSL can be developed for self-use by developers, for example, to automate tasks of analysis, testing, documentation, or deployment of a software system (e.g., utility DSL [74, Section 2.7.1]). Non-technical DSL are capable of empowering non-developer practitioners as *end-user developers* by allowing them to contribute variable and unanticipated parts of a software system via a DSL, including but not limited to tests, automation, orchestration, and monitoring [36, 55].

DSL have been considered key elements (i.e., methodical devices and work artifacts alike) in software-engineering methodologies such as generative software development, model-driven software development, and software product line engineering (see, e.g., [6, 63, 69]).

1.1.1   Modelware and Grammarware

There is a great variety of design and implementation techniques for DSL available. Two families of DSL design and implementation techniques are typically discriminated from each other as archetypes, in particular, for external DSL [61, 76]: grammarware and modelware. In grammarware, a DSL's concrete syntax is defined first, for example, using a well-defined grammar language (e.g., an E/BNF realization, SDF, or ANTLR), and its abstract syntax along with it as a kind of syntax tree or a derivative therefrom. Alternative definition devices are parser combinators and recognition systems. Grammarware DSL are DSL providing primarily textual notations for modeling, i.e., models are represented as structured text derivable from a grammar or detectable by a recognition system. The grammar or recognition definition also drives the development of the DSL tooling (e.g., parsers, editors and editor services, program and model transformations). In modelware, a DSL's abstract syntax is typically defined first, using a (semi-) formal, commonly graphical model ("metamodel") expressed in a well-defined modeling language (e.g., MOF, UML, Ecore). Based on this abstract syntax model, other DSL artifacts are authored (e.g., concrete-syntax definition, model transformations). Modelware DSL have historically used graphical (i.e., diagrammatic) notations for models, primarily as means of domain-specific modeling (see below). Modelware, traditionally, puts a strong emphasis on generic tooling services built around the abstract syntax models that can be reused and tailored to build DSL-specific development tools (e.g., model validation, model diffing, and model persistence, off-the-shelf code generation).

---

[2] As a consequence, DSL are often differentiated in terms of the type of domain they are part of and tailored for: application domains vs. modeling domains vs. execution domains [51]. Alternatively, the predominant business or software-development activity captured by a domain is used to label a DSL. Examples include describing business processes and organizational roles *or* software-architecture description, software testing, software analysis [74, Section 2.7].

The distinction between grammarware and modelware, however, presents mostly a false dichotomy in that DSL development at the state of the art combines properties, methods, techniques, and tooling of both archetypes [9, 38]. Prominent examples are providing a grammar-based concrete syntax to an existing model-based abstract syntax (e.g., as in Xtext); or vice versa. A model-based abstract syntax is defined along with a grammar. Object grammars [72] and the DSL development system presented here, DjDSL, are exemplars for the latter. A translational representation of modelware artifacts (metamodel, model, and transformations) in terms of grammarware artifacts (e.g., attribute grammar, parser, and semantic actions) has also been explored [5]. When integrating separately developed DSL [22] or developing families of integrated DSL [71] the boundary between grammar- and modelware erodes further.

In addition, disciplined procedures of engineering domain-specific software languages apply to both [70, 78] and recurring design decisions widely overlap (e.g., regarding syntax design and language-based tooling; [25]).[3] The ability to vary at the levels of abstract syntax, concrete syntaxes, and semantics in a well-defined and systematic manner has been acknowledged for both, grammarware and modelware DSL [8]. This includes the primary drivers and goals of DSL variability (e.g., composite DSL, DSL evolution, and language-product lines). Therefore, for the scope of this work, the distinction between modelware and grammarware is not maintained.

1.1.2   Languages for Domain-Specific Modeling

A domain-specific modeling language (DSML) is a domain-specific language (DSL) for specifying design-level and platform-independent concerns in a domain of application, rather than implementation-level concerns (see, e.g., [2]). In this context, DSMLs typically provide (but are not limited to) a graphical concrete syntax. A DSML is built on top of a tailored *abstract syntax* (i.e., the core language-model) defined using metamodeling techniques. In addition to a DSML's abstract syntax (metamodel), DSML developers often use formal textual specification techniques to express the DSML's structural and behavioural context conditions [26]. Once the abstract syntax and a corresponding concrete syntax are specified, a DSML is integrated into a model-driven tool chain, such as the Eclipse Modeling Framework (EMF). In recent years, the development of DSMLs based on the Unified Modeling Language (UML [59]) and/or on the Meta Object Facility (MOF [58]) has become a popular choice.

1.1.3   Internal and External DSL

When a DSL is developed as an extension of a general-purpose software language (GPL) and when the DSL uses the GPL infrastructure for processing and for

---

[3]This does not counter the fact that the research communities working on grammarware and modelware, respectively, have long been working in isolation from each other [38, p. 78].

enacting DSL scripts, the DSL is an *internal DSL* and the GPL becomes the DSL's host language [13, 17, 47]. The choice of the host language may include general-purpose programming (e.g., Java, C++, Python) and general-purpose modeling languages (e.g., UML, Ecore). The spectrum of DSL as extensions to general-purpose languages ranges from basic source transformations, annotations (including profile mechanisms for modeling languages), stylized framework APIs, embeddable scripts to metaprograms (including code as data). The abstract syntax of an internal DSL is implemented by means of the host language (e.g., a model of classes and their relationships). The concrete syntax of the host language is adopted to realize a domain-specific notation. The semantics of an internal DSL are inherited and, while tailorable to a large extent (including restrictions), remain dependent on the foundational semantics of the host language (e.g., value vs. reference semantics, model-type or type systems). For enactment, internal DSL scripts (DSL models) can be submitted to the host language's infrastructure directly (e.g., the execution engine). Implementation techniques for internal DSL include but are not limited to embedding techniques ("fluent" API, syntax-representation manipulation, dynamic metaprogramming and reflection) and generative techniques (pre-processing, data as code, static metaprogramming; [17, Section 2.3.1]). Internal DSL share the development tooling (e.g., editor, debugger) with their host language. The host-language tooling can also be made tailorable to better accommodate a domain-specific language extension or internal DSL, even for non-developer practitioners [57].

A DSL developed as a freestanding software language, with abstract and concrete syntax defined in a well-defined manner external to and independent from to the host language (via a grammar, parser definition, a dedicated metamodel), is called an *external DSL* [13, 17, 47]. An external DSL can also involve a separate infrastructure for processing DSL scripts. The semantics of an external DSL can be defined regardless of the foundations of the host language. For enactment, program and model transformations are used to translate external DSL programs (models) into host-language programs (models). This allows for reusing the host's execution engine. Alternatively, integration with the target platform can be achieved by direct transformation, bypassing the host language (e.g., via direct compilation to native code or indirect compilation via a low-level intermediary representation). Implementation techniques and tooling for external DSL include, but are not limited to, language workbenches, parser combinators, and parsing techniques that bind host-language fragments as action items [17, Section 2.3.2]). External DSL require a dedicated development tooling (e.g., a generated editor, a custom debugger) separate from the ones of the host language or the target platform.

In research, internal and external DSL approaches are reported relevant at comparable levels. For example, Kosar et al. [38] report for 291 reviewed scientific publications between 2006 and 2012 that 47.8% addressed methods, techniques, and tools specific to internal DSL, 52.2% covered external DSL.[4] In practice, internal and external DSL become combined to balance comparative benefits and drawbacks

---

[4]For domain-specific modeling languages, when built on top of the UML, this picture changes to a clear predominance of internal DSL approaches (UML profiles). Hoisl et al. [25] found that 76

against each other. For example, an external DSL may be provided as a configuration façade on top of an internal DSL to specify intended and valid compositions of the internal DSL assets (e.g., compile-time templates). Vertical integration of internal and external DSL has also been reported in support of multi-view, multi-stakeholder settings (see, e.g., [29]). DSL engineering approaches consider the choice of internal vs. external DSL a separate design decision [47], rather than as a given at the beginning of a DSL project. As a design decision, it may also become deferred or even revisited. The latter assumes some support for both internal and external DSL by the same DSL development system (see, e.g., [77]).

1.2 DSL Product Lines

The ability to vary at the levels of abstract syntax, concrete syntaxes, semantics, and enactment in a systematic and efficient manner qualifies a DSL as being *variable*. Engineering variable DSL shifts emphasis from developing and analyzing a single DSL to developing and analyzing reusable development artifacts for a family of DSL. A family of DSL typically includes a base DSL and all its possible variants. Developing variable DSL requires methods, techniques, and tools known from domain engineering [6, Section 2.2] applied to software-language development.

In a systematic approach to variable DSL development, required and implemented variability is managed explicitly at all stages of a DSL's life cycle. Language-product line engineering is a recent attempt towards this goal. An efficient approach to variable DSL development facilitates systematic variation of a DSL by building on proven development knowledge and development practice on DSL variability. This involves reuse of design and implementation rationale (reusable design decisions, architectural patterns, design and implementation patterns) and the assisted development of DSL variants. The latter can be facilitated by embodying proven knowledge and practices in dedicated DSL development systems. A DSL development system includes language-level variability implementation techniques, orchestrated tool chains for language development (e.g., parsing frameworks), and integrated tooling such as language workbenches [9].

1.2.1 Drivers Towards Variable DSL

In recent years, there has been a growing interest in adopting and developing a variable DSL. The ambition to develop a variable DSL, in the broader context of language-oriented software development, results typically from a confluence of different developments and of different trends: domain interlock, language kernels, DSL-based modernization, and DSL evolution.

---

out of the 80 reviewed UML-based DSL projects were implemented as internal DSL using UML profiles.

1.2.1.1 Domain Interlock

Domains of applications become related vertically and horizontally [6, 51]. In a *vertical* relationship, one higher-level domain of application involves others, lower-level ones (e.g., modeling, and executable domains). The lower-level ones, therefore, offer potential for reusing DSL developed for them across multiple higher-level ones. A prominent example, both in textbooks, research, and in a surprising multitude of industry projects are (application) domains (e.g., model-based testing, software games) that build on variants of the (modeling) domain described by state machines. Application domains then adapt this core to their particularities by extension or by restriction. Closer looks reveal that application domains build on a common core of state-machine syntax and semantics [46, 75]. Commonalities are nodes for states and pseudo-states, arcs for transitions, events, and regions. Variations include guarded transitions, composite triggers, and history support [46, Appendix A]. Another example of vertically related domains is the application domain of scientific workflows and the executable domain of deployment orchestration [29].

In a *horizontal* relationship, a complex domain of applications is divided into sub-domains that have an overlap in terms of domain concepts and their relationships. Each sub-domain, in addition, requires extensions to its representing DSL. Examples include modeling domains that are decomposed into modeling sub-domains based on a common core, e.g., planning of railway schemes and planning of railway capacity [46]. Different executable domains are also often decomposed into multiple related TECHNICAL SUBDOMAINS (e.g., metamodels for persistence, presentation, business data) [73].

A recent take on horizontal relationships between domains and the corresponding DSL has been labeled *domain globalization* [7]. Here, the emphasis is, at a higher level, on the integration of heterogeneous DSL to support language-oriented collaboration as well as software development and operation in a multi-view, multi-stakeholder setting [55]. This puts emphasis on consistency management and compatibility checking between different and independently evolving DSL; rather than on developing DSL families.

1.2.1.2 Language Kernels

It has long been recognized that there can be a middle ground between compact and verbose domain-specific languages as the two extremes (see [74, Section 2.4] for an overview). A compact DSL provides few but generic (lower-level) and extensible abstractions to serve a domain of application. A verbose DSL has ideally full coverage in terms of high-level domain abstractions. As an alternative, a kernel or language core with dependent extensions can be developed. The kernel may even be relevant for different related domains (see above), while the library extensions are specific to certain targeted domains. An example of this is a kernel-based strategy for language-oriented programming that aims at developing programs specific to niche hardware platforms based on a kernel and a kernel-driven IDE [20]. A kernel and a library of extensions can be developed as a DSL product line.

1.2.1.3 DSL-Based Modernization

DSL are often considered evolutionary vehicles for evolving existing software systems [10]. The aim of DSL-based evolution is to make client applications and developers of an existing software systems benefit from the alleged advantages of a DSL, e.g., improved maintainability and understandability. DSL-based evolution typically occurs at two speeds: First, an alternative frontend syntax to an existing API or framework is added (e.g., a "fluent API" as opposed to a command-query API [13]). Then, second, existing client applications and the existing code base are gradually converted to using the DSL. It has been acknowledged that the adoption of a DSL in this evolutionary setting is facilitated by introducing the DSL in a stepwise manner, one feature at a time [10, 11]. This, again, can be well supported by a reactive product-line approach to developing this DSL.

1.2.1.4 DSL Evolution

Finally, a DSL can become subjected to evolution being a complex piece of software itself [11, 49]. This may be triggered by changes in the domain of application, or because of the overall development setting of the DSL (incremental vs. proactive). A case in point is providing variants of a DSL (over time) optimized for certain spatial or temporal performance characteristics [44]. Such DSL evolution may result in a DSL family being developed over time.

1.2.2 DSL Product Lines

A *software product line* is a family[5] of software products derived from a shared code base, ideally in a widely automated manner. Each product is described in terms of a valid configuration of the product line's variability model (e.g., a feature diagram; [6]). In software language engineering, a variable software language (general-purpose or domain-specific) can be implemented as a product line (or family). Such a *language-product line* [28, 42, 44, 45] can be used to derive software languages (DSL) as its variants (products) or to analyze static properties of the members of a language (DSL) family.

The products of a language-product line are distinguished in terms of the features they provide. A *feature* in domain engineering is a discriminating and user-visible functionality or quality attribute of a software system. Features and feature-level dependencies are ideally modeled by the variability model, as part of a domain definition. Product or language derivation is then guided or even triggered by a selection of features (configuration) from the variability model. Therefore, a product-line variability model expresses the space of all valid configurations and products of a product line. The need for guidance in language configuration has been stressed

---

[5]Throughout this writing, the terms *product line* and *program family* are used interchangeably; although, this is not accurate historically.

Fig. 1.1 Types of features
considered in
language-product line and
language-family engineering:
abstract syntax features,
concrete-syntax features,
language features, tooling
features

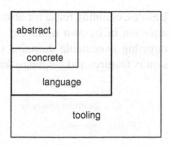

before [42]. For product lines of general-purpose software languages, the targeted users are developers that create programs using one or several language products. For domain-specific languages, and depending on the domain of application, users may include non-developer practitioners (domain experts) or end-user developers. Therefore, depending on the language type, domain, and user audience, different *types of features* of software languages, and in particular DSL, have been considered (see Fig. 1.1).

- *Abstract syntax features* refer to optional elements and relationships of an abstract syntax. Examples are metamodels and metamodel extensions [4], or production grammars and grammar extensions [30] (to the extent grammars define the abstract syntax).
- *Concrete-syntax features* refer to the provision of more than one or different types of concrete syntaxes (graphical, textual) on top of the same variable abstract syntax [45, 77].
- *Language features* [42, 44] refer to optional language constructs and their behaviors. Examples include decompositions according to different concrete-syntactic constructs and their attached behavior as units of expression as perceived by developers (e.g., commands, loop constructs).
- *Tooling features* [44] refer to optional language-based tool functionality and language-oriented tool services. Examples are post-processing optimizations, type checking, and transformations (e.g., for code generation).

As depicted in Fig. 1.1, these feature types typically mesh which each other.[6] An approach aiming at language features absorbs abstract syntax features by definition because variability of the syntax definition is implied. Tooling features might relate to language and abstract syntax features, or not. Tooling aspects such as refactorings and type checking require awareness of any variability at the language-construct level; others might not (e.g., optimization working on an intermediate representation of DSL scripts or models). However, approaches differ in their emphasis on different feature types or in the order they address different types of features. For DSL, abstract syntax features play an important role because the abstract syntax models have a selected and scoped domain of application. Certain drivers towards a variable DSL result from variability within a domain or between domains (*domain interlock*).

---

[6]This has been labeled the multi-dimensional variability of software languages [45, Section 4.1.2].

Besides, enabling reuse for abstract syntaxes as problem-domain models has gained attention in its own right, e.g., when implemented as metamodels [33]. For DSL targeting executable domains (e.g., the infamous expression language), abstract syntax features and language features certainly blend.

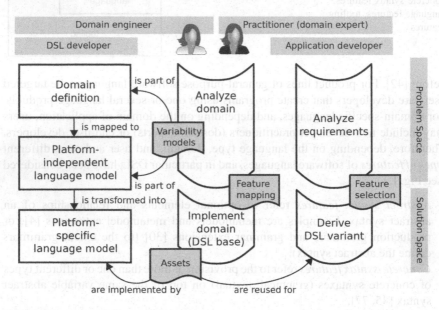

Fig. 1.2 Overview of DSL product line engineering. Domain-engineering tasks (domain analysis, asset development) are carried out by a domain engineer and DSL developer, respectively. Application-engineering tasks (requirements, architecture, design, implementation including DSL derivation) by a domain expert and application developer. Loosely based on [1, Figure 2.1]

In Fig. 1.2, a process of engineering a DSL family using product-line techniques is illustrated (in a simplified form). A *domain engineer* analyzes the application domain of a DSL and creates a problem-domain model as part of a domain definition (e.g., a variant of a class model, or an entity-relationship model). In the same step, the domain engineer identifies commonalities and differences between the required DSL variants. Differences are expressed as optional DSL features. The results are documented in terms of a *variability model*. A variability model specifies the variability of DSL, that is, the number of derivable variants and their properties, in a well-defined and expressive variability modeling language (e.g., a feature diagram). The DSL developer then implements the domain by developing reusable DSL artifacts, the so-called *assets* (e.g., design models, source code, tests, and documentation). The assets are explicitly mapped to the corresponding elements of the variability model (*feature mapping*). This mapping is facilitated by variability implementation techniques that represent features as first-class entities in tools or as language constructs.[7] The roles of domain engineer and of the DSL developer can also be taken in dual role.

To analyze the concrete *functional* and *non-functional requirements* of a DSL-based software system, the practitioners (domain experts) are consulted to investigate their needs. The elicited requirements result in a *feature selection*, based on the feature set defined during the domain analysis (variability model). Based on the selected features, the application developer *derives a DSL* by composing the reusable assets. Feature selection and DSL derivation are ideally guided and even automated to a large extent. Feature selection can be supported by a configurator or by build scripts generated from the variability model. Assuming that a composition or generation technique has been applied that maps features and implementation units explicitly, a generator (at compile time) or weaver (at runtime) can produce a final product (DSL) from a valid feature selection (configuration). Depending on the domain, for end-user developers, the roles of practitioner and application developer can be taken by one subject.

1.2.3 Trajectories to DSL Product Lines

In software product line engineering, different development trajectories to a product line can be taken [1, Section 2.4]: proactive, reactive, and extractive. The trajectory painted in Fig. 1.2 has been referred to as a *proactive* adoption. A proactive development approach develops a DSL product line from scratch and its DSL variants with one leap, using systematic analysis and design procedures (e.g., domain analysis, domain modeling, feature-oriented design). A proactive trajectory presents advantages in terms of an improved quality of the code assets and an increased quality-in-reuse. The required upfront investment, the high lead times, and the presence of portfolios of legacy products (that must be maintained in parallel), however, render an uptake of a proactive approach unlikely in practice.

In a *reactive* trajectory, the DSL developers start with a minimal DSL product line that aims at deriving only very few (one) selected DSL variants. In the sense of incremental software development, each planned iteration then adds to the product line missing feature implementations to complete the family of variants. The overall picture of Fig. 1.2 holds, but phases and steps are repeatedly performed to obtain new increments to all artifacts: domain definition, language models, variability model, and assets. The advantages of reduced upfront investments and limited lead times are countered by the risk of the product-line base not being able to accommodate all feature increments. This might incur costs of corrective refactoring and revisions of the existing code base during each iteration.[8]

Finally, in an *extractive trajectory*, DSL developers depart from a portfolio of existing DSL and turn them into a DSL family in a stepwise manner [42, 46]. Extrac-

---

[7]A general overview of available annotation, composition, and generation techniques is available from Sobernig et al. [66], Apel et al. [1], Czarnecki and Eisenecker [6]. See also Sect. 2.4 for techniques proposed by related work on software language engineering.

[8]Chapter 6 showcases a reactive development of a DSL family using DjDSL.

tion also follows the main phases and steps sketched out in Fig. 1.2. However, it is driven by the documented designs and implementation artifacts of the existing DSL. Tool support for extraction is critical. Tooling is needed to extract commonalities and differences from existing code artifacts and to document the existing variability as a variability model. First, the code bases are used to identify and to mark language constructs (a.k.a. language components). Language components entail all details relevant for a language construct (concrete syntax, abstract syntax, behavioral definitions) deemed a language feature. Second, language components are extracted into dedicated implementation units (e.g., metamodel extensions or modules). Finally, third, based on the extracted dependencies between the implementation units, a variability model is synthesized. This generated variability model can be a starting point for a refinement by the domain engineer and DSL developer.[9] An extractive trajectory leaves the existing products intact; however, it is limited in terms of the variability implementation techniques available for adoption. As a result, an extracted product line will not compare with the quality-in-reuse of a proactively developed one.

Top-Down and Bottom-Up Development
Kühn and Cazzola [41] contrast *top-down* and *bottom-up* paths for product-line development. Top-down, a feature model is created first, guides the decomposition of an abstract syntax (metamodel) into a family and drives code generation. Bottom-up, starting from a language kernel, each existing language variant is decomposed into its parts matched by the kernel and its delta to the base. The delta becomes a feature and is implemented as a language component. Once the collection of components is stable, and all DSL variants have been addressed, a feature model is derived. While having different connotations, a top-down path relates to a proactive one; bottom-up resembles a reactive or extractive path.

As far as language and DSL product lines are concerned, these trajectories merely represent archetypes. A DSL product line project in practice will mesh the methods, techniques, and tools relevant for each of three. For example, extraction techniques can become important when faced with software-language evolution. In an evolutionary setting, functional additions to the common base or new features become added as assets to the product line, without having been anticipated before [42]; much like in a reactive product-line approach. The expectation is that all family members are rebased on top of the extended shared code base; or accommodate the new features as optional ones. To support such a setting, Kühn et al. [42] propose extractive techniques to track changing dependencies between language elements (language components) based on tags and to extract dependency relationships into revisions of the variability model.

---

[9]The suitability of an automatically generated variability model as well as its stability over time has been questioned in extractive or bottom-up approaches [41].

1.3 Empirical Research and Technology Evaluation

Only recently, empirical research on software language engineering and DSL technology evaluations have started being planned, conducted, and reported following systematic research strategies and adopting rigorous designs. For overviews of this small, but growing body of literature, the reader is referred to Hoisl et al. [25, Section 7] and Barišić et al. [3, Section 7.2]. In the following, selected reports on empirical research and technology evaluations are briefly summarized. This is to primarily to show that neither empirical research nor guidelines for technology evaluation, as of today, consider DSL families or variability as a DSL's quality attribute.

1.3.1 Empirical Evidence on DSL

As for empirical research, what follows concentrates on dedicated empirical research projects on DSL *external* quality attributes (e.g., program comprehension, maintainability, developer productivity, ease of use), rather than companions as part of technical reports on DSL development system. The latter commonly stress internal quality attributes (e.g., space and time performance). Despite fundamental claims on the benefits and the drawbacks of DSL, in general, and different DSL types, in particular, evidence collected from rigorous and method-driven empirical studies is very limited. To date, very few empirical studies on DSL have been conducted [14, 21] not to mention in a real-world industrial setting. Most qualitative research is based on opinion statements and experience reports, collected from domain experts in terms of "industry case studies" and from DSL prototype implementation. Important details about collecting and processing the evidence are often missing. Rigorous qualitative research reports, such as the survey by Hermans et al. [21] and Sobernig et al. [68], are exceptions. The few quantitative studies include exploratory evaluations of the maintainability property of the DSL implementations themselves [35, 65], comparing different DSL implementation techniques [37], and DSL syntax styles [23]. None of these efforts or reports touches on DSL variability.

1.3.2 DSL-Aware Approaches to Technology Evaluation

Only recently, the evaluation framework FQAD [32] targeting DSL, which incorporates ideas from DESMET, has been proposed. FQAD suggests a set of 8 quality characteristics of DSL for evaluation (e.g., functional suitability, usability, maintainability) and their sub-characteristics. An evaluator is then supposed to select a number of characteristics based on evaluation goals as part of the evaluator profile and performs the evaluation based on the quantifiable sub-characteristics (e.g., development time). FQAD puts forth a number of assessment components to be composed into assessment processes (e.g., one for assessing DSL success against a baseline process).

On a similar page, the Usability Software Engineering Modeling Environment (USE-ME; [3]) for usability-aware DSL evaluation was documented, tested, and advertised. USE-ME covers the phases of modeling the DSL usage context, modeling the DSL goals, modeling the planned evaluation in terms of usability experiments, modeling surveys for supportive collection of opinions and perceptions, modeling the evaluation tasks under study, and modeling the planned reports. USE-ME provides reusable assets such as a catalogue of "usability metrics" and builds upon (UML-based) model artifacts that is the basis for support tooling for the researchers and expert evaluators.

At a comparable level of detail, experiences on running (controlled) experiments on DSL have been condensed into an integrated DSL experiment environment architecture [19]. The supported phases are experiment planning, conducting, and reporting. Emphasis is on actual software-tool support for experimental researchers: Software support includes an experiment definition language (ExpDSL), simplified data-analysis scripts, and tailored reporting; all developed using MPS [27].

1.4   Single-DSL Development Using NX

This section illustrates the various steps that are typically performed when implementing an *internal* and an *external* textual DSL using the Next Scripting Language (NX; see Fig. 1.3). While NX is a general-purpose object-oriented scripting language, this section and the remainder of this book are limited to NX features relevant or specific to DSL development.[10] In this tutorial, and its running example, the development of a *single-variant DSL* using NX plus helpers, but *without* DjDSL, is highlighted (see Table 1.1). The subsequent chapters, gradually, introduce the reader to the complexity of multi-DSL development and show how DjDSL complements NX to tackle this complexity.

NX is a Tcl-based, object-oriented scripting language. NX is a descendant of XOTcl, a language designed to provide language support for design patterns [54]. For the scope of DSL development and variability support for DSL, two feature areas of NX are of importance: the object system and, more generally, features enabling language-oriented programming (e.g., metaprogramming facilities). Descendants of XOTcl and NX, in particular Frag [77] based on Java, have been proposed in related work on DSL development systems for the same reasons.

The object system of NX is rooted by a single class: nx::Object. All objects are instances of this class. In NX, classes are a special kind of object providing methods to their instances and managing their life cycles. These class objects (simply *classes*, hereafter) are instances of the metaclass nx::Class. NX supports object-specific behavior: Objects can carry behavior distinct from the behavior specified by their class. This behavior can be defined in object-specific methods and by decorator mixins (see per-object mixins in [53]). The object system is highly flexible, the

---

[10]For a primer on NX, please see its introductory tutorial [52]. Tcl is covered by Nadkarni [50], Ousterhout and Jones [60].

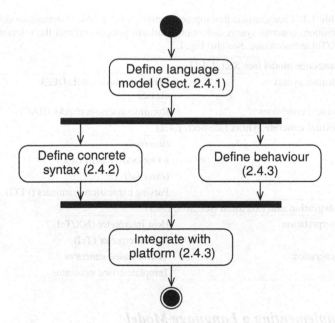

Fig. 1.3 DSL development steps performed in this introductory tutorial

relations between objects and classes and among classes can be changed at arbitrary times.

NX supports dynamic software evolution in terms of runtime state and behavior changes, as well as dynamic changes to program structure and to program composition. In the remainder, we concentrate on the language features of NX relevant for supporting *feature-oriented programming* [66] and advanced object composition [79]. These characteristics of NX are relevant for tackling challenges in implementing domain-specific language models in a feature-oriented manner, allowing internal and external DSL being developed on a common ground, as well as for realizing design patterns as variability implementation techniques.[11]

Fig. 1.4 A minimal language
model for the LEA toy
language, as a minimal
UML2 class (EMOF)
diagram: L(iteral),
E(xpression), A(dd)

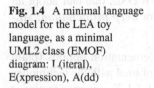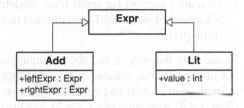

---

[11]The benefits of NX for these tasks are highlighted in Sect. 3.2.3.

Table 1.1 Characteristic development activities for a DSL (language-model definition, concrete-syntax definition, platform integration) and the relevant NX/Tcl infrastructure. See also Fig. 1.3

Language model (see Sect. 1.4.1)	
Abstract syntax	Plain NX classes, ML-DEEP classes
Context conditions	Runtime-assertion checks (RAC)
Textual concrete syntax (see Sect. 1.4.2)	
	(*internal*)
	EXPRESSION BUILDER
	(*external*)
	Parsing expression grammars (PEG)
Integration and execution (see Sect. 1.4.3)	
Interpretation	Host interpreter (NX/Tcl)
	Safe interpreter (Tcl)
Generation	Visitor-based generator
	Template-based generator

1.4.1   Implementing a Language Model

1.4.1.1   Abstract Syntax

Figure 1.4 depicts a possible language-model fragment specified using an EMOF diagram. This language mode can be implemented using the corresponding plain NX class structure in Fig. 1.4. EMOF classes (`Expr`, `Lit`, and `Add`) are turned into the three NX classes and their two superclass-subclass relationships. The EMOF properties (`leftExpr`, `rightExpr`, and `value`) are implemented via the same named NX properties.

Language models may be represented using one of the following alternatives:

- Plain NX classes (see Listing 1.5)
- DjDSL provides a minimal metamodel to implement collaboration-based language models for DSL families (see Chap. 3).
- To realize support for multi-level modeling [40] for a DSL, one can adopt an NX-based object model (metamodel) that provides for *deep instantiation*: ML-DEEP [64].

Please note that any of the above language-model implementation options (plain NX classes, DjDSL collaborations, ML-DEEP) can be combined with the techniques to implement context and consistency constraints (Sect. 1.4.1.2), concrete syntaxes (Sect. 1.4.2), execution (Sect. 1.4.3), and testing (Sect. 1.4.4).

```
1  nx::Class create Expr
2  nx::Class create Add -superclasses Expr {
3    :property leftExpr:object,type=Expr,required
4    :property rightExpr:object,type=Expr,required
5  }
6  nx::Class create Lit -superclasses Expr {
7    :property -accessor public value:double,required
8  }
```

Lst. 1.5 An implementation of the language model modeled in Fig. 1.4 using NX/Tcl

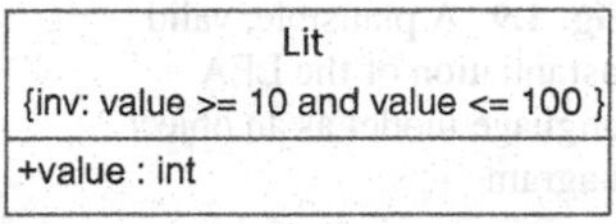

Fig. 1.6 An exemplary context condition (invariant expression) on literals in the LEA language

Lit
{inv: value >= 10 and value <= 100 }
+value : int

1.4.1.2 Abstract Syntax Constraints

To express constraints, especially *context conditions*, which cannot be directly captured by the implemented language model, language-model classes can be decorated using NX *invariant expressions*. Listing 1.7 implements the OCL invariant for the context of Lit as specified in Fig. 1.6: Without DjDSL, NX allows a DSL developer to define and to enforce invariant expressions in terms of runtime-assertion checks (RAC; [48]). Listing 1.8 exemplifies an alternative notation of context conditions, akin to OCL definition blocks. These can also be maintained in a separate sidecar document.

1.4.2 Textual Concrete Syntax

Once defined, the language model can be instantiated in the NX/Tcl host environment, using the NX/Tcl concrete syntax directly. This instantiation is conceptually depicted as an object diagram in Fig. 1.9. Listing 1.10 illustrates how an instantiation of the language model can be defined.

In addition, DjDSL provides for defining complementing or alternative concrete syntaxes for a given language model, either in terms of an internal DSL or as an external DSL.

1.4.2.1 As an Internal DSL

An EXPRESSION BUILDER [13] (BUILDER, hereafter; see also Fig. 1.11) separates the two concerns of actually creating a language-model instantiation (e.g., based on the host-language infrastructure as in Listing 1.10) and of requesting an instantiation using a derived notation. This derived notation is valid according to and embedded

```
Lit invariants set {{${:value} >= 10 && ${:value} <= 100}}
```

Lst. 1.7 An implementation of the invariant constraint modeled in Fig. 1.6 using NX/Tcl

```
1    context: tutorial::Lit \
2        inv: {${:value} >= 10 && ${:value} <= 100} \
3        inv: {${:value} >= 20 && ${:value} <= 50}
```

Lst. 1.8 An alternative implementation of an invariant constraint using NX/Tcl

Fig. 1.9 A plausible, valid instantiation of the LEA language model as an object diagram

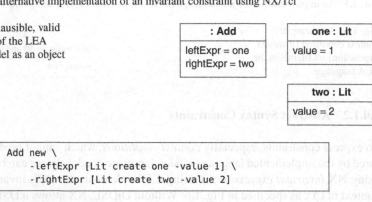

```
1    Add new \
2        -leftExpr [Lit create one -value 1] \
3        -rightExpr [Lit create two -value 2]
```

Lst. 1.10 Direction instantiation of the language-model element Add

with the host-language syntax but deviates from it for the sake of different objectives (e.g., readability, compactness). Consider the example of the LEA language supporting the common operator-prefix notation for its expressions. An expression + 1 2 must be processed such that another instantiation of the language model, as the one created in Listing 1.10, is created on the fly. NX provides techniques such as DYNAMIC RECEPTION to develop a BUILDER for LEA. Tcl leans itself towards the given example because a whitespace-separated input string can readily be consumed as a first-class data structure, a Tcl list, without prior string processing. A BUILDER is realized as an object that is separated from the language model: LeaBuilder (see Fig. 1.12).

This way, a client component requiring an expression to be processed is fully decoupled from the internals of constructing a valid instantiation of the language model. The language model is freed from handling instantiation details, possibly for many different frontend syntaxes and different client applications. The BUILDER implementation is sketched out in Fig. 1.12. The implementation reverses the list of expression elements passed into its method from and turns each element into a message, targeting one of two possible receiver methods: + and the special-purpose method unknown (DYNAMIC RECEPTION). The latter turns operators into Add instances, while the former boxes numeric operands into Lit instances. Lit instances are managed by an operand stack (opds), while Add instances consume the entire stack and are, then, popped onto the stack themselves. The method from

Fig. 1.11 Patterns of hosting an internal DSL in NX/Tcl, as supported by NX and DjDSL; see Sect. 5.1 for more background on these patterns

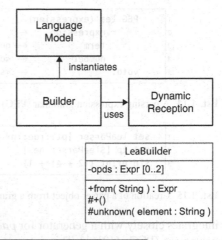

Fig. 1.12 A BUILDER implementation in support of a postfix notation for LEA expressions

```
1  set internalBuilder [AleBuilder new]
2  set expr1 [$internalBuilder from {+ 1 + 2 4}]
```

Lst. 1.13 Instantiating a BUILDER object and processing a LEA expression string

is the only entry point into the BUILDER, accepting an expression string (+ 1 + 2 4) and returning the root Expr (see Listing 1.13).

1.4.2.2 As an External DSL

Once defined, a language model in NX/Tcl can be directly instantiated by using the NX/Tcl host syntax or, indirectly, by creating a BUILDER, an internal DSL syntax. If required, a syntax deemed external to the host language (NX/Tcl) can be defined and processed using a parser infrastructure and a corresponding grammar descriptor. A syntax is said being external when going beyond what is offered by the host language syntax, or when retrofitting it into the host syntax cannot be achieved by proportionate means (e.g., TEXTUAL POLISHING [13]).

Consider the requirement of providing an infix notation for LEA (e.g., (2 + 4)+ 1), which is described by the following E/BNF:

```
1  expression = term, ( '+', term );
2  term = '(', expression, ')' | number;
3  number = digit, {digit};
4  digit = '0' | '1' | '2' | '3' | '4' | '5' | '6' | '7' | '8' | '9';
```

This syntax is genuinely external to the Tcl prefix notation.[12] A language model defined in NX/Tcl can be served by arbitrary parsing engines. NX/Tcl, however,

---

[12]For the sake of running a contrived example, any tactic to transform an infix expression into its pre- or postfix equivalent as a pre-processing step is acknowledged but put aside, deliberately [56].

```
1   PEG lea (expression)
2          expression    ← _ term (_ '+' _ term)?;
3          term          ← number / '(' expression ')';
4          number        ← <digit>+;
5   void: _               ← <space>*;
```

Lst. 1.14 A parsing expression grammar (PEG) for processing LEA expressions

```
1   set leaParser [pt::rde::nx pgen $leaGrammar]
2   set lp [$leaParser new]
3   $lp print {(2 + 4) + 1}
```

Lst. 1.15 Creation of a parser object from a grammar definition and its use

integrates closely with a generator for *packrat parsers* based on *parsing expression grammars* (PEG; [12]).[13] This integration opens up important opportunities in subsequent, more advanced settings. In addition, this integration offers a number of additional advantages such as creating stand-alone, self-hosted language runtimes. The exemplary E/BNF grammar translates, as one option, into the PEG documented in Listing 1.14. This PEG is similar to the original E/BNF in terms of syntax, with some minor deviations, leaving aside important semantic differences (ordered vs. unordered choice; see Sect. 5.2.3):

- Parsing operates in a scannerless manner; in other words, scanning is an integral part of the parsing procedure. Therefore, among others, tokenizing characters and whitespaces must be handled explicitly. See the _ rule on line 5 in Listing 1.14. The recognized input can be automatically removed from the parse result by setting the attribute void.
- The PEG infrastructure comes with predefined character classes, such as <digit> and <space>.
- Mind the minor syntactic differences between the E/BNF grammar and the PEG in terms of sequences (w/ and w/o comma), repetitions, and their default cardinalities, etc.

The PEG can be used as-is to generate a parser for the LEA concrete syntax. Listing 1.15 assumes the PEG from Listing 1.14 to be assigned one-to-one as a value to a variable called leaGrammar. The so-obtained parser can be used to produce the recognized strings into a number of output artifacts (e.g., abstract syntax trees), based on a canonical representation of the recognized string. Technically, this representation is a structure of nested Tcl lists, conceptually akin to the printout in Listing 1.14. This printout is obtained from line 3 in Listing 1.15. The list elements are quadruples that denote the recognized token type (e.g., expression, term, number), the character range corresponding to the recognized token in the input string, and the respective child tokens.

---

[13]See Sect. 5.2.5 for the details.

```
1  set externalBuilder [ExternalBuilder new -parser $lp]
2  set expr2 [$externalBuilder from {(2 + 4) + 1}]
```

Lst. 1.16 Using a BUILDER object to parse and to transform an expression string into an object graph

From this parse representation, one proceeds by defining a BUILDER to derive the corresponding instantiation of the LEA language model: ExternalBuilder (see Listing 1.16). This BUILDER variant for the external syntax serves the same architectural purpose as the one for the internal one (InternalBuilder, see Fig. 1.12).

This BUILDER, however, starts from input of different quality. It operates on a parse tree represented as a hierarchy of Tcl lists, containing the types and input positions of the matched tokens (expression, term, and number):

```
-+= expression :: 0 10
 |-+= term :: 0 6
 |  \-+= expression :: 1 5
 |  |-+= term :: 1 1
 |  |  \--= number :: 1 1
 |  \-+= term :: 5 5
 |     \--= number :: 5 5
 \-+= term :: 10 10
    \--= number :: 10 10
```

This is in contrast to the unqualified expression string treated as a single, flattened Tcl list available to the InternalBuilder.

Given this parse tree, a BUILDER (see Fig. 1.17) may operate as follows: It walks in a bottom-up (postorder) manner the tree structure. Occurrences of token types are turned into method calls to factory methods, which, if applicable, return the corresponding language-model instances (i.e., Add for expression or Lit for number). Factory methods may also decide to drop or promote results of previous factory calls (e.g., term has no correspondence in the language model of LEA).

1.4.3 Integration and Execution

Integration with a target software platform, and one platform-provided host language, can be realized using different forms of interpretation (host and safe interpreters) or using different forms of generation (visitor- and template-based generators). Interpretation and generation can be applied at different artifact levels, such as the different parse representations produced by the internal-syntax processor (ExpressionBuilder) or by the external-syntax processor.

In the following, the emphasis is on *language-model instantiations* as parse representation. This is because, at this level, the concern of integrating and executing a DSL script is independent from the nature of the DSL as an internal or an external one. It goes without saying that, for specific purposes, alternative representations

Fig. 1.17 A BUILDER
implementation in support of
an infix notation for LEA
expressions. It depends on a
generated PEG/packrat
parser: LeaParser

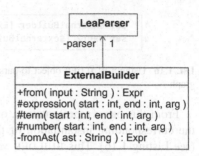

LeaParser

-parser ↑ 1

ExternalBuilder
+from(input : String) : Expr
#expression(start : int, end : int, arg)
#term(start : int, end : int, arg)
#number(start : int, end : int, arg)
-fromAst(ast : String) : Expr

(e.g., builder or parse data) are more suited for platform and host-language integration. Likewise, platform integration is not necessarily about script execution. If a DSL serves as a special-purpose, structural modeling language (e.g., for basic concept modeling), platform integration might gear towards integration with a verification engine, model checker, or a documentation generator. In the following, we look at the basic options of providing an INTERPRETER [16] and a source-code generator [31] for the purpose of script execution (i.e., expression evaluation).

NX allows for integrating the DSL directly with NX itself as the host language using host-language interpretation. Namely, the NX/Tcl host interpreter can be used to interpret and execute DSL scripts (e.g., expressions) directly using the host-language infrastructure (e.g., Tcl's expr command). For this purpose, the language model can be devised to realize an INTERPRETER [16] for its instantiations.[14] An INTERPRETER defines a representation of a DSL script which is traversed to execute ("interpret") the script. The running example of LEA expression trees leans itself towards an INTERPRETER which builds on the language model without indirection, because the tree (composite) structure is reflected in the language model itself (see Fig. 1.18). Alternatively, a derivative of the language-model instantiation must be defined, or, for the external DSL, the tree structure of the parse can be reused for the purpose of implementing an INTERPRETER. Figure 1.18 sketches out a minimal INTERPRETER realization on top of the language model as defined earlier (see Fig. 1.4). The evaluate method is responsible for evaluating a given expression as a Tcl expression using Tcl's expr command. For Add expressions, the implementation of evaluate steps down into its operand expressions (leftExpr and rightExpr). Then, it collects their evaluation results and runs a combined addition. The corresponding method implementations are depicted in Listing 1.19.

---

[14]An enhanced solution relocates the implementation details of INTERPRETER into a separate code structure maintained separately from and composable with the language model, e.g., using a DjDSL collaboration (see Sect. 3.2.3). Another follow-up consideration is to separate the host interpreter from the interpreter executing the DSL in its own, well-defined execution context. For this purpose, NX/Tcl can benefit from Tcl's slave interpreters. They can be controlled and managed from the master interpreter [50, Chapter 20]. This way, one can provide for a tailored interpretation context for a DSL (e.g., distinct command and variable definitions, as well as a separate callstack). Learn how DjDSL leverages this infrastructure for sandboxing internal DSL in Sect. 5.1.

This way, one can request evaluation of any language-model instantiation, whatever its provenance (internal or external), as follows: `$expr2 evaluate` (with `expr2` referring to the variable populated in Listing 1.16).

In (source) code generation, the language-model instantiation representing a DSL script is turned into an executable source representation complying with a programming-language environment other than the DSL's host language (e.g., a system language such as C or C++). The generated code then requires separate compilation. This is unless the representation is directly interpretable. Imagine LEA expressions evolving into a family of expressions that can become complex, and, therefore, evaluate slow when interpreted directly in the host language. Therefore, the objective is to convert LEA expressions into native C expressions. Starting from a language-model instantiation as visualized Fig. 1.9, a generator might produce a C expression (1+2). Additionally, the generator might provide options to explicitly cast operand literals in the generated expression. This helps either unify expression types before evaluation, or to promote and to demote the result type. Consider expressions like `((float)1 + (float)2)` or `(1*1.0 + 2*1.0)`. The resulting expression must then be embedded into a C code skeleton that is (a) compilable, (b) loadable into the running host (Tcl) process, and (c) callable from within the running script.

There are various implementation options available for source-code generators (e.g., template-based, pre-processors; see [31, Chapter 2] for an overview). A frequently adopted one is a code generator based on a VISITOR [16, p. 331]. A VISITOR realizes a code-generating operation on a language-model instantiation, in a way that details of this operation can be modified, or new operations (i.e., visitors) become added, without incurring the need for modifying the language model as such. For this to work, a minimal VISITOR implementation for a language model provides a simple interaction protocol based on double (method) dispatches. On the one hand, `accept` methods of the language-model classes receive visitor objects that, on the other hand, `visit` the language-model objects having accepted them. The visitor's `visit` method then implements the actual operation, namely generating source strings.[15]

Fig. 1.18 LEA language model realizing an INTERPRETER for direct evaluation of LEA expressions as Tcl expressions

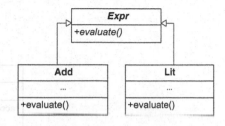

---

[15] As pointed out already for the INTERPRETER, the implementation details specific to the VISITOR roles (`accept` and `visit` methods) can be restructured into separate code units (collaborations). In addition, `accept` propagation can be generalized by using filters [54].

```
1  Add public method evaluate {} {
2    return [expr {[${:leftExpr} evaluate] +
3                  [${:rightExpr} evaluate]}]
4  }
5
6  Lit public method evaluate {} {
7    return [expr {${:value}}]
8  }
```

Lst. 1.19 Implementation of an INTERPRETER for LEA expressions using NX/Tcl

For LEA, `CExprVisitor` implements the family of visitor objects (see Fig. 1.20). It also provides the entry point for evaluating an expression: `evaluate`. The language model is extended to include `accept` methods. The `accept` methods orchestrate the traversal of a visitor through the object structure. For example, Add's `accept` forwards the visitor to its operand expressions. Code generation is realized in the `CExprVisitor` itself. Upon a `visit` on an `Expr` object, depending on its type (`Lit` or `Add`), an adequate `convert` implementation is executed (see Listing 1.21).

For `Lit` expressions, the value is placed and becomes optionally prefixed by a cast operation. The cast target can be set for an entire expression under evaluation. For `Add` expressions, an addition clause in parenthesis is generated. Once the C expression has been assembled, `evaluate` turns it into a combined compilation and script unit, that is, a `critcl::cproc`.[16]

The LEA expression `1 + ( 2 + 4 )` is so processed into the Tcl procedure implemented in C depicted in Listing 1.22.

Fig. 1.20 A VISITOR to convert LEA expressions into C expressions, compiles, loads, and so evaluates them

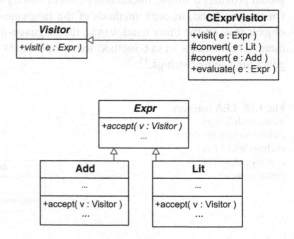

---

[16]Critcl is a Tcl extension which allows for, among others, embedding Tcl commands and procedures implemented in C at the script level. Critcl provides for and deploys the generated Tcl/C extension in a way that makes it directly available from the issuing script.

```
1    :method "convert Add" {e} {
2        set :opnds [lassign ${:opnds} a b]
3        lappend :opnds "($a + $b)"
4    }
5    :method "convert Lit" {e} {
6        set :opnds [list "(${:promoteTo})[$e value get]" {*}${:opnds}]
7    }
```

Lst. 1.21 Implementation of a VISITOR-based C code generator for LEA expressions using NX/Tcl

Lst. 1.22 A LEA expression implemented as a Tcl/C procedure

```
critcl::cproc cexpr {} int {
    return ((int)1 + ((int)2 + (int)4));
}
```

Lst. 1.23 Instantiating a VISITOR to evaluate a LEA expression as an object graph to a result value

```
1    set visitor [CExprVisitor new]
2    $visitor evaluate $expr2
```

With this, code generation and on-the-fly evaluation can be requested as shown in Listing 1.23. The variable reference $expr2 refers to the language-model instantiation obtained from the external LEA script via ExternalBuilder (see Listing 1.16).

1.4.4 Testing

Testing a DSL, whether internal or external, involves different testing strategies (integration vs. unit testing) and different testing scopes [9, 34]. The DSL artifacts and processes *under test* can be the embedded or external concrete syntaxes (i.e., parsing and language-model instantiation), checking the language-model constraints (see Sect. 1.4.1.2), and the DSL integration (e.g., code generators). On top, it can be important to express consistency conditions as tests on the language model itself [67], as well as other DSL-specific phases of processing (e.g., static or dynamic analysis).

In NX, a small testing language is available for defining, executing, and reporting on tests for various of the above scopes (e.g., language-model instantiation). It builds on the native tcltest infrastructure [50, Chapter 24] as testing engine. Exemplary test conditions are processing success ("succeeds"), processing failure ("fails"), and matching patterns of object structures ("to"). Take as examples the following test cases on the two, previously defined BUILDERS. The first two cases put the LeaBuilder as part of the internal DSL under test (see Listing 1.24). A typical test case has the following structure:

- *Description*: Describes the purpose and scope of the test case for the DSL developer or DSL tester.

- *(DSL) Fragment*: Is an embedded program or partial program in the DSL under test (e.g., parts or complete LEA expressions such as + 3 + 1 2 or (1 + 2)+ 3).
- *Condition*: Sets the type of test to be performed on the provided fragment (e.g., build to test a given BUILDER).
- Depending on the selected condition, additional test parameters (e.g., using to pick a specific builder object) as well as different expected results or outcomes are provided (e.g., an object structure to be tested using pattern matching).

```
1   check "Basic LEA expression (left-associative)" \
2       {+ 3 + 1 2} build "succeeds" using $internalBuilder
3
4   check "LEA expressions don't support subtraction." \
5       {- 3 + 1 2} build "fails" using $internalBuilder
```

Lst. 1.24 Exemplary test cases exercising the builder for the internal syntax

```
1   check "Basic LEA expression (left-associative)" \
2       {(1 + 2) + 3} build "succeeds" using $externalBuilder
3
4   check "LEA expressions don't support subtraction." \
5       {(1 + 2) - 3} build "fails" using $externalBuilder
```

Lst. 1.25 Exemplary test cases exercising the builder for the external syntax

The same test-case notation applies to BUILDERS responsible for an external DSL, e.g., ExternalBuilder, by setting the using clause accordingly (see Listing 1.25). This minimal testing infrastructure can be employed in a unit-testing manner. Units here denote structural elements of the overall DSL implementation (e.g., builders, parsers, interpreters, and/or generators) which become under test in isolation from each other. These units can be tested by writing cases on certain test conditions (e.g., build, parse, run). However, it also extends to support integration testing for DSL.[17]

---

[17]Integration testing here refers to tests covering two or more implementation units of a DSL at a time. By providing setup and clean-up clauses as well as different aggregations of test cases, a scenario-based DSL testing approach can be realized (e.g., scenario-based language tests [24]).

References

1. Apel S, Batory D, Kästner C, Saake G (2013) Feature-oriented software product lines, 1st edn. Springer, Berlin. https://doi.org/10.1007/978-3-642-37521-7
2. Atkinson C, Kühne T (2007) A tour of language customization concepts. Adv Comput 70:105–161
3. Barišić A, Amaral V, Goulão M (2018) Usability driven DSL development with USE-ME. Comput Lang Syst Struct 51:118–157. https://doi.org/10.1016/j.cl.2017.06.005
4. Bruneliere H, Garcia J, Desfray P, Khelladi DE, Hebig R, Bendraou R, Cabot J (2015) On lightweight metamodel extension to support modeling tools agility. In: Proceedings of the 11th European Conference Modelling Foundations and Applications (ECMFA'15). Lecture notes in computer science, vol 9153. Springer, Berlin, pp 62–74. https://doi.org/10.1007/978-3-319-21151-0_5
5. Calegari D, Viera M (2015) Model-driven engineering based on attribute grammars. In: Proceedings of the 19th Brazilian Symposium on Programming Languages (SBLP'15). Lecture notes in computer science, vol 9325. Springer, Berlin, pp 112–127. https://doi.org/10.1007/978-3-319-24012-1_9
6. Czarnecki K, Eisenecker UW (2000) Generative programming — Methods, Tools, and Applications, 6th edn. Addison-Wesley, Boston
7. Deantoni J, Brun C, Caillaud B, France RB, Karsai G, Nierstrasz O, Syriani E (2015) Domain globalization: Using languages to support technical and social coordination. In: Proceedings of the International Dagstuhl Seminar on Globalizing Domain-specific Languages. Lecture notes in computer science, vol 9400. Springer, Berlin, pp 70–87. https://doi.org/10.1007/978-3-319-26172-0_5
8. Degueule T (2016) Composition and interoperability for external domain-specific language engineering. Theses, Université de Rennes 1 [UR1]. https://hal.inria.fr/tel-01427009
9. Erdweg S, van der Storm T, Völter M, Tratt L, Bosman R, Cook WR, Gerritsen A, Hulshout A, Kelly S, Loh A, Konat G, Molina PJ, Palatnik M, Pohjonen R, Schindler E, Schindler K, Solmi R, Vergu V, Visser E, van der Vlist K, Wachsmuth G, van der Woning J (2015) Evaluating and comparing language workbenches: Existing results and benchmarks for the future. Comput Lang Syst Struct 44(Part A):24–47. https://doi.org/10.1016/j.cl.2015.08.007
10. Fehrenbach S, Erdweg S, Ostermann K (2013) Software evolution to domain-specific languages. In: Proceedings of the 6th International Conference on Software Language Engineering (SLE'13). Lecture notes in computer science, vol 8225. Springer, Berlin, pp 96–116. https://doi.org/10.1007/978-3-319-02654-1_6
11. Fister IJ, Kosar T, Fister I, Mernik M (2013) Easytime++: A case study of incremental domain-specific language development. Inf Technol Control 42(1):77–85. https://doi.org/10.5755/j01.itc.42.1.1968
12. Ford B (2004) Parsing expression grammars: A recognition-based syntactic foundation. In: Proceedings of the 31st ACM SIGPLAN-SIGACT Symposium on Principles of Programming Languages (POPL'04). ACM, New York, pp 111–122. https://doi.org/10.1145/964001.964011
13. Fowler M (2010) Domain specific languages, 1st edn. Addison-Wesley, Boston
14. Gabriel P, Goulão M, Amaral V (2010) Do software languages engineers evaluate their languages? In: Proceedings of the XIII Congreso Iberoamericano en "Software Engineering"
15. Galster M, Avgeriou P, Männistö T, Weyns D (2014) Variability in software architecture – State of the art. J Syst Softw 91:1–2. https://doi.org/10.1016/j.jss.2014.01.051
16. Gamma E, Helm R, Johnson RE, Vlissides J (1995) Design Patterns – Elements of Reusable Object-Oriented Software. Addison Wesley Professional computing series. Addison-Wesley, Boston
17. Ghosh D (2010) DSLs in action, 1st edn. Manning, Shelter Island
18. Harel D, Rumpe B (2004) Meaningful modeling: What's the semantics of "semantics"? Computer 37(10):64–72. https://doi.org/10.1109/MC.2004.172

19. Häser F, Felderer M, Breu R (2016) An integrated tool environment for experimentation in domain specific language engineering. In: Proceedings of the 20th International Conference on Evaluation and Assessment in Software Engineering (EASE'16). ACM, New York, pp 20:1–20:5. https://doi.org/10.1145/2915970.2916010

20. Hasu T (2017) Programming language techniques for niche platforms. Ph.D. Thesis, University of Bergen

21. Hermans F, Pinzger M, van Deursen A (2009) Domain-specific languages in practice: A user study on the success factors. In: Proceedings of the 12th International Conference Model Driven Engineering Languages and Systems (MoDELS'09). Lecture notes in computer science, vol 5795. Springer, Berlin, pp 423–437

22. Hoisl B, Strembeck M, Sobernig S (2012) Towards a systematic integration of MOF/UML-based domain-specific modeling languages. In: Proceedings of the 16th IASTED International Conference Software Engineering and Application (SEA'12). ACTA Press, Calgary, pp 337–344. https://doi.org/10.2316/P.2012.790-045

23. Hoisl B, Sobernig S, Strembeck M (2014) Comparing three notations for defining scenario-based model tests: A controlled experiment. In: Proceedings of the 9th International Conference on the Quality of Information and Communications Technology (QUATIC'14). IEEE CS, Washington, pp 95–104. https://doi.org/10.1109/QUATIC.2014.19

24. Hoisl B, Sobernig S, Strembeck M (2014) Natural-language scenario descriptions for testing core language models of domain-specific languages. In: Proceedings of the 2nd International Conference on Model-driven Engineering and Software Development (MODELSWARD'14), SciTePress, Setúbal, pp 356–367. https://doi.org/10.5220/0004713703560367

25. Hoisl B, Sobernig S, Strembeck M (2017) Reusable and generic design decisions for developing UML-based domain-specific languages. Inf Softw Technol 92:49–74. https://doi.org/10.1016/j.infsof.2017.07.008

26. Jackson E, Sztipanovits J (2009) Formalizing the structural semantics of domain-specific modeling languages. Softw Syst Model 8(4):451–478. https://doi.org/10.1007/s10270-008-0105-0

27. JetBrains (2017) Meta programming system (MPS). https://www.jetbrains.com/mps/

28. Jézéquel JM, Méndez-Acuña D, Degueule T, Combemale B, Barais O (2015) When systems engineering meets software language engineering. In: Proceedings of the Fifth International Conference on Complex Systems Design & Management (CSD&M'14). Springer, Berlin, pp 1–13. https://doi.org/10.1007/978-3-319-11617-4_1

29. Johanson AN, Hasselbring W (2014) Hierarchical combination of internal and external domain-specific languages for scientific computing. In: Proceedings of the 2014 European Conference on Software Architecture Workshops (ECSAW'14). ACM, New York, pp 17:1–17:8. https://doi.org/10.1145/2642803.2642820

30. Johnstone A, Scott E, van den Brand M (2014) Modular grammar specification. Sci Comput Program 87:23–43. https://doi.org/10.1016/j.scico.2013.09.012

31. Jörges S (2013) Construction and evolution of code generators. Lecture notes in computer science, vol 7747. Springer, Berlin. https://doi.org/10.1007/978-3-642-36127-2

32. Kahraman G, Bilgen S (2015) A framework for qualitative assessment of domain-specific languages. Softw Syst Model 14(4):1505–1526

33. Karsai G, Maroti M, Ledeczi A, Gray J, Sztipanovits J (2004) Composition and cloning in modeling and meta-modeling. IEEE Trans Control Syst Technol 12(2):263–278. https://doi.org/10.1109/TCST.2004.824311

34. Kats LCL, Vermaas R, Visser E (2011) Integrated language definition testing: Enabling test-driven language development. In: Proceedings of the 2011 ACM International Conference on Object Oriented Programming Systems Languages and Applications (OOPSLA'11). ACM, New York, pp 139–154. https://doi.org/10.1145/2048066.2048080

35. Klint P, van der Storm T, Vinju J (2010) On the impact of DSL tools on the maintainability of language implementations. In: Proceedings of the Workshop on Language Descriptions, Tools and Applications 2010 (LDTA'10). ACM, New York, pp 10:1–10:9

36. Ko AJ, Abraham R, Beckwith L, Blackwell A, Burnett M, Erwig M, Scaffidi C, Lawrance J, Lieberman H, Myers B, Rosson MB, Rothermel G, Shaw M, Wiedenbeck S (2011) The state of the art in end-user software engineering. ACM Comput Surv 43(3):21:1–21:44. https://doi.org/10.1145/1922649.1922658

37. Kosar T, López PM, Barrientos P, Mernik M (2008) A preliminary study on various implementation approaches of domain-specific languages. Inf Softw Technol 50(5):390–405

38. Kosar T, Bohra S, Mernik M (2016) Domain-specific languages: A systematic mapping study. Inf Softw Technol 71:77–91. https://doi.org/10.1016/j.infsof.2015.11.001

39. Krueger CW (1992) Software reuse. ACM Comput Surv 24(2):131–183. https://doi.org/10.1145/130844.130856

40. Kuehne T, Schreiber D (2007) Can programming be liberated from the two-level style: Multi-level programming with DeepJava. In: Proceedings of the 22nd Annual ACM SIGPLAN Conference on Object-oriented Programming Systems and Applications (OOPLSA'07). ACM, New York, pp 229–244. https://doi.org/10.1145/1297027.1297044

41. Kühn T, Cazzola W (2016) Apples and oranges: Comparing top-down and bottom-up language product lines. In: Proceedings of the 20th International Systems and Software Product Line Conference (SPLC'16). ACM, New York, pp 50–59. https://doi.org/10.1145/2934466.2934470

42. Kühn T, Cazzola W, Olivares DM (2015) Choosy and picky: Configuration of language product lines. In: Proceedings of the 19th International Conference on Software Product Line (SPLC'15). ACM, New York, pp 71–80. https://doi.org/10.1145/2791060.2791092

43. Lämmel R (2018) Software languages: Syntax, Semantics, and Metaprogramming, 1st edn. Springer, Berlin. https://doi.org/10.1007/978-3-319-90800-7

44. Liebig J, Daniel R, Apel S (2013) Feature-oriented language families: A case study. In: Proceedings of the 7th International Workshop on Variability Modelling of Software-Intensive Systems (VaMoS'13). ACM, New York, pp 11:1–11:8. https://doi.org/10.1145/2430502.2430518

45. Méndez-Acuña D, Galindo JA, Degueule T, Combemale B, Baudry B (2016) Leveraging software product lines engineering in the development of external DSLs: A systematic literature review. Comput Lang Syst Struct 46:206–235. https://doi.org/10.1016/j.cl.2016.09.004

46. Méndez-Acuña D, Galindo JA, Combemale B, Blouin A, Baudry B (2017) Reverse engineering language product lines from existing DSL variants. J Syst Softw 133:145–158. https://doi.org/10.1016/j.jss.2017.05.042

47. Mernik M, Heering J, Sloane AM (2005) When and how to develop domain-specific languages. ACM Comput Surv 37(4):316–344. https://doi.org/10.1145/1118890.1118892

48. Meyer B (1988) Object-oriented software construction, 2nd edn. Prentice Hall, Upper Saddle River

49. Meyers B (2016) A multi-paradigm modelling approach to design and evolution of domain-specific modelling languages. PhD Thesis, University of Antwerp

50. Nadkarni AP (2017) The Tcl programming language: A comprehensive guide. CreateSpace Independent Publishing Platform

51. Neighbors JM (1989) Draco: A method for engineering reusable software systems. In: Biggerstaff T, Perlis AJ (eds) Software Reusability, vol 1, chap 12. Addison Wesley, Boston

52. Neumann G, Sobernig S (2016) NSF/NX tutorial. https://next-scripting.org/xowiki/docs/index

53. Neumann G, Zdun U (1999) Enhancing object-based system composition through per-object mixins. In: Proceedings of the Asia-Pacific Software Engineering Conference (APSEC'99). IEEE CS, Washington, pp 522–530

54. Neumann G, Zdun U (1999) Filters as a language support for design patterns in object-oriented scripting languages. In: Proceedings of the 5th Conference on Object-oriented Technologies and Systems (COOTS'99), USENIX

55. Neumann G, Sobernig S, Aram M (2014) Evolutionary business information systems: Perspectives and challenges of an emerging class of information systems. Bus Inf Syst Eng 6(1):33–38. https://doi.org/10.1007/s12599-013-0305-1

56. Norvell T (1999) Parsing expressions by recursive descent. https://www.engr.mun.ca/~theo/Misc/exp_parsing.htm

57. Nosál M, Porubän J, Sulir M (2017) Customizing host IDE for non-programming users of pure embedded DSLs: A case study. Comput Lang Syst Struct https://doi.org/10.1016/j.cl.2017.04.003

58. Object Management Group (2016) OMG meta object facility (MOF) core specification. http://www.omg.org/spec/MOF, version 2.5.1, formal/16-11-01

59. Object Management Group (2017) OMG unified modeling language (OMG UML). http://www.omg.org/spec/UML, version 2.5.1, formal/17-12-05

60. Ousterhout JK, Jones K (2009) Tcl and the Tk Toolkit, 2nd edn. Addison-Wesley, Boston

61. Paige RF, Kolovos DS, Polack FA (2014) A tutorial on metamodelling for grammar researchers. Sci Comput Program 96:396–416. https://doi.org/10.1016/j.scico.2014.05.007

62. Schaefer I, Rabiser R, Clarke D, Bettini L, Benavides D, Botterweck G, Pathak A, Trujillo S, Villela K (2012) Software diversity: State of the art and perspectives. Intl J Softw Tools Technol Trans 14(5):477–495. https://doi.org/10.1007/s10009-012-0253-y

63. Selic B (2003) The pragmatics of model-driven development. IEEE Softw 20(5):19–25. https://doi.org/10.1109/MS.2003.1231146

64. Sobernig S (2018) Ml-deep. https://github.com/nm-wu/ml-deep/

65. Sobernig S, Gaubatz P, Strembeck M, Zdun U (2011) Comparing complexity of API designs: An exploratory experiment on DSL-based framework integration. In: Proceedings of the 10th International Conference on Generative Programming and Component Engineering (GPCE'11). ACM, New York, pp 157–166. https://doi.org/10.1145/2047862.2047890

66. Sobernig S, Neumann G, Adelsberger S (2012) Supporting multiple feature binding strategies in NX. In: Proceedings of the 4th International Workshop on Feature-oriented Software Development (FOSD'12). ACM, New York, pp 45–53. https://doi.org/10.1145/2377816.2377823

67. Sobernig S, Hoisl B, Strembeck M (2013) Requirements-driven testing of domain-specific core language models using scenarios. In: Proceedings of the 13th International Conference on Quality Software (QSIC'13). IEEE, Piscataway, pp 163–172. https://doi.org/10.1109/QSIC.2013.56

68. Sobernig S, Hoisl B, Strembeck M (2016) Extracting reusable design decisions for UML-based domain-specific languages: A multi-method study. J Syst Softw 113:140–172. https://doi.org/10.1016/j.jss.2015.11.037

69. Stahl T, Völter M (2006) Model-driven software development. Wiley, Hoboken

70. Strembeck M, Zdun U (2009) An approach for the systematic development of domain-specific languages. Softw Pract Exp 39(15):1253–1292

71. Tambe S, White J, Gray J, Hill JH, Gokhale AS, Schmidt DC (2009) Improving domain-specific language reuse with software product line techniques. IEEE Softw 26:47–53, https://doi.org/10.1109/MS.2009.95

72. van der Storm T, Cook WR, Loh A (2014) The design and implementation of object grammars. Sci Comput Program 96:460–487. https://doi.org/10.1016/j.scico.2014.02.023

73. Völter M, Bettin J (2004) Patterns for model-driven software-development. http://www.voelter.de/data/pub/MDDPatterns.pdf

74. Völter M, Benz S, Dietrich C, Engelmann B, Helander M, Kats LCL, Visser E, Wachsmuth G (2013) DSL engineering: Designing, implementing and using domain-specific languages. http://www.dslbook.org

75. Wille D, Schulze S, Schaefer I (2016) Variability mining of state charts. In: Proceedings of the 7th International Workshop on Feature-oriented Software Development (FOSD'16). ACM, New York, pp 63–73. https://doi.org/10.1145/3001867.3001875

76. Wimmer M, Kramler G (2006) Bridging grammarware and modelware. In: Satellite Proceedings of the International Conference on Model Driven Engineering Languages and Systems (MoDELS'05). Springer, Berlin, pp 159–168

77. Zdun U (2010) A DSL toolkit for deferring architectural decisions in DSL-based software design. Inf Softw Technol 52(7):733–748. https://doi.org/10.1016/j.infsof.2010.03.004

78. Zdun U, Strembeck M (2009) Reusable architectural decisions for DSL design: Foundational decisions in DSL development. In: Proceedings of the 14th European Conference on Patt. Lang. Prog. ACM, New York, pp 1–37
79. Zdun U, Strembeck M, Neumann G (2007) Object-based and class-based composition of transitive mixins. Inf Softw Technol 49(8):871–891. https://doi.org/10.1016/j.infsof.2006.10.001

Chapter 2
Variability Support in DSL Development

Developing domain-specific languages is typically situated in the overall development process of a software system [53]. The DSL and DSL-based tooling (e.g., a pipeline for DSL scripts) form a sub-system or component. In this context, DSL play different architectural roles. As a domain-specific modeling language (DSML), they serve as the frontend to a model-driven tool chain. As architecture DSL (ADSL), they help document, define, and analyze the systems' architectural structure and architectural constraints; or documenting architectural design rationale in terms of documented design decisions. In product-line engineering and product development, DSL serve as configuration languages driving product configuration or representing variability models. In the solution space, DSL can take the role of gluing sub-systems and components of the overall system in terms of scripting languages.[1]

Therefore, developing DSL involves design-decision making on the DSL itself in the context of an overall development project [61, 72]. For example, DSL developers can choose from different options on how to realize a DSL's language model (abstract syntax), on the DSL style to be adopted (internal vs. external DSL), on the means to define a DSL's semantics, on the concrete syntax style (e.g., graphical, textual, or both), and on critical technology choices (e.g., host languages, language workbenches, metamodeling infrastructure). The DSL as well as the corresponding infrastructure components (such as parser, generator, or DSL editor) form parts of the respective software architecture, often assisting in realizing a particular architectural style, pattern, or tactic for the scope of the overall system's architecture.

Given that the DSL-based sub-system or component must be integrated with the remainder of the software system (e.g., as the DSL's target platform) and is likely to evolve independently from the rest of the system (e.g., because of changes in

---

[1]Reflecting on DSL-based software development and its architectural dimension (DSL-based architectures, DSL-specific design-decision making) across different methodologies (product-line engineering, model-driven development) was the central theme of a community event co-organized by me [53]: DADA.

© Springer Nature Switzerland AG 2020
S. Sobernig, *Variable Domain-specific Software Languages with DjDSL*,
https://doi.org/10.1007/978-3-030-42152-6_2

the domain covered by the DSL), DSL-based software development often presents challenges beyond typical issues of component integration [22, Chapter 3]. These include failure propagation between and handling across components and also non-functional requirements (e.g., execution performance of DSL scripts).

Performance
It is not unlikely that a DSL must operate under performance requirements that are critical to a business: In a DSL-based energy-trading system developed by Sobernig et al. [56], schedule generation and delivery are time-critical in the range of 1 or 2 min in certain markets. This is because energy trading happens in fixed time boxes (e.g., 15 min after the hour) and price increases tend to grow toward the end of trading windows. Trading, however, is stopped effectively before the end of a time box to create and to deliver the schedule messages reliably for completing the transaction. To optimize an intra-day trading portfolio, the energy seller seeks to minimize schedule-handling times to extend the effective trading time.

Supporting variability must be considered for different scopes of a DSL-based software system and for the DSL as one of its sub-systems:

- Reusable procedures for DSL development (see Sect. 2.1)
- Managing DSL design decisions as architectural knowledge (see Sect. 2.2)
- Challenges pertaining to DSL variability (DSL composition, abstraction mismatches; see Sect. 2.4)

At the time of writing, there is already a respectable body of work in these three areas. This corpus ranges from procedural "models" for DSL development and best-practice guidelines to design-decision documentation and software patterns for DSL design and implementation.

Software Pattern
In software engineering and other engineering fields, a pattern is a time-proven solution to a recurring design problem. A pattern description includes (at least) a *problem description*, a description of the *context* in which the respective problem occurs, and one or more (alternative) *solutions*. Ideally, pattern descriptions also include different *forces* that may influence the choice of a certain solution, *consequences* that arise from a solution, as well as *known uses* of a particular solution [4]. Software patterns are considered at two levels for the scope of this work: (a) As elements of systematic and variable design-decision making on DSL (in the context of managing DSL design rationale) and (b) as techniques to implementing variability. See Sect. 2.4 for an overview. Section 5.1 introduces a pattern-based implementation approach for variable internal DSL syntaxes.

2.1 DSL Engineering Procedures

Developing a DSL involves different characteristic development activities [8, 61]. From a decision-making perspective, each development activity also marks a *decision point*, i.e., a point in time at which particular design-decision problems must be addressed. In doing so, different design solutions based on their assumed or known properties for the DSL design as well as their effects on any subsequent design decisions are assessed. From the angle of design-rationale documentation, a decision point is a point in time for recording an on-going decision-making process.

Supporting variability at the level of a design-decision making involves two levels:

- Reusable and tailorable development procedures (akin to tailorable documentation)
- Deferrable and revocable ("dynamic") design decisions[2]

Tailoring of development procedures by DSL developers means to adjust a flow of (planned) decision-making and developing activities to the requirements of a given DSL project and the requirements of the domain of application. As for dynamic design decisions: A deferrable design decision is one that is taken at a comparably late point in time in a DSL project, despite being mandatory during DSL development and the design-decision process. The goal is to preserve a certain flexibility for the DSL developer and to avoid, in particular, technical lock-ins early in the project. A lock-in leads to a restricted space of options or unwanted consequences for quality attributes of the DSL-based application later on. A revocable design decision is one that can be revisited and, possibly, can be reverted entirely (e.g., by discarding or discontinuing the corresponding development artifacts) without incurring extra effort to modify the remainder of a DSL implementation.

Consider the basic design decision on whether to adopt an internal and an external DSL approach for a given project [71]. Certain early design decisions, especially regarding on DSL development tooling and host languages, may preclude going from one (internal) to the other (external). This is despite the fact that in DSL prototyping, an internal DSL approach may be appropriate while eliciting requirements from the domain may call for an external DSL (e.g., because of restrictions incurred by the host language). Similarly, when a DSL design has matured, it may become unnecessary to further maintain one of the alternative syntaxes (e.g., an internal and external DSL, respectively). Revoking a former decision by decommissioning the implementation of the unneeded syntax, without the risk of tedious reworking the code base, is then advantageous. The same applies to implementations of processing pipelines for DSL scripts in the DSL-based tooling (e.g., analysis, transformation, execution).

DSL product line engineering involves phases of domain and DSL-based application development. In each phase, two different perspectives are relevant: problem space and solution space (see also Fig. 1.2). The problem-space perspective

---

[2]The use of "dynamic" compares with its meaning in terms of a binding mode [10].

puts the spot on the stakeholders (practitioners, domain engineers), problem statements, their articulated requirements, and the family of existing software products (DSL variants; if any). The solution-space perspective corresponds to the perspective taken by DSL developers and application developers. Their emphasis is on concerns of the solution domain, including the DSL architecture as well as DSL-based application architecture, design, and implementation; plus, verification and validation (testing) of these artifacts. In the following, existing reference procedures for *domain engineering*, both from the problem-space and the solution-space perspectives, are highlighted.

2.1.1 Problem Space

Reference procedures for problem-space tasks in DSL product line development have been proposed against a broader domain-engineering background (FODA and FAST mentioned in [44]) and for more specific types of tasks. Examples include requirements gathering and elicitation for a DSL [11]. This also covers more recent contributions to incorporate systematically the quality-in-use (including DSL-based tooling) into iterative DSL development processes (e.g., FQAD ; see Sect. 1.3). Historically, DSL have been integral building blocks and output artifacts of domain-engineering approaches such as Draco [46] and DEMRAL [10].[3] To give an idea, a DEMRAL-inspired process includes the following problem-space tasks and exemplary artifacts as shown below [based on 10, Section 5.7].

Example (DEMRAL)
1. Domain analysis

   (a) Domain definition: terminology documentation (e.g., controlled vocabulary).

      (i) Goal and stakeholder analysis: context diagrams, goal model
      (ii) Domain scoping and context analysis: software-product scenarios (e.g., use cases, interaction scenarios), deployment diagrams

         (A) Analysis of application areas and existing software systems: product-attribute matrices
         (B) Identification of features: nomenclature and feature descriptions
         (C) Identification of relationships to other domains

(continued)

---

[3]For this writing, a deep dive into domain engineering, in general and with emphasis on DSL, is out of scope. This is mainly because the key contributions of this work relate to the solution-space tasks. The interested reader is referred to [10, 44] for respective overviews of domain engineering w/ and w/o DSL. For an example of systematic domain-analysis techniques used in our DSL projects, see, for example, [56] (FODA).

(b) Domain modeling

(i) Identification of key concepts: platform-independent domain or DSL model
(ii) Feature modeling: variability model (e.g., feature diagram)

2. *Domain design (solution space)*
3. *Domain implementation (solution space)*

2.1.2 Solution Space

Reference procedures for solution-space tasks in DSL product line (or, multi-DSL) development can be based on those for single-DSL development [61]. Particularly reference procedures with emphasis on the architectural design of DSL are suited (a) because they integrate with problem-space procedures (to capture the variability aspects of the domain) and (b) because they can be tailored to support proactive, reactive, and extractive paths for developing and for deploying a DSL product line (see also Sect. 1.2).

Strembeck and Zdun [61] distilled recurring DSL development activities based on a review of DSL project experiences. These recurring activities are documented and it is shown how they can be arranged differently in single-DSL development processes. In a complementary contribution, Zdun and Strembeck [72] document three main decisions to be made when applying the DSL development process from [61]. These decisions relate to the choices of a specific type of DSL development process, of a concrete syntax style, and of developing an external versus developing an internal DSL. To render these decision descriptions reusable,

Fig. 2.1 DSL development styles [61, Section 6]: driven by language model (on the left), driven by syntax mock-ups (on the right). The background tutorial in Sect. 1.4 represents an instance of the language-model-driven style (see also Fig. 1.3)

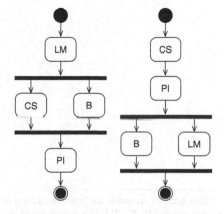

they are documented using a pattern format [72].[4] The recurring development
activities are:

- *Language-model definition* (LM): Input are domain-engineering artifacts on the
  problem space (e.g., domain definition, domain scoping). Output are the core
  language-model (primary abstract syntax) and context conditions plus semantics
  definitions.
- *Concrete-syntax definition* (CS): Input are the language-model artifacts and,
  if available, syntax probes from a domain analysis. Output are definitions for
  graphical or textual syntaxes (e.g., production or parsing grammars).
- *Behaviour definition* (B): Input are the language-model definitions. Output are
  behavior models (e.g., control- or data-flow models) and behaviour definitions
  using an external formalism (e.g., semantic actions of a grammar), supported by
  behavioural context conditions.
- *Platform integration* (PI): Input are language-model and behaviour definitions.
  Output are mapping definitions (e.g., model or program transformations) targeting a given software platform, and platform-specific (executable) artifacts.

Strembeck and Zdun [61] further document characteristic arrangements of these
activities ("styles") that the authors have observed for several projects: driven by a
language model (see Fig. 2.1, on the left), driven by syntax mock-ups (see Fig. 2.1,
on the right). These development styles, if adopted, are commonly tailored to meet
project-specific requirements, including domain-specific requirements (e.g., direct
access to domain experts) and requirements of the overall DSL-based application

Fig. 2.2 A reactive,
incremental development
procedure. Each
across-activity iteration adds
another DSL variant (e.g., one
or several optional features)
as an increment to the family

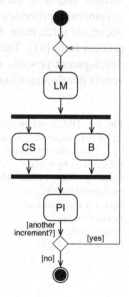

---

[4]This body of recorded and reusable design decisions in support of design-decision making has
since grown [28, 57, 71]. This is elaborated on in Sect. 2.2.

development project (e.g., a software framework made accessible via the DSL under development).

Multi-DSL development procedures, based on a DSL product line, can be thought as variants of these reference procedures by adding within-activity or across-activity iterations. Consider a proactive multi-DSL project [71] involving different concrete syntaxes (internal and external) as alternative frontends. This would be expressed as iterations (one per concrete syntax) within the CS activity. For this purpose, Strembeck and Zdun [61] also provide more detailed models of the four high-level activities, including CS, for adoption. Consider another example. A reactive multi-DSL project, which adds one DSL variant at a time, based on an initial single-variant product line, can be depicted as an across-activity iteration (see Fig. 2.2). Note that each across-activities iteration can include only selected activities and design decisions. In Chap. 6, a detailed example of a reactive development path is given.

A process-oriented perspective on DSL development (whether on the problem space or solution space or both) has immediate benefits. It establishes a shared process vocabulary (e.g., of different development artifacts) and represents common DSL development styles via different flows between development activities (e.g., language-model-driven or mock-up-driven DSL development). On the flip side, a process perspective alone abstracts from DSL development as a result of continuous decision-making by stakeholders (e.g., domain engineers, DSL developers, application developers, practitioners). Such decision-making is always situated in a specific context. This context is shaped by domain requirements and architecture requirements (e.g., a certain modeling technology stack such as a specific DSL development system). And this context spawns a design-decision space at a different level of granularity: decision options and forces on different elements and concerns of a DSL product line and DSL-based application. Therefore, reference procedures must be complemented with reusable design rationale, which is, therefore, covered next.

2.2 DSL Design Rationale

Design rationale (DR) [3, 15] on DSL development includes reasoning and justification of decisions made when designing, creating, and using the development artifacts of a DSL. Relevant artifacts are related to the abstract and concrete syntax, behaviour definition, metamodeling infrastructure, or the DSL-based tool chain. Documenting DR explicitly aims at assisting software (DSL) developers by providing and explaining past decisions (e.g., in a design-space analysis) and by improving the understanding of a particular DSL design choice during development and maintenance (e.g., as a kind of design-process documentation).

Two kinds of DSL design rationale can be distinguished (following [24]):

1. DSL-*specific* DR reflects on the reasoning over different decision options during a particular design process for a single DSL. Examples of such

explicitly documented, specific DR may be found in artifacts created in source-configuration management tools, development-issue trackers, and open-standards artifacts. For general-purpose software languages, examples include Java Community Process documents, the recorded issue votes during the ANSI/CLISP X3J13 specification process as collected in Steele [59], and Tcl Improvement Proposals (TIP).

2. DSL-*generic* DR includes knowledge obtained through developing multiple DSL, for one or several domains of application. Generic DR is commonly found only as implicit knowledge of experienced DSL developers. For example, software patterns have been used in software language engineering to explicitly document generic DR.

Capturing design rationale (DR) on a DSL project can be achieved in different, systematic ways [15]. First, one can recover design decisions by reviewing DSL development artifacts after the fact (e.g., abstract syntax or concrete-syntax definitions). This can be done either by the DSL developers themselves or by third-party experts on DSL development and in DR documentation. Second, DSL designers might record their rationale themselves as a by-product of the decision-making process. A third source are records of communication created by DSL designers, for example, language-user documentation, change/maintenance documentation, and scientific publications. Finally, if available, design-support software can be used for documenting design-decisions (e.g., IDEs including support for design-knowledge management 63). However, contemporary design-support software for DSL (DSL development systems, language workbenches) does not provide DR capturing facilities.

The lack of documented design-decision rationale in software engineering is attributed to the *capture problem* of design-rationale documentation [3, 15]. An important barrier to documenting design rationale (DR) in all necessary detail is the considerable overhead of creating and maintaining DR documentation.[5] Other problems explored in the research on documenting DR include the intrusiveness of documentation techniques, lack of incentives, and cognitive barriers in software-design processes (see, e.g., [15, 19, 29]). As a consequence, new DSL development projects cannot benefit from the experiences gained in prior projects and valuable design knowledge might be lost [24].

Empirical Evidence
In our recent work on UML-based DSL [28], a survey among 80 experts revealed that four-fifth of the participants encountered (at least one of) the

(continued)

---

[5] A study on capturing architectural design knowledge quantified the time effort needed for a project *including* capturing design rationale to be *twice* the time needed for a project *without* that extra effort [5].

candidate barriers, in decreasing order: absence of tool support to document decisions (80.6%), time/budget constraints (79%), lack of standards/requirements to document design decisions (79%), and missing justification for extra work of documenting design decisions (79%). These barriers were also perceived as being the most critical ones.

In this context, two important objectives in software-engineering research are to *limit the effort* for documenting design decisions and to *increase the quality* of the documented rationale [3, 15, 19]. To achieve these objectives, existing documentation approaches distill common or reusable knowledge—similar to software patterns [24]—from decisions made in actual development projects to document and share proven solutions along with their forces, consequences, and (alternative) solutions (see, e.g., [28, 39]). For developing DSL (including DSMLs) prior work has started by gathering DR and best practices. Results include procedural models on systematic DSL development (see Sect. 2.1) as well as software-pattern collections (see, e.g., [58, 72]) and design-decision catalogs [28].

2.2.1 Reusable DSL Design Decisions

In a long-term research effort of 3 years [26, 57], we collected, documented, and systematized generic design rationale from more than 80 UML-based DSLs.[6] The key result is a publicly available catalog of reusable design decisions [27]. The *decision catalog* consists of seven reusable design decisions (*decision records*), each describing a repeatedly observed *decision context* (e.g., a development phase or certain technology choices), a repeatedly reported *design problem* regarding a DSL design element, as well as corresponding *design options* to solve the problem. In total, the catalog documents 35 decision options (see Fig. 2.3). Table 2.1 highlights design decisions relevant to this section. In addition, the reusable design decisions also report on the inter-dependencies between different reusable decisions (e.g., between designing the abstract syntax and the concrete syntax of a DSL).

A reusable design decision is codified as a *decision record*. A decision record provides two or more descriptions of proven solutions to a generic and recurring problem in developing a DSL. The problem described by a decision record must not only recur, that is, be observable for many DSL development projects, but it

---

[6]While certain decisions are specific to UML as the host language (in particular, UML-specific extension techniques), others apply to non-UML and even non-modeling DSL as well (e.g., on concrete-syntax definition). This is also because a DSL development system or a DSL-based tool chain commonly blends model- and grammarware techniques and tools (see Sect. 1.1). The overall proposal of documenting generic DR and of rendering it reusable as well as tailorable is not specific to the UML.

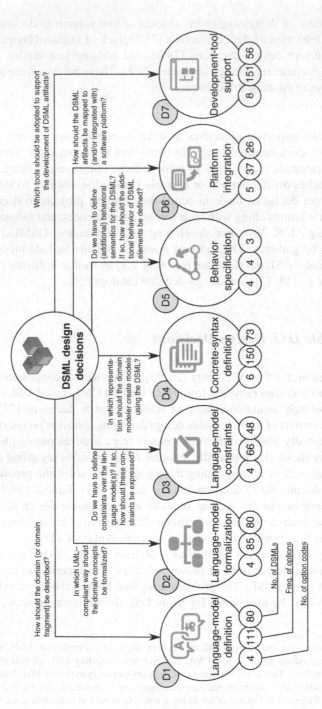

Fig. 2.3 The catalog of reusable design decisions on UML-based DSL covers seven decision points (D1–D7). The circles attached to each decision document the number of decision options per decision point, the number of occurrences of these options in the reviewed DSL designs (absolute frequency), and the number of DSL choosing at least one of these options

---

D4 Concrete-Syntax Definition

Problem. *In which representation should the domain modeler create models using the DSML?*

Context. The concrete syntax serves as the DSML's interface. Different syntax types can be defined and tailored to the need of the modeler ...

Options.
  O4.1 Model annotation: Attach UML comments as concrete-syntax cues to a UML model, containing complementary domain information such as keywords, narrative statements, or formal definitions (see, e.g., [3]). ...
  O4.2 Diagrammatic syntax extension: ...

Decision drivers. An overview of positive and negative links between decision drivers and available options is shown in the table below. ...
  Non-diagrammatic UML notation requirements: Textual notations [1] for the UML are auxiliary representations and act as frontend syntaxes (O4.4).

Driver/Option	O4.1	O4.2	O4.3	O4.4	O4.5	O4.6	O4.7
Non-diagrammatic UML notation requirements	o	o	−	−	−	o	o
Degree of cognitive expressiveness	−	+	+/−	+/−	+/−	−	o
Disruptiveness	−	+	+	+	++	−	+/−
Degree of required modeling-tool support	++	−	+/−	+	−−	++	o

Consequences.
  Usability evaluation: The DSML syntax is especially important from the DSML user perspective. If a DSML is mainly used by non-programmers, a special focus on usability aspects is needed. ...

Application. In our case studies we provide a couple of different concrete syntax definitions such as UML stereotype-specific annotations for reusing symbols (P1, P3, P7, P9, P10). ...

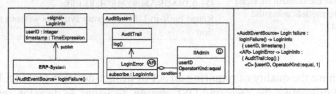

Figure 1: Exemplary graphical and textual concrete syntax [2].

Sketch. Figure 1 shows an example of two concrete syntax definitions ...

Fig. 2.4 An excerpt from the actual decision record on concrete-syntax definition (D4) in Hoisl et al. [27], highlighting the document sections corresponding to the key concepts of a design-decision record

Table 2.1 Thumbnail descriptions of selected (7 out of 35 total) decision options (for 4 out of 7 decision points) relevant to the presentation of examples in this section

	Problem statement	Options (selected)
D1	How should the domain (or domain fragment) be described?	O1.1 INFORMAL TEXTUAL DESCRIPTION Use informal text to identify and to describe domain abstractions and their relationships (e.g., domain-vision statements, domain-distillation lists)
D2	In which UML-compliant way should the domain concepts be formalized?	O2.2 PROFILE RE-/DEFINITION Implement the language model by creating (or by adapting existing) UML profiles (i.e. «profile» packages containing stereotype definitions) O2.3 METAMODEL EXTENSION Implement the language model by creating one or several metamodel extensions (i.e. «metamodel» packages containing new metaclasses and associations) O2.4 METAMODEL MODIFICATION Implement the language model by creating one or several metamodel extensions (i.e. «metamodel» packages containing redefining metaclasses and associations)
D3	Do we have to define constraints over the language model(s)? If so, how should these constraints be expressed?	O3.1 CONSTRAINT-LANGUAGE EXPRESSION Make language-model constraints explicit using a constraint-expression language (e.g., OCL, EVL)
D4	In which representation should the domain modeler create models using the DSML?	O4.1 MODEL ANNOTATION Attach UML comments as concrete-syntax cues to a UML model, containing complementary domain information such as keywords and narrative statements O4.6 DIAGRAM SYMBOL REUSE Reuse built-in UML diagram symbols without modification

must also have the quality of requiring an act of design-decision making. For structuring and presenting the recurring DSL design decisions as decision records, we developed and refined a document template [27]. Each decision record is structured into several sections: decision context, decision problem, decision options, decision drivers, decision consequences, decision applications, and decision sketches. An excerpt from the actual decision record on concrete-syntax definition (D4) is depicted in Fig. 2.4.

A decision record first describes a recurring design-*decision problem* that has been repeatedly observed for several DSL development projects. The exemplary decision record in Fig. 2.4 gives a problem statement frequently observed when deciding on the concrete-syntax style for a DSL: "In which representation should the domain modeler create models using the DSL?" This problem applies to a specific *decision context*. The decision context is primarily set by one of the decision points characteristic for DSL development (D1–D7, above). In addition, a particular metamodeling toolkit (e.g., MOF/UML), the application domain modeled by a DSL, and the target software platform can contribute to establishing the decision context. To give an example: The problem statement in Fig. 2.4 would not apply for a DSL project which is not about providing a particularly tailored or any concrete syntax to modelers. This could be because modelers are expected to work on an abstract syntax representation only.

As its core content, a decision record lists *decision options* which describe solutions to the initial stated decision problem. The excerpt in Fig. 2.4 shows the option MODEL ANNOTATION (O4.1) which is about realizing a tailored concrete syntax by means of model annotations. Next, a decision record documents means to select an option (or a combination of options) in terms of *decision drivers*. An exemplary driver in Fig. 2.4 is the cognitive expressiveness of concrete-syntax styles. These drivers are likely to steer the DSL designer toward a particular option or option combination. This selection decision affects the solution spaces of subsequent decisions. For example, they can set a new decision context. To scaffold follow-up decision-making, a decision record makes the DSL designer aware of known *decision consequences*. Consequences can include the need to evaluate other decision options within the same decision record or in related decision records. However, consequences can also point to follow-up decision problems not covered by the decision-record catalog alone. Such a consequence is the need for usability evaluations in Fig. 2.4.

To provide evidence that the listed decision options are taken from observed practice, a decision record comprises DSL projects as examples of *application* of the individual options or option combinations. In Fig. 2.4, one can see that a number of DSL projects also recorded as part of our decision-record catalog are referenced as applications. A decision record is then closed by replicating one concrete realization *sketch* of one decision option, taken from one DSL application. In Fig. 2.4, an example of providing a combined graphical and textual concrete-syntax is given.

This documentation format has been derived from prior work on documenting design rationale in software engineering. In particular, it is inspired by software-pattern descriptions [4] and architectural design decisions [51].[7] In addition, the format is based on feedback obtained from a survey on expert opinions on DSL development and DR documentation for DSL. For the content of a decision record, in particular the decision options, to qualify as generic design rationale, it must reflect *recurring* practice. As a rule of thumb from the software-pattern community [4, 9]), it was verified that each design option has at least applications in *three* different third-party DSL projects, that is, DSL not developed by the authors.

---

[7] A word of caution: Reusable decisions are not identical to or variants of software patterns. For example, a design decision (recorded decision) lists multiple solution propositions (decision options) rather than one. However, patterns are important decision support during design-decision making and pattern descriptions can be used to facilitate design-decision documentation (e.g., they can be referenced from therein).

2.2.1.1   Complementary Generic DR on DSLs

Design-decision making based on generic DR involves building up an inventory of reusable design decisions. The identification of relevant sources of documented DR is ideally performed in a systematic manner (e.g., using techniques for systematic literature reviews).[8] As for DSL development, there are design-decision collections complementing ours. They are complementary in the sense that they provide for additional coverage of the design-decision space, both in breadth and in depth. However, they are clearly referenced from our design-decision catalog so that a DSL developer can screen those for relevant generic DR. In what follows, two DR collections complementing ours are briefly summarized.

Zdun [71] presents Frag as a development system for textual DSL and provides a discussion of architectural decisions for DSL development. The motivation for Frag is to provide support for deferring and revisiting important design decisions (e.g., internal vs. external DSL syntax) during and even after having designed a DSL in an initial revision.

Key Decisions (Based on Zdun [71, Table 2])

HOW SHOULD THE LANGUAGE MODEL OF THE DSL BE REALIZED?

- Explicit language model: metamodel, a schema definition (DTD, XML schema), grammar
- Implicit language model: packages of host-language classes

SHOULD AN EXTERNAL OR AN INTERNAL DSL BE DEVELOPED?

- Internal-only DSL
- External-only DSL
- Mixed DSL

HOW SHOULD THE DSL'S BEHAVIOR BE DEFINED?

- Generator-based transformations (templates, rules)
- Direct interpretation (scripting language)
- Syntax-directed translation into host-language instructions

HOW SHOULD THE DSL BE INTEGRATED WITH THE HOST LANGUAGE?

- Host-language extension
- Host-language piggybacking
- Host-language specialization
- No integration (sandbox)

(continued)

---

[8]An approach to a systematic identification of reusable design decisions and software patterns was devised, applied, and documented by Lytra et al. [39].

HOW SHOULD THE STRUCTURAL CONTEXT CONDITIONS IN THE DSL BE
REALIZED?

- Constraint-language expressions
- Transformations
- Host-language expressions
- No context conditions

Mernik et al. [44] used the patterns from [58] to conduct a survey on decision
factors affecting the analysis, design, and implementation phases of DSL development. They document decisions, decision options, and references to known cases in
four design-making dimensions: decision, analysis, design, implementation.

Key Decisions (Based on [44, Table XX])
SHOULD A DSL BE DEVELOPED?

- Notation

  - New domain notation
  - Existing domain notation: graphical frontend, frontend for framework
    API

- Task automation
- Product-line adoption
- Data-structure representation
- Data-structure traversal
- Configuration frontend
- Programmable interaction
- GUI construction

HOW SHOULD DOMAIN ANALYSIS BE PERFORMED?

- Informal
- Formal
- Extract from existing software system

HOW SHOULD THE DSL BE DESIGNED?

- Host-language exploitation
- Language invention
- Informal
- Formal

HOW SHOULD THE DSL BEHAVIOR BE IMPLEMENTED?

- Interpreter
- Compiler or generator

(continued)

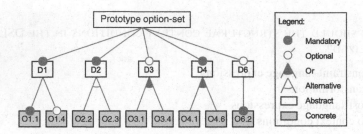

Fig. 2.5 A feature diagram representing the seven prototype item-sets found in the pool of 80 UML-based DSL architectures. These seven prototypical designs include nine different decisions. Each of the seven distilled prototype designs is one of the possible, valid configurations of this feature space

- Pre-processor
- Embedding
- Compiler/interpreter extension
- COTS processing pipeline
- Hybrid (mix of options)
- No execution needed

2.2.2   Excursus: Reusing Design Decisions for UML-Based DSLs

A decision-record catalog resulted from the work reported in [28, 57] that serves as an evidence-based and empirically validated foundation for decision making and design-decision documentation in the context of UML-based DSL projects (and beyond). For the *identification* of key decision problems, decision makers can consult our decision-record catalog, which documents recurring decision contexts and decision problems. The decision options and associations support the *inventory* of suitable design decisions for deriving a selection of candidate solutions. Finally, the *evaluation* of candidate solutions for their fit to domain-specific and domain-generic requirements can be performed using the documented decision drivers and decision consequences. This catalog and the underlying work can facilitate structuring the design space for UML-based DSL, exploring the design space of an existing DSL, and documenting design-decision making during DSL development.

2.2.2.1   Prototype Designs

The space of available (and observed) design decisions for UML-based DSL is vast. Therefore, based on frequency analysis using frequent item-sets, repeatedly observed combinations of design decisions were computed [54]: prototype designs.[9] A prototype design was defined as a frequent item set that represents a largest item subset which was also frequently found to represent a complete transaction. A prototype design is frequently found extended by adding other (frequently or infrequently observed) options. In this sense, it represents an *evolutionary* prototypical design to derive extended UML-based DSL designs. The notion of prototype designs matches DSL design practices commonly described and reflected on in secondary literature on extending the UML and UML-based DSL development: UML extension, UML specialization, and UML piggybacking using UML profiles.

This notion of prototype design is particularly useful for structuring the design space. First, they cover a critical share of the 80 DSL reviewed in [28, 57]. Second, they stress commonalities and differences in terms of decision options between these highly representative option combinations. This differential information be visualized as a feature diagram (see Fig. 2.5). In particular, the seven prototype item-sets characterize 30% of the studied DSL (24/80) in their entirety. Furthermore, they are contained as large proper subsets by 25 extended option sets; therefore, reaching a total coverage of approximately 61% of the DSL included in our study (49/80).

Decisions and decision relationships distilled using frequent item-sets are immediately useful devices to structure and to analyze a design space during decision identification. In addition, we learned that the distilled frequency data can be used to tailor the catalog [19]. This tailorability involves supporting visualizations (e.g., variability models such as feature diagrams; [35]) as well as auxiliary content: decision-making skeletons, prototypical designs, cross-references between related decisions, and frequency data on known uses.

2.2.2.2 Design-Space Analysis

The design-decision catalog facilitates recovering the decision space of an existing DSL using Questions-Options-Criteria (QOC) diagrams. QOC notation is a semi-formal, diagrammatic approach for describing a space of design arguments specific to an existing design [15, 40].

A QOC diagram on a UML-based DSL for modeling system audits (Security Audit) is reproduced in Fig. 2.6. *Questions* deal with features of the designed artifact. In the example from Fig. 2.6, such a feature is the representation of audit rules in the technical domain of system auditing. The DSL should allow domain modelers (a security auditor) to author audit rules. In QOC, *options* capture possible answers to the questions. The exemplary design space shown in Fig. 2.6 of the

---

[9]The relationship between software-pattern description and design-decision description has already been commented on. Similarly, prototype designs relate to the notion of pattern sequences. Pattern languages describe potential or actually observed sequences in which the patterns can be applied [4]. Pattern sequences compare with our notion of sets of co-adopted decision options (including prototype designs) in the sense that option sets can reflect sequences of adopted decision options.

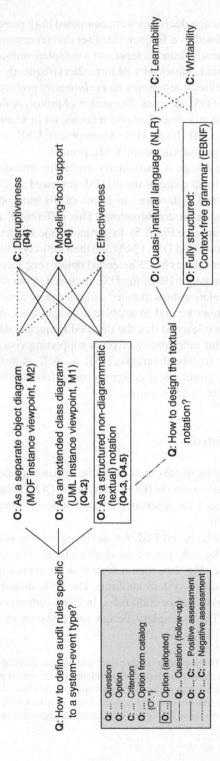

Fig. 2.6 A partial QOC representation of a selected design-space fragment for the DSML SecurityAudit. This example follows the original QOC notation introduced in MacLean et al. [40]; advanced QOC notation elements such as arguments are omitted for brevity

SecurityAudit DSL consists of three options. Clearly, the actual design space of the SecurityAudit DSML was larger. Two QOC options have correspondences to decision options from our catalog, by stating their identifiers from the catalog (D4: O4.2, O4.3, O4.5; see Fig. 2.6). Depending on the design context, a QOC option might map to several decision options in our catalog or vice versa. *Criteria* indicate properties or effects of adopting given options, e.g., to satisfy certain requirements. Our catalog describes decision drivers for adopting or discarding certain decision options (e.g., disruptiveness, modeling-tool support). The decision records enumerate positive and negative links between drivers and options. As such, our catalog offers candidate criteria to be adopted in a QOC analysis. The positive and negative links form the basis for the *assessment* of the QOC options to answer the QOC question. Finally, a QOC *decision* denotes the act of marking QOC options as adopted (see the solid rectangles in Fig. 2.6). Each decision may be followed by another QOC question. In our example, the choice of providing a structured, grammar-based textual notation was succeeded by a question on the concrete-syntax style to be used.

2.2.2.3 Design-Decision Documentation

The catalog of reusable design decisions aims at collecting, systematizing, and documenting DSL design processes, comparable to the role of software patterns in documenting architectural design decisions [24]. A decision-making process typically covers the activities of identifying, of inventorizing, and of evaluating documented generic design decisions. The proposed design-decision catalog can so assist in the following decision-making sequence on a DSL, e.g., also to kick-start or sketch out a design early in the process.

1. Identify closely related and prototype designs: The design-decision catalog maintains annotations that aggregate the included DSL based on their domain of application. Based on these groupings, design-decision makers can approach the catalog content in two ways: (a) by reviewing prior DSL projects assigned to one or more relevant aggregations and/or (b) by identifying the so-called *prototype designs* for the respective application domains: Because reviewing prior DSL might incur substantial overhead in early iterations (for example, this could involve reviewing between 20 and 30 concrete DSL for a given domain), the catalog offers frequently recurring combinations of decisions, so-called *prototype designs* [54] (see also the earlier paragraph in this section).
2. Explore decision associations: Starting from an exemplary concrete design or prototype design, additional decisions can be explored by following the links between decision records.
3. Record a DSL-specific design decision by referencing details from the catalog.

The latter item leads to intermediate and final results of a decision-making step to become recorded using structured text documents following an agreed-upon format.[10] These structured text documents on design decisions and their details (alternatives, arguments) allow for *referencing* a collection of reusable and recurring design decisions.

Table 2.2 shows an example of a structured document used to capture one particular decision on another UML-based DSL: PRDM. This documented, DSL-specific design decision captures the fact that an earlier decision was to implement the DSL by an existing model-driven framework (BusinessActivities) and its corresponding metamodel. This is recorded by the reference to another decision document named ExtendBusinessActivitiesFramework in Table 2.2. This prompted the DSL to be realized as a metamodel extension (O2.3) combined with a metamodel modification (O2.4), adding to the UML profile (O2.2). Based on adopted decision options (inspired either by the prototype design or by project-specific factors), the DSL developer can study documented associations between decision options.

The document template used in Table 2.2 structures the document into predefined sections (e.g., name, status, problem statement, arguments leading to a decision).[11] In order to annotate decision details within unstructured text fragments, dedicated mark-up elements («...») are provided. This way, the decision document and text elements in the document can be tagged to indicate a particular iteration in the decision-making process, the state of the decision, or stakeholder roles, for example.

To recap, the objective is to reduce the time spent on these documentation tasks, by avoiding repetition. Work on generic design knowledge suggests that the effort of specifying such a decision document can be reduced by referencing reusable and generic decisions. In particular, such references allow for focusing on describing additional, DSL-specific decision knowledge only, rather than repeating what is described in the decisions catalog. A complete process documentation of a DSL design consists of a collection of such decision documents, which are interconnected by different relationship types (e.g., «caused by»).

2.3   Variability Challenges

The *composability* of language-definition artifacts (i.a., language model and syntax, context conditions, behavior, integration, and test cases) is a prerequisite for a variable design and implementation of a DSL [18] as a DSL product line. Composability is also required to adhere to the condition of modularity. The modularity condition involves, for example, preserving modular comprehensibility [60] of the language-definition artifacts under composition. A definition is considered modularly comprehensible when a developer can understand what this very definition is doing in isolation from the other composable definitions during a comprehension or maintenance task.

---

[10]See [51] for an overview of document templates.

[11]The document template by van Heesch et al. [65] was selected because it has been used before in empirical studies on documenting and recovering architectural designs.

Table 2.2 An exemplary documented design decision named `UMLIntegration` for the DSML PRDM based on the document template from [65]. Decision options of the catalog (i.e. O2.2, O2.3, and O2.4) are referred to using the «see» tag in the *Decision* and the *Alternatives* sections. Drivers and consequences available from the catalog are referenced using «see» in the *Arguments* section

Name	`UMLIntegration`
Current version	3 (MS2 «Snapshot»)
Current state	«Approved»
Decision group	None
Problem/issue	In which UML-compliant way should the domain concepts be formalized?
Decision	We opt for a combined strategy: First, a UML/BusinessActivities metamodel extension («see» `O2.3`) is created. The reuse of UML-based structural and behavioral features (duty associations to UML operations and properties) makes a slight modification of the UML metamodel necessary («see» `O2.4`). To bind standard UML metamodel elements (e.g., actions) to the extended duty-aware metamodel (e.g., as compensation actions), an auxiliary UML profile providing stereotypes to UML metaclasses is defined («see» `O2.2`)
Alternatives	Use either a UML profile («see» `O2.2`) or a UML metamodel extension/modification («see» `O2.3` and «see» `O2.4`) alone
Arguments	There is a limited overlap between the constructed language model (i.e. the domain concepts) and existing, standard UML metamodel elements («see» `Domain space`). While, for example, concepts such as roles, subjects, and duties under different views (e.g., transition system for duty states, duty hierarchies) are not directly reflected in the UML metamodel, compensation actions for neglected duties can be modeled using standard UML actions. In addition, the BusinessActivities framework, as the basis for the DSML, deploys a UML metamodel extension. Compliance with the framework and its UML compatibility levels is a firm requirement. The integration into standard UML modeling tools is not a critical factor («see» `Tool integration`)
Related decisions	• This decision is «caused by» `DomainModel` • This decision is «caused by» `ExtendBusinessActivitiesFramework`
Related requirements	`Portability`, `MultipleViews`, `ProcessFlowMetaphor`
Related artifacts	[27]
History	

Stakeholder	Action	Status	Iteration
S. Schefer-Wenzl «Developer»	«Propose»	«Tentative»	MS1
S. Schefer-Wenzl «Developer»	«Validate»	«Decided»	MS1
M. Strembeck «Domain expert»	«Confirm»	«Approved»	MS2

Realizing the required composability in a DSL development system is challenged by the need to provide for different *types of composition* and by *abstraction mismatches* that counter the modularity of the resulting DSL implementations.

2.3.1 Types of DSL Composition

Erdweg et al. [17] identify and describe four basic types of software-language composition that equally apply to DSL composition: language extension, language unification, extension composition, and self-extension.[12]

*   *Extension*: The ability of a DSL development system to define and to apply units of extensions to a base DSL in an incremental and modular manner.
*   *Unification*: The ability of a DSL development system to form a unified DSL out of two or more composed DSL; in particular, when the composed ones have not been developed with composition in mind.
*   *Extension composition*: The ability of a DSL development system to, first, compose two or more DSL extensions before enabling them for the base DSL.
*   *Self-extension*: The ability of a DSL to extend itself by defining and by applying extensions in an embedded manner (from within a DSL script or model).

Depending on the goals and the context of a multi-DSL development project (see Sect. 1.2), one or a mix of these composition types may be warranted. Therefore, a DSL development system is required to support at least extension and unification (if not all of them; [18]). This way, the choice of applying a certain composition type is rendered a proper design decision at the discretion of the DSL developer or the integrating application developer. From the perspective of the DSL development system, however, enabling different composition types, and combinations thereof, incurs substantial complexity. This is because support for multiple composition types interferes with other concerns. To give an idea:

For which *scopes* of a DSL design and implementation are compositions supported? Are the different composition types supported both for internal and external DSL?

The scope of composition relates to the types of features (syntax, language, and tooling features; see Sect. 1.2). Ideally, a DSL development system is expected to capture variability and to support the composition type for the scope of abstract syntax, concrete syntax, semantics, and tooling services [18, 31, 42]. The issue of composition scope extends to the composability of single- or multi-faceted language definitions [34, Section 2]. The presence of multiple definition artifacts responsible

---

[12]While the typology of Erdweg et al. [17] has been referred to by the majority of relevant research, as the original definitions leave room for interpretation, there is some disagreement in their readings between the modelware and the grammarware communities (see, e.g., Degueule [12, p. 27]) when it comes to details: restriction as an extension, self-extension for external DSL, etc. In Chap. 5, the composition types are covered in greater detail and by example.

for a feature implementation challenges feature mapping, maintaining trace links between definitions and features, and managing the resulting dependencies between the different types of definition artifacts [16].

When a DSL development is geared towards different DSL styles, such internal *and* external *and* mixed [71], the different composition types must be well supported regardless of the DSL style adopted by a DSL developer. In such a setting, each composition type affects different kinds of DSL definition artifacts (e.g., grammar definitions, built-in syntax processor, or parser combinator). This adds to the complexity introduced by multi-faceted DSL definitions.

2.3.2 Abstraction Mismatches Under Composition

An *abstraction mismatch* describes a situation in which a DSL developer is forced to choose a modeling or programming abstraction to express a concern in the domain of application that is not a perfect match of the abstracted concept or relationship [70, Chapter 3].When looking for ways of implementing a variable DSL, primary concerns are features and configurations and the available abstractions to represent them are provided by different implementation techniques (e.g., objects, classes). Establishing and maintaining correspondences between them has been referred to as *feature mapping* before. Generally, the extent or severity of the mismatch cannot be judged directly. Moreover, the mismatch often does not reveal itself immediately. Typically, the mismatch has negative consequences (over time) on certain quality attributes of the resulting DSL and DSL-based tooling. These include a reduced flexibility and degraded quality-in use for the domain experts, decreased maintainability, or increased architectural and implementation complexity. In this sense, abstraction mismatches contribute to technical debt. In this work, mismatches affecting the composability of DSL definition artifacts negatively are particularly relevant: decomposition mismatches.

A *decomposition mismatch* is an abstraction mismatch that results from separating and composing concerns in the design and the implementation of a software system, such as a DSL using a DSL development system. In object orientation, a frequently observed mismatch results from decomposing a single conceptual entity in the domain into multiple implementation entities. For a variable DSL, mismatches can result from the multiple separation and composition of concerns. Consider a problem-domain model of a small domain of arithmetic expressions, LEA as introduced in Sect. 1.4. This domain exhibits the concerns of expression types (literals, addition, subtraction) and types of operations on the expressions (evaluation). In basic object orientation, one of the concerns must be selected by the DSL developer to become represented by classes, the other by operations owned by the classes. In Fig. 2.7, the DSL developer opted for the expression types as classes. The consequence of expression types becoming the primary or dominant decomposition using classes is that each and every operation (eval) must be implemented for every class. This might certainly be warranted. However, at

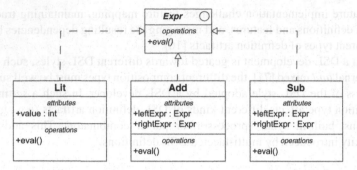

Fig. 2.7 An extension of the LEA model introduced in Sect. 1.4. There are two concerns separated and composed at the same time: expression types (Add, Lit, etc.) and operation types (eval). One becomes the dominant criterion of decomposition (e.g., expression types). This yields an instance of the *expression problem* as a showcase of a decomposition mismatch visible also in developing variable software languages [32, 38, 64]

times, this design decision turns into a mismatch, especially *under composition*. Whenever a new operation type is added (e.g., as the result of adding a new DSL variant to the family), the corresponding operation must be implemented for all classes. Whenever an operation (evaluation) is to be modified, this must happen for all corresponding implementations of eval. In addition, this kind of decomposition mismatch also invites the DSL developer to code clones. If the design decision would have been to promote operation types to classes instead, the mismatch would result from, e.g., adding new expression types. This archetype of a decomposition mismatch is known as the expression problem, resulting from the tyranny of the dominant decomposition.

This form of the expression problem can become virulent for a variable DSL design directly, that is, its language model. More generally, for variable DSL, the relevant and competing concerns are the structure of the modeled problem domain and the structure of features implementations adding to the base structure. This is addressed prominently in Chap. 3 (*collaboration-based decomposition*). When separating a variable DSL into and composing it from language constructs (language components such as loop types) and processing phases (type checking), this can result in a higher-level instance of this decomposition mismatch. When adding a new language component, the relevant filters (passes) in the language-processing pipeline must be adapted; or vice versa [64, Section 4]. Liebig et al. [38] reflect on the two-dimensional decomposition structure between tooling and language features. Adding a new language feature such as string support to an expression DSL (as sketched in Fig. 2.7), the syntax definition, typing and evaluation rules, test cases, and documentation have to be extended to accommodate strings. Inversely, adding a tooling feature like syntax highlighting requires implementation of highlighting rules for all existing language features.

Fig. 2.8 Classification of variability implementation techniques, with selected examples from variable software language engineering. See Sect. 2.4 and Table 2.3 for a more comprehensive list

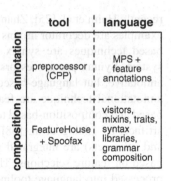

In relevant research, different variability implementation techniques for DSL and software composition, in more general, have been discussed in light of their capacity to balance the forces of and the consequences caused by abstraction mismatches such as the expression problem in its different flavors. The assessment and comparison criteria are often phrased in terms of the expression problem [32, 38].[13]

The relevant variability implementation techniques are often distinguished using the following characteristics [1, Section 3.1]:

- Tool-based versus language-based implementation technique
- Annotation-based vs. composition-based implementation technique

A *tool-based* technique builds on one or a pipeline of tools external to the DSL development system to represent features in the code base and/or to realize the DSL derivation. A *language-based* technique uses first-class mechanisms provided by the host language of the DSL development system to represent features and to implement DSL derivation. An *annotation-based* technique marks regions in language-definition artifacts belonging to a certain feature. DSL derivation then involves removing or ignoring regions specific to deselected features to form a DSL variant. A *composition-based* technique implements features in form of composable units, ideally first-class abstraction units of a host language. Derivation then means composing all feature implementations of the selected features to create a DSL variant.

The overview in Fig. 2.8 gives some exemplary techniques from software-language development. A basic example of a language- and composition-based technique are VISITORS [21] for implementing variability in post-processing, behavior, and platform integration (e.g., visitor-based transformations). See more

---

[13]For example, Kaminski et al. [32] have stated the following criteria based on the expression problem, among others: (1) extensibility in adding new expression types and new operation types; (2) no modification of existing code under composition; (3) independence of extensions from each other under composition.

recently Heim et al. [25], Zhang and Oliveira [73], and Leduc et al. [37]. Advanced examples are decorator mixins [55] and traits [6]. Basic tool-based and annotation-based techniques are syntax pre-processors external to the DSL development system. Syntax pre-processors built into a host language of a DSL qualify as an annotative, but language-based technique. Another example of a language-based annotational technique are feature annotations in MPS [67]. An advanced tool-based and composition-based technique is the FeatureHouse integration of Spoofax artifacts by Liebig et al. [38]. The Spoofax definition artifacts (SDF grammars and rules sets) are integrated with FeatureHouse to run AST-based compositions based on feature selections. The derived definitions (grammar and rules) are then processed into language tooling using Spoofax itself. The distinction is useful, on the one hand, to contrast different approaches and their consequences regarding the presence of abstraction mismatches. For example, tool-based techniques are believed to support a clear separation of concerns between implementing features and implementing the derivation logic.

On the downside, a tool-based technique involves many different definition arti-facts and a complex pipeline between external tools plus coordination artifacts (e.g., build scripts). This multitude of definition artifacts aggravates problems introduced by abstraction mismatches. The distinction, on the other hand, also turns out too limited because advanced techniques can combine the characteristics. An annotative tool-based technique like the one by Liebig et al. [38] using FeatureHouse on top of Spoofax could be extended to incorporate language-based techniques at the level of grammars (e.g., grammar imports).

2.3.3   Development Processes

While the spot of this writing is on composition types for and abstraction mis-matches at different levels of multi-DSL development, there are more general challenges to address. They go beyond being proactive, reactive, or extractive; or top-down or bottom-up development. Kaminski et al. [32] raise the issue of the audience: *Who composes the language features?* Depending on the answer on this question—non-technical domain expert or a developer practitioner—the compos-ability of language-definition artifacts must be assessed in an extended manner. For example, certain implementation techniques with issues in error handling or ambiguous composition results might not be suited for a non-technical audience or even generalist application developers. To the end, variable DSL development aims at realizing software reuse, Zdun [71, p. 734] raises the question on whether DSL development systems should rather facilitate building throw-away prototypes fast or gradually improving *evolutionary prototypes* by supporting deferrable design decisions.

2.4   State of Variability Support

Existing approaches to multi-DSL development [62] have realized composability for various artifact scopes employing different variability implementation techniques underneath. Table 2.3 aims at giving an overview of DSL development systems that support multi-DSL development and that provide for a dedicated infrastructure for capturing and for managing variability of DSL families. More general and comprehensive comparisons between approaches to software-language including DSL development are available from Kosar et al. [33], Méndez-Acuña et al. [42], Şutîi et al. [62], and Erdweg et al. [18].

In Table 2.3, relevant DSL development systems are characterized according to the relevant descriptors of variable DSL introduced in the previous sections:

- Which DSL types are supported: internal, external, both?
- Is the variability representation and management endogenous or exogenous?
- Which variability implementation techniques are provided to the DSL developer (language-based vs. tool-based, composition vs. annotation)?
- Which DSL composition types are supported: extension, unification, extension composition, self-extension?
- Is the DSL development system suited or intended for a particular development trajectory: proactive, reactive, extractive?

Table 2.3 Overview of approaches and DSL development systems aiming at variable DSL. DSL types are int(ernal) or ext(ernal). Variability representation and management can be achieved in an end(ogenous) or exo(genous) manner. Type pairs of implementation techniques are identified as: language-based compositional (LC), language-based annotational (LA), tool-based compositional (TC), tool-based annotational (TA). Composition types: extension (ex), unification (un), extension composition (ec), and self-extension (se)

Approach	Type	Varia.	Impl.	Composition	Path
MetaMod [62]	ext	end	LC/TC	ex/un/ec	proactive (reactive)
MPS [30, 68]	ext	exo	LC/LA	ex/un/ec	proactive
LISA [43]	ext	end	LC	ex/un/ec/(se)	proactive
Melange [12, 13]	ext	(end)	LC/TC	ex/un/ec	proactive
Fusion + Gromp [20, 41]	ext	(end)	LC/TC	(ex/un/ec)	proactive
Neverlang + AiDE [36, 64]	ext (int)	exo	LC/TC	ex/un/ec	proactive, extractive
MontiCore [23, 34]	ext	end	LC	ex/un/ec	proactive
Eco [14]	ext	–	LC	ex/un	proactive (reactive)
MetaDepth [45]	ext	(end)	LC	(ex/ec)	proactive
YAJCo [7]	ext (int)	–	LC	ex/un/ec	proactive
APEG [47]	ext	–	LC	ex/un/ec/se	proactive
Helvetia + PetitParser [48, 50]	ext (int)	–	LC	ex/un/ec/(se)	proactive
Silver + Copper [32, 66]	ext	–	LC	ex/ec	reactive
FeatureHouse + Spoofax [38]	ext	exo	TC	ex/un	proactive
DjDSL	int, ext	exo	LC	ex/un/ec/(se)	reactive

2.4.1 MetaMod [62]

MetaMod is a language- and composition-based (LC) approach in that it allows for decomposing an external DSL into and re-composing its core language-model from abstract syntax units called *groups*. Groups contain definitions of potentially shared abstract syntax elements (concepts, relations) and can be related to each other (i.e., by a structural merge for reuse and by referential sub-typing between groups). The space of valid group combinations is primarily determined via MetaMod's composition mechanisms (endogenous variability management). Composition constraints can enforce restrictions on concept compositions from receiving to providing groups or vice versa (including language restriction). Deferred operation definitions encode behavioral requirements between providing and receiving groups. Otherwise, the language model does *not* render the variability space explicit. Behavioral definitions (*processing units*) describe operations as units of behavior implementation which are owned by groups, rather than the concepts that they operate on (in the spirit of free-standing or generic methods). Group ownership of operations is considered more adequate to support group composition. MetaMod is confined to external and textual DSL development, by building on top of MPS [30]. MetaMod, therefore, supports all composition types but self-extension. MetaMod's application is reported for proactive development only, whereas its infrastructure can most certainly be used for a reactive and iterative path also.

2.4.2 MPS [30, 68]

Völter [68] explores bringing the different composition types (in his classification: referencing, extension, reuse, and embedding) to the Meta-Programming System (MPS; [30]). In this tool context, the emphasis is on external DSL with mixed, textual, symbol-based, and tabular DSL. Context conditions are expressed as type-system rule. Moreover, extended composition support for IDE services beyond the mere concrete-syntax definition is elaborated on. At various stages, MPS received variability-management support for MPS-based DSL. Initially, ideas were explored for single MPS-based DSL (e.g., MEL [69]), however, the ideas generalize to the MPS workbench facilities (workbench DSL) themselves [67]. In essence, MPS was shown to be extensible via a language-based compositional (LC) and annotational techniques (LA). The latter allows for feature annotations (carrying feature expressions) binding DSL syntax blocks (ranges) to configuration features (e.g., a debugging mode). The configuration features themselves are feature toggles, expressed in a slim feature-model DSL [67]. With this, an MPS-based approach manages variability in an exogenous manner. The different MPS-based approaches have been reported for a proactive DSL-family development only.

2.4.3 LISA [43]

In LISA, the different types of language composition based on the notion of composable attribute grammars are elaborated on. Therefore, LISA helps build textual and external DSL. In terms of variability techniques and management, LISA falls into the family of language- and composition-based (LC) approaches by providing composable language-specification units. Composition is realized by borrowing the notion of inheritance and applying a form of inheritance relationship between the attribute-grammar fragments (language plus extends construct). Attribute-grammar composition covers lexing, abstract syntax, concrete syntax, and attributes plus semantic rules. Other than this, no explicit expression or analysis of the configuration space is built into LISA. LISA is claimed to support all composition types including self-extension.

2.4.4 Melange [12, 13]

Melange puts emphasis on external DSL in a metamodeling setting (EMF), being implemented on top of the same technology stack (EMF, Ecore, Xtend). The basic types of composition are supported in terms of a revised notion of (MOF/UML) package merging. Metamodels can be combined using dedicated composition operators (merge, slice). The artifacts under composition are, therefore, (Ecore) metamodels as abstract syntax models. Behavior can be specified using aspect units (Xtend) to be weaved with abstract syntax units, assuming model-based interpretation as the main vehicle of enacting behavior. Melange, therefore, qualifies as a combined language- and tool-based approach using a compositional representation of variable parts of language definitions (TC/LC). Aspects are also used to glue behaviors of the languages under compositions. Concerns other than abstract syntax composition, structural as well as context conditions on the models under composition are *not* addressed, including concrete syntax. In its modelware setting, Melange is claimed to accommodate all composition types but self-extension (which is deemed not applicable in modelware by the authors). The examples provided reflect only on a proactive DSL development path. Explicit variability modeling (in terms of a feature model) is not included.

2.4.5 Gromp + Fusion [20, 41]

In Gromp and Fusion, respectively, the composition of graphical, external DSL is supported. Against a metamodeling background (Ecore, EMF), abstract syntax composition is achieved via the so-called Fusion scripts. Fusion scripts are weaving definitions for imported Ecore metamodels, representing a tool-based compositional approach. This way, Ecore metamodels are model-transformed using add, rename, and removal operations into a merged metamodel. In this context, behavioral definitions are not considered. Concrete-syntax specifications are expressed in a custom, Ecore-based model language called Picture. Picture models are sidecar models to the abstract syntax models. In the spirit of Fusion composition scripts, Gromp scripts can be used to express compositions of two or more Picture metamodels using add, removal, and rename operations to arrive at a merged Picture metamodel. There is no explicit variability modeling, neither at the Fusion nor at the Gromp level. The applications reported by the authors only hint at a proactive development. The authors also do not reflect on the different composition types supported. Given that the approach closely resembles Melange's [12, 13], one can assume similar capabilities: extension, unification, and extension composition.

2.4.6   Neverlang + AiDE [36, 64]

The Neverlang environment and its surrounding tool chain and IDE services have been built with textual and external DSL in mind. Although, through its Neverlang Java API, it is essentially open for use in developing internal and, hence, mixed DSL scenarios. This has, however, not been explored in a systematic manner by Neverlang's creators at the time of writing. Neverlang allows for composing (domain-specific) software languages from a number of language-level building blocks (LC): `modules` group `reference syntax` elements as syntax specifications, which carry production rules to be consumed by a parser generator for bottom-up LR grammars (DEXTER). In addition, `modules` bind semantic-action specifications to `roles`, which represent processing phases of language elements (e.g., type-checking, platform integration). The execution semantics of the semantic actions are realized by a tailorable VISITOR over the composed syntax tree. For actual language derivation from existing modules, a composition `module` imports from language `modules`, borrowing from traits: production rules can be added as well as removed as part of a composition. Elements of production rules (non-terminals) can be renamed. The authors consider all composition types supported, but do not demonstrate self-extension. Variability management ranging from dependency retrieval and analysis to designing families of DSL is well recognized by the creators of Neverlang and has resulted in tooling of AiDE [36]. AiDE allows a DSL developer to derive variability models (feature trees with cross-tree constraints) from tags carried by the Neverlang modules. As an initial product, feature dependency graphs are built from the module tags, which are then enriched by adding syntax-level dependencies (between required and provided non-terminals). These variability models are then the basis for various AiDE services: model navigation, language configurator, dependency resolution, and on-the-fly language recomposition. AiDE has been proposed with an extractive development path in mind, but Neverlang + AiDE equally apply to proactive DSL development.

2.4.7   MontiCore [23, 34]

A language integration framework for MontiCore [34] is presented in [23] in terms of a language-based compositional technique. MontiCore and its extensions target composition of domain-specific modeling languages as external and textual DSL. Primary motivator is the combination for data modeling in and architecture (deployment) descriptors for (domain-specific) software systems. For this purpose, the framework supports language-model aggregation, language embedding, and language inheritance in terms of abstract syntaxes. These abstract syntaxes are defined using MontiCore grammars (ANTLR's flavor of LL(k) grammars) linked to variants of UML class models as domain models (UML/P). Non-terminals can take the role of `interface non-terminals` or `abstract non-terminals` (i.e., deferring the specification of the corresponding production rule) and can extend each other, both at the CS and AS level; or the latter only `astextends`. Associations can be specified explicitly (`association` construct) and are wired automatically, by integrating with an identity-resolution and binding framework. The mapping between concrete-syntax specification (grammar) and the language (domain) model remains implicit. In addition, the framework offers facilities to cross-reference between the integrated language models (e.g., via extended symbol tables). Handling of behaviour definitions under composition is not addressed. Beyond a configuration mechanism for the indented grammar compositions (grammar inheritance, embedding), there is no variability management. Besides, the authors only consider a proactive development path.

2.4.8 Eco [14]

Eco falls into the category of syntax-directed environments and aims at external and textual DSL. The main objective is the support of incremental parsing under switching *language boxes* for language embedding. Eco is based on an LR parser generator. AST nodes can be deferred to bind to different subtrees, each representing another nested language, because the ECO parser only requires knowledge of the token type, not the actual value of a language-box node. A common syntax-tree interface is provided by the concrete-syntax tree, which wraps around the syntax trees of each language box. Each language box is a composition unit including grammar, name binding rules, and rules for syntax highlighting. This way, Eco supports extension and unification. In addition, Eco grammars can cross-reference each other. There is no dedicated variability representation or management. The nature of language boxing is suited for a reactive DSL-family development, but the authors put emphasis on a proactive approach.

2.4.9 MetaDepth [45]

In MetaDepth, the composition of external and textual DSL based on metamodels as abstract syntax models is supported for the scopes of abstract syntax (AS), concrete syntax (CS), and behavioral definitions (PI). Behavioral definitions are attached as operations to metamodel classes, with their bodies implemented as EOL programs. The main composition vehicle are model templates and model-template composition built on top of the Epsilon family of model management languages. Such templates express syntax and semantics specification with explicit require-ments on concepts (as template variables), which, at template binding time, are resolved to elements of input models. After template instantiation, concrete-syntax models are translated into an ANTLR grammar and an associated parser. Variability management beyond template configuration is not addressed. The authors remain silent about the intended composition types, but given a template-based approach, extension and extension composition are plausible.

2.4.10   YAJCo [7]

YAJCo separates between abstract syntax and concrete-syntax definitions. The former is defined in terms of Java classes and their relationships, the latter is derived from Java annotations attached to the model classes. Behavioral semantics defined by Java methods grouped into aspects, which are introduced into the model classes when required. In [7], YAJCo's fit for the different composition types is showcased (extension, unification, and extension composition). There is no variability management, nor any extended notion of modularization units (other than Java classes) in YAJCo. Emphasis is on external and textual DSL; basically, the capacity to realize mixed internal-external DSL based on Java is not addressed.

2.4.11   APEG [47]

APEG is a Java-based parser generator driven by PEG. APEG itself is defined using SDF. The primary objective is to allow changes to a grammar and its parser, respectively, during a parse. APEG is an example of a dynamic or adaptive grammar framework. This way, by one definition, APEG supports self-extension at the level of a syntax definition and the associated parser. APEG allows one to trigger grammar adaptions of a prototype grammar (available as a grammar attribute) from within special-purpose semantic actions (adapt operation). The grammar mixin is an arbitrary string defining APEG rules to derive an updated, out-place grammar from the prototype. The underlying grammar composition is limited to add new PEG rules (non-terminals) and adding to the end of choice expressions. This way, APEG is about external and textual DSLS, with language composition entailing both abstract syntax and concrete-syntax composition as an integrated definition artifact. Reis et al. [47] discuss how APEG can address the different forms of composition identified by Erdweg et al. [17].

2.4.12 Helvetia + PetitParser [48–50]

Emerging from the Helvetia framework [48, 50], PetitParser [49] is a DSL framework targeting textual external DSL development by combining aspects of parser combinators and PEG, originally implemented in Pharo Smalltalk. While internal DSL development is supported due to the embedding of the DSL development tooling in Smalltalk, it is not stressed by the authors nor explored systematically. The main objective of Helvetia is to allow defining different kinds of DSL composition strategies ("pidgins", "creoles", and "argots") while maximizing compatibility of the composed languages with existing host-language features and tool support (parser, compiler, syntax highlighter). Helvetia maps to basic elements of DSL definition to Smalltalk language constructs (grammar rules and transformations to methods) and instruments their life cycle stages (parse, transform, etc.) to inject the intended behavior. Actual DSL to host-language transformations are realized using a custom quoting technique (i.e., mapping DSL syntax to host AST is implemented using quoted Smalltalk methods). This way, language composition is achieved by a mix of method annotations, method combination, and method references in superclass hierarchies, the underlying parser infrastructure. The notion of "language boxes" [48] generalized the idea of Helvetia DSL to host-language structures for more general language composition: A LanguageBox provides an object-oriented programming model (LanguageChange objects) to reference and modify an input grammar into a derived one at predefined extension points (after, before). The underlying grammar semantics are those of a basic PEG-driven parser. PetitParser [49], finally, gives isolated access to the infrastructure for Helvetia and language boxes as well as support for parser combination in terms of chainable parser objects. Basic tooling support (syntax highlighting) is provided by instrumenting the standard Smalltalk services.

2.4.13 Silver + Copper [32, 66]

Silver is a parser-generator framework based on attribute grammars and produces Copper parsers [66]. Silver and Copper have been used to build extension infrastructures for particular general-purpose languages such as C (AbleC; [32]) and Java (AbleJ). There is no dedicated variability representation or management available. While the primary purpose is developing extensions (and extension compositions) to GPL, they do not qualify as internal extensions because they are capable of modifying syntax and semantics of the GPL. The primary application is a reactive development style, given the emphasis on extension and extension compositions to GPL.

2.4.14 FeatureHouse + Spoofax [2, 38]

Combining FeatureHouse + Spoofax in an advanced tool-based and composition-based technique is described by Liebig et al. [38] and Apel et al. [2]. Feature-House [2] is a framework for generic software composition allows for generic composition of different software-language artifacts when processed in a language-independent, internal FeatureHouse AST. Liebig et al. [38] integrate Spoofax definition artifacts (SDF grammars and rules sets) into FeatureHouse. Actual design and composition (superimposition) are then performed in FeatureHouse, including an explicit variability model and model-based configuration. The derived definitions (grammar and rules) are then processed into language tooling using Spoofax itself. Within the limits of FeatureHouse, extension and unification are supported. The emphasis in this combined approach is the proactive development of a variable DSL.

2.5 DjDSL: A Variability-Aware Development System for Mixed DSLs

A systematic comparison of multi-DSL development systems and approaches to variable DSL development in Sect. 2.4 (see Table 2.3) reveals that particular challenges have not been fully or systematically addressed so far. To begin with, none of the reviewed approaches covers internal DSL or DSL that mix internal and external syntaxes (mixed or hybrid DSL; [71]). This is despite the reported importance of internal DSL (see Sect. 1.1). Three approaches (Neverlang + AiDE, Helvetia + PetitParser, and YAJCo) would, however, fulfill basic technical conditions to support internal DSL development.

With regard to variability representation and management, only three attempts were found reported to support first-class and exogenous variability models as part of the DSL development system; MPS, FeatureHouse + Spoofax, and Neverlang + AiDE. The MPS-based solution (e.g., a feature-modeling DSL) formed part of a discontinued proof-of-concept implementation. In Neverlang + AiDE, the emphasis is more on synthesizing a feature model from language-component dependencies. The combo FeatureHouse + Spoofax reuses the FeatureHouse modeling facility as part of a tool-based approach. In summary, there is no comprehensive *language-based* solution available for variability modeling, feature mapping, and feature selection as part of a DSL development system.

Context conditions as part or supplement of abstract syntax and language-model definitions have not been considered by most approaches. This is particularly surprising for modelware approaches such as Melange and Fusion + Gromp given a rich body of techniques on model composition.

Finally, in terms of development styles, there is a predominance of approaches gearing towards *proactive* multi-DSL development. Extractive approaches such as Neverlang + AiDE or approaches open to application in reactive development (Eco,

Silver + Copper) are a minority. As a middle ground, there is a lack of methods, techniques, and tools that aim at reactive multi-DSL development; in spirit of Frag [71] for single-DSL development.

In the remainder of this book, the emphasis is on a number of conceptual contributions plus reference implementations that close these stated gaps in multi-DSL development. In essence, the aim is to design, to implement, and to explore a well-defined and readily applicable *language-based* and *composition-based* DSL development system meeting the following requirements:

- The DSL development system can host internal, external DSL, and *mixed* DSL (i.e., DSL having an internal and an external syntax).
- The DSL development system supports the different DSL composition (extension, unification, extension composition, and self-extension), both for internal and external DSL.
- The DSL development system realizes composition support for all artifact scopes, e.g., language-model and variability-model definitions, context-condition definitions, and concrete-syntax definitions.
- The DSL development system avoids or mitigates abstraction mismatches in DSL implementations *by construction*. This also holds under DSL composition; both, for internal and external DSL.
- The DSL development system provides for modeling (representing) and managing DSL variability in a first-class and exogenous manner.

The result of this long-term effort is DjDSL. DjDSL is developed using NX and Tcl (see Sect. 1.4). DjDSL complements NX and Tcl by leveraging their capabilities for single-DSL development to multi-DSL development and DSL product lines. DjDSL is realized as an integrated bundle of five components (see Fig. 2.9). Implementationwise, each component is organized as a separate NX/Tcl module.[14]

- The component **djdsl::lm** provides for representing and for managing *variable language models* based on the notion of *collaboration-based designs*. Language models can be realized in a platform-independent (UML) or platform-specific (NX/Tcl) manner. The language models can be designed in a decomposition structure that maps to features of a corresponding variability model. See Chap. 3.
- The component **djdsl::vle** provides for representing and for managing *variability models* as well as feature selections as first-class abstractions in DjDSL. It builds on a versatile and canonical *multiplicity encoding* of variability models. A backend encoding of variability models in terms of Binary Decision Diagrams (BDD) enables automated analyses. See Chap. 3.
- The component **djdsl::ctx** provides for defining context conditions on top of DjDSL language models. Context conditions defined this way can be de- and re-composed in a manner facilitating DSL composition. See Chap. 4.

---

[14]Documentation, instructions, and distributions are available from the supplemental repository [52].

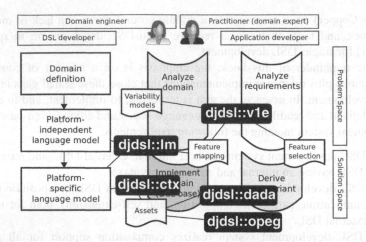

Fig. 2.9 DjDSL aims at supporting DSL product line design and implementation (i.e., asset development) as well as DSL derivation. DjDSL provides five major components: `djdsl::lm`, `djdsl::vle`, `djdsl::ctx`, `djdsl::dada`, and `djdsl::opeg`. For the background on DSL product line engineering, see Sect. 1.2

- The component `djdsl::dada` provides for implementing variable textual syntaxes for *internal DSL* on top of DjDSL language models. All DSL composition types are supported. See Chap. 5.
- The component `djdsl::opeg` provides for implementing variable textual syntaxes for *external DSL* on top of DjDSL language models. Important DSL composition types are supported. External syntaxes are defined using parsing expression grammars (PEG) that tightly integrate with DjDSL language models as the abstract syntax. See Chap. 5.

Chapters 3–5 make deep dives into designing and implementing variable language models, variable context conditions, and variable textual syntaxes. To see DjDSL and all of its components in action, Chap. 6 elaborates on applying DjDSL on a multi-DSL development project. A DSL family for object-to-NoSQL (ONM) mapping is designed and developed over multiple iterations (i.e., in a reactive manner).

References

1. Apel S, Batory D, Kästner C, Saake G (2013) Feature-oriented software product lines, 1st edn. Springer, Berlin. https://doi.org/10.1007/978-3-642-37521-7
2. Apel S, Kästner C, Lengauer C (2013) Language-independent and automated software composition: The FeatureHouse experience. IEEE Trans Softw Eng 39(1):63–79. https://doi.org/10.1109/TSE.2011.120
3. Burge JE, Carroll JM, McCall R, Mistrík I (2008) Rationale-based software engineering. Springer, Berlin

4. Buschmann F, Henney K, Schmidt DC (2007) Pattern-oriented software architecture—On patterns and pattern languages. Wiley, London
5. Capilla R, Nava F, Carrillo C (2008) Effort estimation in capturing architectural knowledge. In: Proceedings of the 26th IEEE/ACM International Conference on Automated Software Engineering (ASE'08). IEEE CS, Silver Spring, pp 208–217
6. Cazzola W, Vacchi E (2016) Language components for modular DSLs using traits. Comput Lang Syst Struct 45(Suppl C):16–34. https://doi.org/10.1016/j.cl.2015.12.001
7. Chodarev S, Lakatoš D, Porubän J (2014) Abstract syntax driven approach for language composition. Open Comput Sci 4(3):107–117. https://doi.org/10.2478/s13537-014-0211-8
8. Clark T, Sammut P, Willans J (2008) Applied metamodelling: A foundation for language-driven development, 2nd edn. Ceteva
9. Coplien J (1996) Software patterns. SIGS management briefings. SIGS Books & Multimedia
10. Czarnecki K, Eisenecker UW (2000) Generative programming—Methods, Tools, and Applications, 6th edn. Addison-Wesley, Reading
11. de Kinderen S, Ma Q (2015) Requirements engineering for the design of conceptual modeling languages: A goal- and value-oriented approach. Appl Ontol 10(10):7–24. https://doi.org/10.3233/AO-150139
12. Degueule T (2016) Composition and interoperability for external domain-specific language engineering. Theses, Université de Rennes 1 [UR1]. https://hal.inria.fr/tel-01427009
13. Degueule T, Combemale B, Blouin A, Barais O, Jézéquel JM (2015) Melange: A meta-language for modular and reusable development of DSLs meta-language for modular and reusable development of DSLs. In: Proceedings of the 2015 ACM SIGPLAN International Conference on Software Language Engineering (SLE'15). ACM, New York, pp 25–36. https://doi.org/10.1145/2814251.2814252
14. Diekmann L, Tratt L (2014) Eco: A language composition editor. In: Proceedings of the 7th International Conference on Software Language Engineering (SLE'14). Lecture notes in computer science, vol 8706. Springer, Berlin, pp 82–101. https://doi.org/10.1007/978-3-319-11245-9_5
15. Dutoit AH, McCall R, Mistrík I, Paech B (2006) Rationale management in software engineering: Concepts and techniques. In: Rationale Management in Software Engineering, Chap 1. Springer, Berlin, pp 1–48
16. Erdweg S, Ostermann K (2017) A module-system discipline for model-driven software development. Art Sci Eng Program 1(2). https://doi.org/10.22152/programming-journal.org/2017/1/9
17. Erdweg S, Giarrusso PG, Rendel T (2012) Language composition untangled. In: Proceedings of the Twelfth Workshop on Language Descriptions, Tools, and Applications (LDTA'12). ACM, New York, pp 7:1–7:8. https://doi.org/10.1145/2427048.2427055
18. Erdweg S, van der Storm T, Völter M, Tratt L, Bosman R, Cook WR, Gerritsen A, Hulshout A, Kelly S, Loh A, Konat G, Molina PJ, Palatnik M, Pohjonen R, Schindler E, Schindler K, Solmi R, Vergu V, Visser E, van der Vlist K, Wachsmuth G, van der Woning J (2015) Evaluating and comparing language workbenches: Existing results and benchmarks for the future. Comput Lang Syst Struct. 44(Part A):24–47. https://doi.org/10.1016/j.cl.2015.08.007
19. Falessi D, Briand LC, Cantone G, Capilla R, Kruchten P (2013) The value of design rationale information. ACM Trans Softw Eng Methodol 22(3):21:1–21:32
20. Flórez H, Sánchez M, Villalobos J (2012) EnAr-fusion. A tool for metamodel composition. Technical Report ISIS-01-2012, Universidad de los Andes
21. Gamma E, Helm R, Johnson RE, Vlissides J (1995) Design Patterns – Elements of Reusable Object-Oriented Software. Addison Wesley professional computing series. Addison-Wesley, Reading
22. Ghosh D (2010) DSLs in action, 1st edn. Manning Publications, Shelter Island
23. Haber A, Look M, Perez AN, Nazari PMS, Rumpe B, Volkel S, Wortmann A (2015) Integration of heterogeneous modeling languages via extensible and composable language components. In: Proceedings of the 3rd International Conference Model-driven Engineering and Software Development (MODELSWARD'15), pp 19–31

24. Harrison N, Avgeriou P, Zdun U (2007) Using patterns to capture architectural decisions. IEEE Softw 24(4):38–45. https://doi.org/10.1109/MS.2007.124
25. Heim R, Nazari PMS, Rumpe B, Wortmann A (2016) Compositional language engineering using generated, extensible, static type-safe visitors. In: Proceedings of the 12th European Conference on Modelling Foundations and Applications (ECMFA 2016). Lecture notes in computer science, vol 9764. Springer, Berlin, pp 67–82. https://doi.org/10.1007/978-3-319-42061-5_5
26. Hoisl B, Sobernig S (2016) Open-source development tools for domain-specific modeling: Results from a systematic literature review. In: Proceedings of the 49th Hawaii International Conference on System Sciences (HICSS'16). IEEE CS, Silver Spring, pp 5001–5010. https://doi.org/10.1109/HICSS.2016.620
27. Hoisl B, Sobernig S, Strembeck M (2016) A catalog of reusable design decisions for developing UML/MOF-based domain-specific modeling languages. Tech. Rep. 2014/03, WU Vienna. http://epub.wu.ac.at/4815/
28. Hoisl B, Sobernig S, Strembeck M (2017) Reusable and generic design decisions for developing UML-based domain-specific languages. Inf Softw Technol 92:49–74. https://doi.org/10.1016/j.infsof.2017.07.008
29. Horner J, Atwood M (2006) Effective design rationale: Understanding the barriers. In: Rationale Management for Requirements Engineering, Chap 3. Springer, Berlin, pp 73–90
30. JetBrains (2017) Meta programming system (MPS). https://www.jetbrains.com/mps/
31. Jézéquel JM, Méndez-Acuña D, Degueule T, Combemale B, Barais O (2015) When systems engineering meets software language engineering. In: Proceedings of the Fifth International Conference on Complex Systems Design and Management (CSD&M'14). Springer, Berlin, pp 1–13. https://doi.org/10.1007/978-3-319-11617-4_1
32. Kaminski T, Kramer L, Carlson T, van Wyk E (2017) Reliable and automatic composition of language extensions to C. In: Proceedings of the ACM SIGPLAN Conference on Systems, Programming, Languages and Applications: Software for Humanity (SPLASH 2017). ACM, New York, pp 98:1–98:29. https://doi.org/10.1145/3133922
33. Kosar T, Bohra S, Mernik M (2016) Domain-specific languages: A systematic mapping study. Inf Softw Technol 71:77–91. https://doi.org/10.1016/j.infsof.2015.11.001
34. Krahn H, Rumpe B, Völkel S (2010) MontiCore: A framework for compositional development of domain-specific languages. Int J Softw Tools Technol Transfer 12(5):353–372. https://doi.org/10.1007/s10009-010-0142-1
35. Kruchten P, Lago P, van Vliet H (2006) Building up and reasoning about architectural knowledge. In: Proceedings of the Second International Conference on the Quality of Software Architectures (QoSA'06). Lecture notes in computer science, vol 4214. Springer, Berlin, pp 43–58
36. Kühn T, Cazzola W, Olivares DM (2015) Choosy and picky: Configuration of language product lines. In: Proceedings of the 19th International Conference on Software Product line (SPLC'15). ACM, New York, pp 71–80. https://doi.org/10.1145/2791060.2791092
37. Leduc M, Degueule T, Combemale B, Van Der Storm T, Barais O (2017) Revisiting visitors for modular extension of executable DSMLs. In: Proceedings of the ACM/IEEE 20th International Conference on Model Driven Engineering Languages and Systems (MoDELS 2017). ACM, New York
38. Liebig J, Daniel R, Apel S (2013) Feature-oriented language families: A case study. In: Proceedings of the Seventh International Workshop on Variability Modelling of Software-Intensive Systems (VaMoS'13). ACM, New York, pp 11:1–11:8. https://doi.org/10.1145/2430502.2430518
39. Lytra I, Sobernig S, Zdun U (2012) Architectural decision making for service-based platform integration: A qualitative multi-method study. In: Proceedings of the Joint 10th Working IEEE/IFIP Conference on Software Architecture and 6th European Conference on Software Architecture (WICSA'12, ECSA'12). IEEE, Piscataway, pp 111–120. https://doi.org/10.1109/WICSA-ECSA.212.19

40. MacLean A, Young RM, Bellotti VME, Moran TP (1996) Questions, options, and criteria: Elements of design space analysis. In: Design Rationale: Concepts, Techniques, and Use, Chap 3. Lawrence Erlbaum Associates, London, pp 53–106

41. Melo I, Sánchez ME, Villalobos J (2013) Composing graphical languages. In: Proceedings of the First Workshop on the Globalization of Domain Specific Languages (GlobalDSL@ECOOP'13). ACM, New York, pp 12–17. https://doi.org/10.1145/2489812.2489816

42. Méndez-Acuña D, Galindo JA, Degueule T, Combemale B, Baudry B (2016) Leveraging software product lines engineering in the development of external DSLs: A systematic literature review. Comput Lang Syst Struct 46:206–235. https://doi.org/10.1016/j.cl.2016.09.004

43. Mernik M (2013) An object-oriented approach to language compositions for software language engineering. J Syst Softw 86(9):2451–2464. https://doi.org/10.1016/j.jss.2013.04.087

44. Mernik M, Heering J, Sloane AM (2005) When and how to develop domain-specific languages. ACM Comput Surv 37(4):316–344. https://doi.org/10.1145/1118890.1118892

45. Meyers B, Cicchetti A, Guerra E, de Lara J (2012) Composing textual modelling languages in practice. In: Proceedings of the Sixth International Workshop on Multi-paradigm Modeling (MPM'12). ACM, New York, pp 31–36. https://doi.org/10.1145/2508443.2508449

46. Neighbors JM (1989) Draco: A method for engineering reusable software systems. In: Biggerstaff T, Perlis AJ (eds) Software Reusability, Vol 1, Chap 12. Addison Wesley, Reading

47. Reis LV, Iorio VOD, Bigonha RS (2015) An on-the-fly grammar modification mechanism for composing and defining extensible languages. Comput Lang Syst Struct 42:46–59. https://doi.org/10.1016/j.cl.2015.01.002

48. Renggli L, Denker M, Nierstrasz M (2010) Language boxes: Bending the host language with modular language changes. In: Proceedings of the Second International Conference on Software Language Engineering (SLE'09). Lecture notes in computer science, vol 5969. Springer, Berlin, pp 274–293. https://doi.org/10.1007/978-3-642-12107-4_20

49. Renggli L, Ducasse S, Gîrba T, Nierstrasz O (2010) Practical dynamic grammars for dynamic languages. In: Proceedings of the Fourth Workshop on Dynamic Languages and Applications (DYLA'10)

50. Renggli L, Gîrba T, Nierstrasz O (2010) Embedding languages without breaking tools. In: Proceedings of the 24th European Conference on Object-oriented Programming (ECOOP'10). Lecture notes in computer science, vol 6183. Springer, Berlin, pp 380–404. https://doi.org/10.1007/978-3-642-14107-2_19

51. Shahin M, Liang P, Khayyambashi MR (2009) Architectural design decision: Existing models and tools. In: Joint Proceedings of the Third European Conference on Software Architecture and the Eighth Working IEEE/IFIP Conference on Software Architecture (ECSA/WICSA'09). IEEE, Piscataway, pp 293–296

52. Sobernig S (2019) DjDSL. https://github.com/mrcalvin/djdsl/

53. Sobernig S, Strembeck M (2014) DSL-based architecting and DSL-based architectures. In: Proceedings of the ECSA 2014 Workshops and Tool Demos Track, European Conference on Software Architecture (ECSA'14). ACM, New York. https://doi.org/10.1145/2642803.2642818

54. Sobernig S, Zdun U (2016) Distilling architectural design decisions and their relationships using frequent item-sets. In: Proceedings of the 13th Working IEEE/IFIP Conference on Software Architecture (WICSA'16). IEEE, Piscataway, pp 61–70. https://doi.org/10.1109/WICSA.2016.9

55. Sobernig S, Neumann G, Adelsberger S (2012) Supporting multiple feature binding strategies in NX. In: Proceedings of the Fourth International Workshop on Feature-oriented Software Development (FOSD'12). ACM, New York, pp 45–53. https://doi.org/10.1145/2377816.2377823

56. Sobernig S, Strembeck M, Beck A (2013) Developing a domain-specific language for scheduling in the European energy sector. In: Proceedings of the Sixth International Language on Software Language Engineering (SLE'13). Lecture notes in computer science, vol 8225. Springer, Berlin, pp 19–35. https://doi.org/10.1007/978-3-319-02654-1_2

57. Sobernig S, Hoisl B, Strembeck M (2016) Extracting reusable design decisions for UML-based domain-specific languages: A multi-method study. J Syst Softw 113:140–172. https://doi.org/10.1016/j.jss.2015.11.037
58. Spinellis D (2001) Notable design patterns for domain-specific languages. J Syst Softw 56(1):91–99. https://doi.org/10.1016/S0164-1212(00)00089-3
59. Steele GL (1990) Common lisp: The language, 2nd edn. Digital Press
60. Stevens WP, Myers GJ, Constantine LL (1974) Structured design. IBM Syst J 13(2):115–139. https://doi.org/10.1147/sj.132.0115
61. Strembeck M, Zdun U (2009) An approach for the systematic development of domain-specific languages. Softw Pract Exp 39(15):1253–1292
62. Şutîi AM, van den Brand M, Verhoeff T (2018) Exploration of modularity and reusability of domain-specific languages: An expression DSL in MetaMod. Comput Lang Syst Struct 51:84–70. https://doi.org/10.1016/j.cl.2017.07.004
63. Tang A, Avgeriou P, Jansen A, Capilla R, Babar MA (2010) A comparative study of architecture knowledge management tools. J Syst Softw 83(3):352–370
64. Vacchi E, Cazzola W (2015) Neverlang: A framework for feature-oriented language development. Comput Lang Syst Struct 43:1–40. https://doi.org/10.1016/j.cl.2015.02.001
65. van Heesch U, Avgeriou P, Hilliard R (2012) A documentation framework for architecture decisions. J Syst Softw 85(4):795–820
66. van Wyk ER, Schwerdfeger AC (2007) Context-aware scanning for parsing extensible languages. In: Proceedings of the Sixth International Conference on Generative Programming and Component Engineering (GPCE'07). ACM, New York, pp 63–72. https://doi.org/10.1145/1289971.1289983
67. Völter M (2010) Implementing feature variability for models and code with projectional language workbenches. In: Proceedings of the Second International Workshop on Feature-oriented Software Development (FOSD'10). ACM, New York, pp 41–48. https://doi.org/10.1145/1868688.1868695
68. Völter M (2013) Language and IDE modularization and composition with MPS. In: Post-conference Proceedings of the International Summer School Generative and Transformational Techniques in Software Engineering (GTTSE'11). Lecture notes in computer science, vol 7680. Springer, Berlin, pp 383–430. https://doi.org/10.1007/978-3-642-35992-7_11
69. Völter M, Merkle B (2010) Domain specific: A binary decision? In: Proceedings of the Tenth Workshop on Domain-specific Modeling (DSM'10). ACM, New York, pp 12:1–12:6. https://doi.org/10.1145/2060329.2060357
70. Zdun U (2002) Language support for dynamic and evolving software architectures. Doctoral thesis, University of Essen
71. Zdun U (2010) A DSL toolkit for deferring architectural decisions in DSL-based software design. Inf Softw Technol 52(7):733–748. https://doi.org/10.1016/j.infsof.2010.03.004
72. Zdun U, Strembeck M (2009) Reusable architectural decisions for DSL design: Foundational decisions in DSL development. In: Proceedings of the 14th European Conference on Pattern Languages of Programs. ACM, New York, pp 1–37
73. Zhang W, Oliveira BCS (2017) EVF: An extensible and expressive visitor framework for programming language reuse. In: Proceedings of the 31st European Conference on Object-oriented Programming (ECOOP'17) (International Proceedings in Informatics). Dagstuhl Publishing, Leibniz, pp 105:1–105:30. https://doi.org/10.4230/LIPIcs.ECOOP.2017.105

Chapter 3
Variable Language Models

Key characteristics of a DSL are an abstract syntax (including context conditions) and semantics (especially semantic mappings) defined at the level of the concepts and their relationships of the problem domain, rather than at the level of the solution domain. This has important implications for the abstract syntax design of a DSL, as opposed to the abstract syntax of general-purpose software languages. First, the different purposes of a DSL abstract syntax are contrasted. Second, different styles of defining concrete and abstract syntaxes are identified. Against this background, the property of a language model of being variable is defined for different scopes, in particular, for design-decision making and for modeling a variable problem domain.

3.1 Some Background on Language Models

3.1.1 Purpose

A software language's abstract syntax is, in general and by definition, meant to enable a particular processing step or language-tooling step. Examples include static analyses based on a syntax tree, visualization for debugging purposes, as well as transformations into another representation. From this end, the responsibility of an abstract syntax design is to abstract from (concrete-) syntax details that are not relevant to the targeted processing or tooling step. For an external DSL, an abstract syntax might take the role of a parse representation. In this role, an abstract syntax is commonly judged regarding its robustness, compactness, and traversability.[1] For a DSL, an additional purpose is that its abstract syntax is defined at the level of the problem domain. The abstract syntax is expected to realize a conceptual model of the problem domain that captures the concepts and their relationships, e.g., possibly using a (semi-) formal structural modeling language. In this role, an abstract syntax

---

[1]In Chap. 5, Sect. 5.2.1, these criteria are elaborated on.

© Springer Nature Switzerland AG 2020

S. Sobernig, *Variable Domain-specific Software Languages with DjDSL*,

https://doi.org/10.1007/978-3-030-42152-6_3

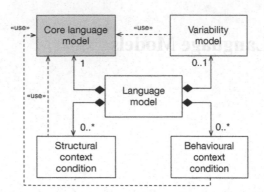

Fig. 3.1 A DSL language model contains a *core language-model* (e.g., the abstract syntax at the level of the problem domain), an optional *variability model*, one or more *structural context conditions*, and one or more *behavioural context conditions*. In the remainder, for brevity, we refer to the *core language-model* as the primary abstract syntax of a DSL as *language model*

is assessed in terms of other quality attributes, for example, its expressiveness. It is important to note that these different quality criteria, depending on the respective purpose, may be opposing each other. For an abstract syntax to qualify as expressive, it may not be compact anymore from the perspective of a syntax processor. For a domain engineer or DSL developer, an abstract syntax that uses homogeneous (abstracted) element types (e.g., nodes) and regular (abstracted) relationships (e.g., parent–child axes) may not be particularly expressive to describe the concepts and their relationships in a domain because, for example, annotations or comments must capture domain details otherwise lost. Such a homogeneous and regular abstract syntax, however, is convenient for implementing traversals [48, p. 89].

These potential tensions (e.g., expressiveness vs. compactness, expressiveness vs. traversability) solicit a decision on the abstract syntax design of a DSL: *Is one abstract syntax sufficient? Or, should a dedicated abstract syntax be provided for each DSL-specific purpose (e.g., problem-domain model, parsing representation)?* For some domains, a single abstract syntax might serve both as a conceptual model and as a parsing representation. Examples include computational domains for algebraic or comparison calculations, in which a (postfix) notation might map to an abstract syntax that allows further processing (expression evaluation) directly. Most higher-level and composite domains of application, however, do not yield an abstract syntax that can serve all-in-one, domain modeling as well as processing and tooling.

As a consequence, for DSL, there is the proven practice of providing and maintaining a primary abstract syntax to capture the problem domain and one or several secondary abstract syntaxes for processing and tooling support. This primary abstract syntax is typically realized using as a model in an object-oriented modeling or programming language. Secondary abstract syntaxes can be derived (automatically) from the primary one as views, for example, to better suit the requirements on traversability for a given analysis procedure.[2] Equally important,

---

[2]It is important to recall that abstract syntax views can result from projections on the primary abstract syntax but can also form supersets of the primary abstract syntax [48].

a secondary abstract syntax may serve as an intermediate representation on the way from a DSL script's (model's) concrete-syntax representation (notation) to its primary abstract syntax representation.[3] For the scope of this work, and in the conceptual framework underneath DjDSL, a DSL's primary abstract syntax is referred to as its *core language-model* (see Fig. 3.1). For brevity, it will be referred to as *language model*.[4] The other parts of a DSL's language model (in the broader sense) such as context conditions and variability model are defined over the elements of the (core) language-model. As a data structure for syntax processing, a core language-model acts as a heterogeneous and irregular parse representation, whether tree or graph [48, p. 99]. It is heterogeneous because it represents a DSL script (model) using different model-types (rather than one abstracted type such as nodes). It is also irregular because references throughout the language model are named. Access to related model elements is not possible in a generic (regular) manner (e.g., collections of children) or without resorting to metaprogramming techniques. From the domain engineer's and DSL developer's perspective, a core language-model is defined using the means of expression of a structural object-oriented modeling language such as EMOF or Ecore, textually or diagrammatically.

3.1.2 Definition Style

Apart from the decision between one or several abstract syntaxes (primary vs. secondary or intermediate), a DSL's primary abstract syntax (language model in DjDSL) can be defined in different ways. Traditionally, modelware and grammarware DSL have been discriminated based on their different approaches. In a *concrete-first* approach (historically, for a grammarware DSL), a concrete-syntax definition precedes the definition of the primary abstract syntax. For example, first, an E/BNF-like grammar definition is provided and a corresponding parser is implemented or generated. Then, representation classes in the host language are defined as abstract syntax representation. This may, or may not, follow from a development procedure that is driven by the concrete-syntax design. In an *abstract-first* approach, the primary abstract syntax is defined first. Concrete-syntax definitions follow by referring to the existing abstract syntax. Again, this may correspond to a DSL development procedure driven by a language model. But this is not necessarily the case. When one of the syntax types precedes the other in their times of definition, a correspondence between the two must be recorded and maintained. Establishing a correspondence may happen implicitly (by derivation) or explicitly (by definition).

The order of definition between syntax types (concrete-first, abstract-first) and how correspondences are established (derivation, definition) form two simultaneous dimensions. Different approaches fall into four different groups along these dimensions (for selection, see Fig. 3.2).

---

[3]The use of such intermediate representations (nested tuples, parse lists, parse trees, parse graphs) is actually the state of things in most syntax-processing pipelines.

[4]Related work has labeled a DSL's primary abstract syntax *problem-domain model*, *semantic model* [30], *domain model*, or *baseline object model* [42].

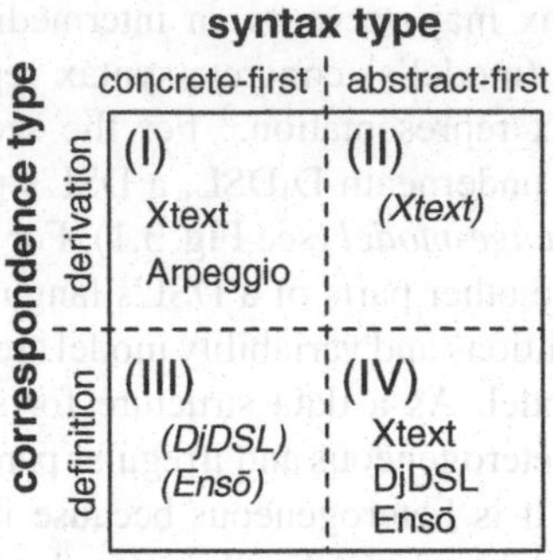

syntax type

	concrete-first	abstract-first
derivation	(I) Xtext Arpeggio	(II) *(Xtext)*
definition	(III) *(DjDSL)* *(Ensō)*	(IV) Xtext DjDSL Ensō

*(left margin label: **correspondence type**)*

Fig. 3.2 As for the definition style of a DSL's abstract syntax, DSL development systems fall into four groups, depending on whether they require a DSL developer to first define a concrete syntax or the abstract syntax, and on whether the correspondences between the two are established per definition (in-place, out-place) or per derivation. DSL development systems commonly support more than one definition style. The chosen example systems (Arpeggio, Xtext, Ensō, and DjDSL) are only indicative

Arpeggio (based on a recognition system) and Xtext (based on a grammar system), both are or can be used as concrete-first approaches. Recognition and grammar definition comes first (a PEG and an Xtext/ANTLR grammar, respectively). From those, an abstract syntax model is derived in a semi-automated manner and partly configurable manner based on generic correspondence rules (e.g., a non-terminal becomes a host-language class). In Xtext, this is referred to as *model inference*; an idea that can traced back to the DSL development system Popart [69]. DjDSL and Ensō (an object-grammar implementation) start from an abstract syntax which is then referenced from within a concrete-syntax definition (a PEG and GLL grammar, respectively). Alternatively, Xtext also allows for building a concrete-syntax based on an existing (imported) abstract syntax (Ecore) model.

DjDSL's, Ensō's, and Xtext's support for defining correspondences between concrete syntax and abstract syntax explicitly is original in that the definition is *in-place*. An in-place definition involves the statement of correspondences between parsed input and a language-model instantiation, or vice versa, along with the definition of either the concrete or abstract syntax. Production or parsing rules (including alternates for Ensō and DjDSL) declare correspondences with language-model elements. In Xtext, this happens on a rule-per-rule basis (`return` keyword). *Out-place* definitions of correspondence, on the contrary, involve third-party definition artifacts, e.g., a weaving model or generator model or transformation. Based on out-place definitions, the translation from parsed input into the abstract syntax representation is typically performed as a post-processing step (rather than as part of parsing). An example for the opposite direction for in-place correspondences, the abstract syntax laying out the concrete syntax, can be found for external diagrammatic DSL. Eugenia [39] allows for annotating abstract syntax (Ecore) models with instructions on how to build a graphical concrete syntax (i.e., GMF diagrams via model annotations such as `@gmf.diagram`, `@gmf.node`, and `@gmf.link`).

3.1.3   Variability and Variability Modeling

For the scope of this writing, a variable (core) language-model as a DSL's primary abstract syntax can vary in terms of the problem-domain concepts and relationship it models. In its form as a model expressed using a structural object-oriented programming or modeling language (e.g., an EMOF or Ecore model), means of defining variants of a base model in a systematic and efficient manner are of interest. The drivers for maintaining variants of a language model follow from the general drivers towards variable DSL (domain evolution etc.; see Sect. 1.2).

In DjDSL, a language-model variant is derived from a base model that is realized as a composed set of collaborating model elements (*collaboration* of *classifiers*). The structural and behavioral features defined by a model element for a given collaboration reflect different *roles* played by a model element [4, 6]. For DSL designs, collaborations can represent features of a variable language model, behaviors implementing a processing phase, or behaviors implementing an analysis phase.

At the level of variable DSL design-decision making, the separation into primary and secondary (intermediate) abstract syntaxes empowers the domain engineer and DSL developer in decision-making. In particular, the decision between internal or external DSL (syntax), as well as maintaining one or several syntaxes per DSL, can be rendered dynamic this way.[5] In Chap. 5, the gain in flexibility is exemplified for DSL developed using DjDSL.

Modeling the variability of a core language-model is an important step in developing a variable DSL and, in particular, a DSL product line. The variability model documents a DSL variability in terms of the DSL variants deemed valid. DjDSL attaches an explicit variability model to a language model (see also Fig. 3.1). The variability model results from the analysis of the problem domain but is put to use in the solution domain. It models the space of language-model variants in terms of features common and optional for all variants. Features map to the element types of a language model, i.e., collaborations. In addition, the variability model allows for querying the language model for the presence or absence of a feature in a configuration. DjDSL offers a textual syntax to define a variability model that encodes the variability in terms of choice cardinalities. This encoding is capable of representing many common types of variability models, including feature diagrams. For visualization, the Czarnecki-Eisenecker notation [21] is used throughout this writing. For variability-aware analyses, the variability model can be integrated with a binary-decision diagram (BDD) engine. Section 3.3 provides the details on variability modeling in DjDSL.[6]

---

[5]Fowler [30, p. 111] puts this as follows:

> "On thing I do want to stress, however, is that experimenting in both directions [internal, external DSL] need not be as expensive as you think. If you use a SEMANTIC MODEL (159), it's relatively easy to layer on multiple DSL, both internal and external."

[6]Variability models play also an important role in other areas of variability-aware DSL engineering. In Sect. 2.2.2, a variability model (feature diagram) is used to structure the space of reusable design decisions on DSL. Variability models can also help analyze grammar definitions for external DSL (e.g., to explore the space of derived instantiations in terms of the abstract syntax).

3.2 Feature-Oriented Decomposition and Composition of Language Models

A variable core language-models in DjDSL is realized as a *collaboration-based design*. In object-oriented modeling and programming, a collaboration groups objects and classes that interact by exchanging messages for the scope of a given collaboration. In this sense, the features exposed by the collaborators and the implemented behavior between them is an encapsulated piece of functionality. A collaborationwise encapsulation of structure and behavior is considered beneficial towards the property of *modularity* of a model or a software system. The notion of collaboration-based designs goes back to approaches of role-oriented modeling, in particular OOram [50]. In objected-oriented modeling (e.g., UML), collaborations can be directly modeled in terms of the same-named concepts: collaborations and collaboration parts. In object-oriented programming, and its more recent offspring such as feature-oriented programming, advanced structuring techniques such as mixin layers, delegation layers, and teams have been proposed to implement collaboration-based designs.[7] In the following, the common example of a Graph-Product Line (GraphPL) is adopted to illustrate our approach. As a variability model, the GraphPL is shown as a feature diagram in Fig. 3.3.[8]

A variable DjDSL language model describes a family of concrete language models, that is, a family of language-model variants. Each variant is formed from one or several collaborations. In Fig. 3.3, a collaboration is depicted informally as a horizontal bar (Graph, coloured, weighted). A variant is created composing a base collaboration (e.g., Graph) and a number of additional collaborations. The base collaboration implements the problem-domain elements and relationships common to all variants of the language model: a container element Graph, as well as Edge and Node classes as the building blocks for different graph representations.

As shown in the feature diagram in Fig. 3.3 (on the right), the variable language model is expected to provide for four valid variants. The two sub-features coloured and weighted are both optional (depicted by the empty dot markers) and simultaneous. That is, this variability model allows for four valid configurations: plain graphs, coloured graphs, weighted graphs, and, both, coloured *and* weighted graphs.[9]

The implementations of these two features are realized as additional collaborations to become composed with the base collaboration to form one of those four variants (see the lower to bars in Fig. 3.3). Variants with coloured have support for colouring graph's edges. Variants with weighted take labels to graph edges, e.g., to

---

[7]Sobernig et al. [62] provide a systematic overview of these techniques. See also Sect. 3.4 on related work.

[8]The GraphPL is a family of variants of a graph library that implements different types of graphs (coloured, weighted, directed, undirected, edge-labeled, etc.), different representation strategies (e.g., edge or neighbor lists), and support algorithms (e.g., for graph traversals). In this chapter, the emphasis is on selected features, as highlighted in Fig. 3.3.

[9]See Sect. 3.3 for more background on variability models, including feature diagrams. A general introduction to the feature-diagram notation used can be found in Apel et al. [6, Section 2.3.2] or Czarnecki and Eisenecker [21, Chapter 4].

store and to attach weightings to edges if the representation condition of the graph requires it. Collaborations for implementing features contain again (partial) classes (called *roles* or *refinements*) that incorporate structural and behavioral extensions into the base elements when two or more collaborations are composed to derive a variant of the language model. The respective role (refinement) elements applicable to a base element form a refinement chain. See the chain of the base element Edge and the two same-named roles contributed by the two feature collaborations in Fig. 3.3 rendered visible as a vertical dashed bar. Feature collaboration can also introduce new language-model elements (e.g., Colour and Weight) which are not present in the base collaboration; hence called *introductions*.

Collaborations in a collaboration-based design and implementation of a language model are not limited to realizing the (varying) features of a language-model family in the sense of varying concepts and relationships from the problem domain. Collaborations can be equally employed to implement the behavior for platform integration (e.g., a direct interpreter on top of the language model) or processing stages or phases that operate on the primary abstract syntax directly. This has also been called *layering* of application-level, analysis-level, and tool-level abstract syntax refinements [49, p. 36]. Beyond a variable design of the primary abstract syntax, a collaboration-based design has also been suggested for the scope of language components and language pipelines by Vacchi and

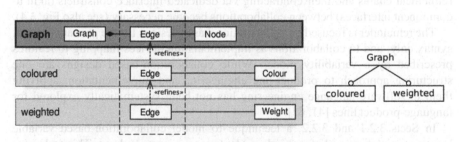

Fig. 3.3 Graph-Product Line (GraphPL): A conceptual sketch of a collaboration-based design of a language model (on the left) and a corresponding feature diagram as the variability model (on the right)

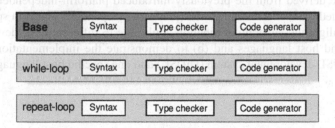

Fig. 3.4 Language componentization [67] considers collaboration-based designs at a different level: Language components are pluggable and behavioral language components (e.g., loop constructs) that require integration and refinement at all levels of a language pipeline (syntax, type checking, and code generation). Language-component interfaces must contract dependencies within and between the language components (e.g., while-loop, repeat-loop), beyond refinement chains

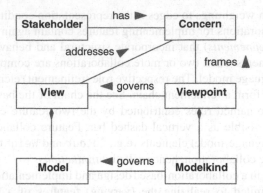

Fig. 3.5 Overview of basic elements of describing a multi-view approach to collaboration-based language models [36, 68]. A key contribution of DjDSL is defining viewpoints on language models based on the idea of collaborations. This viewpoint is implemented using the metamodel in Fig. 3.6 and a corresponding UML extension. The actual views on a language model are represented by a number of interrelated models (e.g., asset and composition models) for a DSL family

Cazzola [67]. Each collaboration (base, feature) spans syntax definition, type checking, to platform integration (e.g., code generation). In such collaboration-based (or layered) pipelines, however, more sophisticated dependency types beyond refinement chains and their contracting via dedicated interface constructs (akin to component interfaces) between collaborations become necessary (see also Fig. 3.4).

The remainder is focused on collaboration-based designs for the primary abstract syntax only; and to collaborations as implementation devices mapping to features prescribed by a variability model. While collaboration-based designs are one structuring approach to product-line engineering and implementation, applying them to software language engineering has not been systematically explored for language-product lines [41, 67].

In Sects. 3.2.1 and 3.2.2, a technique to model collaboration-based variable language models in a platform-independent manner is worked out. This technique is designed and implemented as a UML-based (internal) DSL.[10] In Sect. 3.2.3, a platform-specific realization of variable language models for DjDSL is introduced, that can be derived from the previously introduced platform-independent models in an assisted manner. This separation (platform independent, platform specific) is (a) to highlight the general contribution applicable to different DSL development systems and host languages and (b) to demonstrate the implementation for one concrete DSL development system (DjDSL) and one specific host language (NX).

---

[10]More precisely, it is an internal DSL using UML piggybacking with profiles and context conditions. See also Sect. 2.2.2.

3.2.1 Collaboration-Based Designs of Language Models

A *collaboration*-based design decomposes a variable DSL's language model into collaborations. A collaboration is a bounded collection of interacting program entities (e.g., objects and classes) that interact to implement a scoped and self-contained unit of problem-domain description. A collaboration-based language model comprises a base collaboration and, possibly, one or more collaborations that implement optional DSL features. In this sense, a variable language model is referred to as a feature-oriented one.

A collaboration-based design of a language model emphasizes three major concerns: asset definition, composition definition, and variability definition. Each of these concerns is relevant to one or several groups of stakeholders in a variable DSL design: product-line or asset developer, DSL developer, and a practitioner (domain expert) as the adopter and user of the DSL (see also Fig. 3.5).

DjDSL offers views on a language model which address these concerns. These views are represented as development artifacts themselves (models). The conventions and rules for constructing, interpreting, and using these model-based views when designing a DSL in a collaboration-based manner (i.e., a viewpoint) are established by metamodeling techniques and a dedicated UML extension. Touching on these three concerns, a conceptual overview of a collaboration-based design of a language model is detailed in Fig. 3.6 as an EMOF model.[11] The model is structured into three packages, one covering for each of the three concerns: `assets`, `compositions`, and `djdsl::vle`.

3.2.1.1 Structure of Variable Language Models

The key definitions of a variable language model are given as a conceptual (EMOF) model in Fig. 3.6.

A **Feature** is a unit of DSL or DSL-tooling functionality or behavior directly visible to the DSL developer and/ or DLS users. This visibility is typically clearly marked by the feature being contained by the variability model. In language-product lines, for example, a language feature describes a particular language-definition artifact (e.g., a construct definition at the abstract and/ or concrete syntax level), a developer-visible phase of language processing (e.g., different analyses, debugging, testing, refactoring activities), or both. In addition, a feature of a variable language model must affect the structure of the common language model (e.g., by adding new language-model elements or refining existing ones). Adding new expression operations or expression types, for the LEA example (see Sect. 1.4), may be considered a proper DSL feature. This is because they are not only directly visible to practitioners employing the now extended expressions, but they also add new or refine existing language-model elements to implement new expression types or operations. For the graph-specification language, supporting weight labels and

---

[11] The model is available as a supplement in its repository format (XMI).

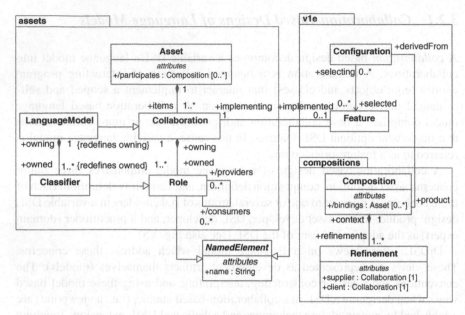

Fig. 3.6 A conceptual model of feature-oriented language models in terms of an EMOF model. The emphasis in this section is on the `assets` and the `compositions` packages. The elements specific to the `djdsl::vle` package are elaborated on in Sect. 3.3

element colouring is visible from the graph modeler's perspective and modifies the language model for the feature-enabled variants (see Fig. 3.3).

A DSL **Configuration** is one valid selection of features, set by a variability model, which resolves all dependencies at the level of the variability model. A configuration is realized by a single variant, that is, one concrete language model which is based on all the collaborations (feature implementation) corresponding to the configuration.

A **Composition** is derived from a configuration and defines the way a language model and additional collaborations are composed to form a derived language model which can be instantiated.

A **Collaboration** implements a DSL feature. For this, a collaboration groups roles that are related in a structural or behavioral manner to implement a given DSL feature. A collaboration **Role** implements the responsibilities of a language-model element (e.g., typically as a class or a partial class) in the context of a collaboration.

A **Refinement** relates two collaborations as a supplier of and a client of provided structural and behavioral features in the context of a given composition. Refinements must adhere to the configuration (i.e., match the dependencies between features).

A **Language Model** is a specialization of a **Collaboration** that realizes the base collaboration for a family of language-model variants. A key property is that it is meant to represent a usable language model, as opposed to a **Collaboration**. In contrast to a **Collaboration**, rather than containing partial entities (roles), it

```
1  context Refinement
2  -- no loops
3  inv FLM_1a:  Composition.allInstances()->forAll(c |
4                   c.refinements->forAll(client <> supplier))
5  -- no duplicates
6  inv FLM_1b:  Composition.allInstances()->forAll(c |
7                   c.refinements->forAll(r1, r2 |
8                       r1.client <> r2.client and
9                       r1.supplier <> r2.supplier))
10 -- no pairs of inverted
11 inv FLM_1c:  Composition.allInstances()->forAll(c |
12                   c.refinements->forAll(r1, r2 |
13                       r1.client = r2.supplier implies
14                       not (r1.supplier = r2.client)))
```

Lst. 3.7

consists of completed entities (classifiers) which allow for instantiating the language model as-is, without further collaborations being added.

A **Classifier** is a language-model element common to all language-model variants and, under composition, the result of integrating (composing) the feature-specific roles into completed and instantiable elements to represent a given variant of a DSL family. For example, classes formed from class fragments, or concrete classes inheriting from abstract ones, which then define the commonalities and the differences in valid DSL programs. The minimum goal is to obtain a language model that can be subjected to instantiation (directly or indirectly via factories). This implies that certain implementation decisions, e.g., behavioral definitions needed for platform integration, may still be deferred in the language model.

3.2.1.2 Context Conditions

In addition to the structure of language models defined above, the following conditions must hold. They are implemented as OCL invariant constraints on the EMOF model from Fig. 3.6.[12] Their main purpose is to express certain conditions on the sanity of a variable language model (no circular relationships) and its consistency with the related artifacts, i.e., the variability model and the compositions.

- A Composition forms a dependency network of refinements that is represented by a directed graph without loops, no duplicate edges (multiples between the same source and the same target), and there are no pairs of inverse refinements. This is captured by the three invariant constraints in Listing 3.7, for the scope of each and every Composition.
- A Composition must include at least one LanguageModel as a client, i.e., the base collaboration being refined by feature collaborations (see Listing 3.8).

---

[12]The context conditions are available as a CompleteOCL script applicable on the supplemental EMOF model.

```
1 context Composition
2 inv FLM_2: refinements->any(client.oclIsKindOf(LanguageModel))
```

Lst. 3.8

```
1 context Collaboration
2 def: allIncluding(c : Composition) : Set(OclAny) =
3       let clients = c.refinements->select(supplier = self).client in
4       clients->closure(allIncluding(c))
5
6 context Collaboration
7 inv FLM_3:  Composition.allInstances()->forAll(c |
8                 self.allIncluding(c)->notEmpty() implies
9                 not self.allIncluding(c)->includes(self))
```

Lst. 3.9

```
1 context LanguageModel
2 inv FLM_4: Composition.allInstances()->forAll(c |
3                 includes(c)->size() = c.derivedFrom.selected->size())
```

Lst. 3.10

```
1 context Role
2 inv FLM_5:  consumers->notEmpty() implies
3                 not self->closure(consumers)->includes(self)
```

Lst. 3.11

- A given Collaboration (including a LanguageModel) cannot reference itself (also not transitively) via refinements. The corresponding OCL constraint in Listing 3.9, first, computes the set of all collaborations that include a given Collaboration via Refinements (allIncluding()) and then, second, evaluates whether the given Collaboration is contained by that set. This invariant constraint also covers for the absence of circular structures in the derived refinements network.
- The number of collaborations included by the language model must match the number of selected (non-base) features of the corresponding configuration. This is a matter of consistency (see Listing 3.10).
- A given Role cannot reference itself (also not transitively; see Listing 3.11).
- A Role can only be dependent on (consume from, provide for) roles within the same collaboration (see Listing 3.12). This is the owning collaboration of all roles (see also Fig. 3.6). The relationships between roles as consumers or providers in a given collaboration abstract from different possible relations set by the implementation techniques of the host language used (e.g., sub- and superclassing with and w/o method combination, property types). The rationale for this restriction is that a collaboration captures a piece of functionality which is understandable within the context of a given collaboration.

Redefinitions of the structural context conditions above are available for the implementation as a UML profile (see Sect. 3.2.2).

```
1 context Role
2 inv FLM_6:  consumers->union(providers)->
3              forAll(r : Role | r.owning = owning)
```

Lst. 3.12

To summarize: DSL features and configurations belong to the problem domain of a variable DSL design, while collaborations and compositions form the key notions of the solution domain of a DSL design (see Fig. 1.2, Chap. 2). A DSL implementation is said feature-oriented, when its features map to collaborations.[13] These collaborations form the assets of a DSL product line, from which a number of products (DSL variants) can be formed by composition. In this, a collaboration implements the core feature of a DSL, one or several (optionally present) DSL features, and the finally composed product implementation (i.e., one valid DSL model corresponding to a configuration). Forming a product implementation from these assets can be achieved by different implementation techniques [7], depending on the host language and the intended de- and recomposition semantics (e.g., structural superimposition [7], dynamic subclassing [62]).[14]

3.2.1.3 Feature Binding

Including a (DSL) feature into a base language model is referred to as *binding* the feature. Feature binding can occur at several binding times. Programming languages and their runtime environments provide a characteristic set of binding times (pre-processing time, compile time, load time, program execution time) in certain binding modes (i.e., fixed, changeable, or dynamic; [21]). A DSL development system (e.g., a language workbench or a DSL toolkit) typically comes with binding times more specific to the development steps for a DSL (e.g., language-model driven development). The details of these binding-time models, however, may vary substantially depending on the background (e.g., grammarware vs. modelware).

Static feature binding occurs at an early binding time (e.g., when defining or compiling the language-model assets) and represents an irrevocable inclusion of a feature into a program. Forms of dynamic feature binding allow for deferring feature inclusion to later binding times (e.g., during program execution) and for revoking the inclusion decision during the lifetime of a program. In DjDSL, there is a dedicated binding time referred to as *composition time*. This is the time

---

[13]It is noteworthy that not all collaborations necessarily implement a feature. For example, a solitary language model without variations does not map to a feature in the variability model. This is unless, by convention, is represented as a mandatory *base* sub-feature. Similarly, providing a collaboration may be required to realize functionality invisible to the DSL user (e.g., maintaining traceability links between models).

[14]Please refer to Sect. 2.4 for a more thorough overview of variability implementation techniques, including those eligible to implement a collaboration-based design.

of instantiating a Composition when setting up a DSL pipeline. By removing a particular composition (i.e., destroying the corresponding object at runtime), a particular binding of feature collaborations to a base collaboration is revoked again, leaving all other possible and co-present compositions in the same runtime scope untouched (see also the paragraph on product quantification in Sect. 3.2.3). Therefore, DjDSL realizes a dynamic binding mode for features.

Class and objects are the two main levels of composition in object-oriented, collaboration-based designs [61], because they represent and implement the language model itself and its instantiations. At the model level, the derived language model is represented by a single composed class or a composed, collaborative class structure to be instantiated. At the instantiation level, the language model is embodied by a single composed object or a composed object collaboration. In a DSL development system such as DjDSL, the basic composition level is the model level. This is because the internal- or the external-syntax processors in the pipeline for processing a DSL script (model) assume a composed language model representing a specific DSL variant as an instantiable (i.e., class) structure. In this, each DSL script (model) maps to one instantiation of a composed language model. Once instantiated, such a representation is meant to remain conforming to the DSL variant responsible for its construction.

To summarize, DjDSL supports the dynamic model-level composition of base collaborations and feature collaborations. Note, however, that the notion of a collaboration-based design applies to other combinations of composition-level and binding modes as well, e.g., static model-level instantiation. For a complete overview of possible combinations of feature composition that can be realized on the basis of NX, and therefore in DjDSL, please refer to Sobernig et al. [62].

3.2.1.4 Collaboration-Aware Conflict Resolution

Collaborations in a variable language model consist of classifiers and roles, respectively. For the scope of a given collaboration (e.g., the base collaboration Graph or the feature collaboration weighted), the contained classifiers and roles

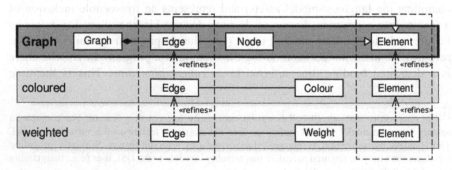

Fig. 3.13 A revised variable language model of the GraphPL. A class Element is a common ancestor for Node and Edge for the scope of the base collaboration. In addition, Element becomes refined by the feature collaborations

can form generalization and specialization hierarchies to model the problem domain and the feature-specific fragment of the problem domain. See an extended language model of the GraphPL in Fig. 3.13 that features a common ancestor Element for nodes and edges. At the same time, between collaborations, roles supplied by feature collaborations refine classifiers in the base collaboration [5]. This way, also generalizing classifiers like Element in Fig. 3.13 can end up with dedicated refinements. As a consequence, a collaboration-based design of an object-oriented program, in general, and for a variable language model, in particular, must reconcile two orders of precedence when computing lookup orders for structural features (e.g., fields, properties) and behavioral features (e.g., methods, initializers)[15]: the order incurred by per-collaboration generalizations and specializations as well as the order incurred by between-collaboration refinements (a.k.a. refinement chains). This represents a corner case in the field of (automated) *conflict resolution* under multiple class-based inheritance [59].

Consider the schematic of a resolution order in Fig. 3.14. The Base collaboration lays out a basic specialization hierarchy between classifiers C, B, and A (in that very order). The two feature collaborations add roles as refinements on top of this hierarchy, in terms of four refinement chains (the vertical bars in Fig. 3.14). When looking up a feature (property or method), DjDSL traverses the combined specialization and refinement hierarchy of a class (C in Fig. 3.14) and selects the left-most, bottom-most feature implementation found.

When following the super-reference (e.g., in method combination), this resolution order is continued to the next left-most, bottom-most candidate. This combined resolution order results in the total precedence as illustrated by the lookup arrow in Fig. 3.14. This resolution mechanism is an extended variant of the one devised for Feature Featherweight Java (FFJ; [5]). The mechanism results from two noteworthy design decisions:

(A) DjDSL searches for a feature implementation first in the refinement chain of a given classifier (i.e., C in Fig. 3.14). If no feature implementation is found in the refinement chain of a given class, or the class itself, the resolver proceeds by examining, the generalizing classifiers are searched next. For each general classifier (e.g., B and A), again the respective refinements chains are traversed first. This yields the left-most, bottom-most search behavior. See the paths labeled "(i)" in Fig. 3.14. To this extent, the mechanism corresponds to the state of the art set by FFJ [5].

(B) DjDSL allows roles (refinements in FFJ) to maintain their own generalizations or specializations that are local to a collaboration. For example, the role Feature1::B is defined as a subclass of classifier Feature1::D, i.e., a classifier introduced with this collaboration. This yields a situation conceptually comparable with resolving precedence conflicts in multiple class-based inheritance. From this angle, the refinement chain of B plus the classifier B itself can be considered a single unified class: B' in Fig. 3.15. The resolution

---

[15]Beware that the term "feature" is here used differently, in the sense of features of classifiers, and not features defined by variability model.

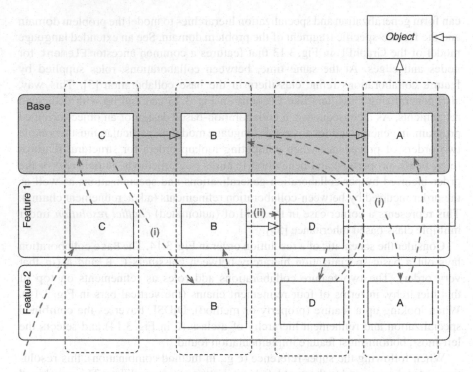

Fig. 3.14 Resolution order of classifier-features (e.g., properties and methods) taking into consideration refinement chains (i) and collaboration-local class precedence (ii). Loosely based on [5, Figure 2]. Horizontal bars (solid) represent collaborations, the vertical bars (dashed) the resulting refinement chains from the perspective of a given composition

mechanism (or, the DSL developer) must decide which generalizing classifier, A or D, takes precedence in feature resolution. This is further complicated by the possibility of roles for D becoming added by other features (see `Feature2::D` in Fig. 3.14.) The extended resolution mechanism in DjDSL gives precedence to local over global generalizing classifiers. That is, from the perspective of B in the context of collaboration `Feature1`, the generalizing classifier D is picked. See the lookup path labeled "(ii)" in Fig. 3.14. A and its refinement chain follow last. Preserving collaboration-local precedence orders is an original addition to the state of the art as represented by FFJ [5].

This extended collaboration-aware feature-resolution mechanism in DjDSL, therefore, gives three guarantees to the developers of a variable language model (whether responsible for the base or a feature collaboration). First, any collaboration-local generalizations and specializations (classifier `Feature1::D` for role `Feature1::B`) will be respected as defined by the developers of this collaboration. Second, the refinements of any base classifier (or classifier introduced by a feature collaboration) are considered before the classifiers themselves. Third, the generalizations and specializations set by the base collaboration will be respected in the sense that they

Fig. 3.15 In presence of per-collaboration generalizations and specializations, a resolution mechanism is confronted with a situation similar to linearization under multiple class-based inheritance

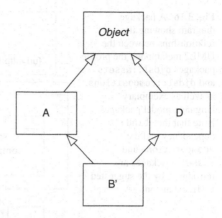

will be searched in their relative order (C followed by B followed by A) in the global resolution order computed by DjDSL.

This collaboration-aware resolution mechanism in DjDSL is built on top of the NX and its automated mechanism of determining the order of precedence among multiple ancestor classes and/or multiple mixins (*linearization*), which define the features (properties and methods) for a given object [59]. NX's linearization is built in a way to avoid counterintuitive results for, e.g., the message-resolution order (MRO) from the developer's perspective in the presence of complex class- and mixin-based inheritance graphs. Violations of intuition can result from features (methods) being looked up in a global order that counters (e.g., reverses) the order between two providers (classes) set for a local scope (e.g., for a class declaration). This is achieved by computing, in essence, a linear order from the inheritance graph equivalent to a global depth-first search constrained by superclass relationships and the class-local precedence orders (a.k.a. *C3 linearization* [10]). NX's C3 implementation is novel as it extends to simultaneously present decorator-mixin hierarchies and superclass heterarchies. Alternative linearization schemes (e.g., Flavor, CLOS, Loops, and Dylan; see [59]) do not guarantee the particular implicit global ordering based on multiple and explicit local orders. DjDSL lifts the properties of C3 linearization to the level of refinement-based linearization (as in FFJ [5]), with collaboration-local precedence orders as an additional linearization constraint.

Table 3.1 A summary of key definitions of a collaboration-based DSL designs and their mapping to a lightweight UML extension to model variable language models in a platform-independent manner

Concept	UML metaclass	Stereotype	Context conditions (OCL)
Asset	Package	«asset»	FLMA_1–FLMA_3
Collaboration	Class	«collaboration»	FLMA_4, FLMA_7
Language model	Class	«languageModel»	FLMA_5
Classifier	Class	«classifier»	FLMA_9
Role	Class	«role»	FLMA_6, FLMA_8

Fig. 3.16 A package
diagram showing the
relationships between the
UML2 metamodel, the profile
packages djdsl::assets
and djdsl::compositions,
as well as exemplary
language-model packages.
Note that the «bind»
dependency and the
«composition» and
«asset» packages are
introduced by the suggested
UML extension

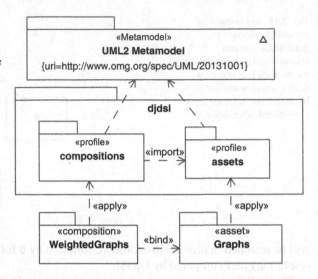

3.2.2 A UML Extension for Feature-Oriented Language Models

The idea of separating variable language models into and then composing them
from collaborations is independent from host language used to implement the assets
and the language-specific composition techniques [7]. Therefore, it is important to
capture the essence of a collaboration-based design independently from a particular
host language (e.g., NX/Tcl for DjDSL).

To this end, the proposed approach is defined as an extension to UML class
models. The extension contains two UML profiles: djdsl::assets and djdsl::
compositions (see Fig. 3.16). This way, the extension clearly separates the two
concerns identified before: asset definition and composition definition. The separation of concerns also reflects the separation of duties between a DSL (product)
developer and a DSL product line developer. The UML extension is part of DjDSL
to design a DSL language model and to reflect on the design, in a systematic manner.
Reflection includes the static analysis of prerequisites as defined by the structural
context conditions, as an example. Figures 3.17 and 3.29 give the corresponding
profile diagrams. Table 3.1 documents the most important correspondences between
the conceptual model of variable language models and the realization as extensions
to UML metaclasses (i.e., Class, Package, and Dependency). The rationale
guiding design and implementation of the UML profiles is as follows. In the
following, the design and implementation of both packages is elaborated one.

3.2.2.1 Assets

The profile djdsl::assets allows for collaborations to be defined using minimal and restricted UML class models. These class models are based on UML

(nested) classes to capture the conceptual elements of a collaboration, as introduced before.

The main asset concepts (Asset, Collaboration, Role, LanguageModel, and Classifier) map to the corresponding and equally named stereotypes: «asset», «collaboration», «role», «languageModel», and «classifier»; respectively (see Table 3.1).

The «asset» extends the Package metaclass. This way, asset collections can be defined as stereotyped UML packages for collaborations (see Graphs in Fig. 3.16). The remaining stereotypes extend the Class metaclass. Extended classes are used to represent both collaborations (language models) and roles (classifiers). Roles (classifiers) are represented as nested classes. This is because UML classes can be used to model various language-level implementation constructs (e.g., object-classes, partial classes, mixins, aspects), without introducing (additional) abstraction mismatches between model and implementation. The relationships (references and associations) between these four concepts (stereotypes) map to property pairs typed by the mirrored stereotypes.[16]

A number of structural context conditions must hold for «asset» packages. They do not only relate to the fundamental conditions defined earlier for the conceptual model. In addition, they establish a sane ground by verifying prerequisites on such a package's content and constrain the use of UML class models to modeling a variable language model only.

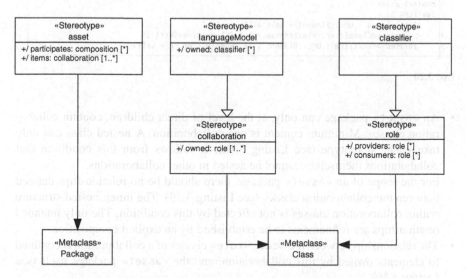

Fig. 3.17 The profile diagram showing the implementation details of the djdsl::assets profile. The underlying profile model is available from the supplemental Website. The corresponding derivation rules for the derived properties (e.g., owned) of the stereotypes (e.g., languageModel) are defined in a side-car CompleteOCL document

---

[16]As a general implementation decision, all properties owned by the defined stereotypes (e.g., owned of «collaboration») are defined as *derived* oncs. The accompanying OCL documents provide the corresponding derivation rules.

```
 1  context assets::asset
 2  def: allAssets() :
 3      Set(UML::Class) = self.base_Package.ownedElement
 4          ->select(oclIsKindOf(UML::Class) and
 5          (getAppliedStereotypes().qualifiedName->includes('assets::collaboration') or
 6          getAppliedStereotypes().qualifiedName->includes('assets::languageModel')))
 7          .oclAsType(UML::Class)->asSet()
 8  inv FLMA_1a:
 9      self.allAssets()->notEmpty()
10  inv FLMA_1b:
11      self.allAssets()->notEmpty() implies
12          not (self.allAssets()->forAll(
13              getAppliedStereotypes().qualifiedName
14              ->includesAll(Set{'assets::collaboration',
15                              'assets::languageModel'
16                              })))
```

Lst. 3.18

```
1  context asset
2  inv FLMA_2:
3    let relations : Set(UML::Relationship) =
4      self.base_Package.ownedElement->select(oclIsKindOf(UML::Relationship))
5          .oclAsType(UML::Relationship)->asSet() in
6      relations.relatedElement->excludesAll(allAssets())
```

Lst. 3.19

```
1  context asset
2  inv FLMA_3:
3      let related : UML::Element = self.allAssets()
4          ->nestedClassifier.relationship.relatedElement->asSet() in
5      related->forAll(re : UML::Element | re.owner = c or re = self)
```

Lst. 3.20

- An «asset» package can only, at the level of direct children, contain collaboration classes. Minimum content is one collaboration. A nested class can only take either stereotype (see Listing 3.18). It follows from this condition that collaborations themselves cannot be nested in other collaborations.
- For the scope of an «asset» package, there should be no relationships defined between the collaboration classes (see Listing 3.19). The inner, nested structure within collaboration classes is not affected by this condition. The only intended relationships are refinements to be established by an explicit composition.
- The relationship between the nested «role» classes of a collaboration is confined to elements owned by this collaboration; and the «asset» package itself (see Listing 3.20).
- «collaboration» classes must contain at least one nested class («role» or «classifier»). On top, there must be at least one «role» class. This follows directly from the requirement that a language model must be instantiable, without any prior composition (see Listing 3.21).

```
1  context collaboration
2  inv FLMA_4a:
3    self.base_Class.nestedClassifier->size() > 0
4  inv FLMA_4b:
5    self.base_Class.nestedClassifier->notEmpty() implies
6    self.base_Class.nestedClassifier->forAll(oclIsKindOf(UML::Class))
7  inv FLMA_4c:
8    self.base_Class.nestedClassifier->notEmpty() implies
9    self.base_Class.nestedClassifier->forAll(
10     getAppliedStereotypes().qualifiedName->includes('assets::role')
11       or
12     getAppliedStereotypes().qualifiedName->includes('assets::classifier'))
13 inv FLMA_4d:
14   self.base_Class.nestedClassifier->notEmpty() implies
15   self.base_Class.nestedClassifier->one(
16     getAppliedStereotypes().qualifiedName->includes('assets::role'))
```

Lst. 3.21

```
1  context languageModel
2  inv FLMA_5:
3    self.base_Class.nestedClassifier->notEmpty() implies
4    self.base_Class.nestedClassifier->forAll(
5      oclIsKindOf(UML::Class)
6        and
7      getAppliedStereotypes().qualifiedName->includes('assets::classifier'))
```

Lst. 3.22

```
1  context role
2  inv FLMA_6:
3    collaboration.allInstances().base_Class.nestedClassifier->select(
4      getAppliedStereotypes().qualifiedName->includes('assets::classifier'))
5    ->any(name = self.base_Class.name)
```

Lst. 3.23

- A «languageModel» as a specialized collaboration must contain «classifier» classes only. This follows directly from the requirement that a language model must be instantiable, without any prior composition (see Listing 3.22).
- Each «role» class contained by a «collaboration» class must correspond to a same-named «classifier» class provided by a language model, or by another «collaboration» class (see Listing 3.23).

  This restriction captures the fact there cannot be an orphaned role, without a given classifier to enter a potential refinement relationship with.
- A nested class cannot take «classifier» and «role» at the same time (see FLMA_7 in Listing 3.24).
- A role class must be set abstract. A classifier class must be set concrete (see FLMA_8 Listing 3.24).
- A given classifier class must be unique in the collection of assets. This last context condition represents the firm expectation that there are only refinement chains with single classifiers as the chains' tails (see FLMA_9 in Listing 3.24).

```
 1  context collaboration
 2  inv FLMA_7:
 3    self.base_Class.nestedClassifier->notEmpty() implies not
 4    self.base_Class.nestedClassifier->forAll(
 5      getAppliedStereotypes().qualifiedName->includes('assets;;role')
 6        and
 7      getAppliedStereotypes().qualifiedName->includes('assets::classifier'))
 8
 9  context role
10  inv FLMA_8a:   self.base_Class.isAbstract
11  context assets::classifier
12  inv FLMA_8b:   not self.base_Class.isAbstract
13
14  context classifier
15  inv FLMA_9:
16      collaboration.allInstances().base_Class.nestedClassifier->select(
17        getAppliedStereotypes().qualifiedName->includes('assets::classifier'))
18      ->forAll(name <> self.base_Class.name)
```

Lst. 3.24

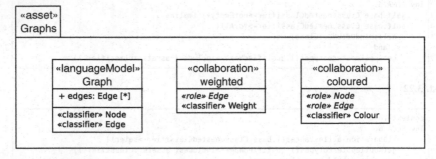

Fig. 3.25   Content of the «asset» package Graphs

The above conditions are completed by derivation conditions that define the properties of stereotypes based on the underlying, stereotyped elements. The complete
suite of OCL context conditions are provided as a supplemental CompleteOCL
document.

To illustrate the profile's application, an «asset» package for the running
GraphPL example may be modeled as depicted in Fig. 3.25.

1. The package Graphs is set to «apply» the djdsl::assets profile package
   (Fig. 3.26), and is marked as an «asset» package.
2. The «asset» package Graphs is then populated with classes (Graph, weighted,
   and coloured) that capture the three collaborations (see also Fig. 3.3). Accordingly, they are marked as «languageModel» and «collaboration», respectively.
3. The internal structure of the collaborations classes is established using nested
   classes, e.g., Graph::Node and Graph::Edge. The nested classes act either as a
   «classifier» or as a «role».

The actual collaborations can then be modeled using a dedicated class diagram per
collaboration. Figures 3.27 and 3.28 show the contents of two selected collaborations: Graph and weighted. coloured is omitted for brevity. The language model

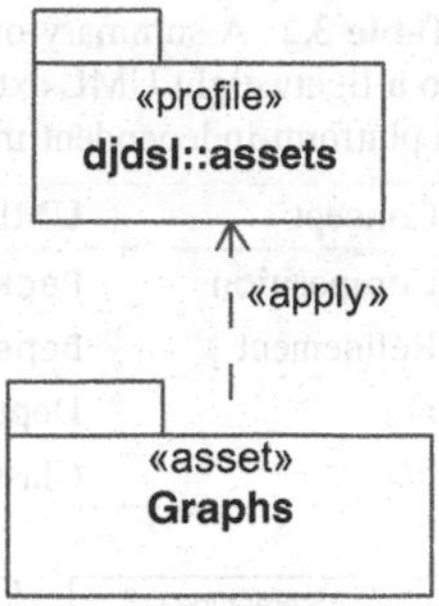

Fig. 3.26 Profile application

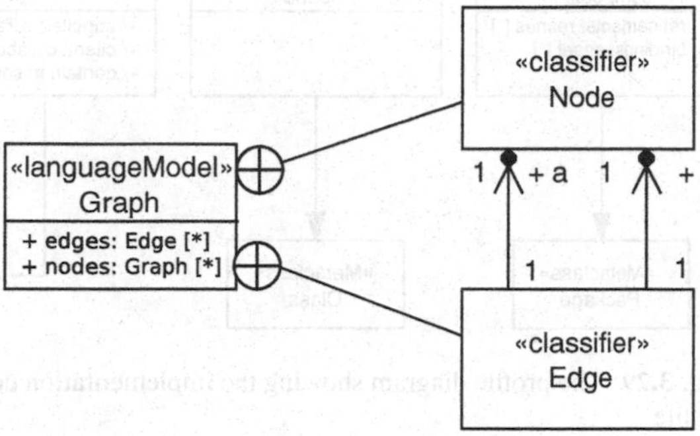

«profile»
djdsl::assets

⫶ «apply»

«asset»
Graphs

Fig. 3.27 Content of the
«languageModel» class
Graph

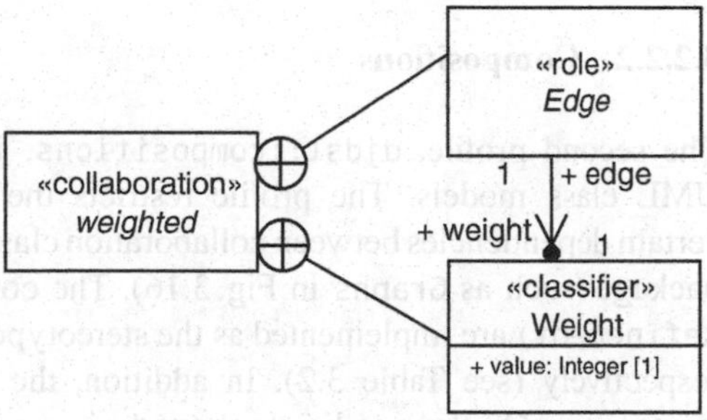

«classifier»
Node

«languageModel»
Graph
— — — — — —
+ edges: Edge [*]
+ nodes: Graph [*]

1   + a   1   + b

1   1

«classifier»
Edge

Fig. 3.28 Content of the
«collaboration» class
weighted

«role»
Edge

«collaboration»
weighted

1   + edge

+ weight   1

«classifier»
Weight
— — — — — —
+ value: Integer [1]

Graph provides two «classifier» classes, one for nodes, the other for edges. This is because, in this GraphPL variant, graphs are represented via edge lists. Note that the circled-plus notation is used to depict the nesting between the parent class and its children. Between parent and children, as well as between children, any relationship or dependency type can be modeled. The collaboration weighted, on the contrary, involves a «role» class and a «classifier» class. The role provides a refinement to the Edge classifier, to reference a weight. The edge weight is represented by the Weight class.[17]

---

[17] In a UML modeling tool (e.g., Papyrus or MagicDraw), the asset-package view (Fig. 3.25) and the collaboration views (Figs. 3.27 and 3.28) are realized as separate but cross-referencing class diagrams drawing from the same class model (e.g., using hyperlinks from one to the other in Papyrus).

Table 3.2 A summary of key definitions of collaboration-based DSL designs and their mapping to a lightweight UML extension (djdsl::compositions) to model variable language models in a platform-independent manner

Concept	UML metaclass	Stereotype	Context conditions (OCL)
Composition	Package	«composition»	FLMC_1, FLMC_2
Refinement	Dependency	«refines»	FLMC_3, FLMC_4, FLMC_6
n/a	Dependency	«bind»	FLMC_7
n/a	Class	«bound»	FLMC_5

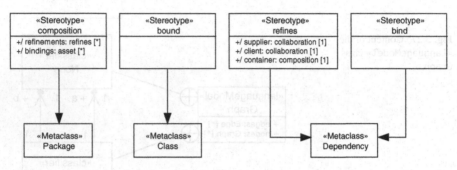

Fig. 3.29 The profile diagram showing the implementation details of the djdsl::compositions profile

3.2.2.2 Compositions

The second profile, djdsl::compositions, is also based on a small subset of UML class models. The profile restricts the use of class models to declaring certain dependencies between collaboration classes, defined in a corresponding asset package (such as Graphs in Fig. 3.16). The composition concepts (Composition, Refinement) are implemented as the stereotypes «composition» and «refines», respectively (see Table 3.2). In addition, the profile provides for two auxiliary stereotypes. On the one hand, «bound» is used to identify classes as the collaboration classes under composition. On the other hand, «bind» establishes a reference to an asset package, whose collaboration classes are referenced from within a given composition. «composition» extends the Package metaclass. A stereotyped UML package acts as a container for all refinements defined for the scope of a given composition (see WeightedGraphs in Fig. 3.16). In this container, only UML classes and UML dependencies are permitted. The stereotypes bind and refines extend the Dependency metaclass. For the scope of a «composition» package, first, a «bind» dependency to asset package must be declared (see Fig. 3.16). Then, second, «bound» classes referring to existing collaboration classes in the previously linked asset package(s) are placed. For this purpose, «bound» extends the Class metaclass. Between bound classes, «refines» dependencies can finally be declared (Fig. 3.29).

```
1 context composition
2 def: binds() : Set(UML::Package) = self.base_Package.ownedElement->select(
3     oclIsKindOf(UML::Dependency) and
4     not (getAppliedStereotype('compositions::bind').oclIsUndefined()))
5     ->oclAsType(UML::Dependency).supplier->oclAsType(UML::Package)->asSet()
6 inv FLMC_1a: self.binds()->notEmpty()
7 inv FLMC_1b: self.binds()->notEmpty() implies self.binds()->forAll(
8     getAppliedStereotypes().qualifiedName->includes('assets::asset')
9 )
```

Lst. 3.30

```
1 context composition
2 def: deps() : Set(UML::Dependency) =
3     self.base_Package.ownedElement->select(
4         e : UML::Element | e.oclIsKindOf(UML::Dependency)
5     )->oclAsType(UML::Dependency)->asSet()
6 inv FLMC_2a:
7     self.deps()->notEmpty() implies
8     self.deps()->forAll(
9         getAppliedStereotypes().qualifiedName->includes('compositions::refines')
10        or
11        getAppliedStereotypes().qualifiedName->includes('compositions::bind'))
12 inv FLMC_2b:
13    self.deps()->notEmpty() implies
14    self.deps()->forAll(getAppliedStereotypes()->size() = 1)
```

Lst. 3.31

In addition, the following structural context conditions must hold for «composition» packages. The conditions establish the prerequisites for compositions and render explicit when a composition can be considered valid.

- A composition package must bind at least one «asset» package (see Listing 3.30). As outlined earlier, this is because a «composition» package establishes «refines» dependencies between (previously) defined assets, that is, collaborations in «asset» packages. This way, multiple compositions and their packages can be based on one collection of asset packages. Compositions can also be based on a single asset package, provided that it contains several collaborations for composition.
- A «composition» package must contain refinement and binding dependencies only. All contained refinements and dependencies may only carry a single stereotype (see Listing 3.31). This condition limits the use of composition packages to the one concern of defining compositions.
- There must be exactly one supplier and one client to a refinement dependency. Suppliers and clients to a refinement dependency must be bound classes only (see Listing 3.32). Note that the first sub-condition (FLMC_3a) still allows for having one asset (collaboration) acting as a refinement supplier to two or more client collaborations. This is necessary to model derivatives, i.e., compositions between collaborations which are then to become integrated with a language model in a second step.
- Refinement dependencies must not form cycles (see Listing 3.33).
- A bound class must correspond to a collaboration class in one of the asset bindings (see FLMC_5 Listing 3.34).

```
1  context refines
2  inv FLMC_3a:
3      self.base_Dependency.supplier->size() = 1 and
4      self.base_Dependency.client->size() = 1
5  inv FLMC_3b:
6      self.base_Dependency.supplier->any(
7          e : UML::Element | e.oclIsKindOf(UML::Class) and
8          e.getAppliedStereotypes().qualifiedName->includes('compositions::bound')
9      )
10 inv FLMC_3c:
11     self.base_Dependency.client->any(
12         e : UML::Element | e.oclIsKindOf(UML::Class) and
13         e.getAppliedStereotypes().qualifiedName->includes('compositions::bound')
14     )
```

Lst. 3.32

```
1  context refines
2  inv FLMC_4:
3      not self.base_Dependency.supplier->closure(clientDependency.supplier)
4      ->includes(self.base_Dependency)
```

Lst. 3.33

- A refinement must only relate two bound classes owned by the composition package owning the refinement dependency (see `FLMC_6` in Listing 3.34).
- A «bind» dependency must only relate «composition» packages as its source (client) and «asset» packages as its target (supplier; see `FLMC_7` in Listing 3.34).

There are additional conditions necessary to define the relationships between stereotypes via properties. As these are not critical to understanding the essence of this UML extension, they are provided along with the supplemental CompleteOCL document.

Against the background of the structural rules and context conditions, a composition in the running GraphPL example may be modeled as depicted in Fig. 3.35. Such a package diagram for defining a composition (`WeightedGraphs`) involves the following steps:

1. The package `WeightedGraphs` is set to «apply» the djdsl ::compositions profile package.
2. The composition package `WeightedGraphs` is related to the previously defined «asset» package `Graphs` using a «bind» dependency.
3. The composition is then populated with classes (`Graphs::Graph` and `Graphs::weighted`) that must correspond to equally named collaboration classes in the now related «asset» package (i.e., `Graphs`).
4. The «bound» classes can finally be connected using «refines» (see Fig. 3.36). Once set, the refinement chains between classifier classes at the consumer end of the «refines» dependency and role classes at the supplier side are established.

The djdsl::compositions profile package, therefore, offers two complementary views on compositions: A package diagram is used to declare the «bind»

```
 1 context bound
 2 inv FLMC_5:
 3     base_Class.owner.oclAsType(UML::Package).extension_composition.binds()->any(
 4       ownedElement->select(
 5         oclIsKindOf(UML::Class) and name = self.base_Class.name
 6       )->notEmpty())
 7
 8 context refines
 9 inv FLMC_6a:
10     self.base_Dependency.relatedElement->forAll(
11       oclIsKindOf(UML::Class) and
12       not (getAppliedStereotype('compositions::bound').oclIsUndefined()))
13
14 context refines
15 inv FLMC_6b:
16     self.base_Dependency.client.oclAsType(UML::Class).owner = self.container.
           base_Package
17
18 context refines
19 inv FLMC_6c:
20     self.base_Dependency.client.owner = self.container.base_Package
21
22 context bind
23 inv FLMC_7a:
24     self.base_Dependency.client->forAll(
25       oclIsKindOf(UML::Package) and
26       not getAppliedStereotype('compositions::composition').oclIsUndefined())
27 inv FLMC_7b:
28     self.base_Dependency.supplier->forAll(
29       oclIsKindOf(UML::Package) and
30       not getAppliedStereotype('assets::asset').oclIsUndefined())
```

Lst. 3.34

Fig. 3.35 Profile application and asset binding

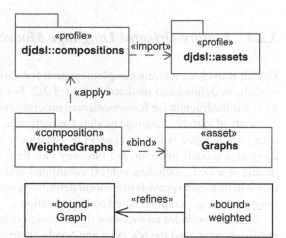

Fig. 3.36 Content of the «composition» package WeightedGraphs

relationship, a class diagram serves for recording «refines» relationships between then «bound» classes. UML modeling tools (e.g., Papyrus) allow for maintaining cross-references between the corresponding view diagrams. Alternatively, a single diagram may be used containing all in one, bindings and refinements.

Table 3.3 Correspondences between the UML extension and the DjDSL constructs for implementing variable language models. Assisted integration via a MOFM2T transformation from «asset» packages into a corresponding NX/Tcl package for DjDSL is available (as indicated)

UML metaclass	Stereotype	DjDSL metaclass	Transform. av.
Class	«asset»	`::djdsl::lm::Asset`	✓
Class	«languageModel»	`::djdsl::lm::LanguageModel`	✓
Class	«collaboration»	`::djdsl::lm::Collaboration`	✓
Class	«classifier»	`::djdsl::lm::Classifier`	✓
Class	«role»	`::djdsl::lm::Role`	✓
Package	«composition»	`::djdsl::lm::Composition`	
Dependency	«refines»	`::djdsl::lm::Composition` (property refines)	

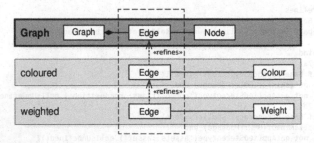

Fig. 3.37 The running example of a GraphPL: The conceptual sketch of a collaboration-based design of a language model, on the left, is implemented as a variable language model in DjDSL

3.2.3 Feature-Oriented Language Models in DjDSL

DjDSL provides a reference implementation for variable and composable language models, as defined and modeled in Sect. 3.2.2. For this purpose, DjDSL builds on an NX infrastructure for feature-oriented programming (FOP; [62]). The conceptual elements of variable language models (in particular, collaborations, classifiers, and roles) are mapped onto first-class FOP constructs (e.g., Collaboration classes). Language models implemented this way can be directly used to define the other details of a DSL, including context conditions and concrete syntaxes. In addition, they can be used to provide behavioral definitions and continue by a step of platform integration (e.g., template-based code generation).

Table 3.3 provides an overview of the basic correspondences between the UML profile elements and the NX language-level constructs (i.e., metaclasses).

There are, however, noteworthy challenges when mapping the platform-independent language models to a host-language environment such as NX/Tcl for DjDSL: decomposition mismatches, composition locality, quantification, and host-language blending.

3.2.3.1 Avoiding Decomposition Mismatches

In an object-based decomposition of a tiered, collaboration-based design, the collaborations (Graph, coloured, and weighted in Fig. 3.37) and the collaboration parts (Graph::Edge, weighted::Edge) are represented by distinct runtime objects. For the client of a collaboration-based language-model instantiation (a weighted graph object), the parts of a complex collaboration form single runtime entities. The directly accessible one is the composed, most refined edge kind which then forwards client messages to edge objects along a refinement chain. This decomposition mismatch can entail a self-problem during method combination and method forwarding [43, 46]. The latter might end up broken in unexpected ways.

3.2.3.2 Composition Locality

Critical operations (e.g., message sends during object construction) on and within a composed collaboration (a weighted graph) should be local to the composed collaboration. The composed collaboration so sets the context for, e.g., constructor calls [46, 60]. This issue is closely related to the object decomposition of collaboration roles. For any given feature composition (e.g., weighted graph), object construction should resort to the composition-specific refinements of the respective collaboration role (e.g., weighted::Edge) rather than the most general (as defined in a constructor call, e.g. Graph::Edge). The same must hold for class hierarchies (and the method lookup order on top) within a collaboration to be refined by other collaborations [46].

3.2.3.3 Product-Bounded Quantification

In feature-oriented programming and software composition, in more general, quantification [28] refers to evaluating selection predicates over a program structure (an AST, an interpreter state) to match code units (objects and methods in the base program) for performing transformation, weaving, and intercepting operations on them. In dynamic feature binding (as in DjDSL), one can create multiple products (language-model compositions) and product instantiations (language-model instantiations) side-by-side; for example, multiple graph products each with a different feature configuration. This requires the client code to manage multiple feature compositions. Reconfiguring selected products (e.g., unbinding the coloured feature) must preserve the feature composition of the remaining products through tailorable quantification statements. Unbounded quantification over an object graph might also cause unwanted interactions: For example, by selecting a class for refinement through a class fragment in a feature implementation, all instances of this class (and its subclasses) existing prior to activating the feature for a given product (and therefore future instances of the selected class) are affected.

3.2.3.4 Host-Language Blending

The language-model implementation resulting from a feature composition step should be usable directly from native applications written in the host language. Any unwanted interactions between the FOP infrastructure (e.g., collaborations) and the host language features used to implement them (e.g., classes and class inheritance systems, the type system) must be controlled [61]. For example, if the product derived was represented by a collaboration structure implemented by a set of (nested) classes, these classes would have to remain refinable by means of native subclassing (the inheritance hierarchy) without breaking the collaboration semantics (the refinement hierarchy). Likewise, if products were represented as objects and the host language allowed one to specify object-specific behavior (e.g., methods and accessors), this object-specific behavior should not interfere with the overall product behavior (e.g., through unwanted method hiding). Consider, for example, the requirement that an NX class representing the language-model element Graphs::Graph should not only serve as representation vehicle, but should also contain behavior implementation.

In the following two subsections, the provided DjDSL infrastructure for variable language models is elaborated on. The infrastructure allows one to implement reusable language-model assets (language models and collaborations) and, then, to define asset compositions to derive actual language models as products. The language-model assets are defined in a manner agnostic about the feature-binding strategy being requested. Finally, the stated challenges (mismatches, locality, quantification, and integration) are revisited, to highlight how DjDSL accomplishes to tackle these.

These implementation techniques build on native NX mechanisms. The adopted NX mechanisms include object and class aggregations, as well as changeable superclassing. They honor the previously identified requirements on variable language models (see Sect. 3.2.1). While NX is capable of accommodating feature composition for different binding modes (static vs. dynamic) and scopes (per-class, per-object), for variable language models, emphasis is on per-class compositions and, given the environment of a dynamic host language (Tcl), dynamic feature binding.[18] The central steps (asset definition and composition) are illustrated by referring to the running example of the GraphPL.

3.2.3.5 Common Assets

In the first step, the assets of a language-product line for a family of graphs are created. The assets consist of the collaboration implementing a basic graph, the language model Graph, and the collaborations that match features in the GraphPL feature model such as weighted. Conceptually and in their implementation, the

---

[18]For a broader background on feature-oriented programming in NX, with variable feature composition, the reader is referred to [62].

Fig. 3.38 Content of the
«languageModel» package
Graph

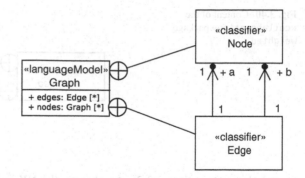

```
 1   Asset create Graphs {
 2     LanguageModel create Graph {
 3       :property name:alnum
 4       :property -incremental edges:object,type=Edge,0..n
 5       Classifier create A
 6       Classifier create Node
 7       Classifier create Edge {
 8         :property -accessor public a:object,type=Node
 9         :property -accessor public b:object,type=Node
10       }
11     }
12     Collaboration create weighted {
13       Classifier create Weight {
14         :property -accessor public {value:integer 0}
15       }
16       Role create A
17       Role create Edge -superclasses A {
18         :property -accessor public weight:object,type=Weight
19       }
20     }
21   }
```

Lst. 3.39 An «asset» package plus language model and collaboration implemented using DjDSL; see the models in Figs. 3.38 and 3.40

collaborations within assets (e.g., Graph) are represented as aggregations of NX objects (Graph::Node and Graph::Edge). See Fig. 3.38 and Listing 3.39. This allows one to address and to handle the assets as first-class citizens (objects) in an NX/Tcl environment. This way, the product-line assets can be easily introspected and modified using standard programming idioms. For instance, some of the conceptual relationships (e.g., ownership between collaborations and their roles in terms of the opposite properties owned and owning) map directly to introspection calls on NX objects: info parent and info children, respectively.

The collaboration classes (Graph) are both class objects and namespaces. As namespaces, they add namespace qualifiers (Graph::*) to disambiguate the objects representing collaboration roles (e.g., Graph::Edge vs. weighted::Edge). This is akin to the model-level collaboration classes serving as UML namespaces for the

Fig. 3.40 Content of the
«collaboration» package
weighted

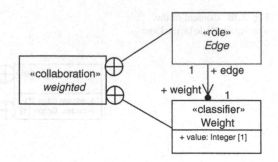

nested classes (see Sect. 3.2.2). As objects, the NX collaboration classes provide a collaboration interface to clients. Most importantly, the collaboration interfaces expose factory methods (new edge(), new node()) to instantiate refined, collaboration-specific variants of the contained objects. The generated factory method contributes to establishing composition locality for clients.

Likewise, collaboration classes matching features, such as weighted, are also contained by a dedicated or a shared asset class. In Fig. 3.40, the corresponding UML class is tagged as a «collaboration». In contrast to language models, collaborations (and their internal structure) are not meant to be instantiated directly. Collaborations are intermediate and abstract. Accordingly, collaboration classes and their role classes are marked *abstract* in their UML representation (see Fig. 3.40). As a consequence, the previously mentioned factory methods are not generated after having included each feature module, but rather for the composed, concrete collaboration. For the same reason, asset classes do not provide for factories of collaborations.

Language-model assets defined using the DjDSL extension to UML class models can be transformed using standard model transformations. As a reference implementation, DjDSL provides a MOFM2T transformation available from the DjDSL distribution. This reference implementation documents the conceptual correspondences (summarized in Table 3.3) and produces a ready-to-use language-model implementation that can be directly sourced from within a DjDSL-based DSL implementation (i.e., as a deployable Tcl module).

3.2.3.6 Composition

A composition of assets and their collaborations takes a language model as its base and provides a configurable means to add feature-specific collaborations into the composition. The ultimate goal of this step is to derive a class structure from the selected collaborations (Graph and weighted for a weighted graph) that forms the composed language model, i.e. the product. In DjDSL, a class structure representing the composition product is built on the fly. This involves generating a derived language model (i.e., the *resulting* language model) based on the assets (Fig. 3.41).

The composition WeightedGraphs in Listing 3.42 realizes weighted edge support from the GraphPL by setting the base collaboration to Graphs::Graph and

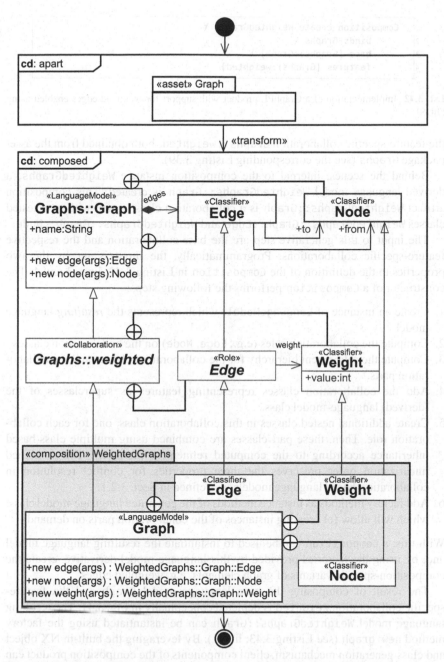

Fig. 3.41 Exemplary composition forming weighted graphs. The illustration adopts a model-transformation diagram (MTD) as introduced by [71]. Using an MTD, the procedure of weaving superclass relationships dynamically to implement the refinement chains is depicted in a declarative manner. The underlying implementation also establishes and preserves the conflict-resolution order for feature lookups in co-presence of refinement chains and inheritance relationships between classifiers and roles (see Sect. 3.2.1)

```
1   Composition create WeightedGraphs \
2       -binds Graphs \
3       -base [Graphs::Graph] \
4       -features [Graphs::weighted]
```

Lst. 3.42 Implementation of a GraphPL product with support for weighted edges enabled using DjDSL

the feature-specific collaboration Graphs::weighted, both obtained from the asset package Graphs (see the corresponding Listing 3.39).

Behind the scenes, internal to the composition instance WeightedGraphs, a derived language model WeightedGraphs::Graph is created. This composition artifact WeightedGraphs::Graph is a collaboration class, again, with two nested classes WeightedGraphs::Graph::Edge and WeightedGraphs::Graph::Node.

The input to this generative step are the base collaboration and the respective feature-specific collaborations. Programmatically, the input is set by the two properties to the definition of the Composition in Listing 3.42, lines 3 and 4. The constructor of a Composition performs the following steps:

1. Create an instance of LanguageModel, which represents the *resulting* language model.
2. Compute the collaboration roles (e.g., Edge, Node) on the collaboration classes.
3. Compute the refinement hierarchy for the collaboration classes and the collaboration parts.
4. Add the collaboration classes representing features as superclasses of the (derived) language-model class.
5. Create additional nested classes in this collaboration class, one for each collaboration role. Then, these part classes are combined using multiple class-based inheritance according to the computed refinement hierarchy. The combined linearization order preserves the three properties for conflict resolution in collaboration-based language models, as defined in Sect. 3.2.1.
6. Add factory methods as instance methods of the generated language-model class, which will allow for creating instances of the collaboration parts on demand.

With this, a Composition can be used to instantiate the resulting language model and, by using the factories provided by this language-model derivative, create the composition-specific variants of graph elements, e.g. weighted edges.

The result of composing the base language model Graph and the feature-specific collaboration weighted is depicted conceptually in Fig. 3.41. The resulting language model WeightedGraphs::Graph can be instantiated using the factory method new graph (see Listing 3.43; line 1). By leveraging the built-in NX object and class generation mechanism, client components of the composition product can use it as an ordinary class. The language-model class WeightedGraphs::Graph can be subclassed. The same holds for its parts (WeightedGraphs::Graph::Edge, WeightedGraphs::Graph::Node). At this point, there is no need to be aware of their specifics as language models or feature-specific collaborations, they can serve as ordinary NX classes. Internally, NX's built-in object system introspection is used

```
1   set wg [WeightedGraphs new graph -name "wg"]
2   set n1 [$wg new node]
3   set n2 [$wg new node]
4   set e [$wg new edge \
5                 -a $n1 \
6                 -b $n2 \
7                 -weight [$wg new weight -value 1]]
```

Lst. 3.43 Use of the readily composed GraphPL product for defining a new graph

during the above transformation steps to query the child objects of the collaboration classes and to extract their object names.

The use of explicit composition classes internal to a Composition allows DjDSL to guarantee product-bounded quantification. A chosen configuration of features and the corresponding composition of assets is so bounded by the runtime context set by a dedicated Composition object; allowing for the parallel use and runtime modification of further compositions based on the same assets. Also note that, at the time of writing, there is no model-to-text transformation support for DjDSL composition models into their NX-based composition implementations, as introduced in this section.

3.3   Rendering DSL Variability Explicit

In engineering variable software, there are two distinct concerns of representation: the concern of describing (prescribing) variation in a piece of variable software and the concern of containing the variation as part of a program representation [27]. In language-product line engineering, the former relates to modeling the variability (e.g., via feature models), the latter to implementing the variability (or variability-aware programs). In this section, variability modeling in terms of describing and prescribing the variations of a language model, the corresponding DSL product line, is at focus (see also Fig. 3.44). To model variability, different notations and languages have been proposed including feature diagrams (with and without constraints) and propositional formulas [6, 21]. Such a variability model does not necessarily contain variation itself, it describes at the level of the problem domain the variational structure of a DSL product line, for instance.[19]

In software language engineering, different paths to represent variability (e.g., endogenous, exogenous) and to obtain a variability model (e.g., top-down, bottom-up) have been considered. An endogenous variability representation takes variability data into the DSL implementation (e.g., configuration files, build

---

[19]This is not to say that variability models could not be subjected to variation themselves (e.g., in the context of modeling multi-product lines); or that variability-modeling techniques could not be used as part of the solution space, e.g., to derive configurators, or build and deployment descriptors.

scripts, implementation of a project-specific generator). An exogenous variability representation, the variability model is a stand-alone, processable first-class model artifact, expressed in terms of well-defined variability modeling language or a lower-level formalism capable of encoding the variability (e.g., CSP, BDD).

Exogenous variability modeling has been attributed having characteristic advantages and disadvantages, as does its endogenous counterpart: On the one hand, an explicit variability model allows for analyzing the variation space in its own right (e.g., using static analysis [66]) and to consider different variability implementation techniques in the language model and the DSL. It also allows one to capture design decisions while deferring actual decision-making during DSL implementation (e.g., on concrete-syntax variability; [70]). On the downside, an explicit variability model requires an extra mapping of the prescribed configuration space into the solution domain. The DSL developer must ensure that the structure and constraints between features are respected and maintained in the implementation. This task is not trivial, as there are frequently no direct correspondences between features and their implementations; as well as higher-order mismatches (e.g., implementations of features must be patched to operate in a given composition). Likewise, the variability model and the domain details might not be accessible (usable) from within the DSL implementation (e.g., to support dynamic analyses aware of the variability).[20]

Obtaining a variability model on a DSL family *bottom-up* (rather than top-down) has also been considered [40, 44]. In a top-down path, a feature model is created first by the domain engineer and the DSL developer, guides the decomposition

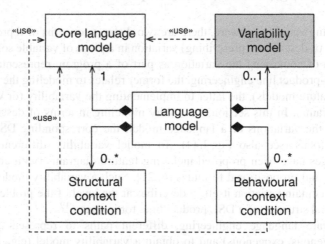

Fig. 3.44 The *variability model* is part of the language model (in the broader sense). It represents the space of valid DSL variants (configurations and products). It maps to implementation units of the primary abstract syntax or *core language-model* (e.g., collaborations)

---

[20]Rendering program representations aware of program variability is the ambition of a current on *variability-aware programming* [27]; as well as variability-aware runtime analyses.

of an abstract syntax (metamodel) into a family, and drives subsequent steps in the language pipeline. In a bottom-up path, first, a collection of language components is established. From dependencies between language components, either inferred automatically or obtained from annotations, a variability model is synthesized. While created automatically and reflecting directly implementation-level dependencies, variability models obtained this way have been found to exhibit a counterintuitive structure for the DSL developer or the application developer to make configuration decision (sometimes also inadequate for static analyses). In addition, they suffer from structural variation over time, when re-generated [40].

As a consequence, providing for techniques and tools to define exogenous variability models in a top-down manner is a building block of approaches to language-product lines [44, Section 4.1.2]. Exploring the design space of modeling DSL and language-model variability, the following requirements on variability-modeling support in a DSL development system like DjDSL emerge: multi-dimensional variability, feature mapping, encoding for automated analyses, concrete-syntax style.

Multi-Dimensional Variability
A variable DSL can vary regarding abstract syntax, concrete syntax, language constructs including behavior, and tooling support. A variability-modeling technique must be able to represent several dimensions of variability at the same time [44]. Examples include decomposition of a variability model (e.g., feature tree) into sub-models (e.g., sub-trees); or to form a composite from its parts.

Feature Mapping
A variability-modeling technique must allow the DSL developer to maintain a correspondence between the product-line assets (source code, tests, documentation) realizing and the model elements representing features. The correspondence can be enacted explicitly or implicitly. An implicit link are correspondences implemented by matching names or identifiers. An explicit link involves first-class references between features as model elements and as implementation constructs (e.g., model-level associations, annotations). At the same time, a variability model may employ pure representational modeling constructs without correspondence in the product-line implementation (e.g., to structure or to partition a model). The distinction between *abstract feature* and *concrete feature* in feature-modeling languages [66, p. 6:5] can serve as an example.

Encoding for Automated Analyses
An automated analysis based on variability data is relevant at different stages, for different objectives [6, 11, 66]. One objective, during domain analysis, are sanity checks on and the refinement of variability model itself, being under construction, e.g.: Are there features that cannot be selected? Can mandatory features be promoted into the base? More generally, two variability models can be compared and identified as generalizations, specializations, or equivalents (e.g., to guide refactorings or to characterize model changes over time). Another objective are, during architecting and designing the DSL-based application, validity checks of

feature selections, e.g.: Is a partial selection of features valid? Which mandatory features remain to be considered? Finally, a third objective are variability-aware analysis, optimization, and inspection tasks at the level of assets (e.g., source code and tests). To enable such variability-aware analysis, the DSL development system must provide an encoding of variability models as input to an analysis engine. Examples include an encoding as propositional formula to enter propositional SAT or BDD solvers; or as an encoding as a constraint program to be exercised by a CSP solver [11, Section 6].

Concrete-Syntax Style
The rich body of variability-modeling techniques and languages offers different visual (graphical) and textual concrete syntaxes to borrow from. Depending on the DSL developer audience and the domain of application, more than one syntax must be supported (e.g., a graphical and a textual). Besides, one syntax should allow variability models (or fragments thereof) to be embedded with implementation artifacts or managed along with them in a seamlessness manner (e.g., in an SCM repository). The latter is also prompted by the feature-mapping requirement above.

Additional baseline requirements have been identified by related work on DSL for (textual) variability modeling [16, 18]. DjDSL provides a first-class variability modeling environment djdsl::vle, which allows one to model DSL variability using a variant of feature models, in a textual notation, and to embed the resulting model along with the language-model implementation. djdsl::vle is implemented as internal DSL for the domain of variability modeling on DjDSL DSL families. This renders the model accessible as a standard NX/Tcl data structure (e.g., an object graph plus utilities) from within DjDSL language models; and beyond.

3.3.1 Abstract Syntax

In DjDSL, a feature model is represented by a structure of four concepts: Model, Choice, Feature, and Constraint. The abstract syntax is minimal, both in terms of element types and their relationships and its core semantics (multiplicity constraints). Yet, it is capable of representing different flavors of feature models in use, also as its frontend. This is a convenient property shared with abstract syntaxes of the so-called *canonical* feature-modeling languages, namely varied feature diagrams (VFD; [58]) and neutral feature diagrams (NFT; [34]).

The main promise of a canonical abstract syntax is avoiding typical pitfalls of feature-modeling languages (lack of expressiveness vs. succinctness), while offering a language kernel that can be easily extended to include modeling features to support another type of feature models. In the following, the four tenets of modeling in djdsl::vle are introduced one by one (see also Fig. 3.45).

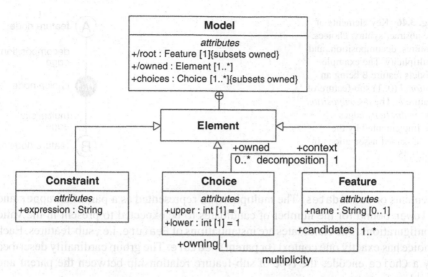

Fig. 3.45 Overview of the key concepts of the djdsl::vle representation of feature models, in particular Choice and Feature

Table 3.4 Representing common relationships between parent and child features using a multiplicity-based encoding (e.g., djdsl::vle choices, vp-nodes in VFD or NFT). $CAND$ is the set of candidates features for a given choice, with $|CAND| \in \mathbb{N}_{>0}$

Optional sub-feature	0..1	$|CAND| = 1$
Mandatory sub-feature	1..1	$|CAND| = 1$
Inclusive-or group of sub-features	1..j	$j \in \mathbb{N}_{>0}, j \geq 1, |CAND| > 1$
Exclusive-or group of sub-features	1..1	$|CAND| > 1$
And group of sub-features	s..s	$s \in \mathbb{N}_{>0}, s = |CAND|$
Absent (negated) sub-feature	0..0	(for constraints)

3.3.1.1 Models

A Model is the central container, factory, and lifetime context for model elements, in particular instantiations of Choice and Feature. A Model maintains references to a minimum of one Choice that represents the root element of the model. The root Feature, a key tenet of description of a feature model, is derived from this root Choice. Models are also the central entry point to model-based analysis operations (see Sect. 3.3.4).

3.3.1.2 Choices

A Choice is the model element that represents a number of presence options in terms of sub-features for the valid configurations of a feature model, along with a specific constraint on the group cardinality (multiplicity) of its child

Fig. 3.46 Key elements of
the abstract syntax: choices,
features, decomposition, and
multiplicity. The example
models feature B being an
optional (0..1) sub-feature of
feature A. The *decomposition*
and *multiplicity* edges
are implemented by the
same-named associations in
Fig. 3.45

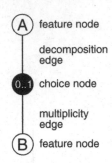

elements or `candidates`. The multiplicity is represented as a pair of an `upper` and
a `lower` bound for the number of candidates to be expected to present in the valid
configurations. The candidates are instantiations of `Feature`, i.e., sub-features. Each
choice has exactly one context (or parent) `Feature`. The group cardinality described
by a `Choice` encodes the type of sub-feature relationship between the parent and
children features.

Whereas most feature-modeling languages have explicit abstract syntax elements
for the common mandatory, optional, or, and xor dependencies between (sub-
)features, `Choice` generalizes them as a unified modeling element.[21] Table 3.4
provides an overview of the multiplicity-based encoding of the most common
(hierarchical) feature-model dependencies. Figure 3.46 exemplifies how an optional
sub-feature is modeled using this multiplicity-based encoding.

3.3.1.3 Features

`Features` are those model elements that represent the (problem space) features of a
DSL product line. As stated earlier, a DSL feature is a unit of language or language-
tooling functionality or behavior directly exposed to the developer of a DSL script
(model). A `Feature` having `owned` instantiations of `Choice` is also referred to as a
decomposition feature. Otherwise, a `Feature` is said to be a *primary* one. Primary
features must be named.[22]

Decomposition features can also be unnamed, which is the case of *auxiliary*
features as artifacts of certain model transformations.[23] For named features, the

---

[21]Choices as well as their equivalent *card*(inality) nodes and operators are not limited to those.
They are eligible for encoding cross-tree (non-hierarchical) constraints, including the required
absence or negation: (0..0).

[22]The notions of decomposition and primary feature compare with those of abstract and concrete
feature, respectively [6]. However, their definitions in terms of the underlying abstract syntaxes are
different.

[23]For example, a typical transformation in the problem space is turning all primary features into
actual leaves of the tree structure. This requires intermediate, in `djdsl::vle` unnamed, feature
elements. See Heradio-Gil et al. [34, Section 2.4].

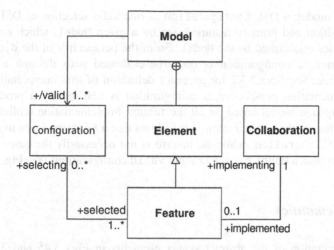

Fig. 3.47 The concept of a Configuration links a Model and different (invalid/ valid) combinations of Feature instantiations. See also Fig. 3.6

Model is the naming scope and authority. A name assigned to a feature must be unique within the model. Primary features always map to implementation units (i.a., collaborations and roles) in DjDSL that carry the same name. Decomposition features can but do not necessarily have to have a correspondent in the implementation.

3.3.1.4 Constraints

A (non-hierarchical) Constraint represents an expression string defined in an expression language external to djdsl::vle. Generally speaking, a constraint expression encodes presence or absence of certain Feature combinations in addition to the Choice structure of the Model. Expression operands represent (named) instantiations of Feature of the model, expression operators the presence (absence) conditions between Feature instantiations. Examples include subsets of the Object Constraint Language (OCL) expressions or standard formulas in a propositional-logic (PL) language.

When constraints are omitted, a model forms a tree structure (i.e., each element has only one parent and the structure is free of cycles). In presence of constraints, the model is described by a directed acyclic graph (DAG).

3.3.1.5 Configurations

The djdsl::vle abstract syntax is an extension to DjDSL's abstract syntax for *feature-oriented language models* in Fig. 3.6. The natural extension points of the model depicted in Fig. 3.6 are Feature and Configuration. In the view of a variability model, a DSL Configuration is one valid selection of DSL features (decomposition and primary features), set by a given Model, which resolves all dependencies established by the Model. From the perspective of the djdsl::vle representation, a configuration is one true-evaluated path through a Choice-Feature tree. See Sect. 3.3.2 for an exact definition of this interpretation. From the implementation perspective, a configuration is realized by a product. That is, one language model based on all the feature implementation (collaborations) corresponding to the configuration.[24] It follows that a Feature maps to an implementing Collaboration, while the inverse is not necessarily the case.[25] Against this background, a Model has one or more valid configurations (see Fig. 3.47).

3.3.2 Semantics

The interpretation of the abstract syntax elements in Figs. 3.45 and 3.47, most importantly of Choice and Configuration, is as follows:

3.3.2.1 Multiplicity Encoding of Variation Points

A Choice represents a collection of sub-features into which a parent feature is decomposed. The cardinality of this collection (i.e., the candidates Fig. 3.45) is the number of Feature instantiations contained in that collection. In Table 3.4, the cardinality is denoted as $|CAND|$. A Choice represents additionally a constraint on the cardinality of this collection. This constraint is referred to as the multiplicity, setting valid cardinalities of the constrained collection. A cardinality is valid provided that it is not less than the lower bound and not greater than the upper bound maintained by a Choice. Typical bounds and their interpretation in terms of feature modeling are documented in Table 3.4. There are two important qualifications to multiplicities in djdsl::vle. The qualifications render them different from cardinality constraints in other environments:

1. The are no unbounded cardinalities, in which case there was no constraint on the upper bound of a Choice.
2. The upper bound of a Choice cannot be greater than the cardinality of the represented collection.

---

[24] In the problem space, the term *product* is related to that of a configuration: A product is the subset of primary (leaf, terminal) features of the configuration set. In the solution space, the product is an implementation of one valid configuration. The latter is relevant to this discussion.

[25] It was repeatedly stated that a collaboration in DjDSL can also provide for the implementation of structure and behavior that do not correspond to a feature.

Fig. 3.48 Example of an *and*-decomposition, in Czarnecki-Eisenecker notation (i.e., concrete syntax!); top: and-group of mandatory sub-features; bottom: and-group including optional sub-feature

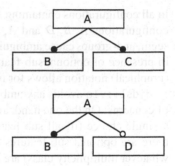

3.3.2.2 Configuration Validation

Based on the abstract syntax and the interpretation of multiplicities represented by a Choice, a given Configuration is considered valid iff the following conditions hold:

1. Every element of a Model is assigned a Boolean value, which is computed according to the subsequent steps.
2. All Model-level choices evaluate to true.
3. A Choice evaluates to true if at least the lower bound and at most the upper bound of its candidates features evaluate to true.
4. A Feature evaluates to true

   - if it is included by the Configuration under evaluation *and*
   - if its owned Choice instantiations evaluate to true, if any.

This generic and cascading evaluation procedure implies that all Constraint instantiations evaluate to true, whether they are represented as Choices directly or otherwise. It also follows that, to become valid, the configuration must contain the root feature. While this evaluation procedure can be implemented at a known complexity, djdsl::vle reformulates the evaluation of configurations into a satisfiability problem as part of its platform integration (see Sect. 3.3.4).

3.3.2.3 And-Groups vs. And-Choices

In an *and*-group of sub-features, or *and*-decomposition, all grouped sub-features must be present in a configuration, in which the parent feature is also present, to render the configuration valid. In (graphical) notations of feature models, they are typically identified by freestanding decomposition edges, not connected by an arc (as opposed to arcs for or- and xor-groups). Such and-groups may contain both mandatory and optional sub-features. The feature model at top of Fig. 3.48 indicates that B and C must be present in all configurations containing A (or, there is just one valid configuration A, B, C). The feature model at the bottom exemplifies an and-group including an optional sub-feature D. It interprets as follows: B must be present in all configurations containing A, B can be present or absent (or, there are two valid configurations A, B, D and A, B). As straightforward as their interpretation may seem, and-groups cause ambiguity in semantics (e.g., for their multiplicity encoding in presence of optional sub-features[26]) and also notational ambiguity, e.g., when a (graphical) notation allows for multiple groups per feature.

djdsl::vle avoids any ambiguities (semantical and notational) by a separation of concerns: On the one hand, an explicit *and*-decomposition can be modeled using a single choice (iff all sub-features are mandatory) or using different choices (if there are optional sub-features involved). On the other hand, multiple groups (of whatever multiplicity class) are represented using distinct choices per group.

- Model and Feature can have multiple associated Choice instantiations. All choices must evaluate to true, for the Model or Feature to evaluate to true, subsequently.[27]
- *And*-groups in terms of feature modeling translate into djdsl::vle as follows:
  - Sub-features are all mandatory: A single Choice with a multiplicity constraint limiting the cardinality (lower and upper bounds) to exactly the number of candidate features. In djdsl::vle, this is referred to as an *and*-choice. Figure 3.49a is a djdsl::vle abstract syntax representation of Fig. 3.48, top part.
  - At least one sub-feature is optional: The mandatory sub-features are grouped by an *and*-choice. The optional ones by a separate choice with a lower bond of 0 and the upper bound equal to the cardinality of the subset of optional sub-features. Figure 3.49c is a djdsl::vle abstract syntax representation of Fig. 3.48, bottom part.[28]
- When needed for expressing a domain, or transcribing models from group-aware feature-modeling languages as frontend, djdsl::vle can contain multiple choices, including choices encoding and-groups as above, at a given decomposition level such as the root feature.

Hence, *and*-groups and *and*-choices are distinct modeling elements, with the latter capable of embedding the former, depending on the kind of sub-features (mandatory, optional). It should be noted that a single *and*-choice can be rewritten as a number

---

[26]For example, Classen et al. [16, Section 5.2] explore in detail the consequences of a (false) multiplicity encoding of and-decompositions including optionals. The mitigation proposed is a refined configuration validation, which corrects the bounds for the presence of optionals. Such mitigations are not required in djdsl::vle.

[27]One may consider this an *implicit* form of *and*-group. However, explicit grouping in feature modeling implies that a whole feature is grouped (decomposed) into parts directly.

[28]Note that a [1, 2]-choice as in Fig. 3.49b does represent the and-decomposition incl. an optional sub-feature. This is because in an inclusive-or group such as [1, 2] any sub-feature is possibly optional (B and D); not just a particular one (D). In other words, the described configuration space differs (2 vs. 3 valid configurations). If encoded that way, multiplicity evaluation can be adjusted. However, the structural information on the optional sub-features would get lost [16].

of [1, 1]-choices (see Fig. 3.49d); so can choices of optional subfeatures be defined as separate [0, 1]-choices.

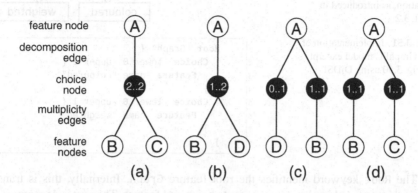

Fig. 3.49 Various examples on encoding *and*-decompositions in djdsl::vle; (**a**) *and*-choice representing the top model in Fig. 3.48; (**b**) an inclusive-or choice; (**c**) two-choice representation of the bottom model in Fig. 3.48; (**d**) split but equivalent representation of (**a**)

3.3.3 Concrete Syntax

djdsl::vle provides multiple textual concrete syntaxes. First, direct instantiation of the language model is supported. Second, indirect instantiation via an internal DSL syntax is offered. Additional textual syntaxes can be added using internal or external DSL techniques.[29] While djdsl::vle can accommodate graphical concrete syntaxes as well, the emphasis is on textual ones. This is because the initially stated requirements include that djdsl::vle model forms part of a DjDSL language model. This does not preclude the adoption of a supporting graphical notation, though, even if only for visualization purposes.[30]

In the following, an overview of the built-in textual notation is given. This overview aims at reiterating over the most important syntax elements, as defined in Sect. 3.3.1, while highlighting important contributions of the concrete syntax (e.g., structuring techniques). The overview builds on small or abstracted examples, including the excerpt from a GraphPL feature model (see Fig. 3.50).

Listing 3.51 implements the GraphPL model excerpt, which includes a root feature Graph and two optional sub-features: coloured and weighted.

---

[29]Defining and using such a *frontend syntax* closely resembling another textual variability-modeling language (TVL; [16]) is possible as an exercise of self-application in DjDSL.

[30]The majority of variability-modeling languages offer (or are even limited to) a graphical notation inspired or derived from the original FODA notation. Textual notations have been proposed for uses in SLE and for application generators; and gained momentum when it comes to modeling large domains [16].

Fig. 3.50 The GraphPL model excerpt, in Czarnecki-Eisenecker notation, as introduced in Sect. 3.2

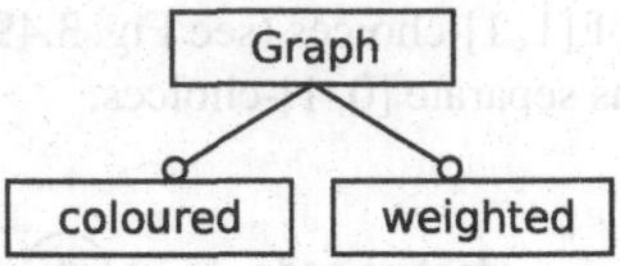

```
                    ┌─────────┐
                    │  Graph  │
                    └─────────┘
                     ○       ○
            ┌──────────┐  ┌──────────┐
            │ coloured │  │ weighted │
            └──────────┘  └──────────┘
```

Lst. 3.51 Implementation of the GraphPL model excerpt in Fig. 3.50 using DjDSL

```
1  Root "Graph" {
2    Choice -lower 0 -upper 1 {
3      Feature -name "coloured"
4    }
5    Choice -lower 0 -upper 1 {
6      Feature -name "weighted"
7    }
8  }
```

The `Root` keyword identifies the root feature `Graph`. Internally, this is transformed into a combined structure of root choice and feature. The root is decomposed into two optional sub-features. In `djdsl::vle`, an optional sub-feature corresponds to a `Choice` of multiplicity 0..1 with one `Feature` as its child element. See also Table 3.4 for a reference. Recall that a parent feature (`Graph`) can carry multiple instantiations of `Choices` (two in Listing 3.51). Semantically, this corresponds to an *implicit* and-decomposition.

3.3.3.1 Constraints

`djdsl::vle` allows for defining additional constraints on the hierarchical structure of `Choice` and `Feature` instantiations, which run across the hierarchy, in terms of an auxiliary, external textual constraint sub-language and/or extra `Choice` instantiations owned by the `Model` (i.e., at the top level, outside the root hierarchy).[31]

Textual constraints provide a small subset of Boolean expressions, including the binary operators and and or as well as the unary operator not. These operators work on operands which represent (named) features. Compound expressions must be grouped explicitly using pairs of parentheses. The core of the constraint language is kept minimal, additional operators are modeling using the primitives (implication etc.). Syntactic sugar is provided, though. The corresponding (parsing expression) grammar is documented in Listing 3.52.

Consider the exemplary textual constraint in Listing 3.54. It imposes an additional validation condition on the `djdsl::vle` model in Listing 3.53. Any valid configuration including the feature MST must also include `weighted`, but not necessarily vice versa. This is an example of an implication, modeled as using not/or. Textual constraints cannot define new feature. Only references by name to those defined as part of the hierarchy under the root are permitted.

---

[31] These choices are *extra* in the sense of adding to the one, mandatory root choice present in every `Model`.

```
1           Expression    ← _ Term (_ BinaryOp _ Term)?;
2           Term          ← NotOp? _ (Variable / '(' Expression ')');
3 leaf:     BinaryOp      ← AndOp / OrOp;
4           AndOp         ← 'and' / '&&';
5           OrOp          ← 'or' / '||';
6           NotOp         ← 'not' / '-';
7           Variable      ← <alnum>+;
8 void:     _             ← <space>*;
```

Lst. 3.52 A parsing expression grammar (PEG) for textual constraints on DjDSL's variability models

Lst. 3.53 Implementation of another GraphPL model excerpt using DjDSL

```
Root "Graph" {
    Choice -lower 0 -upper 1 {
        Feature -name "Algorithm" {
            Choice -lower 1 -upper 2 {
                Feature -name "MST"
                Feature -name "ShortestPath"
            }
        }
    }
    Choice -lower 0 -upper 1 {
        Feature -name "weighted"
    }
}
```

Lst. 3.54 A textual constraint expressed over the variability model in Listing 3.53

```
Constraint {not MST or weighted}
```

Lst. 3.55 Constraint implementation using an explicit choice

```
1  Choice with -lower 1 -upper 2 {
2      Feature with {
3          Choice with -lower 0 -upper 0 {
4              Feature with -name "MST"
5          }
6      }
7      Feature with -name "weighted"
8  }
9  }
```

Constraints can also be represented directly as Choice instantiations owned by a Model in addition to the root choice. Both constraint types have the same expressiveness. See Table 3.5 for an overview of the correspondences between djdsl::vle textual constraints and choices. For instance, the textual constraint in Listing 3.54 corresponds to the Choice structure in Listing 3.55, and vice versa.

Listing 3.55 exhibits two noteworthy details. First, a Feature can be used in an unnamed manner (see line 2). This allows for encoding a unary operator such as *not*.

Table 3.5 An overview of basic correspondences between the two constraint notations: textual and choices

Textual	Choice

A **and** B	`Choice -lower 2 -upper 2 {`
	`    Feature -name "A"`
	`    Feature -name "B"`
	`}`

A **or** B	`Choice with -lower 1 -upper 2 {`
	`    Feature with -name "A"`
	`    Feature with -name "B"`
	`}`

not A	`Choice with -lower 0 -upper 0 {`
	`    Feature with -name "A"`
	`}`

Fig. 3.56 A feature model (Czarnecki-Eisenecker notation) showing three levels of decomposition, starting from the root R. The example was adopted from [16, Figure 2]

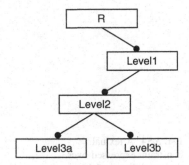

This is one use of a `Feature` as an auxiliary construct. The second detail is the use of a [0, 0]-choice as the multiplicity encoding of the *not*-operator itself (see line 3).

3.3.3.2 Structuring

`djdsl::vle` models in the provided textual notation are directed by the nesting of its abstract syntax. Consider the feature model in Fig. 3.56. The three levels of decomposition (levels 1–3) translate into corresponding nesting levels in the implementing `djdsl::vle` script depicted in Listing 3.57 given the inline declaration of `Feature` instantiations. Given the presence of `Choice` as notational elements, one extra level of nesting becomes added.

Having such a syntax-directed notation has advantages. For example, models reflecting decompositional hierarchies of a domain are expressive to this end. However, such a notation also risks rendering models of even medium size unwieldy. Therefore, `djdsl::vle` allows one to define `Feature` instances representing any nesting level (e.g., `Level1`) outside the `Root` block. These out-of-line `Feature` declarations can be referenced to declare the intended hierarchy, see, e.g., `%Level1`

Lst. 3.57 Nested implementation of the feature model in Fig. 3.56

```
 1    Root "R" {
 2      Choice -lower 1 -upper 1 {
 3        Feature -name "Level1" {
 4          Choice -lower 1 -upper 1 {
 5            Feature -name "Level2" {
 6              Choice -lower 2 -upper 2 {
 7                Feature -name "Level3a"
 8                Feature -name "Level3b"
 9    }}}}}
10    }
```

Lst. 3.58 Flattened implementation of the feature model in Fig. 3.56

```
 1    Root "R" {
 2      Choice -lower 1 -upper 1 {
 3        %Level1
 4      }
 5    }
 6
 7    Feature -name "Level1" {
 8      Choice -lower 1 -upper 1 {
 9        %Level2
10      }
11    }
12
13    Feature -name "Level2" {
14      Choice -lower 2 -upper 2 {
15        Feature -name "Level3a"
16        Feature -name "Level3b"
17      }
18    }
```

and %Level2 in Listing 3.58.[32] Listing 3.58 depicts the result of using out-of-line Feature declarations. The resulting models from Listings 3.57 and 3.58 are equivalent. Note that the djdsl::vle notation does not prescribe any particular order of declaring Root and Feature blocks, or Feature and Feature blocks, relative to each other.

3.3.4   Integration: Binary Decision Diagrams

A variability model defined using djdsl::vle can be subjected to different prede-fined or developer-provided automated analysis operations. The need for analysis procedures at different stages of language-product line engineering has already

---

[32]Using the Feature identifiers before declaring them acts as a kind of forward reference. Implementationwise, as an internal DSL in NX/Tcl, there are no forward references, actually. The relative evaluation of the script blocks is scheduled accordingly to achieve this effect.

been stated (e.g., static product-line analyses, validation of feature selections, perfective maintenance of the model, model comparisons, and guidance for code inspections [6, 11, 66]). Imagine, as a concrete example during development, that the developer of a DSL-based application is to select features from a given DSL family, implemented in DjDSL, by defining a Composition (see Sect. 3.2.3). DjDSL offers a built-in mechanism to establish whether the feature selection passed to the Composition constructor is actually allowed under the ruling variability model. Depending on the result of the selection test, construction proceeds or is interrupted by an exception. Alternatively, DjDSL can present further features as suggestions for inclusion to arrive at a valid configuration.

Such selection validation and other analysis operations can be achieved, to a limited extent, by building on the abstract syntax structure of a variability model itself (e.g., using graph analysis), or by reformulating the variability model using more suitable external formalisms. DjDSL offers built-in support for recoding a djdsl::vle into corresponding formulas of Boolean algebra[33] A Boolean formula is recognized or generated by the following grammar:

$$F \leftarrow X \mid \text{'0'} \mid \text{'1'} \mid \text{'}\neg\text{'}\ F \mid F\ \text{'}\wedge\text{'}\ F \mid F\ \text{'}\vee\text{'}\ F \mid F\ \text{'}\Rightarrow\text{'}\ F$$
$$\mid F\ \text{'}\Leftrightarrow\text{'}\ F$$

Operators include negation, conjunction, disjunction, implication, and bi-implication (in order of appearance above).[34] Operands are the literals 0 and 1 as well as a range of Boolean variables denoted by x. A Boolean variable takes a value out of the set $\{0, 1\}$. The interpretation of operators follows the standard truth tables. Note, however, that in this setting, their interpretation will be normalized, beyond a succinct rewrite in terms of conjunction, disjunction, and negation only, in terms of an if-then-else normalization (INF).

Starting from a djdsl::vle model, the following steps are performed to obtain a corresponding (non-normal) Boolean formula [11]:

1. Each *primary feature* maps to a same-named Boolean variable.
2. Each choice maps to an operator, depending on the multiplicity set and its number of candidate sub-features (see Table 3.6 for an overview).
3. Each textual constraint is processed as-is (given that they build on a subset of Boolean algebra and the syntactic structure allows for direct processing).
4. The overall formula is the conjunction of all sub-formulas, established by iterating the choices and any constraints.

---

[33] Here, for the scope of this writing, a shortcut is taken: The reformulation of the variability model is actually interpreted as a formula in *classical* propositional (or sentential) logic [65], which then is mapped to its corresponding Boolean formula for operationalization, with Boolean algebra being one model of classical propositional logic. For an overview of alternative formalism and encodings, rooted in propositional formulas or not, the reader is kindly referred to [6, 11, 56].

[34] Actual operator precedence can be implemented either by the ordering of alternates (e.g., in a parsing expression with ordered choice), some priority encoding, or by a concrete syntax employing explicit ordering (e.g., parentheses as in djdsl::vle textual constraints).

Table 3.6 Correspondences between the multiplicity encoding of djdsl::vle model (choices) and the operators used in the corresponding Boolean formula. Different encodings of *atmost-k* constraints are supported (e.g., binomial, binary [31])

Optional	$0..1$	$|CAND| = 1$	Implication ($\Leftarrow$)
Mandatory	$1..1$	$|CAND| = 1$	Bi-implication ($\Leftrightarrow$)
Inclusive-or	$1..j$	$|CAND| > 1$	Disjunction ($\vee$)
Exclusive-or	$1..1$	$|CAND| > 1$	Atmost-one (e.g., binomial enc.)
And	$s..s$	$s = |CAND|$	Conjunction $\wedge$
Absent (negated)	$0..0$	n/a	Negation $\neg$

From such a corresponding formula, DjDSL internally computes a binary decision diagram (BDD) [14, 38]. A BDD takes the structure of a rooted, directed acyclic graph or a binary tree with shared sub-trees. This property results from the node and edge sets: There is a maximum of two sink nodes labeled $\bot$ (for false or 0) and $\top$ (for true or 1), respectively, with an out-degree of zero. Each non-sink or *branch node* is labeled by a Boolean variable and maintains exactly two outgoing edges, connecting two successors. The edges or successors are called the *low* and *high* edge and successor, respectively. The low edge models the consequence of assigning the variable represented by the source branch node to 0, the high edge models the variable assignment of 1. This way, a BDD represents a model of a function that maps a Boolean formula to a resulting truth value, 0 or 1, based on a given variable assignment. An assignment is one allocation of 0 and 1 to the Boolean variables of a formula (represented by branch nodes in the corresponding BDD).

The construction of a BDD from a Boolean formula can be modeled as two subsequent steps, one of normalization, one of reduction: First, all Boolean operator occurrences are rewritten as their if-else-then equivalents using recursive application of the Shannon expansion (assuming a previously decided fixed order of variables under expansion). This results in the if-then-else normal form (INF) of the formula. Second, the set of if-then-else sub-formula is then reduced based on identical test conditions (RHS) to obtain a close progenitor of the final BDD. Intuitively, each sub-formula of an INF formula maps to a branch or sink node of the BDD, with the low edge representing the else-branch and the high edge the then-branch of the if-construct. In this reading, a BDD models a Boolean function effectively as a decision graph [14].

The resulting BDD has convenient properties: It can be stored effectively (using beads [38, Section 7.1.4]) and allows for directly answering satisfiability or enumeration questions. Formulations of advanced questions interesting in language product line engineering (see, e.g., [65]) can be encoded this way in their documented forms without but minor syntactic modifications. This also includes different encoding styles of multiplicity constraints as Boolean formulas [31] and optimizations on the BDD encoding based on the hierarchical variability model. Alternatively, formulas once encoded as BDD can be exported in their CNF (or DNF). DjDSL uses the Tcl extension tclbdd as BDD encoder and BDD engine.

Fig. 3.59 Related work on
variable language models

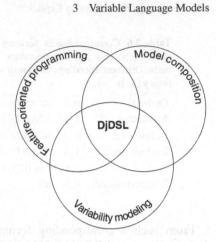

3.4 Related Work

For realizing variable language models, DjDSL builds on three areas of related
work (see Fig. 3.59): model composition (with emphasis on model-based software
product line engineering), feature-oriented programming (for enactment), and
variability-modeling techniques (to render variability models first-class entities in
a DSL development system).

3.4.1 Model Composition and Model-Based Software Product
Lines

When the primary abstract syntax (or, core language-model) of a DSL is defined
using a metamodel (i.e., a flavor of class models), methods, techniques, and tools
for metamodel and model composition become relevant [22, Section 3.3.1]. This
is because metamodels are models themselves in their respective metamodeling
system. In what follows, a selection of related work on model composition is presented. The selection has been made according to whether a composition approach
has been applied to engineering variable model-based DSL in a compositional
manner.[35] For more comprehensive surveys on the extensive body of model-
composition approaches, the reader is referred to [17, 22]. Model-composition
techniques can be broadly grouped along two dimensions: How do they establish
correspondences between two or more models under composition (e.g., using
operators, using pattern matching)? What is the interpretation (intention) of establishing these correspondences (e.g., overlapping, crosscutting) [17, Section 1.2]?
To realize variable language models, DjDSL combines model-based composition
techniques in an original manner: Correspondences between assets (base and feature

---

[35]This selected scope excludes, for example, techniques for metamodel pruning as a form of
language-model specialization. In metamodel pruning, an effective metamodel in an automated
manner [35]. Please consult Atkinson and Kühne [9] for an overview of this line of research.

collaborations) are established using pattern matching (in the simplest form: by element-name matching) and using a dedicated *correspondence model*. The latter is represented by the internal structure of a «composition» class that represents one feature configuration (see Fig. 3.28). Once established, these correspondences are interpreted in terms of a crosscutting augmentation [17, Section 1.2.2.2]: Augmenting combines the structure (properties) and behavior (methods) of two collaborations to implement a particular mix of features forming a language-model variant. The composed collaborations are said cutting across a shared—dominant and heterogeneous [4]—object-oriented structure at the core of the modeled problem domain (e.g., Graph, Node, Edge). Having these characteristics, DjDSL's take on model composition is markedly distinct to related work.

To begin with, the UML and its language architecture (including MOF; [19]) provide two implementation techniques for UML-based (internal) DSL that build on model composition (package merging, profile application). These are language-model extension and language-model piggybacking.[36]

A DSL can be defined as a *language-model extension* [64] of UML. In this scenario, the UML metamodel is extended and modified in an additive manner. This can be achieved by first introducing new metamodel packages, which contain new or redefining metaclass definitions. To create an actual UML metamodel derivative, they are then structurally merged into the UML metamodel package [15, 24]. UML's package merging includes a traversal of the merged and receiving packages to unify the common elements (based on name and element type) and to copy the unique elements to form a resulting package.

A second option to use UML as the base and attach DSL-specific elements to existing metamodel elements (*language-model piggybacking*; 64). This can be achieved using UML profiles [32, 47], which decorate models defined using the UML metamodel.

Outside of UML, the generic modeling environment (GME; [37]) provides model-composition operators for class models as metamodels including model union, multiple class-based inheritance, an extended inheritance relationship: GME allows for interface inheritance or implementation inheritance. In addition, the extended inheritance relationship covers the composition relationships the progenitor classes are involved with (e.g., as composition containers; [37, Section V]). Kompose [29] sets out to implement model composition based on a reusable composition framework. The framework provides extension points for different metamodels (e.g., Kermeta, Ecore) in terms of the STRATEGY pattern for defining match policies (Mergeable interfaces) for their models and a (extensible) library of merge operators applicable to the integrated models. Template-based composition of models has also been considered [26]. In such an approach, abstracted model templates define generic and reusable facets relevant to different base models. In a process of template instantiation, templates become completed (bound) by models under composition.

---

[36]The reader is kindly referred to Hoisl et al. [35], Sobernig et al. [63] for a comprehensive coverage of UML-based techniques for DSL development, including model composition.

```
define DoDAFextension extending DoDAF:dodaf {
  modify class dodaf.SystemFunctionSymbol {
    add property FunctionType type String
  }
  modify class dodaf.DataFlowSymbol {
    filter property SASymHasFromArrow
    filter property SASymHasToArrow
  }
}
```

Lst. 3.60 An excerpt from a metamodel-extension definition, as supported by MoNoGe (see Figure 3 in [12]). The notation and the underlying composition behaviors resemble closely those available for collaboration-based composition mechanisms in FOP (e.g., FFJ)

The approaches to model composition the most comparable with DjDSL's, at the time of writing, are the ones for MoNoGe project [12] and its successor EMF Views (that is, its metamodel extension language, MEL). In MoNoGe, an original metamodel (DjDSL: «languageModel» class) can receive one or more metamodel extensions (DjDSL: «collaboration» classes) to form the extended metamodel (DjDSL: «composition» class). Extensions can apply a number of extension operations, including addition (e.g., new, special, general classes), modification (e.g., adding or modifying properties), and filtering (i.e., hiding existing classes and their features).

Apart from filters, this array of operations matches DjDSL's one. Extensions themselves can be defined in a textual manner, very much akin to notations for defining artifacts in collaboration-based designs in feature-oriented programming. See Listing 3.60 and its striking similarity with FFJ's refines [5]. The MoNoGe composition approach has been absorbed within EMF Views [13] as the Metamodel Extension Language (MEL). In this context, the composition mechanism benefits from an infrastructure for nursing virtual metamodels and virtual models (needed for view generation) as MEL's correspondence model.

Model composition has also been explored and applied in the context of model-based software product lines. A software product line is deemed *model-based* if the primary development artifacts of the product line are models expressed in a modeling language (e.g., Ecore, UML) and the corresponding model transformations expressed in model-transformation languages. To the extent a language-product line is (partially) based on models (i.e., language models in terms of DjDSL's UML extension or the product line is about a family of domain-specific modeling languages), approaches and techniques to model-based SPLs apply. In broad terms, approaches, techniques, and tools fall the two common categories: annotation based vs. composition based. Emphasis below is on model kinds relevant to define the various aspects of language models (e.g., types of class models).

In composition-based approaches [7], there is a clear separation of implementation artifacts (solution space) into implementation units mapping to features in the variability model (problem space). A dedicated step of composition is needed to assemble a product from the product line, which realizes one valid configuration.

Apel et al. [6, 7] developed and maintain FeatureHouse, a framework for generic software composition supported by a tool chain to bring feature-oriented programming using superimposition to different software languages, including the UML. Feature compositions are expressed and perform using a language-independent model, either based on a feature-aware grammar (FeatureBNF) or XML schema. FeatureHouse can be extended to support new languages by providing a plug-in (i.e., grammar or schema plus structural composition rules). UML models are supported based on their XMI representation [7].

In annotation-based approaches [1, 20], the product line (all variants and products) are superimposed, that is, represented by one integrated model (sometimes referred to as the "150% model"). Annotations attached to model elements denote presence conditions of elements in certain configurations. In a dedicated transformation step, these presence conditions are evaluated (against a given configuration) and the output model represents one product (variant). Alternatively, the annotations can point to model transformations explicitly (rather than acting as guard expressions), which are then executed to obtain a product or variant model.

In fmp2rsm [20], a modeler creates a single UML model (i.e., activity and class models) as a *model template*, which contains all variants, along with an explicit feature model. Based on a selection of features from the model, the model template is traversed and the presence conditions (explicit, implicit; expressed as Boolean formulas or XPath expressions) are evaluated. Based on this, a removal and patch analysis is performed to identify those model elements which will end up in the template instance, or variant model.

FeatureMapper [1, 33] allows for annotating Ecore models using presence conditions (feature expressions), guided by an Eclipse UI plugin. These feature-expression annotations link an Ecore model and a variability model. This has in particular been applied to Ecore models describing textual languages in terms of EMFText. During product instantiation, model elements associated with absent (unselected) features are removed to form the output model.

3.4.2 Collaboration-Based and Feature-Oriented Object Orientation

The notion of *collaboration* and *roles* in object-oriented modeling and programming can be traced back to the work by Reenskaug et al. [50] towards Object Oriented Role Analysis and Modeling (OOram). OOram originated in experiences on Smalltalk-based framework design and implementation and was centered around a technique of *role modeling*. In role modeling, the emphasis is on collaborating objects and their collaboration-specific roles; rather than their birth classes. Collaborations are the primary building blocks and classes are derived from composing collaborations and the object-roles contained therein. Collaborations can be added to existing compositions as needed, and the participating classes are updated for their new roles to play accordingly. This closely resembles the notion of collaboration-based design as employed in this work and in feature-oriented programming (FOP).

Compositional approaches to feature-oriented programming (FOP) of software product lines (SPLs) typically support one or several feature decomposition and feature-binding strategies as defined in Sect. 3.2.1. Below, the ones which directly influenced the implementation of DjDSL and the underlying FOP framework for NX [62] are reviewed. A more complete account on binding support in FOP, including annotational approaches, is given in [6, 54].

Apel et al. [5] discuss issues of guaranteeing type compatibility throughout all products of a SPL by leveraging a type system with product-line awareness. Their work is based on a condensed version of Feature Featherweight Java (FFJ). While this paper mainly focuses on the typeful aspects of feature composition, compositional requirements on method and field combination are also discussed. Interestingly, the method-lookup mechanism proposed for FFJ is, modulo Java and NX specifics, equivalent to the one achievable in NX by using decorator-like mixins. In NX, sets of mixins can model refinement layers in FFJ and result in comparable lookup orders. In contrast to refinements in FFJ, the decorator mixins are integral, built-in language constructs of NX for a variety of compositional purposes beyond FOP (e.g., implementation vehicles for GoF design patterns; see [72] for details).

Rosenmüller et al. [53, 54] propose code generation from a single asset base integrating both static class-level and dynamic object-level feature bindings in FeatureC++. The framework allows for switching between static class-level and dynamic object-level feature bindings at SPL build time. These assets (class refinements) are organized in a flat folder structure. For static binding, these class structures are merged by superimposition. For dynamic binding, feature classes as part of a GoF Decorator pattern idiom are generated. These feature classes are then organized in decorator chains to implement layered designs, based on method forwarding, using an application-level super-reference list. This entails decomposition issues such as the self-problem. Limitations are due to the host language C++ (e.g., not supporting dynamic class-level composition).

Ostermann [46] puts forth a collaboration-based and layered implementation technique based on prototype delegation (to realize refinement chains) and a variant of virtual classes (to represent collaborations with composition locality). The result allows for dynamic, object-level compositions. Multiple binding schemes are not supported. This delegation layer compares with dynamic, object-level technique using NX decorator mixins. For example, decorator mixins share the rebinding of the self-reference under delegation.

Smaragdakis and Batory [60, 61] present an implementation technique for collaboration-based designs using mixin layers. Their notions of collaboration-based design and of coarse-grain modularization for stepwise refinements is also a central motivation for FOP in NX. As for the implementation techniques for collaboration-based designs and the notion of mixins, besides C++, Smaragdakis and Batory [60] explore the use of CLOS mixins (i.e., the CLOS variant of multiple class-based inheritance with linearization). Their CLOS implementation study compares with our NX study as NX's OO system is closely modeled after CLOS (e.g., the linearization scheme used).

In CaesarJ [8] (and the Beta family of languages) the concept of family classes as collections of virtual classes attracted our attention towards the issue of composition locality and influenced the NX implementation of collaboration classes based on constructor generation and object nesting. Also, NX provides comparable means to navigate family classes. The NX helper command info parent allows one to access the enclosing object, similar to the pseudo variable out in gbeta. Further similarities result from CaesarJ and gbeta composing superclass hierarchies upon binding family classes (and their nested classes) to each other. The nested classes are a variant of abstract subclasses.

In DeltaJ [55] refinements are limited to the class level. A program is generated given a product configuration. We, therefore, classify DeltaJ as a static, class-level approach only. While in our dynamically typed language setting, we stress software compositional issues, Schäfer et al. investigate (static) type safety under feature composition.

3.4.3 (Textual) Variability Modeling

A general introduction to variability and feature modeling is provided in [6, 21, 56]. A comparative overview of different variants of feature-modeling languages, including syntaxes and semantics, is provided by [57, 58]. In the following, the emphasis is on closely related work that (a) influenced design decisions taken on the abstract syntax of djdsl:vle and (b) approaches to primarily textual variability modeling. Moreover, the review concentrates on approaches to defining (modeling) variability rather than containing it in terms of, e.g., variational data structures [27].

Riebisch et al. [51, 52] reviewed graphical feature-modeling languages at the time (e.g., FODA, Czarnecki/ Eisenecker, FeatuRSEB) and suggested to add syntax and semantics of group cardinalities (multiplicities) as known from the UML. In essence, the resulting feature-modeling language was rebased to build on (groups of) optional subfeatures that carry multiplicities. In addition, certain non-hierarchical relationship types between features were considered (e.g., requires, refines). The motivation was twofold: First, the authors had recognized the potential of streamlining otherwise (partially) redundant modeling elements at the abstract syntax level. Second, adding multiplicities promised to increase the expressiveness of feature models beyond predefined (multiplicity) classes.

Schobbens et al. [57, 58] defined, as a result of the critical-analytical review of feature-modeling languages, the feature-modeling language varied feature diagrams (VFD). VFD was meant to comply with three previously established goals: embeddability, succinctness, and non-redundancy. The abstract syntax of VFD itself was defined on the basis of a canonical, abstracted representation of feature models (free feature diagram, FFD) providing a design space for graph types (DAG, tree), operators, (non-hierarchical) constraint types, and presence/absence of textual constraints. Using FFD, VFD are defined as trees with a single operator *card* ("group cardinality" or multiplicity). During configuration, the *card* operator evaluates to true iff features contained by feature group, denoted by the corresponding node, are selected in accordance with specified cardinality. The authors demonstrate that the resulting abstract syntax can embed all alternatives with a linear increase in complexity (size). In addition, VFD is reported more succinct than alternatives, in terms of a decrease of syntax elements (e.g., nodes and edges) needed to model a domain when transforming from VFD to an alternative model (i.e., at the same level of expressiveness). Finally, VFD is not redundant in the sense that it does not define superfluous language constructs that could not be defined using existing ones. The key to these properties is the choice of a single and versatile operator (node type) representing feature groups and group cardinalities. DjDSL shares these beneficial properties with VFD.

Neutral feature diagrams (NFT; [34]) are a derivative of VFD that restricts variability models to a tree shape. NFT assumes concrete or primary features, which have a correspondence in terms of feature implementations, to be modeled as terminal nodes of variability trees (whereas VFD is neutral about this). The main motivation of Heradio-Gil et al. [34] is to provide for a "backend representation" of VFD in support for analysis operations centered on computing *commonality* measures. These measures aim at capturing a ratio of reuse in a family to rank features (from frequently to rarely reused, for instance). NFT is reaped to compute the total number of products using recurrent relations [34, Section 4]. This is not to be confused with generating (enumerating) all products. NFT demonstrates the benefits of a canonical abstract syntax and applying useful transformations (e.g., from a DAG to a tree, non-terminals to terminals using auxiliary nodes) that are also supported by djdsl::vle.

As for textual feature-modeling languages, a number of suggestions have been put forth. Eichelberger and Schmid [25] provide a structured overview of approaches to textual variability modeling, ranging from early exemplars (FDL, GUIDSL) to more recent ones (Clafer, FAMILIAR, Velvet, TVL) regarding different dimensions, e.g., support for modeling in the large and supported constraint types. From a bird's eye perspective, DjDSL is unique in adopting a canonical representation (multiplicity encoding) throughout the syntax (concrete to abstract) down to the backend encoding (BDD). At the same time, DjDSL is limited to variability models without attributes because of its application on variable language models.

FAMILIAR [2, 18] has been realized both as an external (Xtext) and as internal (Java/ Scala) DSL to implement the domain of feature-modeling, around the core abstractions of feature model, feature, and configuration. In addition, the implemented domain supports analysis operations and importing from and exporting into different representations. A key objective is the support of managing composite feature models using aggregate, merge (in different modes), slice, and diff operations. The operations are based on traveling back and forth between the FAMILIAR representation of models and their logic or Boolean homologues (e.g., by model synthesis). Key differences to djdsl::vle are that FAMILIAR is not rooted in a canonical representation of variability models. djdsl::vle, on the other hand, currently does not support composition and reconstruction of variability models based on a backend representation. Note that the BDD-backed implementation of merging in FAMILIAR, for instance, is applicable to DjDSL, though.

TVL [16] is a variability-modeling language with a textual concrete syntax backed by an abstract syntax and semantics derived from VFD, like djdsl::vle. Similar to Familiar, it comes in different implementation flavors (e.g., as a Java library, as an external DSL implemented via ASF+SDF). The TVL engine integrates with a SAT (Sat4J) as well as a CSP solver (CHOCO), the latter for numerically attributed variability models. A key difference to DjDSL is that DjDSL exposes the canonical representation (including multiplicity encoding) directly as a syntactic frontend while TVL hides these details. DjDSL allows for defining a TVL-like frontend with in-house means as a secondary concrete syntax; at least for a TVL subset excluding attributed variability models (see Sect. 3.5).

PyFML [3] is a recent addition to the examples of textual variability modeling notations, based on a PEG-driven DSL development system (textX; [23]). This way, PyFML was developed in a notation-first, grammar-based manner. PyFML supports arbitrary multiplicities and feature-level attribute annotations. The abstract syntax is based on a canonical representation and can therefore not accommodate different feature-model flavors. The underlying tool chain integrates with CSP for analysis operations for and based on the variability models.

3.5 Summary and Discussion

The language model of a domain-specific language (DSL) is the central development artifact in single-DSL and multi-DSL development. In DSL product line engineering, it is a major outcome of the domain-engineering phase; together with its variability model (see Sect. 1.2). The language model is the point of reference for the other development artifacts (i.e., context conditions, syntax processors, transformations for platform integration). As such, the language model may also be the first development artifact to be created by a DSL developer (see Sect. 2.1). Design-decision making centered on the language model spawns a complex space of decision options and decision consequences on its own (see Sect. 2.2). The decisions taken on the language-model design and its implementation affect most other decision-making phases including tooling decisions.

Designing and implementing a *variable* language model is challenged by the risk of introducing abstraction mismatches when adopting inadequate variability implementation techniques. Decomposition mismatches in implementations of language models include variants of the *expression problem*, for example (see Sect. 2.3.2). Abstraction mismatches negatively affect import quality attributes of a language-model implementation, such as unmodified reusability and feature traceability In addition, variable language models must accommodate different types of DSL composition: extension, unification, and extension composition.

DjDSL delivers a conceptual framework and a reference infrastructure (djdsl::lm) to model and to implement language models as *collaboration-based designs* (see Sect. 3.2.3). As such, they allow for mapping features in a variability model directly to implementation units (i.e., Collaboration and LanguageModel); and vice versa. A variability model itself can be directly represented in DjDSL using a built-in variability-modeling language: `djdsl::vle`. Using this language, different variability-modeling dialects can be captured using a canonical, multiplicity-based variability encoding. The `djdsl::vle` models can be refined using constraints and analyzed themselves as binary decision diagrams (BDD). Feature selections map to corresponding compositions of feature implementations (collaborations). This way, DjDSL is fully equipped to model, to implement, and to analyze a variable language model. Chapter 6 demonstrates the suitability of collaboration-based language models implemented using DjDSL for DSL extension in a complex application example. Chapter 5 features examples of extension, unification, and extension composition; both for internal and external DSL.

DjDSL offers two paths of language-model development, both on the grounds of collaboration-based designs. First, there is a platform-independent approach using extended UML class and package diagrams (see Sect. 3.2.2). For this purpose, DjDSL defines two UML profiles. Based on a profiled class model, a battery of model-to-text transformations can produce a corresponding `djdsl::lm` implementation of the model; or it can be mapped to another DSL development system. Alternatively, as a platform-specific approach, `djdsl::lm` can be developed directly as sketched out above.

UML Collaborations

The notions of collaboration, collaboration roles (parts), and collaboration uses native to the UML metamodel are not a conceptual fit for collaboration-based designs as employed in DjDSL or feature-oriented programming, in more general. This is because of a misfit in terms of certain UML meanings regarding collaborations [45, Section 11.7]: First, a UML collaboration does not own the classifiers (classes) that form the collaboration parts. This implies that classifiers can participate in different UML collaborations. This is not compatible with the meaning of collaboration as units of composition and product quantification in DjDSL, as established earlier. Second, UML collaborations themselves cannot act as elements of a language model (i.e., having properties other than its collaboration parts or even operations).

References

1. Aßmann U, Bartho A, Bürger C, Cech S, Demuth B, Heidenreich F, Johannes J, Karol S, Polowinski J, Reimann J, Schroeter J, Seifert M, Thiele M, Wende C, Wilke C (2014) Dropsbox: The Dresden open software toolbox. Softw Syst Model 13(1):133–169. https://doi.org/10.1007/s10270-012-0284-6
2. Acher M, Collet P, Lahire P, France RB (2013) Familiar: A domain-specific language for large scale management of feature models. Sci Comput Program 78(6):657–681. https://doi.org/10.1016/j.scico.2012.12.004

3. Al-Azzawi Fouad A (2018) PyFml: A textual language for feature modeling. Int J Softw Eng Appl 9(1). https://doi.org/abs/1802.05022

4. Apel S, Batory DS, Rosenmüller M (2006) On the structure of crosscutting concerns: Using aspects or collaborations? In: Proceedings of Workshop on Aspect-oriented Product Line Engineering (AOPLE). http://www.softeng.ox.ac.uk/aople/

5. Apel S, Kästner C, Größlinger A, Lengauer C (2010) Type safety for feature-oriented product lines. Autom Softw Eng 17(3):251–300. https://doi.org/10.1007/s10515-010-0066-8

6. Apel S, Batory D, Kästner C, Saake G (2013) Feature-oriented software product lines, 1st edn. Springer. https://doi.org/10.1007/978-3-642-37521-7

7. Apel S, Kästner C, Lengauer C (2013) Language-independent and automated software composition: The featurehouse experience. IEEE Trans Softw Eng 39(1):63–79. https://doi.org/10.1109/TSE.2011.120

8. Aracic I, Gasiunas V, Mezini M, Ostermann K (2006) An overview of CaesarJ. In: Transactions on Aspect-oriented Software Development I, pp 135–173. https://doi.org/10.1007/11687061_5

9. Atkinson C, Kühne T (2007) A tour of language customization concepts. Adv Comput 70:105–161

10. Barrett K, Cassels B, Haahr P, Moon DA, Playford K, Withington PT (1996) A monotonic superclass linearization for Dylan. In: Proceedings of the 11th ACM SIGPLAN Conference on Object-oriented Programming, Systems, Languages, and Applications (OOPLSA'96). ACM, pp 69–82. https://doi.org/10.1145/236337.236343

11. Benavides D, Segura S, Ruiz-Cortés A (2010) Automated analysis of feature models 20 years later: A literature review. Inf Syst 35(6):615–636. https://doi.org/10.1016/j.is.2010.01.001

12. Bruneliere H, Garcia J, Desfray P, Khelladi DE, Hebig R, Bendraou R, Cabot J (2015) On lightweight metamodel extension to support modeling tools agility. In: Proceedings of 11th European Conference Modelling Foundations and Applications (ECMFA'15). Lecture notes in computer science, vol 9153. Springer, pp 62–74. https://doi.org/10.1007/978-3-319-21151-0_5

13. Brunelière H, Perez JG, Wimmer M, Cabot J (2015) EMF views: A view mechanism for integrating heterogeneous models. In: Proceedings of 34th International Conference on Conceptual Modeling (ER 2015). Lecture notes in computer science, vol 9381. Springer, pp 317–325. https://doi.org/10.1007/978-3-319-25264-3_23

14. Bryant RE (1995) Binary decision diagrams and beyond: Enabling technologies for formal verification. In: Proceedings of IEEE International Conference on Computer Aided Design (ICCAD'95). IEEE, pp 236–243. https://doi.org/10.1109/ICCAD.1995.480018

15. Burgués X, Franch X, Ribó JM (2008) Improving the accuracy of UML metamodel extensions by introducing induced associations. Softw Syst Model 7(3):361–379

16. Classen A, Boucher Q, Heymans P (2011) A text-based approach to feature modelling: Syntax and semantics of TVL. Sci Comput Program 76(12):1130–1143. https://doi.org/10.1016/j.scico.2010.10.005

17. Clavreul M (2011) Model and metamodel composition: Separation of mapping and interpretation for unifying existing model composition techniques. Theses, Université Rennes 1. https://tel.archives-ouvertes.fr/tel-00646893

18. Collet P (2014) Domain specific languages for managing feature models: Advances and challenges. In: Proceedings of 6th International Symposium on Leveraging Applications of Formal Methods, Verification and Validation. Technologies for Mastering Change (ISoLA 2014). Lecture notes in computer science, vol 8802. Springer, pp 273–288. https://doi.org/10.1007/978-3-662-45234-9_20

19. Cook S (2012) Looking back at UML. Softw Syst Model 11(4):471–480

20. Czarnecki K, Antkiewicz M (2005) Mapping features to models: A template approach based on superimposed variants. In: Proceedings of 4th International Conference on Generative Programming and Component Engineering (GPCE'05). Lecture notes in computer science, vol 3676. Springer, pp 422–437. https://doi.org/10.1007/11561347_28

21. Czarnecki K, Eisenecker UW (2000) Generative programming — Methods, Tools, and Applications, 6th edn. Addison-Wesley, Boston
22. Degueule T (2016) Composition and interoperability for external domain-specific language engineering. Theses, Université de Rennes 1 [UR1]. https://hal.inria.fr/tel-01427009
23. Dejanović I, Vaderna R, Milosavljević G, Vuković Ž (2017) TextX: A python tool for domain-specific languages implementation. Knowl Based Syst 115:1–4. https://doi.org/10.1016/j.knosys.2016.10.023
24. Dingel J, Diskin Z, Zito A (2008) Understanding and improving UML package merge. Softw Syst Model 7(4):443–467. https://doi.org/10.1007/s10270-007-0073-9
25. Eichelberger H, Schmid K (2013) A systematic analysis of textual variability modeling languages. In: Proceedings of 17th International Software Product Line Conference (SPLC'13). ACM, pp 12–21. https://doi.org/10.1145/2491627.2491652
26. Emerson M, Sztipanovits J (2006) Techniques for metamodel composition. In: Proceedings of 6th OOPSLA Workshop on Domain-specific Modeling (DSM'06), pp 123–139. http://www.dsmforum.org/events/DSM06/Papers/13-Emerson.pdf
27. Erwig M, Walkingshaw E (2011) The choice calculus: A representation for software variation. ACM Trans Softw Eng Methodol 21(1):6:1–6:27. https://doi.org/10.1145/2063239.2063245
28. Filman RE, Elrad T, Clarke S, Akşit M (2004) Aspect-oriented programming is quantification and obliviousness, Chap 2. In: Aspect-oriented Software Development. Addison-Wesley, Boston
29. Fleurey F, Baudry B, France R, Ghosh S (2008) A generic approach for automatic model composition. In: Workshop Proceedings of International Conference on Model Driven Engineering Languages and Systems (MoDELS'07). Lecture notes in computer science, vol 5002. Springer, pp 7–15. https://doi.org/10.1007/978-3-540-69073-3_2
30. Fowler M (2010) Domain specific languages, 1st edn. Addison-Wesley, Boston
31. Frisch AM, Giannaros PA (2010) SAT encodings of the at-most-k constraint: Some old, some new, some fast, some slow. In: Proceedings of the 10th International Workshop on Constraint Modelling and Reformulation
32. Giachetti G, Marín B, Pastor O (2009) Using UML as a domain-specific modeling language: A proposal for automatic generation of UML profiles. In: Proceedings of 21st International Conference on Advanced Information Systems Engineering (CAiSE'09). Lecture notes in computer science, vol 5565. Springer, Berlin, pp 110–124
33. Heidenreich F, Kopcsek J, Wende C (2008) Featuremapper: Mapping features to models. In: Companion Proceedings of 30th International Conference on Software Engineering (ICSE'08). ACM, pp 943–944. https://doi.org/10.1145/1370175.1370199
34. Heradio-Gil R, Fernandez-Amoros D, Cerrada JA, Cerrada C (2011) Supporting commonality-based analysis of software product lines. IET Softw 5(6):496–509. https://doi.org/10.1049/iet-sen.2010.0022
35. Hoisl B, Sobernig S, Strembeck M (2017) Reusable and generic design decisions for developing UML-based domain-specific languages. Inf Softw Technol 92:49–74. https://doi.org/10.1016/j.infsof.2017.07.008
36. ISO/IEC/IEEE. (2011). ISO/IEC/IEEE systems and software engineering— Architecture description. Standards document 42010-2011, ISO/IEC/IEEE. https://doi.org/10.1109/IEEESTD.2011.6129467
37. Karsai G, Maroti M, Ledeczi A, Gray J, Sztipanovits J (2004) Composition and cloning in modeling and meta-modeling. IEEE Trans Control Syst Technol 12(2):263–278. https://doi.org/10.1109/TCST.2004.824311
38. Knuth DE (2009) The art of computer programming, vol 4, 1st edn. Addison-Wesley, Reading
39. Kolovos DS, García-Domínguez A, Rose LM, Paige RF (2017) Eugenia: Towards disciplined and automated development of GMF-based graphical model editors. Softw Syst Model 16(1):229–255. https://doi.org/10.1007/s10270-015-0455-3
40. Kühn T, Cazzola W (2016) Apples and oranges: Comparing top-down and bottom-up language product lines. In: Proceedings of 20th International Systems and Software Product Line Conference (SPLC'16). ACM, pp 50–59. https://doi.org/10.1145/2934466.2934470

41. Kühn T, Cazzola W, Olivares DM (2015) Choosy and picky: Configuration of language product lines. In: Proceedings of 19th International Conference on Software Product Line (SPLC'15). ACM, pp 71–80. https://doi.org/10.1145/2791060.2791092
42. Lämmel R (2018) Software languages: Syntax, Semantics, and Metaprogramming, 1st edn. Springer. https://doi.org/10.1007/978-3-319-90800-7
43. Lieberman H (1986) Using prototypical objects to implement shared behavior in object-oriented systems. SIGPLAN Not 21(11):214–223
44. Méndez-Acuña D, Galindo JA, Combemale B, Blouin A, Baudry B (2017) Reverse engineering language product lines from existing DSL variants. J Syst Softw 133:145–158. https://doi.org/10.1016/j.jss.2017.05.042
45. Object Management Group. (2017). OMG unified modeling language (OMG UML). Available at: http://www.omg.org/spec/UML, version 2.5.1, formal/17-12-05
46. Ostermann K (2002) Dynamically composable collaborations with delegation layers. In: Proceedings of 16th European Conference on Object-oriented Programming (ECOOP'02). Springer, pp 89–110. https://doi.org/10.1007/3-540-47993-7_4
47. Pardillo J, Cachero C (2010) Domain-specific language modelling with UML profiles by decoupling abstract and concrete syntaxes. J Syst Softw 83(12):2591–2606
48. Parr T (2009) Language implementation patterns: Create your own domain-specific and general programming languages, 1st edn. Pragmatic Bookshelf, Raleigh
49. Ratiu D, Voelter M, Molotnikov Z, Schaetz B (2012) Implementing modular domain specific languages and analyses. In: Proceedings of Workshop on Model-driven Engineering, Verification and Validation (MoDeVVa'12). ACM, pp 35–40. https://doi.org/10.1145/2427376.2427383
50. Reenskaug T, Wold P, Lehne O (1995) Working with objects: The OOram software engineering method. Manning Publications
51. Riebisch M, Böllert K, Streitferdt D, Philippow I (2002) Extending feature diagrams with UML multiplicities. In: Proceedings of 6th International Conference on Integrated Design and Process Technology (IPDT'02). Society for Design and Process Science. https://doi.org/10.1007/978-3-540-25934-3_16
52. Riebisch M, Streitferdt D, Pashov I (2004) Modeling variability for object-oriented product lines. In: Buschmann F, Buchmann AP, Cilia MA (eds) Workshop Proceedings of 17th European Conference on Object-oriented Technology (ECOOP'03). Springer, pp 165–178. https://doi.org/10.1007/978-3-540-25934-3_16
53. Rosenmüller M, Siegmund N, Saake G, Apel S (2008) Code generation to support static and dynamic composition of software product lines. In: Proceedings of 7th International Conference on Generative Programming and Component Engineering (GPCE'08). ACM, pp 3–12. https://doi.org/10.1145/1449913.1449917
54. Rosenmüller M, Siegmund N, Apel S, Saake G (2011) Flexible feature binding in software product lines. Autom Softw Eng 18:163–197. https://doi.org/10.1007/s10515-011-0080-5
55. Schaefer I, Bettini L, Damiani F (2011) Delta-oriented programming of software product lines. In: Proceedings of 10th International Conference on Aspect-oriented Software Development (SPLC'10). ACM, pp 43–56. https://doi.org/10.1007/978-3-642-15579-6_6
56. Schaefer I, Rabiser R, Clarke D, Bettini L, Benavides D, Botterweck G, Pathak A, Trujillo S, Villela K (2012) Software diversity: State of the art and perspectives. Int J Softw Tools Technol Transf 14(5):477–495. https://doi.org/10.1007/s10009-012-0253-y
57. Schobbens PY, Heymans P, Trigaux JC (2006) Feature diagrams: A survey and a formal semantics. In: Proceedings of 14th IEEE International Requirements Engineering Conference (RE'06). IEEE CS, pp 136–145. https://doi.org/10.1109/RE.2006.23
58. Schobbens PY, Heymans P, Trigaux JC, Bontemps Y (2007) Generic semantics of feature diagrams. Comput Netw 51(2):456–479
59. Simons AJH (2005) The theory of classification, part 17: Multiple inheritance and the resolution of inheritance conflict. J Object Technol 4(2):15–26
60. Smaragdakis Y, Batory D (1998) Implementing layered designs with mixin layers. In: Proceedings of the 12th European Conference on Object-oriented Programming (ECOOP'98). Springer, Berlin, pp 550–570

61. Smaragdakis Y, Batory D (2002) Mixin layers: An object-oriented implementation technique for refinements and collaboration-based designs. ACM Trans Softw Eng Methodol 11(2):215–255

62. Sobernig S, Neumann G, Adelsberger S (2012) Supporting multiple feature binding strategies in NX. In: Proceedings of 4th International Workshop on Feature-oriented Software Development (FOSD'12). ACM, pp 45–53. https://doi.org/10.1145/2377816.2377823

63. Sobernig S, Hoisl B, Strembeck M (2016) Extracting reusable design decisions for UML-based domain-specific languages: A multi-method study. J Syst Softw 113:140–172. https://doi.org/10.1016/j.jss.2015.11.037

64. Spinellis D (2001) Notable design patterns for domain-specific languages. J Syst Softw 56(1):91–99. https://doi.org/10.1016/S0164-1212(00)00089-3

65. Thüm T, Batory D, Kastner C (2009) Reasoning about edits to feature models. In: Proceedings of the 31st International Conference on Software Engineering (ICSE'09). IEEE CS, pp 254–264. https://doi.org/10.1109/ICSE.2009.5070526

66. Thüm T, Apel S, Kässtner C, Schaefer I, Saake G (2014) A classification and survey of analysis strategies for software product lines. ACM Comput Surv 47(1):6:1–6:45. https://doi.org/10.1145/2580950

67. Vacchi E, Cazzola W (2015) Neverlang: A framework for feature-oriented language development. Comput Lang Syst Struct 43:1–40. https://doi.org/10.1016/j.cl.2015.02.001

68. van Heesch U, Avgeriou P, Hilliard R (2012) A documentation framework for architecture decisions. J Syst Softw 85(4):795–820

69. Wile DS (1997) Abstract syntax from concrete syntax. In: Proceedings of the 19th International Conference on Software Engineering (ICSE'97). ACM, pp 472–480. https://doi.org/10.1145/253228.253388

70. Zdun U (2010) A DSL toolkit for deferring architectural decisions in DSL-based software design. Inf Softw Technol 52(7):733–748. https://doi.org/10.1016/j.infsof.2010.03.004

71. Zdun U, Strembeck M (2006) Modeling composition in dynamic programming environments with model transformations. In: Proceedings of the 5th International Symposium on Software Composition (SC'06). Lecture notes in computer science, vol 4089. Springer, pp 178–193. https://doi.org/10.1007/11821946_12

72. Zdun U, Strembeck M, Neumann G (2007) Object-based and class-based composition of transitive mixins. Inf Softw Technol 49(8):871–891. https://doi.org/10.1016/j.infsof.2006.10.001

Chapter 4
Variable Context Conditions

Defining and implementing *context conditions* [9, 14] for a DSL's structure (e.g., its language model) and for a DSL's behavior are important steps in design-decision making for and developing a DSL [24]; whether internal or external (Fig. 4.1). Context conditions enforce additional constraints on instantiations of the language model (once composed) and/or the implemented behavior. The former are sometimes referred to as invariant conditions, the latter to pre- and post-conditions. Explicit context conditions become necessary when the underlying assertions over the language model or the intended behavior cannot be expressed directly using the means of expression of a language model itself; or when the assertions cut across the chosen decomposition of the language model.

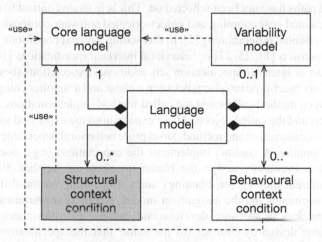

Fig. 4.1 Structural and behavioural *context conditions* are part of the language model (in the broader sense). They represent additional conditions on instantiations of the core language-model that cannot be expressed in an endogenous manner or that should be maintained separately, e.g., for convenience or to allow for reuse and for composition of the context conditions. Context conditions use the core language-model as their value domain of element types and relationships

© Springer Nature Switzerland AG 2020   137
S. Sobernig, *Variable Domain-specific Software Languages with DjDSL*,
https://doi.org/10.1007/978-3-030-42152-6_4

4.1   Some Background on Context Conditions

Context conditions can be implemented in a variety of ways. Options include (sub-)languages for constraint expressions and assertion checking, with constraints being attached to the language models, as part of model transformation taking the language model as input, or constraints expressed using the host or target language. The informed decision on the actual approach adopted must be made by the DSL developer, although the decision often follows from adopting a particular DSL development toolkit. Deferring or revising this decision, once made, is often not possible or incurs a substantial effort of rewriting [28]. While context conditions are vital to capture a domain in terms of an enriched language model, under de- and recomposition of a language model, a number of issues arise on the intended composition semantics for the context conditions themselves. Should context conditions under composition become weakened (more permissive) or strengthened (more restrictive)? How should the order of condition checking be derived from the overall composition order (e.g., between features) and for different definitional scopes of the conditions (e.g., per-collaboration vs. per-class). Beyond capturing the structural context conditions of a DSL model, context conditions play also a role in static program analyses (e.g., verification via model checking) and can also contribute to runtime-assertion checking (RAC).

In research on modelware, entailing approaches to developing domain-specific modeling languages, handling context conditions, which come attached to meta-models and models (e.g., in terms of OCL or EVL expressions), under *model composition* [4, 5] have only attracted little attention. If addressed, the intricacies of the adopted paths have not been reflected on. This is in sharp contrast to the currents in object-oriented programming and object-oriented software composition, including feature-oriented programming [2]. In this setting, context conditions are realized as part of *contracts* [11, 25, 27] or behavioral interface specifications [10, 16].

A contract or interface specification sets additional expectations (beyond that of a signature or object-type interface) between a client and a supplier component, typically, between method callers and the called method implementations, or between object callers and the called objects. These expectations are expressed as constraints on behavior (constructors and methods) to capture behavioral dependencies between client and supplier. A contract implements the expectations (e.g., assertions) and is checked to eventually assign the blame on client or supplier. Blaming can occur at different binding (or, blaming) times. Depending on the different times of blame assignment and the assignment modes, contracts are building blocks for different practices in software development: runtime-assertion checking (RAC), language-level design-by-contract (in the sense that the specification is crafted prior to an implementation), static analyses, test-case generation, and program verification [10, 27].

4.1.1 Context Conditions under Feature Orientation

In this design-decision space, the following dimensions on context conditions as part of feature-oriented language models (as introduced in Chap. 3) are relevant to decision-making and raise challenges:

- *Condition constructs*: What are adequate definition units for context conditions? How should definitions of context conditions be managed? An endogenous context condition is part of the conditioned language-model unit (e.g., collaboration, classifiers). An exogenous context condition sits aside, in a dedicated definition artifact. Consider the requirement of context conditions providing for the complete implementation of an optional feature, without the need of language-model refinements. Another design decision is whether context conditions should be decomposable into or recomposable from building blocks themselves (e.g., clauses)?
- *Condition scopes*: At which level of de- and recomposition should the DSL developer be allowed to define context conditions? Should the DSL developer be allowed to define context conditions not only for the scope of the language model (asset, classifier, role), but also for the scope of compositions? Besides, the language model defines important context conditions intrinsically (e.g., as part of attribute and method records). How can these intrinsic conditions be integrated?
- *Condition composition*: Wherever defined, how should contracts be composed under language-model composition when deriving concrete DSL as products of a language-product line? What are the available composition techniques, and how do they compare in terms of import quality attributes (e.g., avoiding duplicated definitions)?
- *Condition enforcement*: Wherever and however defined, when should the (composed) context conditions be checked against a given language-model instantiation? There a number of characteristic points in the lifetime of a DSL as candidates. For example, at object-construction time of a language model or upon completion of a builder? Or, once syntax processing as been completed? Or, lazily, before entering some post-processing or a transformation? Also, should contract definition and/or enforcement be available at certain points in time only (e.g., as part of DSL test cases)? How to best signal the provenance of violated conditions (once composed) to the blamed participant, such as the responsible feature implementations (e.g., collaborations in DjDSL)?

As stated several times, preserving a certain flexibility in decision-making for the DSL developer [28] has been identified as an important property of a DSL development system (e.g., in terms of which composition technique to apply). Similar observations have been reported on the need to mix contract-composition techniques at the developer's discretion to reach certain quality goals (e.g., avoid duplicated contracts; [26]). These are motivating drivers that helped shape the support for context conditions as available in DjDSL.

A general challenge is the *crosscutting structure* of context conditions [3, 19]. Being crosscutting, especially at the level of a language model, is their defining

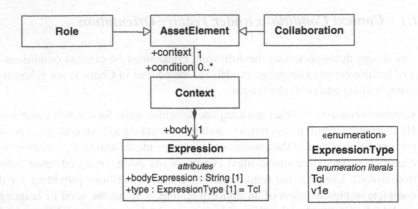

Fig. 4.2 An overview of *invariants* as context conditions on asset elements of DjDSL language models. Context conditions are modeled and implemented as an extension to the conceptual model introduced in Chap. 3, see Fig. 3.6. The extension point is the AssetElement metaclass, which enables context conditions to become attached (scoped) for roles and collaborations alike

property. This is in contrast to method pre- and post-conditions, for example, that are constrained to the narrower context of a message (either by convention or by implementation). Their crosscutting structure follows the same archetypical forms identified for the contracted components: They can be *homogeneous* or *heterogeneous* crosscuts [2]. The type of crosscut dictates the consequences of crosscutting, including types of scattering (e.g., clones) and tangling of contract definitions. For example, a context condition to be applied to a number of language-model elements (classifiers or roles) must be replicated for each and every element because the contracted elements do not share a common ancestor class. Adding feature decomposition on top, as in feature-oriented language models for DjDSL, adds to these unwanted consequences.

4.1.2   Context Conditions for DSL

For the scope of DSL language models, there is the need to define, to enforce, and to document context conditions on the assets making up a DSL product line. These assets and their asset elements are roles, classifiers, collaborations, and language models (see Chap. 3 and also Fig. 4.2).

At a conceptual level, on the one hand, this renders context conditions on DSL product line assets distinct from the notion of contract or contractual interface as applied to (advanced) object-oriented modeling and programming [26]. The latter are attached to methods (pre- and post-conditions), objects, classes as well as components (invariants), and advanced object-oriented language constructs such as pointcuts.

At a second glimpse, on the other hand, as language-model elements are realized as classes (both at the modeling and implementation level), the notion of context conditions in DjDSL maps to contracts in terms of *class invariants* in

Fig. 4.3 Content of the
«languageModel» package
Graph

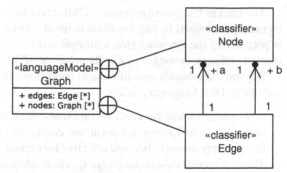

Lst. 4.4 An exemplary OCL
invariant constraint over the
language model in Fig. 4.3

```
1  context Graph
2  inv A('Is unbalanced'):
3      (edges->notEmpty() and
4      nodes->notEmpty()) implies
5      edges->size()*2 = nodes->size()
1  inv B('Contains isolates'):
2      (edges->notEmpty() and nodes->notEmpty()) implies
3      nodes->forAll(n | edges->select(
4          e : Edge | e.a = n or e.b = n)
5      ->notEmpty())
```

advanced object-oriented programming; and the composition of invariants [26]. An *invariant* links to an object-class and imposes expectations and restrictions on this class (or its instances, for that matter). Such a class invariant is an assertion that must be established by the generator or constructor, and from there, every method of a class can rely on the invariant when called. In turn, every method implementation must (re-)establish the invariant on return [25, Section 2.1.1]. Expectations and restrictions typically involve the class attributes and their value domains. Capturing conditions of consistency throughout an object graph are also an important application. For these purposes, an invariant consists of an expression which evaluates to a Boolean value (i.e., a Boolean expression, for short). The body expression may be formulated using different implementation languages. Conceptually, the expectations and restrictions captured by the invariant's expression must hold at any point in time of its instances life spans. Practically, and depending on the life cycle model of the host language and the relevant binding times, invariants are enforced and their expressions evaluated at selected points in time (at instantiation, after instantiation, or before entering model transformations). When invariants are employed as runtime assertions, relevant binding times are both on entering and on leaving methods, for instance.[1]

Consider the example of the OCL invariant constraints in Listing 4.4. These two invariant constraints express basic conditions over a given Graph instantiation which cannot be captured directly in the language model as shown in Fig. 4.3 (e.g., by their property definitions or by their multiplicities): A Graph is deemed unbalanced if there are isolated nodes. The two invariant constraints set context conditions on Graph instantiations.

---

[1] For this reason, and depending on their deployment, class invariants are sometimes considered and even implemented as post-conditions pertaining to object factories, generators, or constructors.

The `context` keyword points to a UML classifier type (`Graph`), that is, the model element constrained by any invariant defined subsequently. An invariant constraint is prefixed by the keyword `inv`, with optional constraint names (e.g., `A` and `B`) and custom violation messages (e.g.,: "Is unbalanced").[2]

Beyond these basics uses of context conditions, this chapter also highlights uses specific to DSL language models:

- *DSL specialization via context conditions*: Imagine that the two context conditions shown in Listing 4.4 form the complete implementation of an optional feature, only meant to become effective for certain DSL variants (configurations). This is a special case of *language specialization*, in which the language model is further restricted by additional conditions only; without any refinements.
- *Intrinsic context conditions*: The feature-oriented language models implemented based on NX classes and their properties set basic constraints on their own. These include multiplicities on properties, as well as type specifiers (i.e., nominal object-types). In the typical life cycle of an object, these constraints are enforced during instantiation and upon accessing the object's states (e.g., using accessor and mutator methods). `djdsl::ctx` collects and submits these basic constraints, intrinsic to the language model, along with the explicit context conditions to validation.
- *Auxiliary context conditions*: At times, in presence of certain abstraction mismatches between an abstract syntax definition and a concrete-syntax definition, context conditions can be used to resolve ambiguities caused by abstraction mismatches. This is addressed in Chap. 5, Sect. 5.2.1.

DjDSL provides an extension to its language-model infrastructure, `djdsl::ctx`, allowing one to define context conditions and to attach them to language models. Figure 4.2 highlights the structure as an extension to feature-oriented language models, i.e., their abstract syntax model from Chap. 3. A `Condition` can constrain `Role` and `Collaboration` instantiations as the two basic asset elements. Multiple `Condition` instantiations can apply to roles and collaborations. Each `Condition` maintains a `bodyExpression`, that is, an expression string valid in a chosen expression language.

For DjDSL, exemplary expression types are expressions expressed in Tcl's `expr` sub-language or `vle` textual constraints (see Sect. 3.3). The latter is required when an invariant sets conditions that reference an associated variability model. The built-in concrete syntax is defined as an internal DSL in front of the abstract syntax defined in Fig. 4.2. It resembles the concrete syntax of OCL invariant constraints.

The remainder is structured as follows:

- Section 4.2 covers the different composition strategies available for variable context conditions: introduction-only, chaining, combination, and templating. Their pros and cons regarding important quality attributes in variable software are discussed briefly.

---

[2]Violation messages are extensions to the OMG OCL invariant constraints [17, Section 12] as introduced by Eclipse's Complete OCL variant.

- Section 4.3 gives the details of the corresponding implementation of variable
  context conditions in DjDSL: `djdsl::ctx`. This includes details on binding
  (blaming) time and on the role of the (total) composition order.

4.2 Composition Strategies

The state of the art in literature [25–27] differentiates between the following composition strategies for context conditions and contracts: introduction-only composition, chaining composition, combination composition, and template composition.
Each exhibits characteristic advantages and disadvantages given a collaboration-
based design of the conditioned language model.

When contrasting the different composition techniques, there are two relevant
perspectives on a context condition (cc): the perspective of the *suppliers* (S) and
the perspective of the *clients* (C). The suppliers (e.g., object generators, language-
model factories, and language-model classes) have the obligation to establish and
to maintain the constraints on a language-model instantiation during its lifetime.
The clients can rely on the context conditions during an instantiation's lifetime (at
least at stable times). The clients (e.g., a template-based generator, a transformation)
are obliged to (contribute to) fulfilling the context conditions upon requesting an
instantiation (e.g., by providing configuration and instantiation data). The suppliers
can rely on the client's contribution at instantiation time. The suppliers also serve
as the context elements of the conditions. Context elements are either introductions
(I) or refinements (R). See Figs. 4.5, 4.6, Listing 4.7, Figs. 4.8, 4.9, and 4.10. The
context condition that is subject to refinement is referred to as *original context
condition* and its refinement as the *refining context condition*.

4.2.1 Introduction-Only Composition

In this strategy, context conditions are defined only at the level of language models
and of classifiers. That is, only conditions having a language model or a classifier
as context are defined. Note that the latter can also be contained by collaborations
implementing features. From the implementation perspective, language models

Fig. 4.5 A schematic of
introduction-only
composition. The supplier S
incorporates the introduction
I and a refinement R. The
context conditions (cc) set by
the introduction I equal the
resulting context conditions
to be guaranteed to the client
(C)

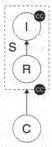

and classifiers in DjDSL are referred to as *introductions*, as opposed to refinements. Language models and collaborations can introduce classifiers as new classes into a composition, while other collaborations provide refinements on previously introduced ones. With context conditions being exclusively defined on introductions, under composition, refinements may not modify the conditions set by the refinements. Consider the example of the composition in Fig. 4.6. With introduction-only composition, only Graph and its classifiers (e.g., Graph::Node and Graph::Edge) carry conditions (before and after any composition). No context conditions, however, may enter the composition via the collaboration

Fig. 4.6 An exemplary composition to represent weight-enabled graphs

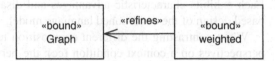

weighted itself, or its constituent Role instantiations. Note, however, that feature-specific collaborations like weighted can come with introductions (classifiers like weighted::Weight) that can be constrained by new context conditions.

This introduction-only composition strategy can be realized by convention or by construction. By convention, DSL developers limit context-condition definitions to introductions. By construction, the programming or, more specifically, the DSL development system identifies introductions and reports any violating condition definitions on refinements. In DjDSL, the emphasis is on context conditions on classes, for which there is a discriminating nomenclature: roles and classifiers can be distinguished starting with their definition.

This nomenclature is reflected in the language-model instantiations and so can be automatically queried for compliance. Technically, DjDSL can verify whether the conditions in Listing 4.7 for a given collection of assets or compositions hold, or report otherwise.[3]

In general, if introductions were extended to also include elements at the sub-class level such methods and properties, or introductions and refinements were not structurally detectable, it is established that each asset element can only be unam-biguously qualified as an introduction or as a refinement under two conditions [1]. First, a collection of selected features (e.g., a product or partial product) must be given. Second, total composition order of features can be computed by the DSL development system.

Introduction-only composition establishes a clear separation of responsibilities between defining context condition (introductions) and complying with a context condition (refinements, compositions) that cannot change under composition. The latter facilitates any static analysis on context conditions. It also avoids barriers to program comprehension for a DSL developer, because context conditions on refinements do not have to be taken into account when developing a client of the

---

[3]DjDSL benefits from the built-in introspection facilities of NX/Tcl to decide on the appropriate or inappropriate "ownership" of context conditions at different processing times.

Lst. 4.7

```
context Condition
inv:   self.context.oclIsKindOf(LanguageModel) or
       self.context.oclIsKindOf(Classifier)
```

Fig. 4.8 A schematic of context-condition chaining, conjunctive on the left, disjunctive on the right. The supplier S is made of the introduction I and a refinement R. In chaining, enforcement of the chained context conditions (cc and cc') is managed *externally*, by the DSL development system, according to the respective composition operator (conjunction, disjunction)

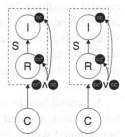

conditioned language model. On the downside, introduction-only composition is maximally restrictive in terms of DSL language-model reuse. A refinement may only operate when fully compliant with the original context conditions. Certain feature-specific refinements might violate existing conditions. For instance, an optional feature on graphs might impose a more relaxed representation condition that allows for isolates to be recorded (e.g., because isolates are meaningful in terms of the network studied or the goal of analysis). In the above example, under introduction-only composition, the refinement could overrule the conditions detecting isolates. Graphs with isolates would not come into existence, in the first place.

4.2.2 Chaining Composition

Chaining context conditions allows for defining additional conditions on refinements (i.e., roles in DjDSL). These refining context conditions are enforced along with the original ones, set by the introductions (classifiers in DjDSL). In this strategy, a chain of context condition can be processed differently:

- *Conjunction*: The chain of context conditions is evaluated as the conjunction of the chained context conditions.
- *Disjunction*: The chain of context conditions is evaluated as the disjunction of the chained context conditions.[4]

Disjunction requires that the refinement order (refinement chain) is reflected in the evaluation order of the chained conditions. The use of conjunction renders every

---

[4]One has to bear in mind that DjDSL is primarily concerned with class invariants. For this reason, many of the options on method contracts (subcontracting vs. contract subtyping) or issues pertaining to assignable clauses do not apply.

refinement (role) responsible for ensuring the refining and the original context condition at the same time. The former cannot influence or overrule the latter. This has the consequence that the refinement can be used according to the original context condition by all clients. The use of disjunction renders fulfillment of context conditions selective from the perspective of the caller: The client can decide which context condition (refining or original) to fulfill. This may be used to either weaken or to strengthen the original context condition. Strengthening requires that the original conditions are reproduced (duplicated) in the refinements, down the refinement chains.

A general benefit of chaining, in whatever mode, is that there is no implementation action required by the DSL developer and the condition's expressions are not polluted with refinement logic (see *combination composition* below).[5] When using conjunctive chaining, the key benefit is that chains of context conditions are evaluated unconditionally, without any refinements interfering (i.e., feature-specific collaborations in DjDSL). Likewise, clients to language-model instantiations can rely on specific context conditions being respected despite the varying presence or absence of other features that might bring additional context conditions into play. To this end, conjunctive chaining helps avoid replicating previously context conditions.

The resulting, composed context conditions are straightforward to understand and to interpret, as if they were the result of mere concatenation. The main downside of conjunctive chaining is that a client must be aware of all context conditions (e.g., as part of an interface description) and, therefore, all the active refinements in advance. On the flip side, suppliers must comply with all context conditions. This makes it impossible to understand, to modify, or to analyze client interactions with suppliers from the perspective of one set of context condition (per feature) alone. In the worst case, all possible feature compositions relevant for a given introduction (classifier or language model) must be considered by the DSL developer or the DSL development system.

4.2.3   Combination Composition

In OOP, along paths of inheritance, structural and behavioral features such as methods can be shared (inherited) between objects. A feature of one object can be entirely replaced by the feature of another object (overriding) or both can be combined by the replacing one explicitly calling out to the overridden one (by following the *super*-reference). As for methods, the latter is referred to method combination [20]. In analogy, context conditions (contracts) along a refinement chain can be replaced (overridden) or become combined (see Fig. 4.9). In context-condition overriding, introductions and refinements can carry context conditions. During composition, the refinement condition (cc') fully replaces the introduction-specific context condition (cc). Along a refinement chain, only the most-specific

---

[5]This is most likely the main explanation why composition of context conditions has been treated this way in approaches to model composition.

Fig. 4.9 A schematic of
combination composition.
The supplier S is made
of the introduction I
and a refinement R; both
carrying context conditions
(cc and cc'). In context-
condition combination,
enforcement of the context
conditions (cc and cc')
along the refinement chain
is orchestrated *internally*,
starting by the most-specific
refining context condition
cc' and continuing from
there up the chain, on a
conditional basis

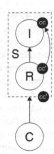

context condition will be enforced from the perspective of the client. This way,
overriding represents the inversion of introduction-only composition. Overriding
provides for a basic means to encode varying context conditions. Refinements and
their context conditions do not have to adhere to the original context conditions.
On the downside, pure overriding puts an extra burden on suppliers and clients
to the language-model instantiation (during comprehension or analysis): As every
refinement may completely change the ultimately ruling context conditions, they
must be aware of any possible composition of context conditions. This renders
introspection on a given feature selection and on the valid combinations of the
embedded variability model necessary, both for suppliers and clients, to rule out
impossible compositions of context conditions. In addition, pure overriding may
lead to cloning existing context conditions down the refinement chain because this
is the only option to preserve conditions. Also, two and more refinements might
introduce conflicting or contradicting conditions.

In context-condition combination, an original context condition is effectively
overridden, but the overriding condition refers to the original context conditions
along the refinement chain. This is analogous to the super-reference in method
combination [20]. The presence of super-references is optional though. Therefore,
refining context conditions without super-reference demote to overriding, as introduced before. The opportunity to combine different (partial) context conditions
into one composite condition avoids cloning and lowers the risk of contradicting
conditions. This is because combination allows for composing context condition
at a fine-grained level of detail, i.e., the level of positioning within condition
expressions. The latter assumes that the refinement chain is free of contradictions
as such.[6] Context-condition combination allows the DSL developer to fully control
reuse and refinement, ranging from overriding, combining to full reuse of ancestor
conditions (without refinements). This can happen separately for every refinement
chain and for each level at a refinement chain. On the negative side, combination

---

[6]This is the case for DjDSL's because of the overall linearization applied to refinement chains (see
Sect. 3.2.3).

Fig. 4.10 A schematic
of template composition.
The supplier S is made of
the introduction I and a
refinement R; both may carry
context conditions (cc).
In templating, the context
conditions reach out to
other behavioral features
(methods) as part of the
context implementations
(expressions). This way, the
context condition acts as a
template and defers details of
its implementation to others.
Without dedicated means of
context-condition refinement,
context conditions become
refinable as long as the called
methods can be refined
systematically

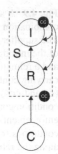

adds to the complexity of reasoning about overriding: The fine-grained control
requires that each and every condition refinement must be known and become
inspected because some might combine while others do not. At the expression
level, the original conditions can become subjected to logical rephrasing, including
negation. When compared to chaining, it is also the DSL developers' responsibility
not to break a chain of refining context conditions unintentionally. Likewise, unless
the super-reference is guaranteed to point to an introduction-level context condition
(i.e., to the tail of the refinement chain), super-references may become dangling
given the composition order under certain feature selections. For example, the
ancestor collaboration in two different composition may or may not include a
receiving feature to bind the super-reference.

4.2.4 Template Composition

The implementation of context conditions may use sub-expressions including
method-call expressions. While in direct evaluation, an expression can be evaluated
based on an immutable set of values, expressions including method calls require
the prior execution of those methods and prior collection of their return value.
For the purpose of this section, method calls are assumed to add Boolean values
to the evaluation environment of an expression. Evaluation is used for both kinds
of expression evaluations (direct and indirect). Consider the example of an OCL
invariant constraint in Listing 4.11.

The expression contains an operation-call sub-expression hasIsolates(). In
djdsl::ctx, this is valid for Tcl expression bodies of context conditions containing
NX method calls, for example. The corresponding method implementations may be
supplied by the asset element owning the context condition (e.g., an introduction)
and/or refinements. In the OCL example, an implementation of hasIsolates may

Lst. 4.11 The invariant constraint B from Listing 4.4, rewritten to use templating

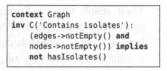

```
context Graph
inv C('Contains isolates'):
    (edges->notEmpty() and
    nodes->notEmpty()) implies
    not hasIsolates()
```

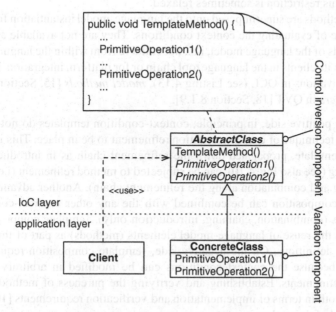

Fig. 4.12 An implementation variant of the GoF TEMPLATE METHOD pattern [8, p. 327]. See Sobernig and Zdun [21] for a background discussion on the more general INVERSION-OF-CONTROL architectural pattern

be provided by the language-model class `Graph` (i.e., the introduction) or by any of this classifier's refinements (e.g., the `weighted` collaboration class).

From an architectural point of view, context-condition templates realize the *inversion-of-control* principle [21]: A more general context condition calls on a more specialized operation as part of its evaluation. Here, "general" and "specialized" refer to the relative position in a refinement chain (higher and lower, respectively). Designwise, template composition between context conditions can be seen as a variant of the TEMPLATE METHOD design pattern [8, p. 327] (see Fig. 4.12). The context condition (C) takes the role of the `TemplateMethod`, containing calls to actual one or several `PrimitiveOperations`. Any refinement to a `PrimitiveOperation` (i.e., method overriding or combination in OOP) modifies the overall context condition. There are typically two or three restrictions imposed on methods to form part or be called from a context condition:

- They are free of (observable) side effects on the application state and they are guaranteed to terminate. Examples are operations and methods of UML classes qualified using their `isQuery` attribute [17, Section 7.5], as well as *pure* methods in JML [15, Section 7.1.1.3].

- Their result type is Boolean or can be coerced into a Boolean value when evaluating a condition's expression (in accordance with the host-language's type system). This is because the return value should enter direct expression evaluation. Depending on the capacity of the condition-expression language used, this restriction is sometimes relaxed.
- The methods are superimposed onto the language-model instantiation for the sole purpose of evaluating the context conditions. They are not available as genuine methods of the language model, i.e., not callable from within the language model or from its clients in the language tool chain or for platform integration. Examples are derivations in OCL (see Listing 4.13), *model methods* [15, Section 7.1.1.2], or *helpers* in QVT [18, Section 8.1.9].

On the positive side, in principle, context-condition templates do not require a dedicated technique of context-condition refinement to be in place. This is because a single template, propagated down the refinement chain as in introduction-only contracting (see also Fig. 4.10), can be subjected to method refinement (i.e., method overriding and combination along the refinement chain). Another advantage is the template composition can be combined with the any other contract-composition techniques (combination, chaining, introduction-only). Template composition also advertises the reuse of language-model elements (methods) as part of the context-condition definitions. On the negative side, template composition requires more attention because the context conditions can be modified in arbitrary ways by method refinements. Establishing and verifying the pureness of methods is challenging, both in terms of implementation and verification requirements [10], and an active field of research.

4.3   Design and Implementation in DjDSL

DjDSL provides a reference implementation for (de-)composable context conditions as defined in the previous section: djdsl::ctx. This implementation is integrated with DjDSL's language-model infrastructure.[7] It allows a DSL developer to define

```
context Graph::hasIsolates() : Boolean
post: result = nodes->forAll(
         n | edges->select(e : Edge |
              e.a = n or e.b = n
         )->notEmpty())
```

Lst. 4.13 Specificationwise definition of a method to be used by a context-condition template, using OCL as an example. Note, technically, an OCL post constraint can only *complement* an already declared or defined method [17, Section 7.5.2]

---

[7]See also Fig. 4.2 for the conceptual and structural design.

Table 4.1 Decision options, advantages, and disadvantages of adopting different composition techniques on context conditions, as available in DjDSL

How to organize (decompose) and apply selectively (compose) context conditions for given a DSL product line?			
Options provided by DjDSL	**Pros**	**Cons**	**Discussed in**
Introduction (trimming)	Original context conditions hold unconditionally, separation of responsibility (introduction vs. refinement), base-only analysis sufficient	Restricts possible refinements and DSL reuse, must be enforced (ideally, by construction)	Section 4.2.1
Chaining	Independent from DSL developer, conjunction: all context conditions are evaluated, disjunction: selective fulfillment, avoid clones	Client awareness of refinement chains, familywise analysis required, disjunction: clones	Section 4.2.2
Combination	Renders original context conditions replaceable, fine-grained control over reuse, avoid clones	Risk of logical rephrasing, chains can be broken by local refinements, dangling super-references, familywise analysis required	Section 4.2.3
Templating	Works with standard method combination, combinable with other techniques, reuse of existing methods	Risk of accidental method refinements, pureness of methods not guaranteed	Section 4.2.4

what constitutes a valid state of a language-model instantiation in terms of context conditions. The DSL developer can choose different points in time for enforcing the context conditions, reporting violations and, if any violations, assigning the blame accordingly by using different means to invoke context-condition validation.

It was established previously that different forms of contract compositions are available, ranging from introduction-only and chaining to combination and templating (see Sect. 4.2). DjDSL presents the fully array of options in this design-decision space to the DSL developer. In fact, it also generalizes introduction-only to a technique referred to as *trimming*. In addition, the different composition options can be mixed in a systematic manner. To guide design-decision making, Table 4.1 summarizes the decision, decision options as well as positive and negative consequences. In this section, the options are reiterated by referring to examples of context-condition composition on the GraphPL running example.

Listing 4.14 exhibits a first concrete-syntax example for a context-condition definition. The value following the context keyword identifies the contextual asset element, for which the condition must hold and will be validated for. From the execution perspective, an instance of this contextual asset element (the class Graphs::Graph) will act as the self-reference during evaluating the body expression. The cond label declares the following value to act as the body expression of

Lst. 4.14 An exemplary context condition defined using DjDSL. The condition captures the requirement that each edge's nodes are well contained by the nodes collection of the Graphs::Graph instance under validation

```
context Graphs::Graph {
  cond {
    ![:edges isSet] ||
    [:edges forAll e {
      [$e a get] in [:nodes get] &&
      [$e b get] in [:nodes get]
    }]
  }
}
```

Fig. 4.15 A visualization of trimmed (collaborationwise) context-condition resolution. weighted is the anchor level, all context conditions resolved for the composition scope of weighted and Graph will be checked. Conditions provided by other levels (coloured, composition-specific ones) will be omitted

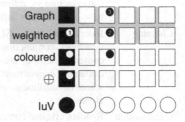

a new Condition. A single context block can contain more than one cond labels and corresponding expression blocks.

4.3.1 Trimming (Including Introduction-Only)

DjDSL generalizes the technique of introduction-only context conditions to defining and to enforcing context conditions selectively for the different composition levels of a language-model composition. Given a composition and a language-model instantiation therefrom, the DSL developer or DjDSL internally can set a certain composition level (e.g., a collaboration) as the starting level for context-condition resolution. From this angle, introduction-only context conditions are the only one option available to the DSL developer that can be taken early or late, at any time, for each and every validation run, if needed. Consider the visual schematic of a collaboration-based decomposition of a DjDSL language model in Fig. 4.15 and the corresponding Listing 4.16. The *instantiation under validation* (IuV) has been created from a composed language model ($\oplus$). The collection of context conditions for the scope of this composition (and its instantiation) includes conditions defined on the collaborations Graph, weighted, coloured, and the composition itself; as well as those defined on their classifiers and roles (see Fig. 4.15). In line with the overall design, any collaboration class that participates in the composition can be selected to invoke the validation procedure on the instantiation, that is, to act as the anchoring validator: */collaboration/* isValid */instantiation/*.

Lst. 4.16

```
Graphs::weighted isValid $IuV
```

Lst. 4.17

```
Graphs::Graph isValid $IuV
```

Fig. 4.18 A visualization of trimmed (collaborationwise) context-condition resolution. Graph is the anchor level, all context conditions resolved for the *introduction* scope of kwGraph will be checked. Composition-specific conditions, as well as those on weighted and coloured, if any, will be omitted. Introduction-only context conditions in DjDSL are a particular application of trimming, or anchoring, validation

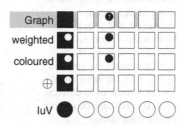

This way, in Listing 4.16, the language-model instantiation referenced by variable IuV (an instantiation of a graph composed from all features *including* coloured) is tested for compliance with the context conditions available for weighted and Graph only; context conditions provided by coloured and the composition are omitted. The resulting evaluation order (including the propagation between asset elements) is depicted by the numbering in Fig. 4.15.

Introduction-only context conditions, as described earlier in this Section, are just a particular use of trimming as provided by DjDSL. By explicitly setting the base language-model class (Graph) as the validator, only context conditions as introduced by the base collaboration will be considered. See Listing 4.17 for a syntax snippet and Fig. 4.18 for the corresponding schematic.

DjDSL's approach to trimmed context-condition evaluation has important consequences. First, DjDSL does not require the DSL developer to restrict herself to introduction-only context conditions, to begin with. Second, trimmed validation allows for tailored and stepwise validation of a language-model instantiation (e.g., when working on one feature-specific collaboration implementation in isolation from the others). Third, there is an important subtlety: Anchoring the invocation of validation using a collaboration class (e.g., Graphs::Graph, Graphs::weighted) does not limit validation to this collaboration only.

Given an overall composition order ($O = (coloured, weighted, Graph)$ in Fig. 4.15), validation subsets the composition order starting at and including the selected collaboration class, e.g., $(weighted, Graph) \subset O$. As a result, for alternative composition orders $(weighted, coloured, Graph)$, and therefore other instantiations under validation, the same anchor (e.g., weighted) will yield a different validation. This is also visualized by the schematic in Fig. 4.19 to contrast with Fig. 4.15. The same anchor validator weighted::Graph will result in different

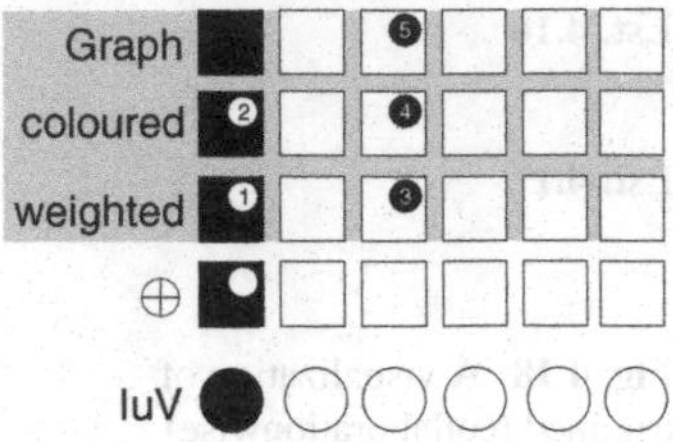

Fig. 4.19 A visualization of trimmed (collaborationwise) context-condition resolution. weighted is the anchor level, all context conditions resolved for the composition scope of weighted, coloured, and Graph will be checked. Composition-specific conditions, if any, will be omitted. As opposed to Fig. 4.15, the same anchor validator resolves to different context conditions depending on the composition

```
1    ${enrichedGraphs}::Graph isValid $IuV; # using conjunction (default)
1    ${enrichedGraphs}::Graph isValid -or $IuV; # using disjunction
```

Lst. 4.20

validation behavior given a different underlying composition. This is in accordance with a given composition order and results from a conscious design decision that reflects the nature of a collaboration: A collaboration always builds on other collaborations and, ultimately, on a base language-model. Its structure and behavior, including context conditions, is typically dependent on its ancestors. For language models, typically at the tail of a composition order (refinement chain), the chosen behavior converges to yielding introduction-only validation as shown above.

4.3.2 Chaining

Chaining of context conditions across collaborations is orchestrated extrinsically by DjDSL validation engine. This is in contrast to contract combination that is intrinsically triggered from within the contracts (context conditions) themselves; much like in method combination. Chaining can be realized using either conjunction or disjunction of condition expressions. The decision on whether to use a conjunction (strengthening) or a disjunction (weakening) of the refined contracts under composition can be taken by the validating client, or, internally by DjDSL. Disjunction is requested by setting the or flag (see Listing 4.20).

Chaining is the default composition technique applied and is assumed by trimming to work as expected (see above). The composition semantics of chaining under conjunction or under disjunction can be mapped to equivalent context-condition combinations. This can be achieved by appending an extra expression clause to each and every context condition:

Lst. 4.21 Overriding

```
1  context Graphs::capped {
2    cond {[:MAXEDGES isSet] &&
3      [:edges size] < [:MAXEDGES get]}
4  }
```

- for conjunctive chaining: ((...) && [next])
- for disjunctive chaining: ((...) || [next])

Key differences remain elsewhere, however. These include for chaining central orchestration as well as avoidance of preplanning and sanity-checking effort, as opposed to contract combination.

4.3.3 Combination

Contract combination between a refinement (collaboration, role) and an introduction (language model, role) involves that (1) a context-condition refinement overrides the context-condition introduction and (2) the refining context condition (optionally) includes the overridden context condition into its evaluation, in an explicit manner. Overriding means that the shadowed context condition is not considered during validation, unless (re-) included by the refinement. Step 2 or combination is achieved by DjDSL by providing the command next to be used as part of a (Tcl) context-condition expression in the refining condition. This command next resembles the next command available for NX method combination. The djdsl::ctx combination semantics closely resemble those of NX's basic next. Both build on the internal feature-resolution order between NX classes, but there are some implementation-specific differences.[8] For example, arguments are allowed for the latter, but not the former as not needed. djdsl::ctx's next also guarantees to return a Boolean value only.

Listings 4.21 and 4.23 provide examples of context-condition overriding and context-condition combination, respectively.

The context condition in Listing 4.21 is defined for the context of the Graphs:: capped collaboration. When active, this collaboration is meant to signal the limitation of the number of allowed edges in a given graph to MAXEDGES. For this purpose, the collaboration implementation defines and sets a property MAXEDGES (see line 2 of Listing 4.22). The property is referenced from within the context condition's expression and compared with the size of the edges collection (see line 3 in Listing 4.21). The collaboration Graphs::capped effectively shadows the context condition provided by Graphs::Graph in the sense that the latter is not submitted to evaluation. As explained before, the main benefit of overriding is the ability to rewrite original context conditions in their entirety. For instance, in

---

[8]Recall that next is the syntax representation for the super-reference [20]. Aligning the means of method and contract combination has been suggested before, see, e.g., the original keyword in a FOP-aware variant of JML [25] and FOP method refinements [1].

Lst. 4.22

```
1  Collaboration create capped {
2  :property -accessor public {MAXEDGES:integer 10}
3  }
```

Lst. 4.23 Combination

```
1    context Graphs::capped {
2      cond {
3        [:MAXEDGES isSet] &&
4        [:edges size] < [:MAXEDGES get] &&
5        [next]}
6    }
```

Fig. 4.24 A visualization of
context-condition
combination. capped (1)
overrides and combines with
the context conditions
provided by Graph (2) via
next

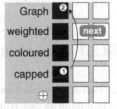

case a context condition is not relevant anymore for a certain selected feature. The
downside, if still relevant, is the need to replicate a context condition to preserve it
as part of the overriding one.

Listing 4.23 shows an extended variant of the Graphs::capped context condition. This variant includes a next call on line 5. This call refers to the shadowed
or overridden context condition, if any. This way, the otherwise discarded context
condition is combined with the overridden one. See also Fig. 4.24. The availability
of context-condition combination via next opens up a range of opportunities to the
DSL developer. A solitary next in Listing 4.23 corresponds to an exact reuse of
the overridden condition. This helps avoid cloning conditions several times. When
it is one of several clauses, it is an actual revision of the original condition; possibly
inverting its meaning. Finally, omitting next yields overriding. This compositional
flexibility can have negative consequences: The DSL developer must be aware of
the overridden context conditions in all details, to combine them without having the
composite evaluation result in an unintended way.

4.3.4 Templating

Context conditions and their body expressions can send self-messages, i.e., messages to the instantiation currently under evaluation, as part of their evaluation.
These self-messages must be matched by method implementations either provided
by the instantiation under evaluation itself, or provided otherwise (e.g., as extrinsic
helpers). Practically, a context condition's expression in DjDSL can call an arbitrary

Lst. 4.25

```
context Graph
inv A('Is unbalanced'):
   (edges->notEmpty() and
   nodes->notEmpty()) implies
   edges->size()*2 = nodes->size()
```

```
1  context Graphs::Graph {
2    # condition incl. self-call to model method
3    cond {[:hasIsolates]}
4    # model-method definition
5    op hasIsolates {} {
6      expr {!([llength ${:edges}] && [llength ${:edges}]) ||
7           [llength ${:edges}]*2 == [llength ${:nodes}]}
8    }
9  }
```

Lst. 4.26 A definition of a model method hasIsolates that is called as part of a template context-condition. The body of hasIsolates is an exemplary translation of the OCL constraint in Listing 4.25, as introduced earlier, to the Tcl expr sub-language

NX method available for the contextual instantiation, including basic built-in ones available to all objects. This is, on the one hand, very convenient because introspection methods, for example, allow for capturing certain constraints on a language-model instantiation. On the other hand, defining such methods, to be used from context conditions exclusively as mere and scoped helpers, on the language model or a collaboration does not separate the concerns between abstract syntax definition and DSL validation, causing a pollution of the abstract syntax object-types.

To separate between methods as genuine constituents of the language model (i.e., the behaviour definition) and helper operations for context-condition implementation and templating, DjDSL allows for defining *model methods*. Recall the OCL constraint in Listing 4.25. Listing 4.26 depicts a model method realizing this OCL constraint: hasIsolates (lines 5–8). The value following the op keyword (or, *operation*) is the model-method name (hasIsolates), followed by method parameters (any NX parameter definition is permitted), and the method body. Like a context condition, a model method is defined for a given context, i.e., a DjDSL asset element (Graphs::Graph in Listing 4.26, line 1). The model method then becomes available for instantiations of this contextual asset element, during validation execution only. For example, the condition expression in line 3 of Listing 4.26 calls out to the model method defined for the same context.

A key characteristic of templating using model methods is that, without modifying, refining, or duplicate context conditions per se, a refinement of context conditions can be achieved using method combination. This involves combining ordinary methods and model methods alike. Consider that, for weighted graphs or analysis operations on them, the context condition testing for (the absence) isolated nodes in a graph should be hardened to exclude isolates nodes in the sense of loop edges (Fig. 4.27). A loop edge is an edge that connects one and the same

Fig. 4.27 hasIsolates in
weighted (1) overrides
hasIsolates provided by
Graphs::Graph and (2)
re-combines the overridden
model method using next

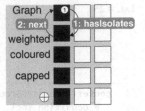

Lst. 4.28 A model method
hasIsolates called as part
of and from within a
context-condition template

```
1   context Graphs::weighted {
2     # model-method combination (using [next])
3     op hasIsolates {} {
4       expr {![:hasLoopEdges] && [next]}
5     }
6     op hasLoopEdges {} {
7       set loopEdges [list]
8       foreach e ${:edges} {
9         if {[$e a get] eq [$e b get]} {
10          return 1
11        }
12      }
13      return 0
14    }
15  }
```

node. In Listing 4.28, a contract refinement implementing this hardened contract
is exemplified.

Note that Listing 4.28 does not introduce a new context condition (cond), which
would be become tested using chaining or combination. Instead, line 3 features an
op definition hasIsolates. This model method, first, overrides any same-named
model method in the refinement chain (e.g., hasIsolates in Graphs::Graph,
Listing 4.26). Then, second, by using a super-reference call via next, the overridden
model method can be invoked (see line 4; see also Fig. 4.27 for a visualization).
Listing 4.28 also demonstrates how a sibling method (hasLoopEdges) can be used
like a standard NX method from within a model method.

A DSL developer must mind the following details about context-condition
templating in DjDSL:

- Method bodies of model methods can be arbitrary NX/Tcl scripts, with their
  return value qualifying as a Boolean value. See hasLoopEdges in Listing 4.28
  (lines 6–14) as an example that features usages of the Tcl foreach and the Tcl
  if commands.
- To render model methods into *pure* features, the overall validation run (isValid,
  validate) must be executed as an outplace validation. Out-place validation
  refers to executing the entire validation run on a deep and throw-away copy
  (clone) of the instantiation under evaluation (including clones of all referenced
  objects), rather than the originals: Graphs::Graph isValid -outplace $IuV
- Templating using model methods is fully compatible with trimming of context
  conditions. Overriding model methods outside the scope set by an anchoring

```
1   Asset create Graphs {
2     LanguageModel create Graph {
3       :property name:alnum
4       :property -incremental edges:object,type=Edge,0..n
5       Classifier create A
6       Classifier create Node
7       Classifier create Edge {
8         :property -accessor public a:object,type=Node
9         :property -accessor public b:object,type=Node
10      }
11    }
12    Collaboration create weighted {
13      Classifier create Weight {
14        :property -accessor public {value:integer 0}
15      }
16      Role create A
17      Role create Edge -superclasses A {
18        :property -accessor public weight:object,type
            =Weight
19      }
20    }
21  }
```

Lst. 4.29 This is a DjDSL asset definition on a GraphPL, already introduced and described as a running example in Chap. 3. Here, it serves for exemplifying the need for handling *intrinsic context conditions*

validator are not enacted during condition evaluation. For example, calling `Graphs::Graph isValid $IuV` rather than `::enrichedGraphs isValid $IuV` will not have the stricter variant of `hasIsolates` executed.

Beyond support for trimming, chaining, combination, and templating, the DjDSL reference implementation of variable context conditions features two more details: intrinsic context conditions and custom binding (blaming) times.

4.3.5 Intrinsic Context Conditions

The DSL developer will see that a number of additional constraints are tested as context conditions without having them specified explicitly.[9] These context conditions are created implicitly by DjDSL upon executing a validation. They originate from the property specifiers of the NX classes that form the language model. Context conditions will be derived from the following class and property details. The description is accompanied by examples taken from the language model defined in Sect. 3.2.3.

---

[9]This type of context conditions (or invariant constraints) is also available in validation engines of metamodeling tool chains, e.g., the *basic* EMF constraints [22, Section 18.4].

• The cardinalities of the object variables are tested against the multiplicity bounds of the corresponding properties defined in the language model. On line 5 of Listing 4.29, the property `edges` sets a multiplicity of lower bound of 0 and an unrestricted upper bound.
• The object variables are tested for compliance with the type specifiers defined by the corresponding properties. There are two important kinds of type specifiers.

  – NX object-types: The `type=` specifier identifies the expected nominal object-type of a property. In Listing 4.29, various properties carry this specifier (see lines 4, 8–9, as well as 18). For instance, the property `weight` at line 18 expects an instance of a class `Weight`.[10]
  – Bit-representational and Tcl value-types: The type specifiers can nominate a number of built-in and custom type checkers. Most importantly, Tcl built-in type checkers[11] can be used (including `integer`, `double`, and `boolean`). Take line 17 of Listing 4.29 as an example of an `integer` property.

In addition to these conditions derived from multiplicities and type specifiers, the following context conditions are automatically tested for:

• Multi-valued vs. single-valued properties: If a language-model property qualifies the managed object variables as multi-valued (e.g., by providing a multiplicity class or having set the `-incremental` option), the object variables will be tested whether they can be processed as valid Tcl lists. This is, for example, the case for the property `edges` on line 5 of Listing 4.29.
• Properties that set default values for the managed object variables will be turned into constraints on the required existence of the so-called variable in the tested object (i.e., a check for the object variable state of being defined). Such a check would be conducted for object variables corresponding to property `value` of class `Weight`, line 17 in Listing 4.29. This is because a default of 0 is stipulated.

Any violation of intrinsic context conditions is reported in terms of the authoritative property object and the validated object. With this, the corresponding violation report can be selectively processed or even suppressed. In addition, enforcement of built-in context conditions can be configured separately. The order of evaluating the intrinsic and extrinsic context conditions, as well as the different types of intrinsic context conditions (relative to each other), is as follows:

1. All intrinsic context conditions

  (a) Object-variable existence (if applicable)
  (b) Multi-valued fitness (if applicable)

2. All extrinsic context conditions

---

[10]Note that the object-type specifier may also be used to trigger the context-condition checks on language-model elements referenced by type-specified properties. However, this option has a number of restrictions in terms of design (e.g., object-type specifiers may point to any super-type in a refinement chain) and of implementation. To avoid redundant checks, extra book-keeping would be required in a cyclic object graph. Therefore, `djdsl::ctx` propagates validation differently.

[11]These correspond 1:1 to built-in `is` options of the Tcl string command.

The rationale for this *intrinsic-first* evaluation order is that intrinsic context conditions likely cover basic defects that might also explain violations to extrinsic context conditions. For example, without successfully parsing as a Tcl list, checks for multiplicity or multi-valued checks are pointless. The above order ascertains that possible root causes are signaled prior to other violations.

4.3.6 Composition Order

Whatever the composition technique applied (or a mix thereof), the underlying order of composition for chaining, combination, and templating directly results from the combined linearization order for a given composition as computed by DjDSL (see Sect. 3.2.1). As it is a conflict-resolution scheme based on linearization, the resulting order of composition is conflict-free. In addition, as collaboration- and class-local precedence orders are preserved (even under changing feature selections!), the risk of unintended chainings, combinations, or model-method resolutions under templating is minimized.

4.3.7 Binding Times and Modes

The examples in this section demonstrate that validation in terms of evaluating the composed context conditions can be triggered at the discretion of clients to the language-model instantiation (e.g., a code generator). DjDSL does not come with a predetermined or fixed set of binding times. The general recommendation is, similar to contract validation in OOP, that a validation is scheduled at *stable times* [16, Section 11.8]. Typical examples in the context of DjDSL are after syntax processing (e.g., upon completion of a builder, upon obtaining the parse representation) or before entering a post-processing step (e.g., direct interpretation, a traversal of the language mode, or a transformation). As for the binding mode, context conditions can be attached and removed from asset elements during runtime, by clients and suppliers alike. Also language-model composition can be adapted at runtime, which changes the evaluation plan for context conditions (e.g., under trimming). Therefore, technically, context-condition evaluation is dynamic.

4.4 Related Work

DjDSL's take on rendering context conditions as part of language models variable relates to two areas of software-engineering research that have developed in striking isolation from each other (see also Fig. 4.30). On one side, there are model-composition techniques (as covered in Sect. 3.4) that support structural and behavioural context conditions as artifacts under composition. On the other, contracts and their composition in feature-oriented programming (FOP).

Fig. 4.30 Related work on
variable context conditions

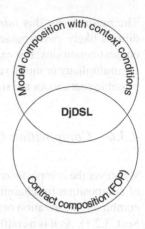

4.4.1 *Composing Model-Based Context Conditions*

There is a rich body of literature of metamodel and model composition techniques
and tools available today, as part of implementing variable primary abstract
syntaxes for DSL and beyond. See Sect. 3.4. Context conditions on model structure
and behaviours, however, have only scarcely been addressed. For example, in
Melange [5, 6] as a model-driven DSL development system, context conditions
(OCL constraints) on the composed metamodels are not handled explicitly (see
also Sect. 2.4). If considered at all, their treatment turns out rather elementary
compared to the sophistication of the composition operations on models. The few
research reports explicit about context conditions or model constraints, on classes
or properties, to the best of my knowledge, default to conjunctive chaining of
invariants [7, 23]. Alternatives are not considered, besides referring to the generic
possibility of customizing the merge operation on context conditions. DjDSL
contributes to closing this conceptual gap.

Another relevant research line on context conditions or model constraints (e.g., in
terms of OCL and EVL) are techniques and tools to allow for the semi-automated or
assisted co-evolution (patching) of constraint expressions along with the changing
metamodels and models [13]. These approaches and techniques, previously also
considered for co-evolving OCL expressions (or similar) as part of model transformations (see, e.g., [12]), deal with detecting changes and change types in model
elements (e.g., promotion or demotion of multiplicities, retyping of properties),
locating a changed model element within context conditions (e.g., context or
body), further resolving the dependency context of the impacted condition, and
generating patching candidates or resolution hints. Given the inherent limits to
automation of these approaches and their focus on change over time (evolution),
they do not directly apply to context-condition composition in collaboration-based
designs of models and metamodels. However, their techniques to identify and
to classify types of conflicts between context conditions and their conditioned
models (e.g., multiplicities, retyping) can complement analysis and verification for

reasoning about composed context conditions. As a highlighted disadvantage of some composition techniques, the need to be aware of many if not all feature configurations (even at a fine level of granularity when combining context conditions) requires tool support. Examples include identifying context conditions affected by the underlying language-model composition or spotting duplicated conditions as refactoring candidates by tracking co-references starting from the language model.

4.4.2 Composing Contracts in FOP

Thüm et al. [26] explored systematically, in a critical-analytical manner, the role of contracts (method pre- and post-conditions, class invariants) in terms of runtime-assertion checking for OO programs, namely contracts for Java programs defined and implemented using the Java Modeling Languages (JML). Contract composition is here considered in terms of feature-oriented programming (FOP) involving class- and method refinements [2]. First, the authors draw a design space of five different contract-composition techniques: plain contracting, explicit contract refinement, consecutive contract refinement, contract overriding, and pure-method refinement. These approaches are reviewed analytically, by identifying characteristic advantages and disadvantages and by giving selected examples. In addition, second, the composition strategies are assessed against selected criteria: strictness (strengthening, weakening), expressiveness, complexity (in terms of the local comprehensibility of contracts), and the propensity to yield code clones. Thüm et al. [26] is relevant conceptually, because the composition techniques map to the ones discussed in Sect. 4.2; with a different emphasis, though: contract composition. In addition, Thüm et al. [26] found that mixtures of composition techniques can be beneficial, especially pure-method refinements and consecutive refinement.

Rebêlo et al. [19] explore and propose ways of extending JML to include the means of expressing JML contracts in terms of aspect-oriented software composition. This is achieved by allowing for combining AspectJ's pointcut definitions ("pointcut designators") with JML specifications. This way, pointcut designators can carry pre- and post-conditions for the scope of the designated join points (i.e., well-defined points during program execution). There is tool support and integration with AspectJ. The aim is to support selected reuse scenarios for contracts when their nature is cutting across base program in an *homogeneous* manner, i.e., the identical contracts and their conditions apply to different join points, potentially. At the same time, certain properties or pitfalls of AOP are claimed to be tamed: modular reasoning, obliviousness, and loss of in-place documentation (mainly because of relocating contracts into aspect definitions). Heterogeneous crosscutting contracts as in Thüm et al. [26] are not considered.

4.5   Summary and Discussion

Structural and behavioural context conditions are an integral part of a domain-specific language (DSL) model (see also Sect. 1.1). Context conditions help model details of the problem domain that cannot be unambiguously or comprehensively captured by the language model alone. At the same time, context conditions are full-fledged feature-implementation techniques themselves. Certain features of a DSL family might be best implemented using additional context conditions, for example, to implement a DSL restriction. In grammarware, this use of context conditions is sometimes referred to as semantics restrictions. Finally, defining and enforcing context conditions is necessary to disambiguate parse representations and abstract syntax representations.[12]

Despite their importance, *context conditions under DSL composition* have barely been addressed by modelware and grammarware approaches. Therefore, DjDSL sets out to close this conceptual gap and to provide to DSL developers fine-grained means of composing context conditions, along with their associated language models. Departing from ideas on *contract composition* in feature-oriented programming (FOP), the validation framework for DjDSL language models (djdsl::ctx) introduces four different techniques of context-condition composition: trimming, combination, chaining, and templating. DjDSL's trimming is original in that it generalizes from introduction-only contract compositions, as proposed in FOP for collaboration-based designs. In addition, the validation framework (djdsl::ctx) also covers for intrinsic context conditions (as available in metamodeling environments like EMF). The DSL developer can choose from different blaming times and can request a validation guaranteed to be free of side effects.

An important point to stress is that these four composition techniques can be combined by a DSL developer when using DjDSL. Experience shows that certain combinations are particularly advantageous. In Chap. 6, the combined use of trimming and templating is highlighted. Trimming allows for evaluating all context conditions from the perspective of a given feature selection and of a corresponding composition of feature implementations (collaborations). Template conditions use deferred or overridable *model methods* as extension points. The template conditions themselves are defined as introductions (i.e., on the base collaboration). For coarser-grained reuse, the mix of templating and conjunctive combination of context conditions was found useful. Interestingly, these experiences match observations on contract composition in FOP (see, e.g., [26, p. 13]).

References

1. Apel S, Kästner C, Größlinger A, Lengauer C (2010) Type safety for feature-oriented product lines. Autom Softw Eng 17(3):251–300. https://doi.org/10.1007/s10515-010-0066-8

---

[12]This role of context conditions is prominently covered in Sect. 5.2.1 of the next chapter.

2. Apel S, Batory D, Kästner C, Saake G (2013) Feature-oriented software product lines, 1st edn. Springer, Berlin. https://doi.org/10.1007/978-3-642-37521-7

3. Balzer S, Eugster PT, Meyer B (2006) Can aspects implement contracts? In: Proceeding of 2nd International Workshop on Rapid Integration of Software Engineering Techniques (RISE'05). Lecture notes in computer science, vol 3943. Springer, Berlin, pp 145–157. https://doi.org/10.1007/11751113_11

4. Clavreul M (2011) Model and metamodel composition: Separation of mapping and interpretation for unifying existing model composition techniques. Theses, Université Rennes 1. https://tel.archives-ouvertes.fr/tel-00646893

5. Degueule T (2016) Composition and interoperability for external domain-specific language engineering. Theses, Université de Rennes 1 [UR1]. https://hal.inria.fr/tel-01427009

6. Degueule T, Combemale B, Blouin A, Barais O, Jézéquel JM (2015) Melange: A meta-language for modular and reusable development of DSLs a meta-language for modular and reusable development of DSLs. In: Proceeding of 2015 ACM SIGPLAN International Conference on Software Language Engineering (SLE'15). ACM, New York, pp 25–36. https://doi.org/10.1145/2814251.2814252

7. France R, Fleurey F, Reddy R, Baudry B, Ghosh S (2007) Providing support for model composition in metamodels. In: Proceeding of 11th IEEE International Enterprise Distributed Object Computing Conference (EDOC'07). IEEE, Piscataway, pp 253–253. https://doi.org/10.1109/EDOC.2007.55

8. Gamma E, Helm R, Johnson RE, Vlissides J (1995) Design Patterns – Elements of Reusable Object-Oriented Software. In: Addison Wesley Professional Computing Series. Addison-Wesley, Reading

9. Harel D, Rumpe B (2004) Meaningful modeling: What's the semantics of "semantics"? Computer 37(10):64–72. https://doi.org/10.1109/MC.2004.172

10. Hatcliff J, Leavens GT, Leino KRM, Müller P, Parkinson M (2012) Behavioral interface specification languages. ACM Comput Surv 44(3):16:1–16:58. https://doi.org/10.1145/2187671.2187678

11. Helm R, Holland IM, Gangopadhyay D (1990) Contracts: Specifying behavioral compositions in object-oriented systems. In: Joint Proceeding of European Conference on Object-oriented Programming and the International Conference on Object-oriented Programming Systems, Languages, and Applications (ECOOP/OOPLSA'90). ACM, New York, pp 169–180. https://doi.org/10.1145/97945.97967

12. Hoisl B, Sobernig S, Strembeck M (2013) Higher-order rewriting of model-to-text templates for integrating domain-specific modeling languages. In: Proceeding of 1st International Conference on Model-driven Engineering and Software Development (MODELSWARD'13). SciTePress, Setúbal, pp 49–61. https://doi.org/10.5220/0004321100490061

13. Khelladi DE, Bendraou R, Hebig R, Gervais MP (2017) A semi-automatic maintenance and co-evolution of OCL constraints with (meta)model evolution. J Syst Softw 134:242–260. https://doi.org/10.1016/j.jss.2017.09.010

14. Lämmel R (2018) Software languages: Syntax, Semantics, and Metaprogramming, 1st edn. Springer, Berlin. https://doi.org/10.1007/978-3-319-90800-7

15. Leavens GT, Poll E, Clifton C, Cheon Y, Ruby C, Cok D, Müller P, Kiniry J, Chalin P, Zimmerman DM (2013) JML reference manual. Draft available at: http://www.jmlspecs.org/refman/jmlrefman.pdf

16. Meyer B (1988) Object-oriented software construction, 2nd edn. Prentice Hall, Upper Saddle River

17. Object Management Group (2014) Object constraint language specification. Formal/14-02-03; Available at: http://www.omg.org/spec/OCL/2.4/

18. Object Management Group (2016) MOF2 Query/View/Transformation specification. formal-16-06-03; Available at: http://www.omg.org/spec/QVT/1.3/PDF

19. Rebêlo H, Leavens GT, Bagherzadeh M, Rajan H, Lima R, Zimmerman, M D, Cornélio M, Thüm T (2014) AspectJML: Modular specification and runtime checking for crosscutting contracts. In: Proceeding of 13th International Conference on Modularity (MODULARITY'14). ACM, New York, pp 157–168. https://doi.org/10.1145/2577080.2577084
20. Simons AJH (2004) The theory of classification, part 10: Method combination and super-reference. J Object Technol 3(1):43–53
21. Sobernig S, Zdun U (2010) Inversion-of-control layer. In: Proceeding of 15th Annual European Conference on Pattern Languages of Programming (EuroPLoP'10). ACM, New York. https://doi.org/10.1145/2328909.2328935
22. Steinberg D, Budinsky F, Paternostro M, Merks E (2009) EMF: Eclipse modeling framework 2.0, 2nd edn. Addison-Wesley, Reading
23. Straw G, Georg G, Song E, Ghosh S, France R, Bieman JM (2004) Model composition directives. In: Proceeding of 7th International Conference on the Unified Modeling Language (UML'04). Lecture notes in computer science, vol 3273. Springer, Berlin, pp 84–97. https://doi.org/10.1007/978-3-540-30187-5_7
24. Strembeck M, Zdun U (2009) An approach for the systematic development of domain-specific languages. Softw Pract Exp 39(15):1253–1292
25. Thüm T (2015) Product-line specification and verification with feature-oriented contracts. University of Magdeburg, Magdeburg (PhD thesis), Available at: wwwiti.cs.uni-magdeburg. de/iti_db/publikationen/ps/auto/Thuem15.pdf
26. Thüm T, Schaefer I, Kuhlemann M, Apel S, Saake G (2012) Applying design by contract to feature-oriented programming. In: Proceeding of 15th International Conference on Fundamental Approaches to Software Engineering (FASE'12). Lecture notes in computer science, vol 7212. Springer, Berlin, pp 255–269. https://doi.org/10.1007/978-3-642-28872-2_18
27. Thüm T, Apel S, Zelend A, Schröter R, Möller B (2013) Subclack: Feature-oriented programming with behavioral feature interfaces. In: Proceeding of 5th Workshop on MechAnisms for SPEcialization, Generalization and InHerItance (MASPEGHI'13). ACM, New York, pp 1–8. https://doi.org/10.1145/2489828.2489829
28. Zdun U (2010) A DSL toolkit for deferring architectural decisions in DSL-based software design. Inf Softw Technol 52(7):733–748. https://doi.org/10.1016/j.infsof.2010.03.004

Chapter 5
Variable Textual Syntaxes

In software language engineering, language composition and the corresponding support for language-development systems are commonly grouped into different composition types [16]: language extension, language unification, extension composition, and self-extension (see Sect. 2.3 for more background). It is important to draw a line here: The perspective in this chapter is centered around DSL as base languages and extension languages, rather than a host language or general-purpose languages being subjected to composition (e.g., to implement an internal DSL). Naturally, properties of the latter extend to properties of the former for internal DSL. In this chapter, these four basic types of DSL composition are reviewed with emphasis on DjDSL's support for these DSL compositions. Language and, more specifically, DSL composition must be tackled at different levels of DSL definition and DSL processing. The emphasis in this chapter is on the syntax-level composition, constrained by other concerns of composition. Especially, language-model composition was covered in terms of collaboration-based designs in Sect. 3.2.3 as a prerequisite. DSL composition at the notational level does not only raise its genuine challenges, but also reveals subtle and non-trivial interactions with the other composition dimensions (e.g., language models, context conditions). Furthermore, this chapter has the firm prerequisite that the DSL definition artifacts and syntaxes subjected to a composition are all realized using DjDSL as the DSL development system and NX/Tcl as the host language.

Textual-syntax design in DjDSL unifies commonly separated approaches of providing an external DSL syntax or of providing an internal DSL syntax. Each DSL project in DjDSL offers an (internal) NX/Tcl syntax *free house*. This syntax can be used for the direct instantiation of a language model, for instance. In addition, further internal syntaxes (for indirect instantiation) or external syntaxes can be implemented (see also Fig. 5.1). All syntaxes, whether internal or external, are based on a common core of language model, variability model, and contracts. In addition, internal and external syntaxes can be implemented and used side-by-side in a DSL

© Springer Nature Switzerland AG 2020

S. Sobernig, *Variable Domain-specific Software Languages with DjDSL*,
https://doi.org/10.1007/978-3-030-42152-6_5

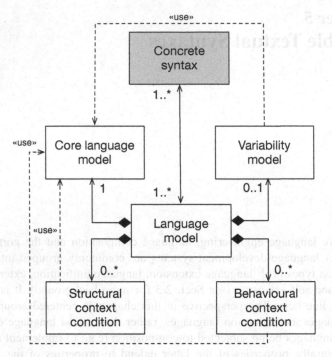

Fig. 5.1 A language model defined in DjDSL serves as a primary abstract syntax behind one or several alternative concrete syntaxes. A concrete syntax, whether designed and implemented as internal or external syntax, can act as the frontend to one or several language models, if needed

script to form a *mixed* DSL.[1] Section 5.1 introduces how additional internal DSL can be designed, implemented, and managed to realize DSL compositions. Section 5.2 demonstrates how external textual syntaxes can be designed and implemented using an advanced grammar-based parsing infrastructure unique to DjDSL.

5.1   Internal DSL: Pattern-Based Variability Implementation Techniques

Software patterns play an important role as variability implementation techniques for DSL product lines, as they do for software product lines in more general [4]. This is mainly because they are readily applicable to implementations in (object-oriented) host languages and because they genuinely document ways of implementing runtime variability using proven solutions [9]. The latter is decisive when implementing variable internal DSL that can be composed with the host language, other DSL, or

---

[1]Chapter 6 shows DjDSL in action for defining a mixed DSL over several iterations. DjDSL shares this capacity of combining and of mixing internal and external syntaxes in a complementary manner with closely related and advanced DSL development systems, for example, Frag [70].

DSL extensions in a disciplined manner. In Sect. 2.4, the necessary background on software patterns for implementing variability is provided. Relevant software patterns and pattern languages describe recurring problems and solutions for architecting a DSL (architectural patterns), for designing the main DSL components and their interactions (language and DSL patterns), and for implementing the internals of the DSL components (design patterns and idioms).

Pattern-based approaches apply to and are equally relevant to developing external DSL [19] and their internals. However, their role for developing internal DSL based on and embedding with a host language, render them more prominent in design-decision making for internal DSL. The following patterns are relevant for architecting, designing, and implementing composable *internal* DSL for different language-composition scenarios. In subsequent sections, it will be shown that they also help move between internal and external DSL (syntaxes) for a given implementation. It will also be shown that both, internal and external, syntaxes in front of a single language model can be realized using DjDSL. The emphasis will be on mitigating issues pertaining to conventional (design) pattern implementations. These include a) examples of abstraction mismatches (object schizophrenia and design fragmentation), the preplanning problem, and the traceability problem [9, Section 7.4.6]. NX, its predecessor XOTcl [38], and their offspring (Frag [70], TclOO) allow for addressing these deficiencies by providing dedicated language-level support to implement design patterns, their underlying object compositions, and object interactions. These include composition filters [40], decorator mix-ins [39], and means of runtime metaprogramming.

The structure and the behavior of internal-syntax processing in DjDSL follow from applying patterns from different pattern collections and pattern languages [7]. These include architectural design patterns (e.g., INTERPRETER [5]), software-language design patterns (e.g., EXPRESSION BUILDER [19] and MESSAGE REDI-RECTOR [69]), general OO design patterns (e.g., CHAIN OF RESPONSIBILITY [20]), and implementation-level ones (e.g., abstract syntax representation patterns [43] and PROPERTY LIST [52]). In this section, in Tables 5.1, 5.2, and 5.3, thumbnail descriptions of the relevant patterns are provided.

Prerequisites
DjDSL comes with an object-oriented framework for implementing BUILDERS in front of its language models: djdsl::dada. These BUILDERS allow for reusing the Tcl host syntax in a customizable and controlled manner to define internal DSL syntaxes. By reusing the Tcl syntaxes,[2] the DSL developer benefits from generic and reusable syntax elements. For instance, Tcl's command notation might already match some domain requirements.[3] Also, Tcl comments can be used as-is, as well as character escaping and character setting. To cover more deviating

---

[2]The use of the plural is intentional. Tcl offers two complementary syntaxes and their corresponding parsers. The second features infix expressions. See Tcl's expr command.

[3]Imagine the example of the syntax-level requirement to separate DSL statements using either delimiter characters, such as semi-colons, and/ or using newline separators. Both are provided by Tcl's native syntax, while realizing them as external DSL syntax involves implementing grammar or parser carefully, to address common problem cases. See [19, p. 333] for some background.

Table 5.1 Thumbnail descriptions of relevant patterns for syntax processing for *internal DSL syntaxes*; see Fig. 5.2 for an overview of their relationships

Pattern	Problem	Solution
GOF BUILDER [20, p. 97]	Building a structure from different parts (objects) by connecting them is not trivial (e.g., it depends on the data types of the various parts). In addition, different structures (e.g., representation) should be built from the same set of parts	Separate the building logic of the structure (e.g., an object graph) from the parts under composition into a dedicated builder entity
EXPRESSION BUILDER [19, p. 343]	The behavior to instantiate a language model and to process a DSL script are implemented by the same (model) classes	Separate instantiation and DSL syntax processing into separate, but closely linked (builder vs. model) objects
SEMANTIC MODEL [19, p. 159], a.k.a. language model, domain model	A primary representation of a DSL script is derived from the concrete syntax (concrete-syntax graph or tree), which is not necessarily suited for processing the DSL script	Provide an abstracted (in-memory) representation of a DSL script that is very close to the purpose of processing of the DSL script (its application domain)
DYNAMIC RECEPTION [19, p. 427]	The receiver of an invocation request (e.g., a specific builder) does not provide a method implementation to process the DSL invocation	Trap and handle (DSL) invocations to builder objects without having defined corresponding methods using built-in message interception or redirection techniques
MESSAGE REDIRECTOR [69]	(DSL) Clients requesting a certain behavior (e.g., by sending messages) and (host-language) providers offering the behavior implementation are not (meant to be) known directly to each other (e.g., to realize dynamic method dispatch)	Provide for redirecting (DSL) invocations to host-language objects implementing the invocation behavior
PROXY [20, p. 207]	The receiver of a message (e.g., a specific builder) does not provide a method implementation to process the message; or the actual provider is not available in a given invocation context	Provide a placeholder object for another one to manage access to it

notation requirements, that can still be mapped to Tcl's syntaxes, TEMPLATED GENERATION [19, p. 539] of Tcl from DSL scripts[4] and forms of TEXTUAL POLISHING [19, p. 477] of DSL scripts can be realized.[5] In addition, the DSL scripts can be subjected to syntax processing and evaluation in sandboxed interpreters. If a domain-specific syntax clearly deviates from Tcl's, then djdsl::dada offers support for internal DSL patterns to shape a derived syntax or switch to an alternative infix notation.

---

[4]For example, by using the Tcl command subst.

[5]For example, by using the built-in regular-expression engine via the Tcl command regsub.

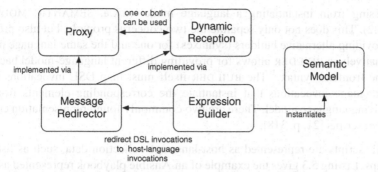

Fig. 5.2 An overview of the pattern relationships specific to the EXPRESSION BUILDER pattern; for brevity, throughout this section, it is referred to as BUILDER; see Table 5.1 for brief pattern descriptions

A sandboxed interpreter (referred to as a *safe* interpreter in Tcl) has restricted capabilities (e.g., removed or hidden base commands) as well as restricted I/O facilities; or none at all. Sandboxed interpreters can be tightly monitored by a master interpreter as their children (slaves), by indirecting invocations between the two, by explicitly sharing I/O resources, or by invoking otherwise hidden commands in the slave context from the master. Master and slaves do not share any state, unless the state becomes replicated from one into the other explicitly.[6]

DjDSL provides a minimal and object-oriented API around these basic facilities (Tcl syntaxes, sandbox interpreter). In addition, it aims at defining two fundamental protocols in support of a DSL developer:

- The *building protocol* allows for implementing EXPRESSION BUILDERS (see Table 5.1) and internal DSL syntaxes based on established patterns for realizing internal DSL syntaxes, such as OBJECT SCOPING and METHOD CHAINING. For this, DjDSL packages selected NX-specific implementation idioms to realize these internal DSL patterns. The aim is also to minimize the effort of implementing a given BUILDER for a domain-specific syntax.
- The *chaining protocol* relates different EXPRESSION BUILDERS to realize syntax-level DSL extension, DSL unification, DSL extension composition, and DSL self-extension.

Chaining will be elaborated on in the subsequent sections. For the remainder in this paragraph, the basic protocol for BUILDERS is at spot.

Builders

At its core, internal-syntax processing is provided by an EXPRESSION BUILDER (BUILDER, hereafter, for brevity; see Fig. 5.2). A BUILDER separates syntax

---

[6]Nadkarni [37, Chapter 20] and Ousterhout and Jones [42, Section 15.11] provide overviews of managing nested Tcl interpreters and the corresponding use of the interp command.

processing from instantiating a language model (a.k.a. SEMANTIC MODEL in
Fig. 5.2). This does not only separate the two concerns properly, but also provides
for providing alternative builders (syntaxes) for one and the same language model.
Alternatively, a BUILDER allows for providing different language-model backends
for one frontend syntax.[7] The BUILDER itself must map DSL invocations to the
host-language invocations that instantiate the corresponding elements from the
underlying language model. There are two commonly found representation choices
for DSL scripts [21, p. 318]:

* DSL scripts are represented as host-language collection data, such as lists and
  maps. Listing 5.3 gives the example of an Ansible playbook represented as a Tcl
  list of lists.
* DSL scripts are represented as a host-language program. Listing 5.5 shows a
  representation of the same Ansible playbook as a Tcl script with nested function
  calls.

For the second case, mappings between different invocation abstractions may
be applicable. In case of the internal DSL being realized based on messages and
methods exchanged between objects (around an object-oriented or "fluent" API),
a mapping is established between DSL messages and host-language messages. For
DjDSL, due to the use of dedicated nested interpreters, the mapped abstractions
are command evaluations at the DSL end and NX messages at the host-language
end. In principle, different invocation abstractions can also be supported. This can
be achieved using intermediary representations such as commands in a COMMAND
LANGUAGE [69]. For the purpose of representing and processing DSL scripts in
terms of native host-language data structures, a number of techniques are applicable
directly in DjDSL based on Tcl as host language. These include LITERAL LIST [19]
and LITERAL MAP [19]. For DSL scripts as host (Tcl) scripts, a BUILDER uses a
MESSAGE REDIRECTOR (see Fig. 5.2). A MESSAGE REDIRECTOR can be realized
by a number of basic language-level techniques (e.g., DYNAMIC RECEPTION via
unknown handlers), advanced ones (e.g., DYNAMIC RECEPTION via composition
filters or traces), or design-level techniques (e.g., design patterns such as PROXY).
In what follows, a concrete example of providing a BUILDER plus MESSAGE
REDIRECTOR is given.

In DjDSL, BUILDERS for interpreted DSL scripts can be implemented as pairings
of dada::Builder and their related dada::Interp (see Fig. 5.4).

dada::Builder provides common behavior and a common method signature
to all builders in DjDSL. A DSL developer starts by defining a subclass of

---

[7]Note that the running examples in this section feature a single BUILDER class per language
model (e.g., BaseGraphBuilder for Graphs::Graph). The design-decision space for BUILDER,
however, involves providing distinct builders even for one language model or one collaboration
(e.g., a builder for the graph, one for edges). Having separate builders for different language-
model entities allows for separating the concern of collecting instantiation data from processing
the internal syntax and the concern of actually running the instantiation. This can be particularly
convenient to avoid issues of circular initialization [56], for instance. See also [19, p. 343] for a
discussion and examples.

Lst. 5.3 An exemplary
Ansible playbook using a
LITERAL LIST [19]
internal-syntax style, that is,
the DSL notation
representation is overlaid
entirely on native Tcl lists and
processed as such (no script
evaluation is involved)

```
1  play {
2    hosts        webservers
3    remote_user admin
4    task {
5      name    "is webserver running?"
6      service {
7        name  http
8        state started}}}
9  play {
10   hosts databases
11   remote_user admin
12   task {
13     name "is postgresql at the
             latest version?"
14     yum  {
15       name  postgresql
16       state latest}}}
```

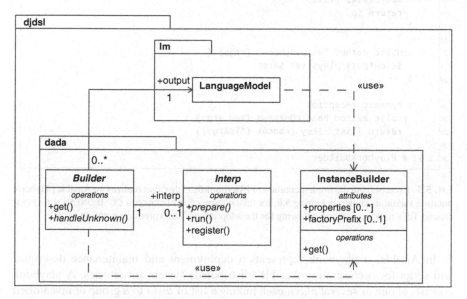

Fig. 5.4 Overview of main structural elements and relationships that form the BUILDER framework djdsl::dada; the collaboration between Builder and Interp realizes a variant of
EXPRESSION BUILDERS, InstanceBuilder serves as CONSTRUCTION BUILDERS and placeholders [56] for different scopes; see Tables 5.1, 5.2, and 5.3 for relevant pattern descriptions

dada::Builder to host an internal-syntax implementation. Optionally, the builder
can be assigned a particular dada::Interp. The latter is responsible for hosting a
DSL script for evaluation and redirecting calls to the builder object.

Consider the example of the PlaybookBuilder in Listing 5.5. It exemplifies
the use of djdsl::dada to implement a notational variant of the Ansible playbook
DSL. The notation snippet supported by this builder is depicted in Listing 5.6.

```
 1   nx::Class create PlaybookBuilder -superclasses Builder {
 2
 3      # entry point
 4      :public method get {script} {
 5        set script [string cat "playbook" "(" $script ")"]
 6        next [list $script]
 7      }
 8
 9      # invocation handlers
10      :variable tasks [list]
11      :public method "<- task" {args} {
12        lappend :tasks [${:output} new task {*}[concat {*}$args]]
13        return
14      }
15
16      :public method "<- play" {args} {
17        set p [${:output} new play -tasks ${:tasks} {*}[concat {*}$args]]
18        set :tasks [list]
19        return $p
20      }
21
22      :public method "<- playbook" {args} {
23        ${:output} plays set $args
24      }
25
26      # dynamic reception
27      :public method handleUnknown {key args} {
28        return [list -$key [concat {*}$args]]
29      }
30   }; # PlaybookBuilder
```

Lst. 5.5 Excerpt from the implementation of `PlaybookBuilder` that realizes an Ansible playbook notation variant as shown in Listing 5.6; for this, it reuses `ExprInterp`, a COMPONENT WRAPPER around Tcl's interp command, allowing for the adoption of Tcl expression notation (expr)

In Ansible, a playbook represents a deployment and maintenance descriptor and script for orchestrating Ansible (distributed) system inventories. A playbook consists of one or several *plays*, each linking a list of *tasks* to a group of inventoried systems or system groups called *hosts* ("webservers", "databases" in Listing 5.6). A task itself defines a call to an Ansible module, such as *service* to check the deployment status of a service application or *yum*, a package manager, to update installations in a single batch on an array of systems.

> **Ansible**
>
> The Ansible playbook DSL is representative for different purposes of a DSL (structural modeling, generation, direct interpretation). In addition, it is also featured in research projects on DSL composition. For example, Johanson and

(continued)

Hasselbring [24] report on combining Ansible playbooks and a DSL to model marine ecosystems driving scientific simulation workflows.

On line 1 of Listing 5.5, the `builder` subclass `PlaybookBuilder` is defined. When instantiated, the builder references a concrete `Interp` (`ExprInterp`) and an instance of the language model to become populated: `Ansible::Playbook`. An `Interp` serves as COMPONENT WRAPPER around Tcl's interpreter commands and is responsible to execute a DSL script in a sealed and controlled environment. The `ExprInterp` is a specialization that wraps around a Tcl interpreter that only accepts Tcl's expression notation. The method `get` (line 4) is the entry point for DSL script evaluation. The main playbook keywords (`play`, `task`) map to DSL invocation handlers implemented as an NX method ensemble. A method ensemble hosts collections of related methods (`play`, `task`) under common name prefixes (`<-`), behaving like ordinary methods. In DjDSL, any method in the `<-` ensemble is automatically registered with the underlying interpreter (via `Interp`) to redirect DSL invocations to these invocation handlers (lines 10–24). These explicitly registered handlers appear as first-class commands in the nested interpreter.

As such, this method ensemble contributes to realizing a PROXY of the builder, managing the access to the builder internals during execution of the DSL script (see also Fig. 5.2). Any DSL invocations not matched by these handler methods are processed via DYNAMIC RECEPTION. The refinable method `handleUnknown` is automatically registered with the underlying interpreter to redirect any unknown calls to the builder and funnel them into this method (or its refinements). In this example, the key-value elements of a playbook (e.g., task names, content of modules) are captured and stored this way with the surrounding play or task objects. With this, the example of `PlaybookBuilder` combines the use of PROXY

Lst. 5.6 An exemplary Ansible playbook using a NESTED FUNCTION internal-syntax style

```
1  play(
2    hosts("webservers"),
3    remote_user("admin"),
4    task(
5      name("is webserver running?"),
6      service(
7        name("http"),
8        state("started")))),
9  play(
10    hosts("databases"),
11    remote_user("admin"),
12    task(
13      name("is postgresql at the
              latest version?"),
14      yum(
15        name("postgresql"),
16        state("latest")
17        )))
```

Fig. 5.7 An overview of the
relationships between
BUILDER, CONSTRUCTION
BUILDER, and PROPERTY
LIST; see Table 5.2 for brief
pattern descriptions

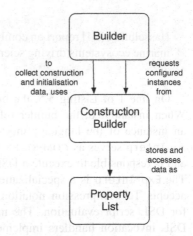

and DYNAMIC RECEPTION to implement the required MESSAGE REDIRECTOR for
a BUILDER (see also Fig. 5.2).

A third component of djdsl::dada is InstanceBuilder (see Fig. 5.4).
This class helps realize different types of CONSTRUCTION BUILDERS for the
scope of syntax processing in DjDSL. A CONSTRUCTION BUILDER provides for
intermediary objects to collect the data required to call a factory, to instantiate
a class, or to obtain a language-model element from within a BUILDER in an
incremental fashion (see Fig. 5.7). This allows for the construction data to be
gathered as it becomes available during DSL script processing through a uniform
programming model. In addition, these intermediaries also help avoid hoarding
data in an ad hoc manner for each and every BUILDER and avoid re-initializing
or cloning already initialized objects to feed them additional initialization data. In
addition, an InstanceBuilder allows for performing the actual instantiation on
request, in a deferred manner, via the factory method get (see Fig. 5.4).

Data collection is organized through a PROPERTY LIST [52] attached to an
InstanceBuilder. The PROPERTY LIST manages a generic and extensible set of
properties to become the initial state of any object commissioned for instantiation
with the CONSTRUCTION BUILDER by the BUILDER. The BUILDER or other
clients may access the properties. Properties may even be added or removed at
runtime. InstanceBuilders can be parametrized by Tcl command prefixes to
support different instantiation procedures, including NX classes or DjDSL language
models. Moreover, they can be used to produce multiple instantiations of a given
class having an identical initialization state.

A companion tutorial covers NX-based and DjDSL-based implementation
techniques for frequently adopted internal DSL syntax patterns, for example,
OBJECT SCOPING and METHOD CHAINING.[8] Against the background of the
("building") protocol for processing internal DSL syntaxes into DjDSL language

---

[8]This tutorial is contained by the DjDSL distribution and is separately accessible.

Table 5.2 Thumbnail descriptions of relevant patterns for `InstanceBuilder`; see also Fig. 5.7

Pattern	Problem	Solution
CONSTRUCTION BUILDER [19, p. 179]	The data to construct a model element is not completely or yet available at the time of instantiating the model class	Have an intermediary object collect incrementally the construction data, as it becomes available during DSL script processing, and have it perform the instantiation on (deferred) request
PROPERTY LIST [52]	A component's or object's state is not known in advance. The state must be modifiable and introspectable by clients at runtime	Provide a data structure (collection) owned by the component or object that manages additional properties and their values that serve as a variable extension to its state. The data structure allows for adding, removing, and introspecting on the extended state

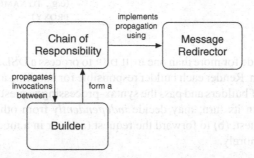

Fig. 5.8 An internal DSL can be extended by one or several others using a structure of BUILDERS connected as a CHAIN OF RESPONSIBILITY. Each BUILDER is responsible for building up the different portions of the (now combined) language model (SEMANTIC MODEL). Refer to Table 5.3 for brief pattern descriptions

models using `Builder` and `Interp` (see also Fig. 5.4), the following four sections shift focus: How to realize the four types of syntax-level DSL composition (extension) based on DjDSL's builders?

Chaining Builders

To realize syntax-level DSL compositions (extension, unification, extension composition, and self-extension), DjDSL implements a variant of the CHAIN OF BUILDERS pattern [59].CHAIN OF BUILDERS is a language-implementation pattern to implement variable internal DSL syntaxes by combining the CHAIN OF RESPONSIBILITY andEXPRESSION BUILDER patterns (again, BUILDER hereafter):

- *Problem*: The BUILDER must be open to extension, in a stepwise manner and without the need for preplanning. Client code to the DSL sub-system, as well as the base BUILDER must not be affected by the unplanned syntax extensions.

Table 5.3 Thumbnail descriptions of relevant patterns for internal DSL extension; see also Fig. 5.8

Pattern	Problem	Solution
CHAIN OF RESPONSI-BILITY [20, p. 223]	The client sending a message does not know the actual provider (e.g., the responsible builder) of the requested behavior	Give more than one (builder) object the chance to act as a provider of the syntax-processing behavior
EXPRESSION BUILDER [19, p. 343]	The behavior to instantiate a language model and to process a DSL script are implemented by the same (model) classes	Separate instantiation and DSL syntax processing into separate, but closely linked (builder vs. model) objects; but also into separate builders for each syntax variant
MESSAGE REDIRECTOR [69]	How to represent DSL invocations and how to implement their propagation between chained BUILDERS?	Provide for redirecting (DSL) invocations from one builder object to another by a built-in or a custom redirection mechanism (e.g., DYNAMIC RECEPTION or a PROXY)

- *Solution*: Provide for more than one BUILDER to process a DSL syntax element or DSL invocation. Render each builder responsible for handling a syntax extension. Form a chain of builders and pass the syntax-processing requests along this chain. Each builder, in its turn, may decide *independently* from other builders (a) to handle the request, (b) to forward the request (as-is or in a modified manner), or (c) to drop it entirely.

In such a CHAIN OF BUILDERS, more than one BUILDER may handle a (DSL) processing request sent by a client. To the client, the BUILDER ultimately responsible is not known beforehand. Each refining BUILDER acts as a potential MESSAGE REDIRECTOR (see Fig. 5.8). The CHAIN OF BUILDERS can be implemented using different host-language environments for internal DSL such as Java [59]. In the following, the emphasis is on DjDSL's implementation of this pattern. This implementation uses decorator mixins [71] as provided by NX/Tcl.

5.1.1   DSL Extension

A DSL developer composes a base language with a language extension. A language extension is an incomplete language fragment which depends directly on the base language for completion (in terms of the concrete syntax, the abstract syntax, and the behaviors; [16]). DSL extensions can be a product of DSL evolution [35]. Consider the running example of a family of graph-modeling languages. The base language is represented by the DjDSL language model Graphs::Graph. A DSL extension, from the perspective of its abstract syntax, is any collaborations (e.g., weighted) that can enter a composition with Graphs::Graph. It is obvious that weighted would not be

Lst. 5.9 A definition of an undirected graph using DOT notation, implemented as an internal DSL syntax in DjDSL in front of the language model defined in Sect. 3.2.3; the corresponding DOT plot is shown in Fig. 5.10 (on the left)

```
1   graph {
2      // node definitions
3      "1st Edition";
4      "2nd Edition";
5      "3rd Edition";
6      // edge definitions
7      "1st Edition" -- "2nd Edition";
8      "2nd Edition" -- "3rd Edition";
9   }
```

complete and operative without being first composed into a base language. From the concrete-syntax perspective of an internal DSL, both language-model assets (base language-model and extension collaboration) provide their own BUILDERS.

Recall that a BUILDER [19, p. 343] is the place to define the syntax-processing logic for an internal DSL. The main motivation is to clearly separate it from the construction or instantiation logic of the underlying language model. Under DSL extension, the dependency relationship between the composable language-model elements (collaborations) will be reflected in a dependency between the corresponding BUILDERS.

A DOT Language
Consider the concrete-syntax example in Listing 5.9 that covers for abstract syntax elements provided by the base language-model Graphs::Graph. The concrete syntax is inspired by the DOT notation fuelling the Graphviz tool chain. Emphasis in this example is on DOT node and edge statements. When processed, the DSL snippet in Listing 5.9 is turned into an instantiation of Graphs::Graph, containing three nodes (labeled 1st Edition, 2nd Edition, and 3rd Edition) and two undirected edges (Fig. 5.10).

In the running example, the BUILDER implements a MESSAGE REDIRECTOR using DYNAMIC RECEPTION via unknown handlers to process DSL invocations.[9] Unknown handlers are a fit to the requirement that DOT node definitions and edge definitions start by a node identifier. Each node and each edge definition is so trapped by the unknown handler, given that there are no corresponding (Tcl) commands 1st Edition, etc., defined.[10] The unknown handler, in turn, implements a straightforward transformation scheme into instantiation calls based on the arity of values trapped by the unknown handler. An arity of one maps to a node definition, while an arity of three maps to an edge definition. The latter is restricted to certain literal strings as second argument (e.g., - or ->). On these grounds, the transformation scheme can be extended to support additional DOT syntax, e.g., the shortcut notation for multiple edges sourced by one node.

---

[9]DjDSL combines different NX/Tcl unknown handlers (per-object, per-ensemble, per-namespace) in an original way to implement a robust type of DYNAMIC RECEPTION.

[10]This is guaranteed by having this BUILDER use an empty Tcl interpreter via EmptyInterp.

Fig. 5.10 DOT
visualizations produced
directly from the snippets in
Listing 5.9 (on the left) and in
Listing 5.11 (on the right)

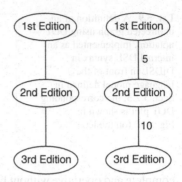

Lst. 5.11 An extended
definition of an undirected
graph using DOT notation
plus weight attributes,
implemented as an internal
DSL syntax using DSL
extension via chained
BUILDERS

```
1  graph {
2    // node definitions
3    "1st Edition";
4    "2nd Edition";
5    "3rd Edition";
6    // edge definitions
7    "1st Edition" -- "2nd Edition" [weight = 5];
8    "2nd Edition" -- "3rd Edition" [weight = 10];
9  }
```

An Extended DOT Notation

Under DSL extension, for example, when extending graphs to include weight
attributes, the notation must be extended accordingly to support (DOT) attribute
statements. Listing 5.11 exhibits the resulting snippet: Edge definitions can carry
attribute statements in-between brackets defining edge weights of 5 and 10,
respectively (see lines 7 and 8 in Listing 5.11). The resulting graph is rendered
in Fig. 5.10 (on the right-hand side). The extended syntax could be implemented
by cloning and enriching the original BUILDER. Preferably, the existing BUILDER
becomes rather reused in an unmodified manner. The objective is the latter. In line
with providing multiple BUILDERS for parts of the same language model, DjDSL
allows for providing additional BUILDERS that link to the original (base) BUILDER
and that process a syntax increment solely. For this purpose, the BUILDERS under
composition form a CHAIN OF RESPONSIBILITY in DjDSL (hence: *chaining protocol*; see also Fig. 5.8). In a CHAIN OF RESPONSIBILITY,more than one BUILDER
may handle a (DSL) message sent by a client and the responsible BUILDER is not
known beforehand to the client. When the chain is managed dynamically, this is
not even known to the chained BUILDERS themselves. Each acts as a MESSAGE
REDIRECTOR [5] of invocation messages. The class diagram in Fig. 5.12 shows
a structural overview of a CHAIN OF RESPONSIBILITY between BUILDERS (on
the right). An abstracted interaction protocol between chained BUILDER objects is
depicted on the left.

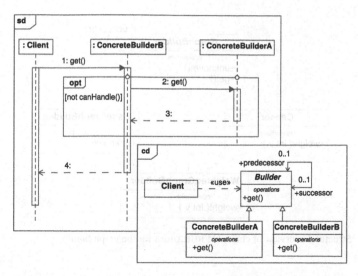

Fig. 5.12 Structural and behavioral overview of a CHAIN OF RESPONSIBILITY between BUILDERS; adapted from [20, p. 223]

From a bird's eye perspective, a BUILDER can maintain a forward reference to a successor BUILDER. Therefore, over several forward references, they form a forward-linked list. A chain of succeeding BUILDER ends with the last BUILDER having an empty `successor` property (see Fig. 5.12, on the left). Maintaining backward references to predecessors might also be necessary (e.g., to allow a kind of call delegation despite changing self-references). The shared BUILDER superclass has a double role: It contracts an object-type to DSL clients, in particular offering a `get` method for DSL scripts. This operation promises as a result an instantiation of the language model. Internally, the `get` operation of the BUILDER superclass realizes the core responsibilities of the BUILDER. These are message redirection and managing the life cycle of a DSL-specific interpreter. In addition, it is responsible for the propagation logic between BUILDERS. DSL invocations must be propagated between predecessor and successor `builders`, if needed. The propagation logic establishes whether to process a DSL script (or fragments of it) locally, with the currently responsible `ConcreteBuilder`, or to forward the script to the successor, if any. This generic decision condition is represented by the `opt` fragment's guard of Fig. 5.12 (on the left). The order of chaining BUILDERS will correspond to the composition order of the collaborations in a given DjDSL composition (Fig. 5.13).

As for the running example, the chain of builders corresponds to the following pairing: (`WeightedGraphBuilder`, `BaseGraphBuilder`). In the interaction depicted in Fig. 5.14, this is realized as the overall ordering between call messages between instances of the two classes. An instantiation of `WeightedGraphBuilder`, specific for the `weighted` collaboration, processes the DSL script shown in Listing 5.11 first. This is to trap the attribute statements (see message 2). The unknown handler (message 3) will then forward any other invocations originat-

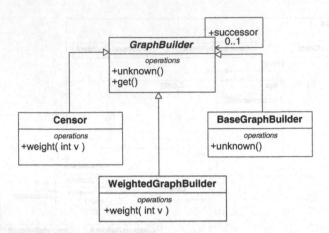

Fig. 5.13 Structural overview of chainable BUILDERS for the graph family

ing from the script to the successor (message 4). Then, an instantiation of the
BaseGraphBuilder is responsible for the pre-processed script for finalization. Its
unknown handler will not forward anymore but will rather realize the final DSL to
host-language mapping (see message 5 in Fig. 5.14).

Taking Responsibility
Conceptually, each BUILDER in a chain is responsible for deciding on whether
to process on its own or on whether to forward a DSL script (element). At
the implementation level, this conceptual canHandle checkpoint (see Fig. 5.12,
on the right) can be realized explicitly or implicitly. DYNAMIC RECEPTION is
one technique to implement the indirection between DSL and host language in
a BUILDER (see above). DYNAMIC RECEPTION is also a candidate to operate
the CHAIN OF RESPONSIBILITY and to conditionally propagate DSL invocations
between different BUILDERS. The propagation condition depends on the kind of
DYNAMIC RECEPTION being used. When DYNAMIC RECEPTION is implemented
using unknown handlers, as in DjDSL, then every chained BUILDER can claim
responsibility for a DSL invocation by implementing a corresponding method. In
this sense, propagation is implemented implicitly because the unknown handler
will only see unhandled invocations. Any message not matched by a method
implementation is then forwarded to the successor BUILDER. The BUILDER at the
tail has then to deal with the ultimately unknown DSL invocations, or report a syntax
failure. A key characteristic of a CHAIN OF RESPONSIBILITY is that, for a DSL
client, it is not observable whether the DSL script submitted for processing contains
such invalid (unhandled) DSL syntax elements. This depends on the processing
capabilities of each BUILDER and the assembly of the chain.

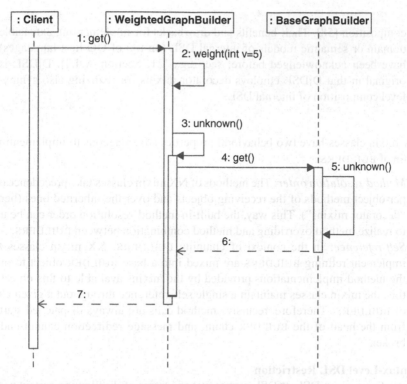

Fig. 5.14 Interaction overview of chainable BUILDERS for the graph family

Chaining Implementation in DjDSL

So far, chaining BUILDERS based on a CHAIN OF RESPONSIBILITY has been considered in terms of a generic object-oriented implementation, with method forwarding between distinct BUILDER objects. This is because the focus is on the design-decision level. On top, this generic structure and behavior can be ported to different host languages. The downside of a conventional CHAIN OF RESPONSI-BILITY implementation, however, are the issues of certain abstraction mismatches such as object schizophrenia. This can lead to broken message redirection across a chain of BUILDERS. DjDSL and its BUILDER framework djdsl::dada, therefore, leverage an alternative implementation technique. BUILDERS are realized as NX classes. As such, they can act as *decorator mixins* for other BUILDERS.

Decorator Mixins

Mixins and their different flavors (abstract subclasses, traits, decorator mixins) are versatile implementation techniques for object-oriented software

(continued)

composition [58]. Their benefits and drawbacks for implementing extensible domain or semantic models of internal DSL (on top of OO host languages) have been acknowledged before; see, e.g., [21, Section A.4.2]. DjDSL is original in that DjDSL employs decorator mixins for realizing also syntax-level composition of internal DSL.

NX mixin classes have two behavioral properties advantageous to implementing a chain of BUILDERS:

1. *Method-resolution order*: The methods of NX mixin classes take precedence over per-object methods of the receiving objects and over the inherited ones (hence: "decorator mixins"). This way, the built-in method-resolution order can be used to realize method overriding and method combination between BUILDERS.
2. *Self-reference*: In the context of chaining BUILDERS, NX mixin classes that implement refining BUILDERS are mixed into a base BUILDER object to make the method implementations provided by the mixins available to this object. In this, the mixin classes maintain a single self-reference throughout a given chain of BUILDERS. Therefore, recursive method calls are always dispatched starting from the head of the BUILDER chain; and message redirection cannot end up broken.

Syntax-Level DSL Restriction

Restricting a given DSL or DSL composition in terms of disallowing certain means of expression can become necessary for educational purposes [16] or as a form of language specialization in its own right [61, Section 4.6]. DSL restriction has been considered a variant of DSL extension, in the sense that a DSL extension imposes additional restrictions on the abstract syntax of the base DSL or DSL composition, or on transformations based on the abstract syntax (e.g., during validation or platform integration; see [16]). At the level of concrete syntax, equivalently, restricting an internal DSL can be realized by prepending special-purpose BUILDERS at the chain's head. Preceding BUILDERS can consume then restricted DSL invocations. The consuming BUILDER can either report the disallowed syntax element or discard it silently, depending on the restriction scenario. This way, no corresponding abstract syntax elements end up in the language-model instantiations, to begin with. This should then be complemented by restrictions implemented at later processing phases [16].

As an example, the BUILDER class `Censor` in Fig. 5.13 can be prepended to precede `WeightedGraphBuilder`. Its handler method for weight attributes consumes and discards the matched attribute statements. This is achieved by effectively overriding the method `weight` early in the chain of BUILDERS.[11]

---

[11] In DjDSL and the mixin-based implementation of BUILDER chaining, this is effectively achieved by conventional method overriding w/o super-reference call.

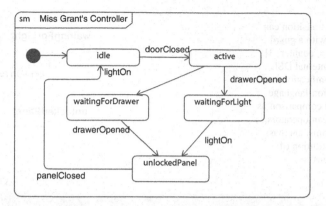

Fig. 5.15 A UML state machine of "Miss Grant's Controller" based on Figure 1.1 in Fowler [19]

5.1.2   DSL Unification

When two or more, otherwise freestanding and independent DSL are composed, this is referred to as *language unification*. Regarding abstract syntax composition, this refers to two or more language models (or composed language models) becoming subjected to composition. Unification further assumes that the composed language fragments are allowed, if needed, to interact with each other. DSL unification also requires that the composed DSL remain intact and unmodified under composition. Any patch code must be orthogonal to the DSL implementations. Such unification is supported by DjDSL's language models (see Sect. 3.2.3).

From the perspective of concrete-syntax composition, when all DSL under composition are realized as internal DSL based on DjDSL, the basics of DSL extension apply also for unification. However, rather than aligning only processing of a composed DSL syntax (e.g., using some form of MESSAGE REDIRECTOR), bidirectional interactions, or even a managed shared state, might be required on top. A pattern-based approach must, therefore, address these challenges inherent to behavioral language integration by rendering known solutions to these problems available to the DSL developer.

To guide the discussion, this subsection adopts the following storyline on unification: Two separately developed DSL are considered. These are a Boolean and Comparison Expression Language (such as LEA from Sect. 1.4) and a State-Machine Definition Language (SMDL) capable of modeling one of the variants of "Miss Grant's Controller" introduced by Fowler [19, p. 4]. See Fig. 5.15.

Fig. 5.16 A transition can
be equipped with a guard
expression: [= counter 3].
The second internal DSL
to enter the unification is a
mini-expression language
with selected comparison as
well as Boolean operators,
numerical atoms, and basic
variable substitution (in
prefix notation)

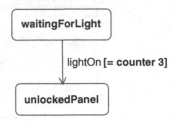

> **Miss Grant's Controller**
> Miss Grant is told to maintain a secret compartment in her bedroom. This
> compartment requires a particular sequence of actions from her side to
> become unlocked for her to open. The corresponding state-machine models
> the modal behavior of the software-based compartment controller, reacting
> to Miss Grant's input actions [19, Section 1.1.1]. This example has been
> widely adopted to demonstrate and contrast *by example* DSL development
> environments (see, e.g., [70]).

These two DSL, fully functional and usable in their own rights, become unified to
implement *guarded transitions*. A guarded transition is a transition that is annotated
by a guard expression and whose firing is controlled by the prior evaluation of the
attached guard expression. If the guard is evaluated to true at that time, the transition
is enabled, otherwise, it is disabled and will not fire. Guarded transitions can be used
to model transitions that are conditional on the event or trigger history maintained
by the state machine.

In Fig. 5.16, the transition potentially triggered by lightOn events is only
enacted when this event type has been encountered three times. The state variable
counter forms part of a state context maintained and passed throughout the state-
machine implementation.

The following, not uncommon bidirectional interactions must be supported:

• The guard expressions and their variable expressions must bind to the values of
  state variables, as provided by a state context, for instance. This is required to
  express stateful guard expressions.
• The state-machine implementations must be able to submit guard expressions
  for evaluation on event occurrence (otherwise opaque to them) and obtain the
  evaluation result to decide on whether to fire a transition or not.
• The so modeled controller is tested using a software simulator of the controlled
  device that takes (user) actions and emits events in response to trigger state transitions. Transition guards must be considered before send actions (commands) to
  the simulator.

Table 5.4 A thumbnail descriptions of relevant patterns for internal DSL implementation and extension

Pattern	Problem	Solution
METHOD CHAINING [19, p. 343]	A basic DSL expression can consist of several clauses that are evaluated, possibly in arbitrary order, when invoking the DSL expression	BUILDER methods implement each possible expression clause. To chain up clause invocations, each preceding clause returns the BUILDER as a receiver of the message resulting from the subsequent clause call
OBJECT SCOPING [19, p. 385]	DSL invocations are processed or redirected in a global invocation environment (e.g., a global namespace). Invocations risk polluting or interacting with this environment in unforeseen ways	Process and evaluate a DSL script in the context of a dedicated object, such as a BUILDER, a controlled environment
LITERAL LIST [19, p. 417]	A (nested structure of) DSL expression(s) consist(s) of a sequence of one or more syntax elements	Represent a DSL expression using a (nested) list data structure offered by the host language (e.g., first-class lists and/or variable argument vectors)

```
 1  when "doorClosed" goto "active" {
 2    when "lightOn" goto "waitingForDrawer" {
 3      when "drawerOpened" goto "unlockedPanel" {
 4        when "panelClosed" goto "idle"
 5      }
 6    }
 7    when "drawerOpened" goto "waitingForLight" {
 8      when "lightOn" goto "unlockedPanel"
 9    }
10  }
```

Lst. 5.17 An excerpt from the state-machine definition of Miss Grant's Controller written using SMDL

Unification of the two DSL mandates that they maintain their functional properties as stand-alone DSL, and still, when composed, interoperate as sketched out above without modifying their implementation. As for syntax composition, state-machine definitions must be extended to include means to express guards and attach them to transition definitions. DjDSL facilitates providing the necessary structural and behavioral *patch code*, both at the level of the abstract syntaxes (language model) and the internal concrete syntaxes (BUILDERS). The latter aspect is at spot in the following paragraphs.

Lst. 5.18 The suite of
comparison operators
supported by BCEL

```
1    and > counter -1 = counter 3
1    and > counter -1 =´counter 3
1    or > counter -1 <> counter -1
1    or > counter -1 = counter -1
```

State-Machine Definition Language (SMDL)

Listing 5.17 exhibits the notation of the State-Machine Definition Language
(SMDL) as implemented by the BUILDER. When–goto phrases represent transitions
and trigger events. Events and states are defined implicitly, when first appearing
in a when-goto phrase. The definition script in Listing 5.17 implements 1:1 the
UML state machine shown in Fig. 5.15. To realize this notation as an internal DSL
syntax, the SMDL BUILDER realizes a mixed strategy: The when–goto phrases are
implemented using a variant of METHOD CHAINING specific to NX/Tcl (Table 5.4).
The transition clauses when and goto map to chained method calls, each executed
on the same BUILDER object. Nesting when–goto phrases one in another is realized
using a variant of OBJECT SCOPING. The top-level and each nested script (e.g.,
line 4 in Listing 5.17) is redirected to be processed using instance evaluation on a
given BUILDER object. This way, the nesting of two script levels also helps encode
pairings of source (ancestor level) and target state (predecessor level).

Boolean and Comparison Expression Language (BCEL)

The lines of Listing 5.18 showcase exemplary expressions in prefix notation, as
supported by the Boolean and Comparison Expression Language (BCEL). Boolean
operations supported are logical or and logical and. The comparison operators
available are greater than (>), less than (<), equality (=), and inequality (<>). The
operator semantics are adopted literally from their Tcl counterparts, because, for
evaluation, the operator expressions are submitted to the host-language interpreter.
BCEL's internal DSL syntax is implemented using a LITERAL LIST to represent and
to process expressions directly as Tcl lists.

On Tcl Lists

Tcl lists are close kins to Lisp lists and have advantages for designing an internal syntax. Among others, they do not require the DSL script or expressions
to be sandboxed. Their use as dominant expression representation, however,
also comes with restrictions on syntax styling. Tcl lists impose constraints
on allowed character combinations and the balancedness of braces. Avoiding
explicit bracing as in a prefix or postfix notation mitigates this. List parsing
will sanitize certain characters with the host-language syntax rules in mind
(e.g., semi-colons will be automatically escaped), which might not be what
the DSL syntax processor expects in corner cases.

```
1      when "doorClosed" goto "active" {
2        when "lightOn" if {= counter 3} goto "waitingForDrawer" {
3          when "drawerOpened" goto "unlockedPanel" {
4            when "panelClosed" goto "idle"
5          }
6        }
7        when "drawerOpened" goto "waitingForLight" {
8          when "lightOn" if {= counter 3} goto "unlockedPanel"
9        }
10     }
```

Lst. 5.19 An excerpt from the state-machine definition of Miss Grant's Controller written using the extended SMDL, featuring a guarded transition using BCEL expressions

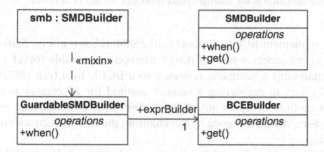

Fig. 5.20 Structural overview of the dependencies realizing a DSL unification in terms of state-machine definitions with guarded transitions. The implementation of the when method that consumes and handles if-clauses of GuardableSMDBuilder is given in Listing 5.21

The BCEL expression lists are processed by the BUILDER elementwise and dispatched to itself in terms of OBJECT SCOPING. In this scheme, the expression operators map to processing methods while literals are captured using DYNAMIC RECEPTION using the BUILDER's unknown handler. The internal processing and construction of an instantiation of the BCEL language model follows a standard stack-based computation driven by the prefix notation.

A Unified Notation

Listing 5.19 exhibits an example of the *unified* notations of the SMDL and BCEL languages. The when–goto phrases now support an optional if clause (see lines 2 and 8 in Listing 5.19). The mandatory syntax element following if carries a BCEL prefix expression that corresponds to the transition guard visualized in Fig. 5.16. At the syntax level, this unification involves defining a BUILDER for the unified syntax that combines with the SMDL BUILDER to add support for if clauses. As hinted at above, the SMDL BUILDER implements the sentential structure of when-if-goto statements in terms of METHOD CHAINING. METHOD CHAINING in DjDSL is open to extension by standard method combination. To implement if clauses, one proceeds as follows (see Fig. 5.20 and Listing 5.21):

```
1   :public method "<- when if" {ifBody args} {
2       # 1) Get (build) if-expression.
3       set exprObj [${:exprBuilder} get $ifBody]
4
5       # 2) Populate the guard reference of the transition under
6       # construction:
7       set tb [lindex ${:currentTransitionBuilder} 0]
8       $tb properties add -guard $exprObj
9
10      # 3) Return any unprocessed arguments to the method chain.
11      return $args
12  }
```

Lst. 5.21 Implementation of the internal-syntax processor for the if keyword

1. Define a refinement BUILDER (GuardableSMDBuilder in Fig. 5.20). This new
   builder (a) introduces a new BUILDER method responsible for if clauses and
   that (b) maintains a navigable reference to a BCEL BUILDER (BCEBuilder in
   Fig. 5.20). Key to registering a handler method for if clauses is to combine
   the when method of GuardableSMDBuilder with the basic one provided by
   SMDBuilder. This is achieved by the chaining the two BUILDERS via the mixin
   relationship.
2. The implementation of the if-handling method obtains the body of the if clause
   (ifBody in Listing 5.21), sends it as client to the referenced BCEL BUILDER
   (line 3), and is responsible for storing the resulting expression object with the
   guard property of the corresponding Transition object (lines 7 and 8).

This example affords two noteworthy details: (a) the use of intermediary objects
as building helpers and (b) the different flavors of (underlying) language-model
unification.

Syntax processing does not necessarily reflect the dependencies assumed by
language-model instantiation. There are typically requirements of circular initialization laid out by a language model that cannot be matched by the flow of syntax
processing [56, 64]; or there are other timing issues. For instance, language-model
elements could be instantiated and initialized only once, in the sense of a read-
only data structure. In such a setting, the incremental gathering of entity data while
processing the input might not be possible using a language-model instantiation
directly [19, Section 3.4]. In the running example, this is apparent for the data of
Transition: source and target states, trigger event, and if-condition. These data
are consumed, processed, and provided by different handling methods (when and,
when goto, and when if). DSL syntax compositions (extension and unification
alike) further add to this complexity. Under composition, it is not necessarily
predetermined which details at all and how they will be provided. For example, will
if clauses be enabled at all? Where will the data corresponding to the different
clauses of a transition definition (when, goto, if) be consumed in the flow of

method invocations, so that the refined `Transition` entity can be fully instantiated, initialized, and included into the web of surrounding object references?

As there is no one-size-fits-all approach to tackle these difficulties, different approaches must be combined. These include generic design techniques such as CONSTRUCTION BUILDERS [19, Section 3.4] and *placeholders* [56]. In the running example, on lines 7 and 8 of Listing 5.21, the use of an intermediate object (`TransitionBuilder`) is exemplified. The intermediary is populated with all instantiation data to enter a future `Transition` instance. The latter will be created at a point in time when it is guaranteed that all data has been fully gathered. In addition, DjDSL and its language models provide built-in factories to obtain such CONSTRUCTION BUILDERS for language-model elements in a standardized manner.

DSL unification in DjDSL assumes, as does DSL extension, that the underlying language model, which is targeted (populated) by the chained BUILDERS, results from a corresponding language-model composition. Alternatively, for DSL unification and under certain conditions, it is possible to limit the integration to establishing references between otherwise freestanding language models. This is the case for the running unification example on SMDL and BCEL in this section. Listing 5.22 illustrates this.

First, the `Collaboration` named `GuardedBehaviours::StateMachine` introduces a refinement of the `Transition` entity to have a `guard` property (lines 5 and 6). Second, this collaboration becomes composed with the base `Behaviours::StateMachine` language model (lines 15–18). This composed language model `GuardableStateMachine` becomes the building target of the interacting BUILDERS. This effectively corresponds to a variant of DSL extension, as covered in Sect. 5.1.1. The major difference is that the DSL extension (`GuardedBehaviours::StateMachine`) references an entity from a second language model (`Expressions::Model::Expression`; see line 6). Alternatively, when composed, an endogenous entity `Expression` would be available for referencing.[12]

5.1.3   DSL Extension Composition

Extension composition is defined as a variant of DSL composition in which two or more extensions are composed with one another, or become combined (unified) into one extension, before entering a composition with a base DSL. Two or more DSL extensions may be composed incrementally (stepwise) into a base language, one at a time. Alternatively, they can be composed first, and the resulting extension becomes merged once with a base. DjDSL with `djdsl::dada` supports both variants of

---

[12]The complementing example on DSL unification using external syntaxes in DjDSL features the case of language-model composition between the SMDL and the BCEL, to complete the big picture. See Sect. 5.2.6.

```
1   Asset create GuardedBehaviours {
2     Collaboration create StateMachine {
3       Role create Transition {
4         namespace import ::djdsl::examples::models::Expressions;
5         :property -accessor public \
6             guard:object,type=[Expressions]::Model::Expression {
7             :public object method value=isSet {obj prop} {
8                 ::nsf::var::exists $obj $prop
9             }
10          }
11      }}}
12
13    Composition create GuardableStateMachine \
14      -binds [list [Behaviours] [Expressions]] \
15      -base [Behaviours::StateMachine] \
16      -features [GuardedBehaviours::StateMachine]
```

Lst. 5.22 Definition and activation of a refinement for transitions to have them carry the guard expressions

```
1   graph {
2     // node definitions
3     "1st Edition";
4     "2nd Edition";
5     "3rd Edition";
6     // edge definitions
7     "1st Edition" -- "2nd Edition" [weight = 5; colour = "#eee"];
8     "2nd Edition" -- "3rd Edition" [colour = "#00f"];
9     "1st Edition" -- "3rd Edition";
10  }
```

Lst. 5.23 A graph definition using DOT must support edge definitions without any or with arbitrary combinations of the supported attributes

DSL extension composition: incremental extension composition and extension unification. As an example, this section returns to the graph-library example from Sect. 5.1.1. A second DSL extension to the DOT-like graph-modeling language, already extended to allow for weight attributes, adds a colour attribute to edge definitions. The aim is to allow for 3-digit hex codes of colours, as depicted in Listing 5.23. An additional requirement is to support any possible attribute variation: no attributes, single attribute (weight, colour), both. See lines 7–9 in Listing 5.23.

5.1.3.1 Incremental Extension Composition

In an incremental composition, an additional BUILDER for handling colour attributes (ColouredGraphBuilder) is inserted as predecessor BUILDER into the chain of BUILDERS (see Fig. 5.24). Method combination will provide for attribute blocks

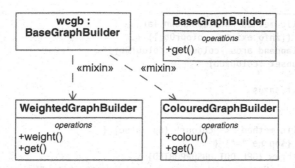

Fig. 5.24 Structural overview of the dependencies realizing an *incremental extension composition* between a base (BaseGraphBuilder) and two extensions (WeightedGraphBuilder, ColouredGraphBuilder). The implementation of the method responsible for consuming and handling the new colour attribute is given in Listing 5.25

with keyword colour to be matched and to be consumed by the method shown on line 9 in Listing 5.25. Processing of the colour and other attributes for each edge definition proceeds as follows: The handler method (line 9) consumes and produces a corresponding language-model element (classifier Colour; line 14). It preserves this instance in terms of a CONTEXT VARIABLE local to this predecessor BUILDER (colourObj). The surrounding edge definition is processed by the unknown handler (handleUnknown) in the sense of DYNAMIC RECEPTION (see lines 1–7). To inject the previously constructed Colour object, held by the CONTEXT VARIABLE into the edge-processing flow, a method refinement for the unknown handler is provided. This way, input matching and processing between chained BUILDERS is implemented via built-in method combination, against a small set of framework methods assumed by all BUILDERS (handleUnknown, handler methods). In addition, all details specific to one feature implementation (extension) are contained locally by a single unit of composition (BUILDER), without affecting other composition units.

5.1.3.2   Extension Unification

Realizing the different configurations resulting from enabling or disabling optional syntax-level features (weighted, coloured) can also be achieved by a different implementation-level variability structure. First, unifying the two extension BUILDERS into a unified extension. Second, the unified extension becomes composed with the base BUILDER. In DjDSL, because chains of BUILDERS are implemented as composition of mixin classes, such an extension unification can be realized using *transitive mixins* [38, 71].

```
1    :public method handleUnknown {args} {
2      if {[info exists :colourObj]} {
3        lappend args -colour ${:colourObj}
4        unset :colourObj
5      }
6      next $args
7    }
8
9    :public method "<- colour" {op value} {
10     if {$op ne "="} {
11       throw {GPL DOT UNSUPPORTED} \
12         "Unsupported operator '$op' in attribute."
13     }
14     set :colourObj [${:output} new colour -value $value]
15     return
16   }
```

Lst. 5.25 Implementation of the internal-syntax processor for the colour attribute

Fig. 5.26 Structural
overview of the dependencies
realizing an *extension
unification.*
WeightedGraphBuilder is
first refined by
ColouredGraphBuilder
and, then, as a unified
extension, composed with
BaseGraphBuilder. The
implementation of the
methods responsible for
consuming and handling the
new colour attribute are
given in Listing 5.25. They
apply for incremental
composition and unification
alike

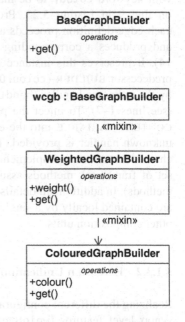

Transitive Mixin
With transitive mixins, it is possible to mix-in class trees into target objects
and target classes explicitly, as well as to apply to the targets implicitly
the extension behavior mixed into the mixin classes themselves Therefore,
multiple layers of mixins are said to become applied *by transition.* Transitive

(continued)

> mixins provide for the orthogonal refinement *between* mixin-based extension
> components (between builders for the coloured and weighted extensions),
> rather than the mixin-based extension of base components alone [38, 71].

The differences to incremental composition are limited to a changed dependency
structure (see Fig. 5.26). The actual implementation (i.e., refinements to unknown
handlers and invocation handlers) is identical and can be applied for both, incremental extension composition and extension unification. This is because, for the scope
of chaining BUILDERS, the resulting method-resolution order from incremental
extensions and unified extensions will be equivalent in terms of the refinement
behavior. A benefit of a unified extension is that the DSL developer of the base
BUILDER is not required to be aware of the composed extensions. The extensions
can be provided by attaching further extensions (mixins) in an unplanned manner to
the one provided extension (`WeightedGraphBuilder`).

A downside could be that coordination code required to make two or more
co-present extensions work together is bundled (tangled) with the implementation
of one extension. Imagine some logic to implement syntax-level restrictions on
the allowed combinations of certain attribute types for edge definitions. In need
of placing and managing provision of coordination code in a clearly separated
manner, a variant of extension unification can be realized: *derivative extensions* [31]
(Listing 5.27).

In DjDSL and its BUILDER framework (`djdsl::dada`), such coordination code
can be hosted by a dedicated and intermediate BUILDER class. This intermediate
class serves for composing other BUILDERS and provides for behavior to accommodate the different extensions (e.g., revised context conditions and patch code
to resolve behavioral conflicts). Implementationwise, derivative extensions build
again on transitive-mixin relationships (see Fig. 5.28). The derivative BUILDER
`AttributedGraphBuilder` is the joint composition target for the two extensions.
When composed into the base object, the method implementations provided by
the two extensions, and the derivative ones, become available for the scope of the
BUILDER. Conveniently, the method-resolution order will place method refinements

```
1   # 1) extension unification
2   WeightedGraphBuilder mixins add ColouredGraphBuilder
3
4   # 2) composition with base
5   BaseGraphBuilder create ::wcgb2 \
6       -interp [EmptyInterp new] \
7       -predecessors [WeightedGraphBuilder] \
8       -output [MultiFeatGraph new graph]
```

Lst. 5.27 Enabling the internal-syntax extension for the `colour` attribute

Fig. 5.28 Structural
overview of the dependencies
realizing a *derivative
extension*.
`AttributedGraphBuilder`,
said derivative, is first refined
by `ColouredGraphBuilder`
`WeightedGraphBuilder`.
The implementation of the
latter two remains unchanged.
The derivative extension
becomes composed with the
base (an instance of
`BaseGraphBuilder`)

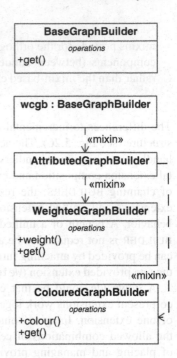

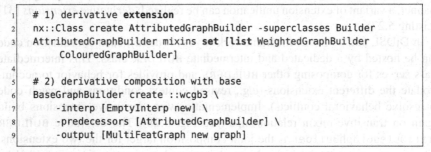

```
1  # 1) derivative extension
2  nx::Class create AttributedGraphBuilder -superclasses Builder
3  AttributedGraphBuilder mixins set [list WeightedGraphBuilder
       ColouredGraphBuilder]
4
5  # 2) derivative composition with base
6  BaseGraphBuilder create ::wcgb3 \
7      -interp [EmptyInterp new] \
8      -predecessors [AttributedGraphBuilder] \
9      -output [MultiFeatGraph new graph]
```

Lst. 5.29

of the `AttributedGraphBuilder` in-between those of the extensions and the base.
Therefore, the derivative can intercept any messages flowing from the former to the
latter, to realize a derived behavior; that is, behavior that is derived from the one
implemented by the two extensions. Listing 5.29 shows this extension-composition
style in action.

5.2 External DSL: Grammar-Based Variability Implementation Techniques

There are different drivers of providing a DSL concrete syntax external to the one of the host language. In the context of the overall development process, an external syntax might become added to a DSL once the language model has been matured, and first tests have been written against the native, internal syntax. That is, it results as a dedicated evolutionary step [70].[13] To the same effect, the phase of domain engineering might have been guided by *syntax mock-ups* that should know be turned into an actual, operative syntax. Syntax requirements expressed this way, by technical domain experts directly (e.g., end-user developers) or indirectly by a legacy system, might simply not be realizable using an internal DSL syntax due to some details of the host-language syntax that cannot be circumvented by the DSL developer. Finally, building or targeting DSL tooling for authoring and analyzing DSL scripts might have an external DSL syntax as a prerequisite or as a consequence.[14] Whatever the drivers, reusing existing external-syntax definitions (e.g., grammar definitions) for DSL variants without modifying the definitions shared by the DSL family remains as a goal and as a challenge, like for internal DSL syntaxes.

5.2.1 Abstraction Mismatches of Parse Representations

DSL tooling and their different ("parsing") pipelines for processing DSL scripts written in an external syntax produce and, then, work with different representations of the processed input: *parse representations*. Parse representation abstract from the concrete-syntax structure of the input to make the DSL script more eligible to run important tasks on them. Parse representations in their role as abstractions can be qualified along different dimensions, for example, their purpose for tooling, their characteristics as data structures, and selected (including non-functional) quality attributes.

Tooling operations on parse representations include analysis operations, code generation, visualization, debugging, and syntax rendering. Each of these operations can be further divided into sub-activities (e.g., syntax rendering can result in a pretty-printed string or an editable projection). Along this dimension, parse

---

[13]For a concrete example, see the story about a DSL for object-to-NoSQL mapping (ONM) in Chap. 6.

[14]Reusing host-language tooling (e.g., IDE) as the infrastructure for tailored DSL-specific tooling is a matter of on-going research [41] but has inherent limits to it. These limits are due to the quality-in-use being highly dependent on the domain-specific context and audience [55, Section 4].

representations are commonly grouped into parse trees and abstract syntax trees (AST; [43, Chapter 4]).

As data structures, parse representations can be devised as trees, graphs with/ without direction, graphs with/ without cycles, as well as COMPOSITE [20] structures with homogeneous vs. heterogeneous elements [43].

As for quality attributes, given a particular purpose, parse representations can be judged according to their compactness, robustness, traversability[15]:

- *Compactness*: Does the parse representation contain elements unnecessary for a given purpose or operation?
- *Robustness*: Is the parse representation robust to changes of the concrete-syntax definition or of the syntax processor (grammar, parser)?
- *Traversability*: Can the parse representation be efficiently and conveniently walked for a given purpose or operation?

Compactness is not only an important in terms of spatial performance, but also refers to the capacity to recognize patterns in the parse representations in a succinct manner. Concrete-syntax artifacts should not be contained by parse representations, if not explicitly required by a given operation.[16] The robustness criterion assumes that the concrete-syntax definition may be further developed or modified as an evo- lutionary step (syntax migration [17]). The targeted parse representation, however, remains unaffected because it has already matured or has been fixed early (e.g., as in language-model-driven DSL development; see Sect. 2.1). Traversability reflects the requirement to be able to implement several passes of a parse representation for running an analysis or a transformation. The aim is to implement a pass not only in a spatially and temporally performant manner, but also using a comprehensible programming model.

DSL development systems are built around several different parse-representation formats (e.g., parse trees, abstract syntax trees, semantic models). The formats avail- able are often predetermined by the adopted parsing infrastructure (e.g., ANTLR abstract syntax trees in Xtext). Ill-choosing the parse-representation format runs the risk of introducing abstraction mismatches. Abstraction mismatches impede the work of a DSL developer who creates, maintains, or tries to comprehend a DSL processing pipeline. An *abstraction mismatch* [68, Chapter 3] of a given parse representation in DSL development systems denotes a misfit of a chosen parse abstraction against a modeling or processing task on DSL scripts in terms of the compactness, the robustness, and the traversability of the chosen representation (see above).[17] An abstraction mismatch can result from different sources. In the

---

[15]Parr [43, Section 4.2] refers to these aspects as "density", "meaningfulness", and "convenience", respectively.

[16]One common example requiring preservation of concrete-syntax details (e.g., the relative positioning in the original input), even in advanced parse representations, is pretty printer or serializers that, otherwise, give minimal round-tripping guarantees.

[17]Regarding parse representations and their fit for semantic analyses, this has also been referred to as an *impedance mismatch* [28].

Fig. 5.30 Single class-based
inheritance

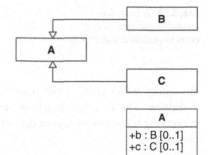

Fig. 5.31 Object
decomposition

context of DSL development, important examples are decomposition mismatches.[18]
In a *decomposition mismatch*, one conceptual entity (i.e., one element of the DSL
language model or a domain model) and operations on them are split and realized
as a collaboration between two or more implementation entities (e.g., two or more
elements of a parse representation).

The inverse is also possible. One implementation entity is made to represent
multiple language-model entities. Under certain circumstances, and given a certain
task, these might be valid optimizations. For different tasks, they require the
DSL developer to use an inadequate abstraction in terms of the three attributes
(compactness, robustness, or traversability) or to handicraft another, intermediate
abstraction. This may be required over and over again, for each and every operation.
For example, a decomposition mismatch in a parse representation of expressions
might lead to emphasizing some concrete-syntax artifacts (e.g., left-recursion
factoring) rather than operators, operands, and their relationships (ordering, precedence). Other prominent examples are elements of concrete-syntax structuring (e.g.,
blocks) having no required (i.e., they can be discarded in the pipeline) or no
exact correspondence (i.e., there are multiple representation option available) in the
abstract syntax.

A group of critical *abstraction mismatches* can be due to mapping a DSL's concrete syntax to an object-oriented language model as the DSL's abstract syntax [27,
Sections 2.1 and 2.2].[19] The consequences regarding compactness, robustness, and
traversability, positive and negative, also depend on the DSL development systems
overall approach to DSL syntax processing and to realizing this mapping.[20] Without
the DSL developer providing additional qualifications, by whatever means, the
mapping between the concrete and abstract syntax remains ambiguous in both
directions of the mapping. In the following, because the context is on providing an
optional external syntax to a DjDSL language model, the emphasis is on (avoiding)

---

[18]Recall the more general introduction to decomposition mismatches in Sect. 2.3.2.

[19]These mismatches are close kins to other OO-related abstraction mismatches in software
engineering, for example, the so-called XML-to-object (X/O) mapping mismatches.

[20]See the introduction of Chap. 3 and the overview of *definition styles*: abstract-first versus
concrete-first, model inference versus explicit model definition (e.g., unified syntax definition).

Lst. 5.32 A presence
condition encoded as a
context condition using OCL

```
context A
inv: (b->size()+d->size()) = 1
```

ambiguity when going from a concrete-syntax definition to the abstract syntax definition. The inverted direction can be equally important. Take the example of preserving telemetry or layout data of the original input to later go from abstract to concrete.

> **On Notation**
> For the discussion, the differences between production rule and parsing expression are not relevant. As DjDSL builds on a parsing infrastructure based on parsing expressions, and for the sake of consistency, I stick to a notation which is supported as-is by DjDSL. Fortunately, it is akin to E/BNF with only minor deviations: ← vs. →, / (choice, ordered alternates) vs. | (alternation, unordered choice).

A starting point to investigate important mismatches is the current practice [6, 27]. This practice involves representing non-terminals as classes in the object-oriented language model and the relationships between non-terminals, such as *alternatives or choices*, as class relationships (e.g., class-based inheritance, references).

Consider the following example of a production rule or parsing expression, more precisely: A ← B / C.

There are several possible language-model correspondences. They implement what in variability-aware programming is referred to as a *singular variation point*. First, one might model the variation point in the syntax using single class-based inheritance. That is, a single superclass captures the parent non-terminal A, two subclasses represent the child non-terminals B and C (see Fig. 5.30). An alternative representation is the literal *object decomposition* into a class A for the parent non-terminal and properties typed by two classes for the child non-terminals B and C. The properties remain uninitialized unless one choice or alternative is processed as part of the input (see Fig. 5.31).

One difference between the two encodings is that the inheritance encoding enforces the cardinality directly. The object-decomposition option, on the contrary, requires a supporting restriction. This restriction could be implemented by some invariant constraint that ascertains that one and only one of the properties has an assigned value (Listing 5.32).

Another required qualification is whether a property denotes a composite aggregation or not. If a non-terminal like A re-appears in different rules (parsing expressions), and so does the corresponding object-type A for more than one

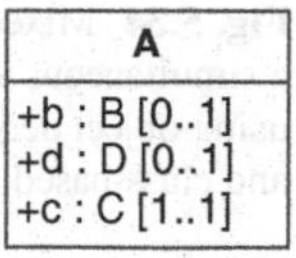

Fig. 5.33 Object
decomposition that flattens
the otherwise nested
concrete-syntax structure. An
additional context condition
is required to encode the
presence condition between B
and D. See Listing 5.32

A
+b : B [0..1]
+d : D [0..1]
+c : C [1..1]

corresponding property, then the DSL developer must make explicit whether a
composite aggregation is intended or not.

Further limitations specific to each representation option become apparent
already when reviewing small extensions to the example: blocks, shared structure,
and associative relationships.

Blocks

A first type of relevant decomposition mismatches relate to the representation of
sub-clauses (sub-expressions) which are used to structure production rules (parsing
expressions) and, accordingly, the allowed input.

The sub-clause (B / D) in A ←(B / D)C cannot be directly represented,
because there is no (explicitly named) non-terminal to be mapped to a subclass
or a property. This leaves the DSL developer with two decision options: (a) to
adopt a destructive encoding (e.g., object decomposition which discards concrete-
syntax details) or (b) to restructure the rule. The former, an encoding based on
object decomposition without structure preservation, is capable of expressing all
variants seen so far in a uniform manner. Separate properties capture the flattened
sub-structure of A, with an additional constraint capturing the overall presence
condition.[21] See Fig. 5.33 for the example.

The latter option involves a dedicated refactoring into two rules (expressions):

```
1   A ← X C
2   X ← B / D
```

The result is a grammar yielding X as an intermediate non-terminal and can be
subjected, again, to an inheritance encoding. The inheritance encoding introduces
artifacts (extra classes) and the language model is patched to contain X elements,
even though not required to model the domain *per se*. See Fig. 5.34. On the upside,
the language model now preserves the nesting structure of the rules (expressions).
This might or not be a prerequisite for certain operations. Depending on the
setting, this is not only a decomposition mismatch, but also introduces a complexity
mismatch (sometimes referred to as composition classes).

---

[21] The need for defining additional constraints on a language model, resulting from the abstraction
mismatches exemplified here, is another case in point for context conditions (see Chap. 4).

Fig. 5.34 Mixed encoding of
a simultaneous variation,
using object decomposition
and class-based inheritance

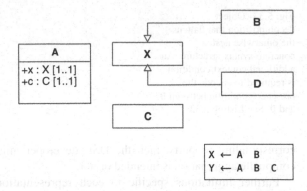

Lst. 5.35 An example of
shared structure between
parsing rules

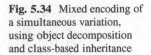

The examples given are not meant to be exhaustive, but they stress the subtle interactions when establishing correspondences between concrete-syntax definitions and abstract syntax definitions. This is particularly the case when building one from the other in *an implicit manner*. By implicit, the one is derived from the other by making certain (well-formedness) assumptions (e.g., using model inference). Two more decomposition mismatches surface when considering more than one production rule (parsing expression) and a language model as instantiation target: shared structure and associations.

Hierarchical Relationships (Shared Structure)
In whatever encoding—inheritance-based, decomposition-based, or mixed—a set of rules (expressions) would map to one class each (i.e., X and Y in Listing 5.35). It is noteworthy that the resulting classes are not related, the mapping is shallow in this respect. However, they appear to share structure (a sequence of A followed by B; or simultaneous variation). It is not unlikely that this sharing is an adequate representation of the targeted domain. A language model that was automatically derived does not necessarily reflect this, whatever the encoding. The sharing could be represented in a number of ways, for instance, by introducing a common superclass or relating X and Y as a pair of direct super- and subclass (see Fig. 5.36). The former option introduces an artifact in the sense that it is not reflected in the concrete syntax. The latter option might have a meaningful correspondence in the modeled domain.

Non-hierarchical Relationships (References, Associations)
An object-oriented language model clearly discriminates between hierarchical (whole-part) and non-hierarchical relationships. They serve for modeling domain relationships of distinct connotations. Production rules (parsing expressions) do not provide this discriminatory means of expression. Their operative semantics (assuming some parsing strategy underneath) typically imply a composite, tree-like relationship that follows from processing the input according to the rule (or by the expression). Therefore, without further qualification or additional means of expression, hierarchical and non-hierarchical relationships cannot be differentiated.

Fig. 5.36 Encoding shared
input structures in terms of a
generalization/specialization
between the classes
representing non-terminals
(rules)

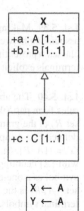

Lst. 5.37 Identical structure
between two non-terminals

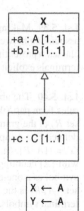

Consider Listing 5.37. X and Y may be considered related either hierarchically (they share some structure, see above) or they may be considered related by association through the mediator concept A. They could also be regarded associated via a specific occurrence of A (i.e., associated by identity for non-terminals or by value, if A stands for a quasi-terminal).

Figure 5.38 exemplifies a possible bidirectional association between the representation classes X and Y. The association is derived based on the identity of the mediator concept A. Depending on the operational context, a parse representation may or may not preserve the mediator elements along with the derived association. In any case, a concrete-syntax definition as in Listing 5.37 alone, without qualification by the DSL developer, cannot render the intended association explicit, nor can it properly differentiate the intended relationship types (Listing 5.39).

DjDSL proposes a technique of defining the language model (or, rather its instantiation) explicitly as integrated part of a grammar definition to avoid any of the above mismatches (blocks, shared structure, or associations). This requires also means to bridge lower-level gaps between the abstractions of concrete-

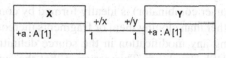

Fig. 5.38 Associations between classes representing non-terminals (X and Y) may be derived, or not, by matching identities (or values) of hierarchically related elements. This assumes that the otherwise implicit and derived association is made explicit (see Listing 5.39) by an act of specification or an act of transformation. Additional and non-derivable qualifications are whether the properties typed A should hold composite aggregations or not

Lst. 5.39 Making an association between two classes representing non-terminals explicit using OCL

```
context X
  inv: y.a = a
context Y
  inv: x.a = a
```

Lst. 5.40 The above rules form part (the multiset R) of the grammar defined as a 4-tuple: $G = (\{A, B\}, \{a, b\}, R, \{A\})$, with $\{A\}$ denoting the start symbol as a one-element set. $\{A, B\}$ is the set of non-terminal symbols. $\{a, b\}$ is the set of terminal symbols

```
1  A ← 'a' B
2  B ← 'b' A
3  // ...
4  A ← 'a' B
5  A ← 'A' B
6  // ...
7  A ← 'a' B / 'A' B
```

syntax and language-model definitions. For example, there is a mismatch between positional matches in a typical parse representation and the named as well as non-positional structural features of language-model classes. These mismatches are challenging when considered in isolation from each other. DjDSL also addresses these mismatches when occurring together and *under compositions* of DSL with external syntaxes (see Sect. 5.2.6).

5.2.2 Composable Parser Definitions

DSL composition can involve one or several external syntaxes, each requiring a dedicated step of syntax processing (parsing). This requires a script written in the combined syntax to be processed as if it were made from different syntax pieces. Each syntax piece is thought of as conforming to one of the original syntaxes or a mix of the original syntaxes, to be processed by an overall or composed parser responsible for these syntaxes. The definition of this overall or composed parser (by a grammar or by a parser combinator) is ideally formed by composing the original parser definitions, rather than cloning them or fragments thereof manually. This has the benefit of tracking any modification in the source definitions without further intervention by the DSL developer. This assumes that the source definitions can be composed as-is, without modification. Reuse without modification is only but one, yet for DSL composition *the* central motivation. Other drivers include separate compilation of fragmented parser definitions, for example.

Parsing of DSL scripts—however realized, by grammar-based parser generators, grammar interpreters, or parser combinators—presents important challenges for rendering the parser definitions de- and re-composable [11, Section 3.3]. This is even more so when the composition of these definitions should adhere to criteria of modularity; for example, that one definition can still be understood by the developer in isolation from the other composed definitions during a comprehension or maintenance task (modular comprehensibility [62]). While important details depend on the parsing approaches and techniques employed (scanner-based vs. scannerless parsing, LL/LR vs. generalized parsing), there are recurring themes. One theme is the *ambiguity under composition*.

For the remainder, a parser definition is made from production or parsing rules (see Listing 5.40).[22] A *rule* consists of a left-hand side (LHS) and a right-hand side (RHS) separated either by a left-headed arrow (parsing rule) or a right-headed arrow (production rule). For what follows, the LHS contains a non-terminal symbol. The RHS contains a production or a parsing expression.[23] The RHS contains a sequence of one or more non-terminal and terminal symbols separated by whitespace and, optionally, enclosed by matching pairs of single quotes. The RHS can also contain special symbols denoting the empty string (ϵ) or a parsing failure (f). For a collection of rules having the same LHS, but different RHS, the RHS are said to be the *alternates* of the non-terminal symbol at the LHS. Lines 4 and 5 in Listing 5.40 exemplify such alternates for non-terminal A. As a shorthand, such alternating rules can be rewritten as a single rule, using the vertical bar | (for production rules) or the slash / (for parsing rules) as delimiters between the alternates (see line 7). A parser definition is called a *grammar* when it is a 4-tuple of the set of non-terminals, the set of terminals, a set of rules, and a start symbol that points to a start rule. The set of rules is formed by all rules' LHS and RHS defined over the domain of non-terminals and terminals.[24]

A composition operation relates a *receiving* parser definition and one or more *composed* definitions. A composition produces a *resulting* parser definition.[25] The variants of composition operations on such parser definitions (grammars) currently available fall into three groups: overriding, combination, and restriction. The individual variants then result from different decisions towards the composition scope (or units under composition), towards symbol qualification, the composition arity,

---

[22]For the presentation in this section, a shortcut is taken that is not warranted in general: a grammar and its grammar definition are not necessarily definitions of the associated parsers. However, the grammar types relevant for the scope of this book—parsing grammars for recognition systems—but also context-free grammars whose languages can be processed using LL parsing closely resemble the parsing logic. In addition, the details of parsing are relevant for the composability of the associated grammar or parser definitions.

[23]Additional rule elements, such as attributes at the LHS or actions at the RHS are not relevant, for now.

[24]For DjDSL, parser definitions containing only parsing rules will be relevant. Such parser definitions are also referred to as *parsing grammars* as opposed to *production grammars* (such as context-free grammars). For the presentation at this point, however, this difference is secondary. The differences [32], however, are critical in terms of the semantics of an associated parser definition.

[25]The application of a composition operation has also been labeled *grammar induction* [25]. Also note that the resulting definition does not necessarily manifest itself as a new definition artifact. It may be a mere runtime artifact, e.g., in dynamic approaches to grammar composition [49].

Lst. 5.41 Disjoint union

```
1  // composed: G0(B)
2  B ← 'b' B
3  // receiving: G1(A)
4  A ← 'a' A
5  // resulting: G1'(G1.A)
6  G0.B ← 'b' G0.B
7  G1.A ← 'a' G1.A
```

the composition order, the self-completeness of the definitions under compositions (complete or partial), and the interaction of composition semantics with parsing semantics.

Given the definition of parser definitions (grammar) above, there are several possible *scopes* for (units of) composition between two or more definitions [25]: all rules, the set of RHS for one or more selected non-terminals, a specific RHS, or selected alternates for a non-terminal symbol. Whatever the unit of composition, a composition will lead to conflicts between non-terminal names. This can be intended or accidental. In the worst, accidental case, these conflicts can cause unexpected results, ranging from an invalid definition, ambiguous parses, or loss of important properties (e.g., closedness under composition). Composition operations, therefore, may qualify symbol names based on their origin definition; or not. When a composition operation allows for two or more composed definitions, a policy must be in place to deal with duplicated units on the way to a resulting definition. The receiving and composed definitions may be complete (i.e., they do not contain undefined non-terminals in their RHS) or partial (i.e., they contain undefined or deferred non-terminals at their RHS). This refers to the role of parser definitions as mere extensions (DSL extensions) or self-sufficient syntaxes (DSL unification). Finally, the parsing semantics underlying the rules will determine the actual composition semantics. In particular, the ordered or unordered choice between alternates affects the composition. Next, the following prototypical composition operations and their variants are reviewed:

- Disjoint union (aliasing, rewriting)
- Overriding (simple union with override)
- Combination
- Restriction (renaming, filtering)

A basic, but not particularly useful composition operation is a *disjoint* union between the rules of a receiving and the rules of one or more composed parser definitions. As a shorthand, the origins of the unified non-terminals are prefixed by their origin definition: G1.A vs. G0.B. This applies at the LHS and RHS of the rules. In Listing 5.41, the resulting definition will have two unconnected rules. In Listing 5.43, despite the commonly named non-terminals at the LHS (A), the receiving definition will again contain two unconnected rules. Assuming the starting symbol G1.A, one of the rules will even be unreachable.

Lst. 5.42 Disjoint union
(extended)

```
1  // composed: G0(A)
2  A ← 'A' A Z
3  Z ← '1' / '0'
4  // receiving: G1(A)
5  A ← 'a' A
6  // resulting: G1'(G1.A)
7  G0.Z ← '1' / '0'
8  G0.A ← 'A' G0.A G0.Z
9  G1.A ← 'a' G1.A
```

Listing 5.42, however, exemplifies an important property of any composition operation regarding the rule on line 3 (Z): By default, all rules of the composed and receiving definitions are carried over into the resulting one. This may be requested explicitly or not, and it may involve modifications. Only restrictive compositions change this default behavior (see below).

To become useful in different DSL composition contexts (e.g., extension, unification), the receiving definition should provide rules from the receiving and the composed ones that connect effectively. This requirement leads to overriding and combination.

Overriding

Overriding yields a resulting definition in which rules, non-terminals, or alternates of the receiving definitions replace entirely rules, non-terminals, or alternates of the composed definition. This leaves the resulting definition without access to the overridden ones. One possible overriding technique for entire rules is a *union with override* between the receiving and the composed definitions [57, Section 5].

Union with Override

It is noteworthy that the application of union with override on parser definitions is a sibling of its application in modeling inheritance in object orientation: record combination [57]. Union with override is also applied uniformly to abstract syntax and concrete-syntax compositions. For example, van der Storm et al. [64] implement a merge operator for their combined definitions of parser and language model ("schemas") as *union with override*.

This union operation does not qualify non-terminals at the LHS (or, RHS for that matter) for their origin (i.e., receiving or composed definitions), but considers just the unqualified non-terminal names. In case of same-named non-terminals between pairs of rules (e.g., A in Listing 5.43), the rule of the receiving definition is carried over into the resulting definition. The composed rule is effectively lost.

Union with override does not require any particular construct support at the level of the parser-definition (grammar) language. The minimum requirement is a

Lst. 5.43 Union with
override

```
1  // composed: G0(A)
2  A ← 'A' A Z
3  Z ← '1' / '0'
4  // receiving: G1(A)
5  A ← 'a' A
6  X ← 'x' A
7  // resulting: G1'(A)
8  Z ← '1' / '0'
9  A ← 'a' A
10 X ← 'x' A
```

Lst. 5.44 Anticipated
overriding

```
1  // composed: G0(A)
2  A ← 'A' A Z
3  Z ← '1' / '0'
4  // receiving: G1(A)
5  A ← G0.A
6  X ← 'x' A
7  // resulting: G1'(G1.A)
8  G0.Z ← '1' / '0'
9  G0.A ← 'A' G0.A G0.Z
10 G1.A ← G0.A
11 G1.X ← 'x' G1.A
```

construct to establish references to composed definitions. Union with override has
the benefit of supporting unanticipated composition. However, it comes with risks of
accidental overriding because it is a blackbox operation: The unit of compositions
are parser definitions in their entirety, there is no control at the level of rules or
below. Imagine a situation, in which non-terminals carrying the same names denote
different concepts (possible under DSL unification, for instance). In its basic form, it
also offers no fine-grained control over the composition, that is, at the sub-definition
level (e.g., rule by rule, within choices). Overriding may also result in duplicated
definitions in case the resulting rule must retain elements from the overridden one.

Applications of union with override can be found in *grammar imports* provided
by ANTLR [44, p. 257]. On a rule-by-rule basis, union with override is also
available from the grammar-module system in *Rats!* [22, Section 4]. *Rats!* allows
for overriding entire rules (including attributes) and selected alternates for a non-
terminal. The latter is a special variant of rule overriding, when considering
alternates written out as separate rules with identical LHS. In *Rats!*, alternates are
labeled for this purpose.

An anticipated variant of overriding can also be realized using references
between definitions when starting from a disjoint union. Recall that to obtain a
disjoint union, all symbols are qualified by their origin definitions. Listing 5.44
demonstrates the basic procedure. On line 5, the RHS of the receiving definition
contains a fully qualified *reference* to the composed non-terminal: G0.A. This
reference ends up in the resulting definition (line 10) as an alias. The alias serves as a

Lst. 5.45 Substitution

```
1  // ...
2  // resulting: G1'(G1.A)
3  G0.Z ← '1' / '0'
4  G0.A ← 'A' G0.A G0.Z
5  G1.A ← G0.A
6  G1.X ← 'x' G0.A
```

Lst. 5.46 RHS extraction
(⇐)

```
1   // composed: G0(A)
2   A ← 'A' A Z
3   Z ← '1' / '0'
4   // receiving: G1(A)
5   A <= G0.A
6   X ← 'x' A
7   // resulting: G1'(G1.A)
8   G0.Z ← '1' / '0'
9   G0.A ← 'A' G0.A G0.Z
10  G1.A ← 'A' G0.A G0.Z
11  G1.X ← 'x' G1.A
```

bridge between any RHS referring to the receiving non-terminal A and the composed one.

This initial type of aliasing between definitions is not ideal because it introduces a superfluous element (G1.A) into a parse representation based on the resulting definition. This extra element must be handled or suppressed. Therefore, this form of overriding can be refined:

- *Alias with substitute*: Occurrences of the aliased non-terminal (G1.A) are substituted for the composed one (G0.A) throughout the RHS of the resulting definition. Substitution is restricted to the RHS of the rules originating in the receiving definition.[26]
- RHS extraction (⇐): The reference to the composed non-terminal (line 5) obtains only the RHS of the referenced rule in an unmodified manner. This is referred to as *importing-by-reference* in ART [25], a parser generator for GLL parsers. See also Listing 5.46.
- *RHS extraction with rewrite* (⇔): The reference to the composed non-terminal (line 5) obtains, again, the RHS of the referenced rule. This time, the extracted RHS is rewritten to change all qualifiers from the composed to the receiving ones (G0 to G1). This is also known as *importing-by-clone* in ART [25]. The benefit is that the rewrite preserves rules with recursion. Without the rewrite, any recursion is lost.[27]

---

[26]Note that the referencing rule G1.A ← G0.A on line 5 in Listing 5.45 is still carried over in its entirety into the resulting definition. However, it is not reachable (after substitution) and is assumed to become pruned by standard cleaning operations.

[27]Another effect is that the rewrite of qualifiers makes the original rule, as carried over into the resulting definition, obsolete. This is also the case when the original rule is recursive.

Lst. 5.47 RHS extraction
with rewrite (⇐)

```
 1  // composed: G0(A)
 2  A ← 'A' A Z
 3  Z ← '1' / '0'
 4  // receiving: G1(A)
 5  A ⇔ G0.A
 6  X ← 'x' A
 7  // resulting: G1'(G1.A)
 8  G0.Z ← '1' / '0'
 9  G0.A ← 'A' G0.A G0.Z
10  G1.A ← 'A' G1.A G1.Z
11  G1.X ← 'x' G1.A
```

In summary, the advantage of RHS extraction (especially with rewrite) is that no indirection is introduced. This way, the compactness of parsing representations is preserved. In addition, recursive rules are preserved, if present. Also note that RHS extraction operates at the sub-rule level (RHS), rather than forming unions of rules sets. The downside of extraction is that extraction must be anticipated when authoring the receiving definitions. The difference between aliasing with substitute and extraction with rewrite is the group of rules that become subjected to modifying the definition qualifiers: the receiving definition's ones and the composed definition's ones, respectively.

Extraction with rewrite can be varied to realize template rules. A *template rule* is a rule in a composed definition that is intentionally left incomplete. It is incomplete in the sense of containing re-definable or even undefined non-terminals at its RHS (like template parameters). This is because extraction with rewrite, in its basic form, orphans composed non-terminals in the resulting definition. For example, in Listing 5.47, non-terminal Z at the RHS of the A rule becomes G1.Z on line 10. This means that non-terminals must be provided for by the receiving definition to complete the composed and rewritten rules (e.g., by a rule effectively defining G1.Z).[28] Alternatively, the DSL developer can use aliases or further extractions from the composed definition to provide the non-terminal definitions.[29]

However realized, overriding allows for reusing parser definitions as-is, but at the risk of accidental compositions and of introducing duplicates.

Combination

Pure overriding is useful for DSL unification in which clearly delimited sections of a given DSL syntax are replaced by a similarly delimited section of another DSL's syntax. DSL extensions or DSL extension compositions involve increments

---

[28]This is sometimes implemented as a construct of *abstracted* or *deferred* non-terminals. See Listing 5.48 that gives the example of an abstract rule for non-terminal Expr in a receiving definition, as provided in Ensō's object grammars [64, Section 3.2].

[29]A variant of the *import-by-clone* operator that fetches all dependent non-terminal definitions of an extracted and rewritten RHS is suggested by Johnstone et al. [25, Section 5] and implemented in DjDSL.

```
1  S ::= [State] "state" name:sym out:T* "when" cond:Expr
2  abstract Expr
3  abstract T
```

Lst. 5.48 *Abstract* non-terminals (Expr, T) in a receiving parser definition that is open for extension by deferring the non-terminal definition to a composed definition, but symbolically closed. The underlying composition procedure, however, can be modeled as a RHS extraction with rewrite. Example derived from [64, p. 14]

Lst. 5.49 Union with override/combine

```
1  // composed: G0(A)
2  A ← 'A' A Z
3  Z ← '1' / '0'
4  // receiving: G1(A)
5  A ← 'a' A
6  X ← 'x' A
7  // resulting: G1'(A)
8  Z ← '1' / '0'
9  A ← 'a' A / 'A' A Z
10 X ← 'x' A
```

to a notation. Increments require that the incremented syntax remains intact, rather than becoming replaced entirely. This is achieved through means of combination. Combination builds on overriding and the different variants thereof (e.g., union with override, aliasing, extraction).

Combination differs from pure overriding by combining the eventually overridden rules or rule elements with the overriding ones. For example, the two RHS of a matching pair of receiving and composed rules are combined *as alternates* to each other in a combined rule in the resulting definition. Consider, for example, Listing 5.49. It adapts the union with override from Listing 5.43 to become a union with *override/combine*. Rather than replacing the receiving rule for non-terminal A (line 5) by the composed one (line 2), the two RHS of the matching rules are combined as alternates (line 9). The same can be applied to aliasing (with or without substitute) and extraction (with and without rewrite).

A distinction must be made between alternates in terms of unordered and ordered choices; and the consequences for alternate combination. For parser definitions with unordered alternates (in particular, production grammars like context-free grammars), the order of combination is irrelevant; alternation as an operation is commutative and does not affect the result of parsing [25]. Implementationwise, this means that combination defaults to simply appending a composed RHS to the receiving one.

On the contrary, for parsing grammars, alternation is a non-commutative operation. Depending on the input and the local order of alternates at the RHS of a rule, certain alternates will not be tested for. Depending on the order of composition, then, one and the same input could be recognized as invalid for a composed language; or a different language becomes described. This requires finer-grained control of the direction of combination (e.g., prepending, appending, inserting), to control for unintended consequences. In *Rats!*, for instance, it is possible to control, on a rule-by-rule basis, whether an selected RHS or alternate is prepended or appended [22, Section 4]. An ill-defined combination with ordered alternates, however, can lead to unexpected or no results.

Restriction

DSL restriction (as a form of DSL extension) can require that a base syntax is reused in a way that intentionally renders syntax elements unavailable in the composed syntax. Restricting a syntax refers to the receiving parser definition being able to selectively mark composed rules or their rule elements for not entering the resulting definition.[30] Restrictions can be implemented in different manners, assuming the following composition flow: (1) A (disjoint) union of the rules from the receiving and from the composed definition is formed, (2) overriding and combination operations are performed, and (3) any *useless* rules (non-terminals) are removed to form the resulting definition.[31] The following restriction variants can be applied:

- *Renaming*: As part of step (2), a dedicated renaming of a non-terminal by the receiving definition can be used to render the non-terminal unreachable in the resulting definition. This effectively removes the entire corresponding rule from the resulting definition. SDF allows for this use of renaming [66].
- *Filtering*: As a dedicated step (4), after having computed the resulting definition, filters may be applied to suppress rules or rule elements based on filtering conditions. Filtering conditions can range from exact matching of rule-element labels (alternates in *Rats!*) to matching rule patterns (applied to RHS in Art [25]).

Restrictions via renaming and via filtering can typically be expressed as dedicated statements that resemble rules with special-purpose operators. Examples are deleters (:/=) in Art [25] or subtraction assignments (-=) in *Rats!* [22].

Depending on the actually supported composition operations (reuse, overriding, combination, and restriction), as well as depending on details of the parsing approach, the following challenges arise when providing for composable parser definitions (see, e.g., [11, Section 3.3.1] for an overview):

- Trade-offs between ambiguity and composability
- Token-level vs. character-level composition
- Anticipated versus unanticipated (de-) composability

Trade-Offs Between Ambiguity and Composability

For the scope of this work, *ambiguity* refers to a property of parser definition (context-free grammar) that will have a corresponding parsing procedure produce

---

[30]Johnstone et al. [25] consider them *filters* that suppress composed rules or rule elements during the import process based on *filter conditions*.

[31]For production grammars, the static analysis procedures of identifying unrealizable and unreachable non-terminals are assumed [1]. For parsing grammars, a conservative analysis incurring false negatives is applied. A false negative is an actually useless non-terminal that cannot be detected as such. See Sect. 5.2.3 for the background.

more than one parse or parsing result, which all are syntactically valid under this grammar. For production grammars (as opposed to parsing grammars based on recognizers) ambiguity refers to the possibility that it produces ambiguous sentences [23, Section 3.1.2]. Ambiguous parsing is particularly critical (*essential* [23]) when each parse presents different and possibly contradicting interpretations in terms of the underlying semantics. But also, earlier when constructing higher-level parse representations such as instantiations of a language model (rather than parse trees), an ambiguous parse cannot be necessarily translated into one expected representation [64, Section 2.2]. Ambiguity can manifest differently. It can surface as parsing failures (e.g., due to state-transition conflicts in a parser), as multiple parsing results (e.g., parse forests)—in worst case scenarios exponential in number, depending on the input—or as a conceptual issue of a missing syntax design-decision.[32]

There is a considerable web of forces and drivers for design decisions to be considered by GPL and DSL developers when it comes to dealing with ambiguity. This involves, among others, balancing trade-offs between (built-in) ambiguity handling (approximative detection, explicit ambiguity resolution) and allowance of grammar features (e.g., left recursion by LR, attribute propagation by LL parsers). Being able to develop an LR parser for a given context-free grammar (CFG) is a one-sided test for the absence of ambiguity in the grammar; failing to do so does not signal the presence of ambiguity, though. Ambiguity conflicts in LR parsing can also be resolved using disambiguation outside inside the parser (extrinsic rules such as precedence orders and associativity [2, Section 6.6]). Such practical approaches to disambiguation are also applied in generalized parsing, but outside of parsing. Generalized parsing approaches (GLL, GLR), while accommodating all grammars including ambiguous ones, require special action to disambiguate as an online or post-processing step (disambiguation or merge filters). In the end, in generalized parsing, ambiguity only surfaces at processing time of the (ambiguous) input.[33]

Composition in this context commonly refers to forming the union of two or more context-free grammars, a.k.a. a grammar union.[34] With composition, the design-decision space towards parsing becomes even more complex. The composability of parser definition themselves may be limited. This is prominently the case for restricted CFG classes, that is, the popular family of grammars that can be turned into LL and LR parsers, respectively, when it comes to a union operation on them. For example, when two grammars amenable to a lookahead LR (LALR)

---

[32]Explicit disambiguation using additional grammar rules and built in disambiguation (ordered choice) can effectively preclude an otherwise important design decision. For developers working with the resulting notation, some ambiguity (keywords vs. identifier, or longest matches) may be real, even though parsing does not run into it due to some inner ruling.

[33]As an extreme example: van der Storm et al. [64] fall back onto treating occurrences of ambiguity as parsing failures, even though tolerated by their generalized (GLL) parser. This is because ambiguity raises issues at the next processing level: automatically creating object graphs as parse representations.

[34]This was referred to earlier as *union with override* as a composition operation.

```
 1 // composed: G0(E)
 2 E → 'a' B D
 3 B → 'b'
 4 D → 'd'
 5 // receiving: G1(E)
 6 E → 'a' B C
 7 B → 'b'
 8 C → 'c'
 9 // resulting: G1'(E)
10 E → 'a' B C | 'a' B D
11 B → 'b'
12 C → 'c'
13 D → 'd'
```

Lst. 5.50 This is an example of a union of override/combine. The composed and receiving definitions can be turned into a parse table for a LALR(1) parser. From a start position on the input stream abc, a lookahead of 1 element (token) suffices to decide on which rule to apply next. This is not the case for the combined resulting grammar: With a lookahead of only one element, both alternates of E match. The generated LALR(1) parser table will end up with conflicts [63, Section 3]

parser generator of some fixed lookahead (k=1) are composed, the resulting grammar cannot be processed by the same LALR(1) parser generator. The generated parser might require an extended lookahead to decide on rules to apply [63]. See Listing 5.50 for an example. As a result, a parser corresponding to composed grammars cannot be used for input valid under the resulting grammar. This is a concrete example for the missingness of the closure under union for restricted CFG. A composition between members of a family of grammars does not yield another member of this family.

Generalized parsing can leverage the closure-under-union property for general CFG, but presents the challenges of ambiguous parsing, at least on ambiguous input. In particular, ambiguity can arise as an unwanted consequence of a composition: Two unambiguous grammars may enter a composition and turn into an ambiguous resulting grammar [14, 64].

DjDSL does not directly address ambiguity, it shuts the above types of ambiguity out beforehand: DjDSL builds on a parsing approach based on a recognition system known as parsing (expression) grammars [18]. They are inherently unambiguous according to the above definition, mainly because parsing expressions build on *ordered choices* and unlimited lookahead. These preclude the possibility of ambiguous parses. However, parsing grammars do not prevent (design-level) ambiguity as perceived by users of the notation and they suffer from non-disjointness under composition: A composition (e.g., combination) may lead to appending a parsing expression e_2 as an alternate to an existing parsing rule $S \leftarrow e_1$, yielding $S \leftarrow e_1/e_2$. This resulting, ordered choice is commutative only if e_1 and e_2 are semi-disjoint expressions, that is, they succeed in consuming input from two languages that are semi-disjoint. Otherwise, the choice is not commutative and the order of composition becomes essential for the parsing result. Intuitively, e_1 and e_2 are semi-disjoint if e_1 does not overlap with any prefix also recognized by e_2 [54, Section 4]. Disjointness must also hold for any super-expression that contains e_1/e_2 like $(e_1/e_2)e_2$.

Example (Adapted from [54, Section 4.2])

Consider the parsing rule S ← ('aa'/'a')'a', with aa as parsing expression e_1 and a as e_2. This rule will successfully consume one input: aaa. Input aa will be rejected, on the ground that the e_1 (aa) is tested first, rejecting any input not having a third a. When flipping the order between e_1 and e_2 from ('aa'/'a') to ('a'/'aa'), only aa will be consumed and aaa becomes now rejected.

   Covering all input, i.e., the language {aa, aaa}, in this one example with a single expression requires an informed re-arrangement. First, the sub-expression (e_1/e_2) must be moved to the right yielding $e_2(e_1/e_2)$. This is equivalent to writing $(e_2e_1)/(e_2e_2)$ according to the distributive property of the ordered choice [18, Section 3.7]. This way, e_2 cannot fail the super-expression unconditionally, the second alternate will be tested when e_2 fails the first one. Second, within the sub-expression, it must be taken care that the expression consuming more of the input (the longer prefix) on success is tested first. This re-arrangement yields S ← 'a' ('aa'/'a').

This has the consequence that a composition can lead to the appended (composed) expression never becoming applied, accidentally and counter the intention of a composition. If e_2 is prepended (e.g., using *Rats!* composition operator), it may effectively shadow the expression introduced by the receiving rule. A DSL developer must, therefore, mind the disjointness of parsing rules to arrive at the intended compositions. This is not only necessary to assess the impact of coarse-grained blackbox composition operations (combination), but also when implementing fine-grained, whitebox compositions. Given that the disjointness property cannot be computed for arbitrary expressions, this can turn into a non-trivial and unsupported task at par with the challenge of an ambiguous CFG. Assuming all input should be consumed by an expression, there is *no* general way of translating an ordered choice into a disjoint form, i.e., rendering its operand expressions disjoint [18, 54].

Token-Level vs. Character-Level Composition

Combining the lexical phase and the parsing phase by incorporating the lexer into a parser yielding scannerless parsers has been considered beneficial for realizing syntax compositions [14]. This is because, first, a character-level grammar as a parser definition is a single unit of composition using the same (context-free) means of expression to tokenize the input as to have those tokens processed into syntactic structures.

ANTLR

ANTLR exemplifies that there can be different units of composition: ANTLR has a fine-granular distinction between lexer rules and parser rules. This is despite the fact that their expressiveness is widely overlapping (e.g., recursion in lexer rules, tokenization by parser rules). In addition, the rules can be organized in pure lexer, pure parser, or combined grammars. For composition, a DSL developer must mind the differences in allowed composition relationships between these three family branches. In addition, composition operations between lexer rules also maintain precedence to avoid tokenization ambiguities (in order of concatenation, with the receiving ones coming first). See Parr [44, p. 257].

Then, second, turning the otherwise one-way interaction of a scanner as a read-only source of a parser into a two-way interaction presents many opportunities for managing syntax composition. In particular, certain types of ambiguity during parsing can be addressed by parametrizing the scanner based on the parsing state.[35]

Despite these advantages for composition, there are also challenges to tackle: All-in-one parser definitions are sometimes deemed too unwieldy because of the details of tokenization [25]. Scannerless parsing introduces character-level ambiguity, in addition to ambiguity types at the token level. These include, as examples, keyword-identifier ambiguity and longest-match ambiguity [53]. Similar to token-level ambiguity, ambiguity has been handled at this level using extra disambiguation rules. Regarding composition, character-level details such as different whitespace conventions and different commenting conventions require special attention under simplistic composition schemes. An example is a grammar union (union with override) that simply merges character-level rules to yield one global configuration of tokenization for a composed syntax which has different local whitespace and commenting conventions.

DjDSL builds on character-level (scannerless) parser definitions. The means of decomposing a parser definition into composable fragments helps manage the extensiveness due to character-level details. Character-level ambiguity also falls into the built-in disambiguation of the recognition system used. Composition operations beyond a union allow to accommodate different local whitespace and commenting conventions.

---

[35]This is advocated and demonstrated by Copper [65].

Example

Consider the parsing rules ID ←[a-z]+ and IF ← 'if'. The former consumes what is to meant to be an identifier or symbol in a DSL, the latter captures a reserved word, or keyword, "if". A separate lexer would first match all keywords, leaving the remainder to be processed for identifiers. In scannerless parsing, and as composed rules, the two rules might end up competing as alternates: S → ID | IF. As unordered alternates, two derivations with different interpretations (keyword vs. identifier) would be suggested for an input containing if. As ordered alternates, S ← ID / IF, the input is always consumed as one kind (identifier), shadowing the other (keyword); or vice versa. This is particularly tricky when identifiers become nested within keywords; or vice versa. A practical approach is to consume keywords first: S ←IF / ID.

Anticipated Versus Unanticipated Composability

A matter of quality generally sought in product-line engineering is minimizing the effort of preplanning [4, Section 3.2.1]. Preplanning involves anticipation of previously unknown features becoming requested (e.g., in a reactive setting) and anticipation of how they are likely to interact with the base and feature assets to this point. Preplanning effort is inherent to a multi-DSL development project (whether proactive or reactive) but can be minimized by employing appropriate variability implementation techniques (see Sect. 2.4).

At the level of a given implementation technique, preplanning effort can be reduced by adopting a technique that allows a DSL developer to leave the existing assets, at the time of adding a new feature implementation, unmodified. Indicators of unmodified reuse are repeatedly stated in challenges and tasks raised for the series of Language-Workbench Competitions [17, Section 6.2.5].

Unmodified reuse is particularly relevant for syntax definitions such as parser definitions and grammars. Take the examples of concrete-syntax and abstract syntax *migration*. In concrete-syntax migration, a requirement might emerge that a purely syntactic change to a textual notation is committed (e.g., renaming of a keyword) that leaves the produced parse representation (abstract syntax) untouched. Is this supported by the DSL development system, allowing for a localized change in the concrete-syntax definition only? In the reverse case, an abstract syntax migration, DSL scripts and models should be carried over unmodified on an evolved abstract syntax (e.g., an abstract syntax entity is split it two related entities).

In what follows, the emphasis will be on the capacity of different composition techniques for grammars and parser definitions (e.g., grammar union, composition operations) to minimize preplanning. This can be achieved by reusing a once defined concrete syntax *as-is* for defining concrete-syntax extensions as part of DSL features becoming added. Unmodified (or unanticipated) reuse as an ideal has the benefits of increasing the commonality of a concrete-syntax fragment in a DSL family (i.e., the reuse likelihood), of preserving backwards compatibility, and of reducing the effort of preplanning—during domain analysis as well as during designing and implementing the initial product line.

5.2.3 Parsing Expression Grammars and Packrat Parsing

A *parsing expression grammar* (PEG; [18]) is defined as a 4-tuple $G = (N, T, R, e_S)$. N denotes the finite set of non-terminals, T is the finite set of terminals, R is the finite set of rules, and e_S is the start expression. Each rule $r \in R$ is a pair (A, e) typically written as a maplet $A \leftarrow e$, with $A \in N$ and e being another parsing expression.[36] A parsing expression defines a pattern to match (recognize) and, if matched, to consume a specified fragment of input. A parsing expression is defined using the empty string (ϵ), the sets of terminals and non-terminals (N, T), as well as operator expressions summarized in Table 5.5.

The meaning of a PEG is given by a recognition program [23, Section 15.7]. A recognition program is a program for recognizing and structuring (including tokenizing, parsing) a string. The (operational) meaning of a PEG-based recognition program can be thought of character-level interpreter of some input that works left-right, top-down to recognize, and if recognized, to consume the matched input. The interpreter always consumes the longest possible matched prefix of some input. A given parsing expression is said to succeed when it consumes what it has recognized; if an expression fails (i.e., it does not recognize anything), it consumes nothing from the input. This is even so when some of its sub-expressions have succeeded.

Parsing expressions can contain operator expressions and operator behaviors not available in other approaches. Most importantly, for a given expression, *alternate* sub-expressions are tried in their order of definition. The first one to succeed wins, any remaining ones are discarded. This is referred to as a prioritized or ordered choice (see operator 2 in Table 5.5). Prioritized or ordered choice has been documented as the key discriminator between PEG and CFG [32]. On top, the choice operator gives rise to all difficulties associated with PEG, also relevant for composition (i.e., ambiguity handling, language hiding, error reporting). Aside from its characteristic choice operator, a PEG's repetition operators proceed in a *greedy* manner, always consuming the longest possible input prefix (see operators 9 and 10 in Table 5.5). In addition, parsing expressions can benefit from lookahead operators, namely *not-* and *and-*predicates. As lookaheads, they do not consume any input even when succeeding.[37]

---

[36]As a structured description of a language, in terms of the concrete and abstract syntax, a PEG resembles closely production grammars such as context-free grammars and their notations (E/BNF). To this end, they are treated the same and what has been said about grammars as parser definitions in Sect. 5.2.6 applies to both. Important differences between CFG and PEG [32] in terms of their meaning (generators vs. recognizers) are pointed out where and when necessary.

[37]*Looking ahead* in a recognition program refers to leaving the read pointer on a stream of input characters or tokens unmodified, while having continued to recognize beyond that position.

Table 5.5 Overview of the operators available for OPEG/PT parsing expressions. Not shown are rule attributes (e.g., void, leaf, value) and built-in character classes (e.g., <alnum>, <digit>, <xdigit>). The three types of *generator* expressions (13–15) are specific to an OPEG. Note that ϵ (epsilon) stands for matching the empty string; $\leftarrow$ indicates a parsing rule as a maplet with a non-terminal as its LHS and a parsing expression as its RHS

	op	Description	Desugared
1	e_1 e_2	Sequence	e_1 e_2
2	e_1 / e_2	Prioritized (ordered) choice	e_1 / e_2
3	'd'	Literal character	'd'
4	'abc'	Literal string	'a' 'b' 'c'
5	[A-z0-9]	Character ranges	[A-z] / [0-9]
6	.	Any character	.
7	(e)	Sub-expression (group)	(e)
8	e?	Optional expression	e / ϵ
9	e*	Inclusive-or (zero-or-more)	e*
10	e+	Inclusive-or (one-or-more)	e e*
11	!e	*Not* predicate	!e
12	&e	*And* predicate	!(!e)
13	\`c\` e	*Instantiation* generator	\`c\` e
14	f:e	*Assignment* generator	f $\leftarrow$ e
15	f:(\`q\` e)	*Query* generator	f $\leftarrow$ \`q\` e

A PEG acts both as a specification of a software language and the specification of a top-down parser for that language [32]. When considered in combination, the characteristics of PEG, as well as their operator types and behaviors yield important properties of a PEG and its corresponding parser:

- A PEG (PEG-based parser) is inherently *unambiguous* in that a recognition program derived from it will produce one parse or parsing result. This is a consequence of the ordered choice and the greediness of expressions when consuming input. While this property makes them unsuitable for natural-language processing, it fits the requirements of defining syntaxes of software languages (e.g., general-purpose and domain-specific ones) and to derive efficient as well as practical parser implementations.
- A PEG (PEG-based parser) has unlimited lookahead. This results from the availability of not- and and-predicates and from the operators' greediness. This is also beneficial to avoid certain types of ambiguity (e.g., longest-match ambiguity).
- A PEG (PEG-based parser) limits the rolling back from unsuccessful (failing) alternates when attempted in top-down, depth-first visits through nested expressions with alternates. The use of ordered choice, as well as the unlimited lookahead, result in this limited *backtracking*.

These operator types, their behavioral meaning, and the resulting PEG properties have another benefit: They allow for a linear-time implementation of a corresponding recognition and parsing algorithm (parser). This parsing style has been referred to as *packrat parsing*. Technically, a packrat parser is a recursive-descent parser that avoids repeated calls to its parsing procedures for already visited input positions and memoizes (caches, "hoards") intermediate parsing results. Cached results are the matches for given input positions. As the size of the former dimension can be considered fixed (number of non-terminals and the input length) and the cached matches are of constant size (position and range), parsers can settle at a temporal complexity that can be considered linear. A packrat parse can be modeled as top-down, left-right walk of a recognition table [23, Section 15.7.2]. Apart from handicraft parsers for a given PEG, PEG-based frameworks have devised different implementation techniques, including grammar interpreters and generators for stack-based packrat parsers. The latter accept a PEG as input and generate a derived parser against a VIRTUAL MACHINE [5, 28, 33].

This is also the case for the *Parsing Tools* (PT) component reused by DjDSL. The VIRTUAL MACHINE for packrat parsers is called PARAM and offers different programming interfaces. These include an object-oriented one that allows for the generative and compositional reuse of stack-based parsing methods (see also Sect. 5.2.5).

Important restrictions of a PEG and a PEG-based parser result from the above properties (in particular, the ordered choice), as well as the underlying parsing techniques. To begin with, *left recursion* is not supported by the basic PEG model given its underlying, recursive-descent interpretation. Practical extensions have been explored and commonly known refactorings to remove direct and indirect left recursion are applicable. On more general terms, handling ambiguity by precluding it from surfacing at all, at any stage of language processing, has been critically appreciated. As for language composition, three complications specific to parsing expressions are particularly relevant for the scope of DjDSL: the issues pertaining to language hiding, grammar cleaning, and error reporting. All of them are consequences of the prioritized or ordered choice operator, surfacing just differently.

Language Hiding

Language hiding is a practical consequence of the absence of *general semi-disjointness* of a choice expression [54] for the scope of the language matched by a PEG.[38] Language hiding occurs when a (greedy) alternate of a choice expression prevents a later alternate from being applied to inputs that it could otherwise succeed on. This is also called a pre-emptive prefix capture [45]. Consider the following two choice expressions, example taken from [46, p. 4]: ('a' / 'aa')'b' versus ('aa' / 'a')'ab'. Further consider that both are exercised on the input aab. One will notice that both will fail on this input, that is to consume the entire input. Both match and consume a and then roll back leaving a suffix unvisited. This is because the first alternates ('a' and 'aa', respectively) win, the second ones will be ignored. This is despite the fact that they would perfectly succeed in consuming the entire

---

[38] See the introduction to the disjointness property as a condition of unrestricted composability of two or more parsing grammars in Sect. 5.2.2.

input, if just tried. Language hiding (or pre-emptive prefix capture) has practical implications for composition operations, in that alternates become automatically (combination) or selectively added (extraction w/ and w/o insertion position). Any added alternate may unintentionally hide others, and, therefore, important fragments of the matched language. DjDSL tries to minimize unintended language hiding for two or more composed grammars, by applying precautionary defaults: For example, alternates introduced by DSL extensions are prepended to those of the receiving grammar. This follows from the assumption that, in extensions, the aim is to capture longer prefixes. Beyond that point, fine-grained control during composition (explicit alternate positioning) is supported.

Grammar Cleaning
In Sect. 5.2.2, it was established that techniques for reducing ("cleaning") grammars from unrealizable and unreachable non-terminals are a building block for modeling and implementing certain composition operations. For production grammars (context-free grammars), this is a matter of static analysis [1, Section 2.4.2]. For parsing grammars, in the general case, finding useless (non-recognizing, undefined, and unused) non-terminals is known to be undecidable (see [23, p. 507] and [18, Section 3.5]). This is, again, due to the issue of *non-disjointness* of the ordered-choice operator [54]: The evaluation of some alternate is conditional on the success or failure of its preceding alternates. The parsing expression with two alternates 'a' / 'ab' is pathological because it will only recognize a in all inputs prefixed by a single a (e.g., aa, ab). The second alternate is realizable (i.e., it recognizes a literal string) but is effectively shadowed by the first alternate ('a'). Therefore, even if an alternate expression can be statically marked as realizable (i.e., it does recognize and possibly consume at least one terminal on the input stream), it may be actually unreachable in the order of any evaluation of a given choice expression. Deciding on whether a choice expression has only disjoint alternates, in general, is not possible either. (Practical) Workarounds are tool-supported manual inspection [48] or leveraging higher-level CFG that are transformed into corresponding PEG, said being *well-behaved* having only choice expressions containing alternates then known to be disjoint [32]. None of these apply to automated grammar cleaning, however. For the scope of this work, a conservative approximation is applied. An approximative cleaning of parsing grammars will lead to false negatives. A false negative is a non-terminal marked as realizable that may still turn out unreachable, conditionally. Therefore, DjDSL is not able to obtain fully reduced grammars and fully optimized parsers (i.e., parsers containing dead code for some input). However, the approximation is sufficient for cleaning resulting grammars from composition artifacts, such as non-terminals becoming undefined.

Error Reporting
As part of a PEG-based parser, parsing procedures (however implemented) emit exceptions under two conditions; one internal to parsing (backtracking), the other specific to the defined syntax. The first, parsing-specific condition occurs as building block of backtracking. When an alternate sub-expression of a choice expression fails to recognize and to consume some input prefix, an exception is the intended

Lst. 5.51 A definition of
Miss Grant's state machine

```
 1   start idle
 2
 3   state idle
 4       on doorClosed go active
 5
 6   state active
 7       on lightOn go waitingForDrawer
 8       on drawerOpened go waitingForLight
 9
10   state waitingForDrawer
11       on drawerOpened go unlockedPanel
12
13   state unlockedPanel
14       go idle on panelClosed
15
16   state waitingForLight
```

start condition of rolling back, to attempt the subsequent alternate of the choice.
The second condition is that an exception returned by a sub-expression (and the
corresponding parsing procedure) is meant to signal a syntax defect found in
the input. Error reporting for PEG-based parsers has, therefore, been considered
challenging, because basic implementations cannot properly discriminate between
the two conditions. This makes actual error reporting to the DSL developer non-
intuitive, or even ambiguous. Practical implementations of PEG-based (packrat)
parsers commonly fall back to a heuristic: Parsing exceptions are reported as syntax
failures when no further alternate is to be tested and not the entire input has been
consumed (i.e., there remains an unmatched suffix). If reported, the farthest-failure
position on the input stream and the corresponding failing expressions [plural!]
on that position are reported to provide the context for inspecting the input for
a defect. While the farthest-failure position heuristic provides more accurate and
localized explanations to the DSL developer, it remains error prone. In addition, it
requires extra effort to localize the defect in the input causing the syntax failure
(e.g., in presence of multiple reported expressions having failed at a given position).
Alternatives have been proposed, such as explicit throw expressions that allow for
placing parsing exits plus failure hints into a parsing expression (a.k.a. "labeled
failures"; [47, Section 5]).

5.2.4 Object Parsing-Expression Grammars (OPEG)

In DjDSL, a parsing grammar is a (packrat) parser definition using parsing
expressions (see Sect. 5.2.3). In addition, and interleaved with the parsing rules, a
parsing grammar contains dedicated expressions to process the consumed syntactic
structure into an instantiation of a DjDSL language mode, i.e., an object graph. This

Lst. 5.52 Examples of an instantiation and an assignment generator

```
         E  ←  `Event` ON name:<alnum>+ ;
void: ON ← WS 'on' WS;
```

way, an OPEG definition lays out two-in-one: (a) input recognition and (b) mapping the recognized input onto objects, their fields, and non-hierarchical relationships (references) between the mapped objects.

In what follows, these capabilities are highlighted and explained by referring to the running example of modeling the state machine driving "Miss Grant's Controller", as introduced in Sect. 5.1. Listing 5.51 depicts the concrete-syntax snippet of a state-machine definition. This syntax snippet is recognized and consumed by the parser defined in this section.

Object Generation

Parsing rules in DjDSL's parsing grammars can contain special-purpose expressions at their RHS that compute one or several instantiations of language-model classifiers when their rule is applied. These expressions are referred to as *instantiation generators*. Listing 5.52 shows a grammar excerpt with two rules E and ON, with WS (not shown) handling and discarding whitespace characters. Rule E consumes trigger-event definitions for state machine transitions of the form on doorClosed (line 4, Listing 5.51). It features the rule element Event enclosed by single grave accents (` ... `). This is an instantiation generator that will translate into an instantiation call for a classifier Event.

To become useful, a parsing rule can be extended to include *assignment generators*. These generators mark recognized and consumed values from the processed input as values to become assigned to the properties of objects created by an instantiation generator. Listing 5.52 shows the example of an assignment generator for a property name. The so-generated assignment binds any value returned from applying the parsing expression <alnum>+, that is, a string of at least one alphanumerical character.[39] In the example, this value will denote the event's name. When E is applied to consume the partial input on doorClosed, the parsing result includes the evaluation result of the following command: Event new -name doorClosed.[40]

Assignment generators do not necessarily apply to objects generated by the same rule. Assignments can propagate up along the rule hierarchy of a parsing grammar.

---

[39]DjDSL benefits from a number of predefined character classes that match those acknowledged by the host language Tcl.

[40]Instantiation and assignment generators compare conceptually with syntax-directed definitions (SDD) working in a bottom-up fashion for construction syntax trees, with semantic rules (instantiation and assignment generators) yielding synthesized attributes (e.g., objects with populated state). See Aho et al. [3, Section 5.3.1]. However, there are important differences in the details. DjDSL's generators tightly integrate with the parsing rules and operate on arbitrary syntax trees.

Alternates

Each alternate at a RHS of a parsing rule, i.e., the operand parsing expressions of an ordered choice, can define an instantiation generator. The instantiation generators can point to the same or different classifiers. Listing 5.53 demonstrates how two alternative writing styles for transitions (i.e., on-go vs. go-on) could be defined as alternates. This is not necessarily achieved in the most compact, but an illustrative manner.

In accordance with the semantics of ordered choices in parsing grammars, only the generator as part of the matching choice branch will be evaluated. For all but the transition definition on line 14, Listing 5.51, the first alternate applies; the second alternate applies then to the input on line 14. It is also permitted that the alternates of a given choice expression do not carry any instantiation generator. Whether this is accepted or not depends on the matching assignment generator in a higher-level rule that consumes (binds) any value returned from the surrounding choice expression. The example in Listing 5.53 also highlights another characteristic of assignment generators. Assignment generators do not depend on their positions in a given RHS or sequence. During object construction, they map directly to non-positional object parameters, as provided by NX.

Associations and References

Assignment generators allow a DSL developer to relate objects, as defined by instantiation generators, in two ways: First, an assignment generator refers to a bare parsing expression. The result computed by this parsing expression will be bound as value of an assignment. Given the hierarchical relationship between parsing expressions, objects are therefore related in a manner reflecting the parsing hierarchy. A `StateMachine` references its `State` instantiations, each `State` maintains `Transitions` that, again, reference a trigger `Event`. This web of relations corresponds to the parsing procedure.

Second, assignment generators can be used to relate objects independently from the parse. This is required because language models typically involve some form of *circular initialization* [56]. In terms of the language model, this refers to associations (references) established between objects beyond those induced by the parse, i.e., at different times of a parse. Circularity requires, to be fully resolved, that all objects to enter circular relationships have been fully initialized before. Alternatively, *placeholders* can take the marginal role of yet to be constructed

```
T ← `Transition` trigger:E GO target:<alnum>+ /
    `Transition` GO target:<alnum>+ trigger:E;
```

Lst. 5.53 Alternates (choices) and instantiation generators

Lst. 5.54 Supporting
forward references

```
1   start idle
2   state idle
```

Lst. 5.55 Example of a
query generator

```
M ← `StateMachine` START
    start:(`$root states $0` <alnum>+)
    states:S+ ;
```

objects [56].[41] Consider the excerpt from the running example in Listing 5.54, whose complete concrete syntax is shown in Listing 5.53. The excerpt puts the spot on a circular dependency between two declaration statements. Setting the start state to idle is in the preamble of the definition (line 1). The state, however, is about to be defined later (line 2).

Using the first form of an assignment generator for the start property will not be able to establish a link to a State object. This is because it has yet to be created when processing line 1 of the input. To defer the assignment, to a moment the remainder of the object graph with all states including idle has been constructed, an assignment operator can be extended into a second form. This second form nests a parsing expression with a *query generator*. In Listing 5.55, the assignment generator for the property start is assigned a parsing expression that contains such a query expression: $root states $0.

A query expression[42] allows for navigating and for accessing the object graph under construction. The first word of a query (e.g., the command) roots the query in the object graph: $root refers to the top-level object corresponding to the root of the parse tree. $parent refers to the ancestor object according to the parse tree. $self is the self-reference to the receiver of the assignment. In addition, a query generator can refer to the parse matches of the surrounding parsing expression in a positional manner. For example, in Listing 5.55, $0 will bind the first value computed by the first sub-expressions <alnum>+, which is a position 0 of the sequence expression.[43] The result of evaluating the query expression in an environment that provides values for the predefined variables (e.g., root, parent, 0) is then assigned to the property denoted by the assignment generator. The generated assignment, however, is deferred to a moment when all objects are guaranteed to being existing, according to the underlying parse tree.

---

[41]For internal DSL development, DjDSL offers CONSTRUCTION BUILDERS that act as placeholders (see Sect. 5.1).

[42]Technically, a query is implemented as a Tcl script containing a single Tcl command (i.e., a sequence of words). The final command to be executed is to be formed by substituting predefined variables (root, 0) for values in a controlled execution environment. The value bindings are provided by the parser.

[43]This example builds around the idea that the state-machine definition contains identifiers (or symbols) for states, which are shared throughout the definition and map to State objects via some accessible keyed collection (states property). The query generators provide the glue to a) resolve objects for identifiers and b) to bind these as values to properties via generated assignments.

```
1    M  ←  `StateMachine` START start:<alnum>+ states:S+ ;
2    S  ←  `State` STATE name:<alnum>+ transitions:T* ;
```

Lst. 5.56 Mapping zero-or-more and one-to-more expressions to multi-valued properties (collections)

```
1       M  ←  `StateMachine` START start:<alnum>+ states:S (states:S)* ;
2       S  ←  `State` STATE name:<alnum>+ TRANS? ;
3    TRANS  ←  transitions:T TRANS*;
```

Lst. 5.57 Mapping *desugared* zero-or-more and one-to-more expressions to multi-valued properties (collections)

Multi-Valued Properties

Parsing expressions can contain repetition operators for consuming zero-or-more
($e*$) and one-or-more ($e+$) occurrences of input matched by the operand expression.
At the level of the language model, these collections of consumed matches naturally
map to multi-valued object properties (0..* and 1..*, respectively, in NX). DjDSL's
object parsing expressions allow for defining multi-valued assignments, across
multiple definition levels of assignment generators, to bind value collections to
multi-valued properties.

Listing 5.56 contains the two top-level parsing rules for the small state-machine
language to describe "Miss Grant's Controller". The RHS of rule M contains an
assignment generator states. The generator's parsing expression S+ will bind one
or more instantiations of the State classifier. This is defined by the corresponding
rule for the S non-terminal (see line 2 of the same listing). The parsing expression
of rule S itself collects zero or more instantiations of the Transition classifier
returned by the T rule (see Listing 5.53).

In accordance with standard normalization rules for these two repetition operators, the two rules can also be rewritten (*desugared*). See Listing 5.57. One may
use multiple occurrences of the same-named and same-valued assignment generator
(see line 1). Even the commonly used right-recursive refactoring is supported (see
TRANS on line 3).

Key to appreciate this idea is that the repeated occurrences of a given assignment
generator in the (intermediate) parse tree are muxed into single, but multi-valued
assignment calls; and not repeated single-valued ones. The latter would effectively redefine the object state, rather than setting a multi-valued property once.
Alternatively, for operand expressions containing instantiation generators (like non-
terminal S in Listing 5.57), one can write a single assignment generator with a
sub-expression holding the desugared repetition, e.g.: states:(S S*).

More Highlights

Parsing rules and their decomposition into alternates and non-terminals are orthogonal to the placement of instantiation and assignment generators. Parsing rules can

```
E    ←  `Event` ON NAME ;
NAME ←  name:<alnum>+;
```

Lst. 5.58 Distributing instantiation and assignment generators over connected parsing rules

be freely re-structured. For example, a refactoring can introduce or factor out sub-expressions into new non-terminals and it can remove non-terminals. The aims are to best organize the syntax definition and to improve ill-defined grammars (e.g., left recursion in parsing grammars), however, *without* affecting the object graph to be generated. Consider a rewrite of the rule defining non-terminal E of Listing 5.52 (line 1) into the two rules in Listing 5.58: E and NAME. The first contains the instantiation generator, and the second features the assignment generator.

The result of the instantiation generator will be exactly the same as with the single rule in Listing 5.52. That is, an instance of classifier Event of name doorClosed. This is despite the fact that the structure of the parse tree differs. Relocating assignment generators into separate rules also has the benefit of reusing syntax and assignment fragments for different instantiation generators (and the language-model concepts). For instance, name or identifier patterns can so be defined in one rule and shared by different language-model elements. This is possible even in the case that the elements are not in a reuse relationship in their language model.

5.2.5   Design and Implementation

The OPEG implementation of DjDSL is realized as an extension to the Tcl package PT (for "Parsing Tools") that forms part of the Tcl Library (tcllib). The extension is itself organized as a Tcl package: djdsl::opeg. The required package pt provides, among others, an NX-based parsing runtime shared by all generated parsers. In this approach, a PEG or an OPEG is not associated with a specific recursive-descent parser [45] or a grammar interpreter [12]. Rather, a grammar, first, is processed to produce a parser program made up of parsing instructions. Parsing instructions deal with character testing, input handling, status as well as error handling. Second, a VIRTUAL MACHINE [5] executes the parsing instructions of a parser program that, in turn, changes the machine's state. The machine's state (in a simplified form) is implemented by a number of stacks for managing the current input position, backtracking positions, etc. In addition, the machine's state contains stores for non-terminal and terminal caches. In pt, this stack-based virtual parsing machine is called PARAM for "PAckRAt Machine".[44] The NX implementation of the PARAM realizes the grammar-specific and the basic parsing instructions as

---

[44]The idea of a virtual parsing machine for processing input according to a PEG has also been considered independently by Kuramitsu [28], Medeiros and Ierusalimschy [33].

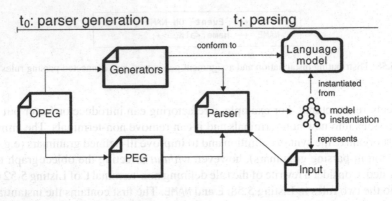

Fig. 5.59 Overview of the processing pipelines in djdsl::opeg: (**a**) parser generation and (**b**) parsing

methods. With this, the PARAM be refined via NX composition techniques (e.g., mixins).

DjDSL extends the parser generator and the PARAM to support *object parsing expressions* as introduced in Sect. 5.2.4. This is achieved without modifying the underlying NX PARAM implementation, nor the implementation of pt. To produce a PARAM parsing program from an OPEG (see *parser generation* in Fig. 5.59), the OPEG is rewritten to break apart generators and parsing expressions. This is the responsibility of the djdsl::opeg::Rewriter component (see Fig. 5.60) which acts as a post-processor on a parsed OPEG. The results are a collection of generators (instantiation and assignment) and an ordinary PEG. The latter is used by the pt parser generator to create a Parser class. This parser is associated with the collection of generators, based on which the parser instruments the virtual parsing machine to indirect selected instruction calls (e.g., when executing choices) to enact the respective generators. For this purpose, the generated Parser class inherits from djdsl::opeg::Engine (see also Fig. 5.60). When clients present input to the generated Parser (see *parsing* in Fig. 5.59), a parse is created that carries embedded annotations about enacted generators. The parse is then consumed in a bottom-up pass to create a language-model instantiation. The actual instantiation is managed by indirection to a ModelFactory (see Fig. 5.60).

Clients defining an OPEG and requesting a parse based on some input interact with three components of djdsl::opeg: djdsl::opeg::Grammar, djdsl::opeg::Engine, and djdsl::opeg::ModelFactory (see Fig. 5.60).

Grammar

The class djdsl::opeg::Grammar is used by clients to define an OPEG. Grammar definition can be achieved by submitting a collection of parsing rules (via new), a complete OPEG script (newFromScript), or by pointing to a grammar file (newFromFile). From this Grammar instantiation, the generation of a parser can then be requested. In addition, Grammar instantiations can be related to each other

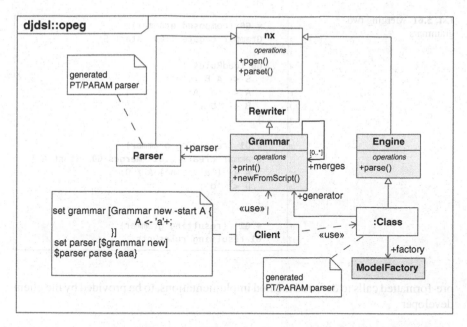

Fig. 5.60 Structural overview of DjDSL's infrastructure for object parsing-expression grammars (OPEG)

via the `merges` attribute. This relationship between `Grammar` instantiations lays the foundation for the grammar-composition technique applied by DjDSL. See Sect. 5.2.6. Besides, `Grammar` provides for utilities to inspect on an OPEG (e.g., rules set) and the resulting parses (e.g., a pretty printer).

Engine
The class `djdsl::opeg::Engine` defines and implements the basic interface of all generated PARAM parsers. Most importantly, it offers different methods to submit input text to parsing. Whatever the parsing facility used by a client, the type of result value is determined by a `ModelFactory`. Internally, the `Engine` class is also responsible for instrumenting the PARAM to set instantiation and assignment generators in motion.

ModelFactory
When instantiation generators are dispatched, this is achieved by indirection via a `djdsl::opeg::ModelFactory`. This allows for plugging-in a different STRATEGY [20]of assembling a language-model instantiation, or a custom post-processor. A client can pick from a set of predefined subclasses of `ModelFactory` (e.g., one for DjDSL's language models, one for plain NX classes) or define a custom subclass or factory object. In absence of a specific `ModelFactory`, the default is to employ a generic TEMPLATE METHOD indirection [60]:Non-terminal matches are turned into

Lst. 5.61 Merging two grammars

```
 1   # G0 (composed grammar)
 2   Grammar create ::G0 -start S
 3
 4   G0 loadRules {
 5     S <- A B / 'a';
 6     A <- 'a' A;
 7     B <- 'b';
 8   }
 9
10   # G1 (receiving grammar)
11   Grammar create ::G1 -merges G0 -start A {
12     A <- ('a' / 'A') A / D;
13     D <- 'd';
14   }
15
16   # G1' (resulting grammar)
17   G1 resulting rules nts
```

pre-formatted calls to deferred method implementations, to be provided by the client developer.

5.2.6　Composing Object Parsing Grammars

The conceptual tenets of grammars as de- and re-composable definitions of context-free languages and parsers were introduced in Sect. 5.2.2. Different types of composition operations, their comparative benefits and drawbacks, were discussed. The covered operations included union with override (a.k.a. grammar union), blackbox combinations, and whitebox operations: aliasing (w/ and w/o substitute), extraction (w/ and w/o rewrite), and restriction (via renaming or removal).

DjDSL's parser definitions (object parsing grammars, OPEG) provide these state-of-the-art operations via a unified programming model. The programming models allows for relating and for modifying parsing-grammar objects (see also Sect. 5.2.5). DjDSL's programming model for de- and recomposing parsing grammars builds on the properties of a recognition system such as parsing expressions under composition. The properties include closure under union, ordered choice, and semi-disjointness. These properties shape many details of the implementation, ranging from cleaning operations on definitions to the transformations themselves. DjDSL offers this spectrum of composition operations and original mixes thereof to accommodate the different DSL composition types (extension, unification, extension composition, and self-extension), as well as to support individual and project-specific design-decision making by DSL developers.

DjDSL allows for relating instantiations of Grammar classes using a single relationship type: *merges*. A receiving grammar can merge one or several composed grammars to obtain a resulting grammar. This closely matches the fundamental

Lst. 5.62 Example of a remove transformation (eager definition)

```
1  # G1 (receiving grammar)
2  Grammar create ::G1 -merges G0 -start A {
3    A <- ('a' / 'A') A / D;
4    D <- 'd';
5  } {
6    # transformations
7    G0::B ==> ; # rule deletion
8  }
```

Lst. 5.63 Example of a remove transformation (lazy definition)

```
1  G1 loadTransforms {
2    # transformations, reloaded
3    G0::B ==> ; # rule deletion
4  }
```

interpretation of composition operations as enumerated in Sect. 5.2.2. For example, the grammar definition in Listing 5.61 defines a merge relationship between two grammars: G1 acts as the receiving, G0 as the composed one. The resulting grammar can be obtained by calling the `resulting` method on the receiving `Grammar` object (see line 17 of Listing 5.61). DjDSL allows for multiple levels of defining merge relationships. Before computing a resulting grammar, the collection of composed definitions is turned into an unambiguous linear order. This linear order preserves local-precedence orders. Violations (e.g., circular merges) under linearization are signaled at definition time.[45] This linearization is then used to resolve dependencies between rules and as the basis for the subsequent transformations. The merges relationship does *not* directly determine which kind of composition operation is to be performed between receiving and composed grammars. This is achieved in a separate step.

In addition to establishing a `merges` relationship, the receiving grammar can also define a script of grammar transformations to implement different composition operations. These include simple union with override in the *absence* of transformations, as well as different variants of extraction and of restriction in the *presence* of transformations. Transformations can be defined either as a closing script block when creating a `Grammar` (see Listing 5.62) or by explicitly calling `loadTransforms` on an existing `Grammar` instance (see Listing 5.63).

The latter can be called repeatedly, causing a flush of the resulting grammar and a rerun of any transformations. The composition behavior in presence of transformations is implemented on the procedure illustrated in an informal manner in Fig. 5.64 (steps a–d). The procedure involves steps of turning unqualified names of non-terminals into qualified names, rule rewriting, and grammar-cleaning operations.

---

[45]Internally, parsing grammars are represented as NX classes and can be related as such: The merge relationship is therefore derived from an ordinary subclass-superclass relationship. This way, DjDSL benefits from the built-in linearization scheme.

First, the set of rules of the input grammars (G0, G1) are processed to turn the non-terminals names into qualified names (**a**): A qualified non-terminal is a non-terminal whose name is prefixed by the name of the its owning grammar. For example, non-terminal A becomes qualified as G0::A. Non-terminal B so becomes G0::B.[46] Second, a union operation is performed with precedence for rules from the receiving grammars over those of the composed one (**b**). Due to prior name qualification, this represents effectively a disjoint-union operation. This has the consequence that the original sets of rules enter the intermediate set of rules in an unaltered and in a complete fashion. Third, the defined transformations (e.g., extraction, restriction) are performed on this intermediate set of rules (**c**). In Fig. 5.64, the example refers to the transformation depicted in Listings 5.61 and 5.62: a removal of the rule with the LHS non-terminal G0::B. Fourth, after completion, standard grammar cleaning is performed, most importantly: unrealizable (including undefined) non-terminals are dropped, then unreachable non-terminals are removed (**d**).

Note that removal of undefined non-terminals is performed at the latest possible, post-transformation stage (i.e., step d in Fig. 5.64). This allows composable grammars or grammar fragments to defer the definition of non-terminals till transformation time (step c in Fig. 5.64). This way, DjDSL's OPEG allow different kinds of deferred non-terminals to implement preplanned extension points. See Sects. 5.2.6.1 and 5.2.6.3 for the details.

As for the actual grammar transformations supported in step c of Fig. 5.64, an overview of the available operators is presented in Table 5.6.

An (**1**) extract w/o rewrite ($\Leftarrow$) selects the RHS expression of the referenced rule (e.g., G0::A) and introduces it into the receiving rules set. Introduction refers to either creating a new rule G1::A with the extracted RHS or adding the selected RHS as an additional alternate to an existing rule. An (**2**) extract w/ rewrite ($\Leftrightarrow$) proceeds as the extract. Additionally, it renames any non-terminals reachable at

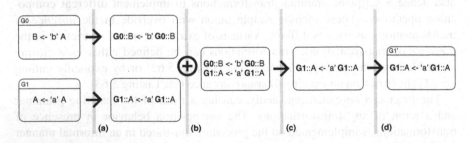

Fig. 5.64 A procedural overview of creating a *resulting* grammar including transforms in four steps (a–d): (a) **narrow**: Non-terminals in the input rules sets are turned into qualified symbols; (b) **compose**: the (disjoint) union of the input rules sets is formed; (c) **modify**: the transformation operations (e.g., append, removal) are performed; (d) **clean**: standard cleaning operations on unrealizable and unreachable non-terminals are performed

---

[46]Johnstone et al. [25] refer to this auxiliary transformation as introducing *name hygiene*.

Table 5.6 Overview of the operators for composing elements of two object parsing-expression grammars (OPEG)

	op	Type	Description	Example
1	$\Leftarrow$	Binary	Extract w/o rewrite	$A \Leftarrow G0::A$
2	$\Leftrightarrow$	Binary	Extract w/ rewrite	$A \Leftrightarrow G0::A$
3	$\overset{*}{\Leftrightarrow}$	Binary	Transitive extract w/ rewrite	$A \overset{*}{\Leftrightarrow} G0::A$
4	$\Rightarrow$	Unary	Remove	$G0::B \Rightarrow$
5	$\leftarrow$	Binary	op. 1 w/o generators	$A \leftarrow G0::A$
6	$\leftrightarrow$	Binary	op. 2 w/o generators	$A \leftrightarrow G0::A$
	None	n/a	Union with override	G1 merges set G0

the extracted RHS expression using the prefix of the receiving grammar (e.g., substituting prefix $G1::*$ for $G0::*$). The (**3**) transitive variant of extract w/ rewrite ($\overset{*}{\Leftrightarrow}$) additionally imports any rules providing definitions for the extracted and renamed RHS non-terminals. These rule dependencies are satisfied from the pool of linearized composed grammars. Finally, (**4**) resulting grammars can be restricted by using the removal operator ($\Rightarrow$). A removal affects an entire rule or a rule alternate. To selectively insert an extracted RHS as a new alternate, the operators 1–3 allow for defining an insertion position, e.g.: $A \Leftarrow G0::A$ 0. The extracted RHS expression becomes inserted at the first (zero-based) position. That is, it is prepended as a new alternate to a rule, if existing. The position qualifier defaults to prepending extracted expressions.[47]

Generators

The generators for instantiations, assignments, and queries are integral parts of the parsing expressions also under transformation. Generators become combined, extracted, and removed with the surrounding parsing expressions or sub-expressions (alternates) according to the stipulated behavior of the first four operators (1–4). This is particularly important for choice expressions. At their top level, generators are elements of each alternate and can become inserted or removed during a transformation affecting the respective alternate. However, to reference and to reuse parsing sub-expressions without their generators (e.g., to attach matches to an alternative generator), there are two transform operators that operate on the plain expressions, without generators (see operators 5 and 6 in Table 5.6).

---

[47]This default is a consequence of the issue of *language hiding* in PEG. See Sect. 5.2.3.

Lst. 5.65 A definition of an
undirected graph using DOT
notation. This is 1:1 reused
from the example exercised
on internal DSL extension,
see Sect. 5.1.1

```
1  graph {
2    // node definitions
3    "1st Edition";
4    "2nd Edition";
5    "3rd Edition";
6    // edge definitions
7    "1st Edition" -- "2nd Edition";
8    "2nd Edition" -- "3rd Edition";
9  }
```

An (**5**) extract w/o rewrite w/o generators (←) selects the RHS expression of
the referenced rule (e.g., G0::A), omitting any generators, and introduces it into the
receiving rules set (see also operator 1). An (**6**) extract w/ rewrite w/o generators
(↔) performs the extraction/ introduction and patches the namespace prefixes (see
also operator 2), again, omitting any generators. See Sects. 5.2.6.1–5.2.6.3 for
concrete applications of these two generator-free operators.

In absence of transformations, a merges relationship defaults to a union with
override. When forming the union, the receiving rules take precedence over the composed ones. The operand values consumed by the six operators listed in Table 5.6
must be qualified (G0::A) or unqualified non-terminal names (A). Unqualified
names, both on the left-hand side and on the right-hand side, will be narrowed
by automatically prepending the enclosing grammar's name. The transformations
are executed in their order of definition, without any particular precedence of one
operator over the other (see, e.g., Listing 5.62). Varying transformations can be
repeatedly applied to obtain different resulting grammars.

In what follows, the application of these basic grammar compositions (union,
extraction, and restriction) is exemplified in the context of the three DSL composition types: DSL extension in Sect. 5.2.6.1, DSL unification in Sect. 5.2.6.2, and
DSL extension composition in Sect. 5.2.6.3. Self-extension will be discussed in
Sect. 5.4. The running examples already introduced on internal DSL composition
are reused (GraphPL, Miss Grant's, and BCEL) with slight extensions to highlight
the capabilities or restrictions of external syntax composition, in general, and for
DjDSL, in particular. This is also to highlight how DjDSL allows for pondering
between providing internal, external, or both syntaxes for a given language model
as a design decision for DSL developers.

5.2.6.1 DSL Extension

A DSL developer composes a base DSL with a DSL extension. A DSL extension
is an incomplete language fragment which depends directly on the base language
for completion (in terms of the concrete syntax, the abstract syntax, and the
behaviors; [16]).

In Sect. 5.1.1, the example of a minimal implementation of an internal concrete
syntax for graph-modeling languages is given using systematically interacting

```
1   G            ← GRAPH OBRACKET StmtList CBRACKET;
2   StmtList     ← (Stmt SCOLON)*;
3   Stmt         ← EdgeStmt / NodeStmt;
4   EdgeStmt     ← NodeID EDGEOP NodeID;
5   NodeStmt     ← NodeID;
6   NodeID       ← QUOTE Id QUOTE;
7   Id           ← !QUOTE (<space>/<alnum>)+;
```

Lst. 5.66 A grammar excerpt specific to DOT graph definitions. The supported constructs are graph and edge statements. Character-level and keyword-level rule definitions (e.g., SCOLON, GRAPH) are omitted for brevity

BUILDERS. The syntax is an excerpt from the DOT syntax as available from the Graphviz tool chain. Listing 5.65 reproduces, as a reminder, one syntax snippet. The example is limited to DOT's node and edge definition statements. Here, an alternative syntax implementation is provided based on an object parsing-expression grammar (OPEG). This has as a positive consequence that the internal syntax and the external one presented here are alternatives on top of one and the same language model. As a starting point, the documented DOT grammar is adopted as a parsing grammar.[48] One possible result of transliteration is reproduced, as a starting point, in Listing 5.66. Note that this grammar definition is a basic parsing grammar *without* the DjDSL's OPEG extensions. The parsing grammar in Listing 5.66 can recognize and consume the snippet shown in Listing 5.65.

Then, generators for instantiations, assignments, and queries are added. The generators establish a mapping between the parsing expressions and the language model. As a result, a parser can be derived that produces language-model instantiations as direct parse results. Key in this step is to align instantiation generators and the available classifiers in a DjDSL language model or a language-model composition. For this example, the target language model is identical to the one introduced in Sect. 5.1.1: a representation model for graphs. From the perspective of the intermediate and ordinary parsing grammar in Listing 5.66, three elementary correspondences must be defined:

1. Matches obtained by NodeStmt (line 5) map to instantiations of the Graph::Node classifier.
2. Matches obtained by EdgeStmt (line 4) map to instantiations of the Graph::Edge classifier.
3. Matches obtained by the top-level or start rule G (line 1) map to instantiations of the Graphs::Graph language-model class.

In addition, the Node instantiations must be initialized to the provided node names. That is, the instantiation procedure of Nodes must be provided with the matched

---

[48]Developing a grammar in one environment driven by a concrete example in another as a guide is common practice [44, Section 5.2].

```
NodeStmt      ← `Node` name:NodeID;
NodeID        ← QUOTE Id QUOTE;
Id            ← !QUOTE (<space>/<alnum>)+;
```

Lst. 5.67 Introducing an instantiation generator into the NodeStmt rule

```
EdgeStmt      ← `Edge` a:(`$root nodes $0` NodeID) EDGEOP
                       b:(`$root nodes $0` NodeID);
```

Lst. 5.68 Introducing query generators into the EdgeStmt rule

```
G             ← `Graph` GRAPH OBRACKET StmtList CBRACKET;
StmtList      ← (Stmt SCOLON)*;
Stmt          ← edges:EdgeStmt / NodeStmt;
```

Lst. 5.69 Introducing an assignment generator edges into the Stmt rule

node names to assign them to the name field of each Node instance.[49] Similarly, the Edge instantiations must obtain references to the Node instantiations identified by the node names given in DOT edge statements. Finally, all Edge instantiations must be assigned to the edges property of the Graph. These requirements can all be tackled uniformly by putting appropriate assignment and query generators in place.

To implement the first correspondence, the parsing rule at line 5 of Listing 5.66 is replaced by the corresponding line in Listing 5.67. The instantiation generator identifies the Node classifier for the scope of the matched expression, with the match consumed by NodeId becoming assigned to the classifier's name property.[50]

The second correspondence for edges requires a more sophisticated parsing rule (see Listing 5.68). Rule matches are turned into instantiations of Edge. The NodeID match left to the edge operator (-) is handled by a query generator that (1) resolves a Node instance using the matched node identifier and (2) assigns the Node to property a of the surrounding Edge in a deferred manner. The same applies to the NodeID match on the right and the property b.

The third correspondence involves prepending an instantiation generator 'Graph' to the start rule (see Listing 5.69). This way, every graph definition block will create a new Graph instance to host nodes and edges as container. All Edge instances originating from within a given graph block are then assigned as

---

[49]Indirection via a ModelFactory allows for supporting different instantiation procedures (e.g., initialization via constructors or dedicated calls to property setters). See also Sect. 5.2.5.

[50]The critical reader will notice that there is no assignment operator for the nodes property: nodes :nodeStmt. For the sake of brevity, Node instantiations are associated with the corresponding graph only internally by the responsible ModelFactory. This is to keep the running example more focused at this point.

```
G            ← `Graph` GRAPH OBRACKET StmtList CBRACKET;
StmtList     ← (Stmt SCOLON)*;
Stmt         ← edges:EdgeStmt / NodeStmt;
EdgeStmt     ← `Edge` a:(`$root nodes $0` NodeID) EDGEOP
                       b:(`$root nodes $0` NodeID);
NodeStmt     ← `Node` name:NodeID;
NodeID       ← QUOTE Id QUOTE;
Id           ← !QUOTE (<space>/<alnum>)+;
```

Lst. 5.70 The completed OPEG rewrite of the PEG grammar from Listing 5.66

```
1  graph {
2      // node definitions
3      "1st Edition";
4      "2nd Edition";
5      "3rd Edition";
6      // edge definitions
7      "1st Edition" -- "2nd Edition" [weight = 5];
8      "2nd Edition" -- "3rd Edition" [weight = 10];
9  }
```

Lst. 5.71 A definition of an undirected *and weighted* graph using DOT notation. This is 1:1 reused from the example exercised on internal DSL extension, see Sect. 5.1.1

a bulk to the edges property of the Graph. The assignment generator edges is a primary example of how multi-valued properties are addressed within an OPEG.

Having completed these three definition steps, one arrives at the OPEG depicted in Listing 5.70. Keyword and literal definitions are omitted for clarity.

In Sect. 5.1.1, the scenario on *DSL extension* involved extending graph definitions to include weight attributes (see Fig. 5.72). The notation must be revised accordingly to support (DOT) attribute statements. Listing 5.71 exhibits the targeted syntactic snippet: Edge statements carry attribute statements in-between brackets defining edge weights of 5 and 10, respectively (see lines 7 and 8 in Listing 5.71). In DjDSL, such an extension can be realized in different manners, e.g., via a straightforward union between OPEG or a grammar transformation. The different options (and their details) have different benefits or drawbacks regarding reuse, in terms of duplicated definition and evolvability (Fig. 5.72 and Listing 5.73).

Whatever the option adopted, all require establishing a *merges* relationship between the original and the revised grammars (see Listing 5.74). In grammar-composition terminology, the original grammar in Listing 5.70 is the composed grammar, the grammar extension in Listing 5.73 acts as the receiving one.

In a union approach, the syntax extension is introduced by overriding the definition responsible for matching and consuming edge statements (EdgeStmt). The overriding definition incorporates weight attributes (WeightAttr) into processing edge statements. This is achieved by referencing additional rules that match the

Fig. 5.72 A structural
overview of the *merges*
relationships for DSL
extension

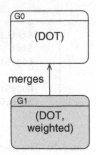

```
EdgeStmt    ←    Edge  a:( $root nodes $0  NodeID) EDGEOP
                       b:( $root nodes $0  NodeID) WeightAttr?;
WeightAttr  ←    OSQBRACKET WEIGHT EQ weight:Weight CSQBRACKET;
Weight      ←    Weight  value:<digit>+;
```

Lst. 5.73 A grammar extension introducing the weight-attribute syntax

```
Grammar create ExtDot \
  -start G \
  -merges $dotGrammar \
  $extDotGrammar
```

Lst. 5.74 Establishing a *merge relationship* between the original OPEG for unweighted graphs
and the revised OPEG for weighted graphs. This implements the dependency structure visualized
in Fig. 5.72

internals of weight attributes (`Weight`, brackets, etc.). The resulting grammar will
match both edge statements with and without weight attributes.

A DSL extension via a union with override can be performed in an unanticipated manner, without devising the composed grammar to be open for extension.
Moreover, a union-based extension presents an intuitive composition operation for
a DSL developer. One downside is the risk of accidental overrides, requiring the
extension developer to be aware of the content (rules) of the composed grammar.
Another becomes visible in this example. The overriding definition of `EdgeStmt`
replicates the RHS of the original `EdgeStmt`. The extension developer will have to
track changes of the original definition to reproduce them in the cloned rule.

A receiving OPEG can perform explicit transformations on the resulting grammar (see Table 5.6). These transformations help reduce the risk of running into
the aforementioned downsides of a union (accidental overriding, duplicates). The
transformation-based option involves providing (a) rules to implement recognizing
and consuming attribute weights, similar to the union-based approach, as well as
providing (b) transforms to implant the new rules into the existing rules set (see
Listing 5.76). Like in the union-based extension, the rules `WeightAttr` and `Weight`
define the actual attribute syntax. The rule for `EdgeStmt` (line 2) links the former
with the surrounding syntax of edge definitions. To this point, the structure of

```
1    # a) receiving rules
2    EdgeStmt    ← `Edge` CoreEdge WeightAttr ;
3    WeightAttr  ← OSQBRACKET WEIGHT EQ weight:Weight CSQBRACKET;
4    Weight      ← `Weight` value:<digit>+;
```

Lst. 5.75 The rules set of an extension OPEG; auxiliary, attribute-specific rule definitions (WEIGHT, EQ) are not depicted for clarity

```
1    # b) transforms
2    CoreEdge        ↔  Dot::EdgeStmt
3    G              ⟺  Dot::G
4    {EdgeStmt end} ⟹
```

Lst. 5.76 DSL extension using explicit transformations

transformation-based extension is similar to the union-based one. The key difference lies in the RHS of the EdgeStmt rule. Rather than cloning and extending the RHS of the original (composed) EdgeStmt, this EdgeStmt is implemented by referencing the original one as-is (via CoreEdge) and amending it. Ultimately, it will also be combined with the original one, if requested, to form the resulting grammar.

Re-consider this, one step at a time: Recall that in presence of transforms, merging produces a disjoint union of two sets of rules, with all rules and non-terminals being prefix-qualified by their originating grammars. Therefore, at the start, there will be effectively two EdgeStmt rules in the intermediate set of rules: Dot::EdgeStmt and ExtDot::EdgeStmt. Based on this intermediate set, the transforms can be used to extract the RHS of Dot::EdgeStmt, park it in a helper rule for ExtDot::CoreEdge, and reference this helper from the RHS of ExtDot::EdgeStmt. This corresponds to what is achieved by the transform on line 2 of Listing 5.76 (↔). Then, to integrate this revised EdgeStmt with the remainder of the composed grammar, line 3 uses the transitive-extraction transform ($\overset{*}{\Longleftrightarrow}$) to draw the entirety of the composed grammar into the namespace of the receiving grammar. This starts from the start symbol Dot::G. The operation will pick up the previously defined, revised ExtDot::EdgeStmt. This, in turn, activates the added syntax for weight attributes. This way, the graph definitions with weights can be processed by creating a parser and by assigning a model factory to obtain the identical result as the union-based extension. However, the use of transformations avoids duplicates. All changes on the composed grammar will be automatically tracked by the resulting one. In addition, accidental overrides are avoided by maintaining the merged sets of rules in separate namespaces. Three details are worth discussing in greater depth: generator extraction, syntax restriction, and extension points.

Extracting Generators, or Not

The developer of the DSL extension can decide on whether to extract RHS expressions of composed rules (e.g., of Dot::EdgeStmt) with or without generators for instantiations ('Edge'). Look at the examples in Listing 5.75 (line 2) and Listing 5.76 (line 2), respectively. The revised rule ExtDot::EdgeStmt contains the instantiation generator. It, therefore, only reuses the bare parsing expression from the composed rule. To achieve this, line 2 of Listing 5.76 employs the extract/rewrite *without* generators (↔), rather than with (⇔). Otherwise, the instantiation generator would end up twice in the resulting grammar: once firing on ExtDot::EdgeStmt, once on CoreEdge matches.

Closure or Restriction

By default, and to maintain closure under composition, (transitive) extraction in DjDSL combines the RHS of a composed and a receiving rule as alternates. This effectively widens the matching space of the resulting grammar as compared to the composed one. The resulting grammar will recognize and consume, in this example, edge definitions with and without weight attributes. If the resulting syntax should be restricted to allowing for the extended edge definitions exclusively, one must restrict the resulting grammar by removing the alternate responsible for the unweighted edge definitions.[51] This restriction can be achieved by employing the remove operator (⇒) on line 4 of Listing 5.76. Therefore, syntax-level DSL restrictions in DjDSL are a variant of DSL extension, as already shown for internal DSL composition in Sect. 5.1.1. Remove operations can generally be used to achieve these restrictive effects.

Extension Points

The extent to which the composed grammar anticipates extensions influences the structure of a DSL extension or restriction. Consider for a moment that the DSL developer had attributes for edge definitions in mind, right from the beginning. The original rules set could contain the following extension points: AttrList and Attr (see Listing 5.77).[52]

The non-terminal Attr realizes what has been referred to as an abstracted or deferred non-terminal or rule. If there is no corresponding definition for the scope of a given grammar, a receiving grammar must provide one. If the latter fails to do so, or the composable grammar fragment is used directly, grammar cleaning will remove Attr and its callers. This will effectively disable the extension points.

Alternatively, a receiving grammar can provide a definition as in Listing 5.78. This will register weight attributes under these extension points. Having an anticipated extension point, only a single transform is necessary (see the last line of

---

[51]Enforcing such a restriction at the syntax level is but one option, an alternative is to be permissive syntactically and enforce validation constraints at a later step.

[52]This is not unlikely to occur in a practical DOT grammar for real use, because DOT attributes are designed as a keyed collection of values in mind; rather than an enumeration over a predefined domain of attribute names and/or values. Besides, it might also be good practice to enforce any restriction on attributes in a later stage of the pipeline (see, e.g., [44, p. 61]).

```
1    EdgeStmt    ←  `Edge` a:(`$root nodes $0` NodeID) EDGEOP
2                          b:(`$root nodes $0` NodeID)
                       AttrList?;
3    AttrList    ←  OSQBRACKET Attr (SCOLON Attr)* CSQBRACKET;
```

Lst. 5.77 Extension points in a base grammar

```
# a) receiving rules
Attr         ←  weight:Weight ;
Weight       ←  `Weight` WEIGHT EQ value:<digit>+;
# b) transforms
                *
G            ⟺  Dot::G
```

Lst. 5.78 Binding the extension points using explicit transformations

Listing 5.78). First, there is no need for an extraction because the extension point
(Attr) serves for this purpose. Second, there is no need for a restriction. This is
because, on the one hand, the composed grammar already declares this an optional
extension (using AttrList?). On the other hand, there is no (dummy) definition of
Attr in the composed rules set becoming combined.[53]

5.2.6.2   DSL Unification

Composing two or more, otherwise freestanding and independent, DSL has been
referred to as *language unification* in Sect. 5.1.2. A unification must preserve the
composed DSL syntaxes, leaving them intact and unmodified. In this setting, the
same basic composition operations provided for DjDSL OPEG apply as for DSL
extension. Differences arise from the fact that unintended or accidental overrides,
for instance, are much more likely. This is because the syntax definitions might
contend over symbol names, whitespace conventions, and literals (e.g., keywords).

In Sect. 5.1.2, a DSL for modeling Miss Grant's Controller (SMDL) and a DSL
for defining Boolean and Comparison Expressions (BCEL) are combined (see also
Fig. 5.79). The objective for the unification is to extend the controller language to
include means of expressing guarded transitions. A *guarded transition* is a transition
that is annotated by a guard expression. Firing a guarded transition is controlled by
the prior evaluation of the attached guard expression. If the guard is evaluated to
true at that time, the transition is enabled, otherwise, it is disabled and will not fire.

This example is replayed here in order to demonstrate DSL unification for two or
more external syntaxes using DjDSL's OPEG. The external concrete syntax for Miss

---

[53]Choosing a parsing expression as a placeholder of an abstracted or deferred non-terminal decides
about the intended extension semantics. For example, ϵ as a placeholder expression is maximally
permissive. A placeholder expression such as end-of-input (!.) will be maximally restrictive.

Fig. 5.79 A structural overview of the *merges* relationships for DSL unification

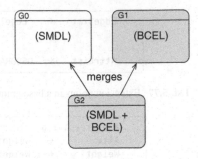

Lst. 5.80 A guarded transition for Miss Grant's Controller

```
state active
  on lightOn go waitingForDrawer
  on drawerOpened go waitingForLight
[ counter > 3 ]
```

Lst. 5.81 A minimal unifying grammar that integrates the SMDL with the BCEL language

```
1  # a) receiving rules
2            T ← `Transition` OrigT OBRACKET
3                guard:Expression CBRACKET;
4    void: OBRACKET ← WS '\[' WS;
5    void: CBRACKET ← WS '\]' WS;
1  # b) transforms
2  OrigT          ↔    MissGrants2::T
3  Expression     ⇐    BCEL::Expression
4  GM             ⇔*   MissGrants2::M
```

Grant's introduced earlier in this chapter is taken as a starting point. For the second DSL under composition, BCEL, an infix notation with mandatory parenthesizing to capture operator precedence and associativity is devised.[54]

Listing 5.80 shows two transitions, one with and the other without a guard expression. A unification is marked by two or more composed grammars being merged by a receiving (unifying) grammar. The running example requires a DSL developer to define a receiving grammar (e.g., GuardedMGC) that merges the BCEL's grammar and the previously defined Miss Grant's grammar (see, e.g., Listing 5.57). The definitional content of the unifying grammar is documented by Listing 5.81. Guard expressions are attached to the Transition instantiations.

Intuitively, the unification is achieved in three transformational steps: First, a revised rule definition for transition definitions is provided. This rule derives from the original definition via the rewrite transform named OrigT. A revamped rule T becomes extended by an assignment generator guard (line 2). Second, the assignment generator is related to the Expression rule of BCEL. This rule becomes

---

[54]While the frontend syntaxes for Miss Grant's and BCEL differ from the internal ones devised in Sect. 5.1.2, the remainder of the languages' expressiveness, their pipelines, and their backend implementation are identical. Being a standard expression notation, the grammar is not documented at this point. The interested reader is referred to the accompanying tutorial.

Fig. 5.82 A structural
overview of the *merges*
relationships for incremental
extension composition

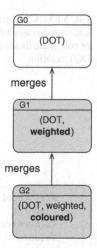

referenced on line 7. Third, and finally, the entire Miss Grant's Controller rules set is dragged into the resulting grammar (on the last line of Listing 5.81).

These transforms resemble closely the ones for a DSL extension, regarding the provision of an extension point in the state-machine language. The main difference comes with the referencing (extract w/o rewrite) of a syntax element from the second composed language: `BCEL::Expression`. As this happens to be the start symbol of BCEL, the entire BCEL rules set is effectively incorporated into the resulting grammar. This is achieved in a way that avoids conflicts with the state-machine rules set.

This unified syntax operates under the assumption that the underlying language models have also been composed so that any `Transition` instantiation provides for a `guard` property. This property is then assigned an `Expression`, or `BooleanOrComparison` instantiation available from BCELs, more precisely. This is identical to the instantiation procedure of the internal DSL unification as elaborated on in Sect. 5.1.2.

The point to stress here is that transformation-based unification in DjDSL allows for the unanticipated, the unmodified, and the controlled reuse of two independently developed syntaxes on top of a unified language model.

5.2.6.3   DSL Extension Composition

Extension composition captures situations in which two or more extensions can be composed with one another or can be co-present as an extension to a base DSL. Two or more DSL extensions may be composed incrementally (stepwise) into a base language, one at a time. Alternatively, the extensions can be composed first, and the resulting grammar becomes merged once with a base grammar. DjDSL and OPEG support both variants of DSL extension composition: incremental extension composition (Fig. 5.82) and extension unification.

Lst. 5.83 A definition of an
undirected graph with weight
or colour attributes using
DOT notation

```
1   graph {
2       // node definitions
3       "1st Edition";
4       "2nd Edition";
5       "3rd Edition";
6       // edge definitions
7       "1st Edition" -- "2nd Edition" [
            weight = 5];
8       "2nd Edition" -- "3rd Edition" [
            colour = #000];
9   }
```

```
# a) receiving rules
EdgeStmt    ← `Edge` CoreEdge ColourAttr ;
ColourAttr  ← OSQBRACKET COLOUR EQ colour:Colour CSQBRACKET;
Colour      ← `Colour` value:('#' <xdigit> <xdigit> <xdigit>);
# b) transforms
G           ⟺  ODot2::G
```

Lst. 5.84 A straightforward implementation of the grammar extension for the colour attribute

Consider the example of a second DSL extension to the DOT-like graph-modeling language. Its aim is to add a colour attribute to edge definitions, just like the weight attribute. Colour attributes carry 3-digit hex codes of colours as part of edge definitions, as depicted in Listing 5.83.

As an incremental composition, one can depart from the weight-enabled OPEG introduced as an example on DSL extension (see Fig. 5.82). From there, one proceeds by defining a second extension grammar to implement the colour attribute syntax in the same spirit. In fact, for this example, the weight-adding grammar fragment from Listing 5.75 is just replicated and rewritten to what is depicted in Listing 5.84.

WeightAttr becomes ColourAttr. The rule for non-terminal Colour lays out the recognized sentential structure for colour attributes (with a signaling keyword, etc.). With this extra grammar merging the weight-enabled grammar (see paragraph on *DSL extension* above), the resulting grammar supports definitions as shown in Listing 5.83.

In DjDSL, the same extended notation can be realized via a different path: *extension unification*. In an extension unification, the points of departure are the extension grammars per se. First, the extensions become composed, then, as a last step the unified (resulting) grammar is merged into the base DSL grammar (see Fig. 5.85). As a matter of fact, an extension unification is a unique mixture of a DSL unification with extensions becoming unified first and a subsequent DSL extension. The unification of two or more extensions is then merged in one step into a receiving (or, *base*) grammar. Extension unification differs from incremental extension composition in that at the time of composing the extensions, they are

Fig. 5.85 A structural overview of the *merges* relationships for extension unification

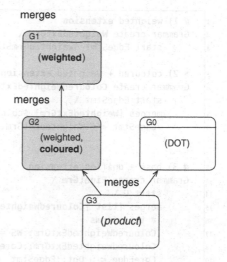

treated in isolation from any base grammar. Most importantly, any undefined or deferred non-terminal definitions must be provided either by the extension grammars themselves or any intermediate (unified) grammar (at least in terms of placeholders). This changes the affordances of defining a unification slightly, as compared to an incremental composition. However, unification also presents immediate benefits. One upside is that the extension unification is defined under a closed-world assumption: The start symbols point to parsing rules introduced by the extension grammars; any deferred non-terminals are clearly marked as such.[55] Another consequence is that an extension unification is symmetric as opposed to incremental composition. Extensions are composed as peers, without one taking precedence over the other in an increment composition with a base. In addition, extension unification provides more control when it comes to enforcing specific variation types for a syntax composition.

The basic flow of an extension unification is exemplified in Listing 5.86 for a colour- and weight-enabled graph syntax. The two main steps are identified as steps (2) and (3). In step (2), a unified extension is created by composing the two grammars documented (as excerpts) in Listing 5.87 (for weight attributes) and in Listing 5.88 (for colour attributes). The actual unification of the underlying rules sets is accomplished by a single, fetch-all transform on line 9 of Listing 5.86:

```
EdgeStmt ↶*↷ WeightedExtGrm::EdgeStmt
```

---

[55]These are not only matters of definitional clarity, but also an implementation-level requirement: Once composed, the resulting grammar will be cleaned from useless non-terminals. To prevent this from happening, there must be placeholder definitions.

```
1   # 1) weighted extension
2   Grammar create WeightedExtGrm \
3       -start EdgeStmt $weightedGrmStr
4
5   # 2) coloured + weighted extension (= unified extension)
6   Grammar create ColouredWeightedExtGrm \
7       -start EdgeStmt \
8       -merges [WeightedExtGrm] $colouredGrmStr {
9           EdgeStmt <*> WeightedExtGrm::EdgeStmt
10      }
11
12  # 3) base + unified extension
13  Grammar create FinalGrm \
14      -start G \
15      -merges [list [ColouredWeightedExtGrm resulting] $dotGrammar] {} {
16          # transforms
17          ColouredWeightedExtGrm::WS ==>
18          ColouredWeightedExtGrm::CoreEdge ==>
19          CoreEdge <-> Dot::EdgeStmt
20          EdgeStmt <*> ColouredWeightedExtGrm::EdgeStmt
21          G <*> Dot::G
22      }
```

Lst. 5.86 An actual extension unification implementation as provided by DjDSL. First, two Grammar instances embody the extension grammars: WeightedExtGrm, ColouredWeightedExtGrm. The latter reifies the unified grammar of the two extensions. Finally, the FinalGrm becomes composed from the unified extensions and the original DOT grammar (whose definition is not shown here)

Lst. 5.87 Excerpt from the extension grammar for the weighted feature, as used for extension unification

```
1   # rules
2   EdgeStmt    ← `Edge` CoreEdge
3                 WeightAttr ;
4   WeightAttr  ← OSQBRACKET WEIGHT
5                 EQ weight:Weight
6                 CSQBRACKET;
7   Weight      ← `Weight`
8                 value:<digit>+;
9   # deferred
10  CoreEdge    ← '';
11  void: WS    ← '';
```

The result of this transform is a unified extension, without dependence on a base (i.e., the DOT) grammar. As already hinted at, to establish this independence, the two extension grammars must be defined in a self-sufficient manner. Most importantly, the start symbols (EdgeStmt) must be defined. Any deferred non-terminals must be matched by placeholder definitions. See WS and CoreEdge in Listings 5.87 and 5.88 for examples. Their definitions contain ϵ expressions as placeholders. In step (3), the base (DOT) grammar is merged together with the unified extension (ColouredWeightedExtension) into a completed and operative grammar (FinalGrm). From this final grammar, a parser can be derived.

Fig. 5.88 Excerpt from the extension grammar for the coloured feature, as used for extension unification

```
1   # rules
2   EdgeStmt    ← `Edge` CoreEdge
3                 ColourAttr ;
4   ColourAttr ← OSQBRACKET COLOUR
5                 EQ colour:Colour
6                 CSQBRACKET;
7   Colour      ← `Colour` value:('#'
8                          <xdigit>
9                          <xdigit>
10                         <xdigit>);
11  # deferred
12  CoreEdge    ← '';
13  void: WS    ← '';
```

Two details are noteworthy about this final compositional step: First, this final receiving grammar does not introduce any new rules. Second, it is the *resulting grammar* of the unified extension becoming merged into the final grammar, and not the receiving grammar of the unification itself. See line 15 of Listing 5.86: ColouredWeightedExtGrm resulting. The rationale for this is elaborated on in the concluding part of this section.

As for the first detail: There are no dedicated rules for the final grammar because its rules set is populated purely from running grammar transformations (see lines 17–21 in Listing 5.86). This is perfectly allowed in DjDSL and corresponds to the nature of an extension unification. The first three transforms (lines 17–19) provide actual definitions for the deferred non-terminals coming with the unified extensions (WS and CoreEdge). Without the upfront removal of the ϵ-placeholders, the resulting grammar would remain dysfunctional. Recall that definitions present in the grammars under composition are turned into alternates of a combined rule. The subsequent two lines 20 and 21 load the sets of rules of the two composed grammars into the final resulting one. This is equivalent to the use of the transitive extract/rewrite transformation, as applied for DSL extension and for DSL unification.

DSL extension composition (whether incremental or unifying) between two or more DjDSL's OPEG exhibits a number of interesting properties that render them characteristically different from plain extension and plain unification. The most important characteristic is that resulting grammars enter another round of composition. They become themselves composed grammars. Another characteristic is the capability to enforce variation-point types (at the syntax level) other than the ones set by the composed grammars (i.e., the individual extensions).

Resulting Grammars as Composed Grammars

Extension compositions involve resulting grammars as their composed grammars. In the example of incremental composition, rather than composing the basic DOT grammar and the weight add-on grammar, the colour add-on as receiving grammar starts from the grammar resulting from composing the two. Looking at the unified extension, the final composition step involved the resulting grammar of the unification to become composed with the DOT grammar. This is an important detail. One the upside, this allows an incremental DSL extension to benefit from the conditions established by a previous composition step. For example, in the incremental composition of the colour extension, the non-terminal `CoreEdge` can be reused, serving as a handle of the basic parsing expression for edge definitions. On the downside, the developer of the incremental extension must be aware of the internals of the resulting grammar as a starting point, and, therefore, the details of the previously mixed extension. For example, the resulting grammar establishes its own namespace of non-terminals and rules, the information about the source grammars is effectively lost. Any changes to the previous extension step might, therefore, break the incremental composition. The same way, because of this, a unified extension appears as a genuine extension rather than a composition.

Intended versus Implemented Variation Points

Extension compositions do not necessarily result in implementing the variation point as intended or expected by the DSL developer. For example: Should edge definitions be permitted without any, colour-only, weight-only, and/ or both attributes? The given examples (incremental and unifying) will permit all arrangements but one: co-presence of both attributes. This is because in both arrangements, three alternates of `EdgeStmt` will end up in the resulting grammar. The two extension grammars provide their specific attribute add-ons (`weight` or `colour`) plus the original edge statement *without* any attributes. The combined use of attributes, even when defined by a variability model, is not implemented by these two compositions. Even worse, combining them would violate the ruling syntax defined by the compositions so far, at least on certain input. For example, chaining up multiple, bracketed attribute fragments as well as multiple key-value pairs within one bracket block will end in incomplete parses or parsing failures. Both features are optional ones (for example, as identified by a variability model) and perfectly usable in isolation from each other. However, when combined, they are likely to break the resulting parser because of the contradicting (e.g., interacting) feature-specific syntax additions. This is an instance of an unexpected *feature interaction* [4, p. 214], surfacing as a syntax or parsing failures.

Derivative Extension

Conflicts between intended vs. implemented variability when features and their corresponding implementations interact with each other must be actively resolved for a given DSL extension composition. The DSL developer must realize a dual goal. A DSL developer must (a) provide for *coordination code* to accommodate the two co-present syntax extensions. In addition, the DSL developer must to (b) implement the coordination code in a way that preserves the intended (modeled) syntax

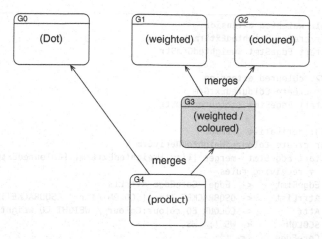

Fig. 5.89 A structural overview of the *merges* relationships when using a derivative grammar (G3, `weighted/ coloured`)

variability. That is, both syntax extensions and their features remain deployable in isolation from each other.

In an ideal setting, the coordination code allows a DSL developer to settle two or more (interacting) features with each other even in an unanticipated setting and to still avoid breaking other configurations. This is an instance of the *optional-feature problem* [26]. This leads to a particular employment of DSL extension composition as supported by DjDSL: *derivative extension composition*. In DjDSL and its parsing grammars, coordination code maps to a dedicated grammar (*derivative* grammar). This grammar provides for extra rules and transforms to resolve unwanted interactions such as syntax failures of two or more DSL syntax extensions (grammars).[56]

A derivative grammar (G3 in Fig. 5.89) imports and manipulates the rules from two or more extension grammars. It then usesDjDSL transformations to resolve any syntax-level conflicts between them (G1 and G2). Then, in a second step, the derivative grammar (G3) is fused with a base grammar (G0) to form the product grammar (G4). Applied to the running example, this could be implemented as printed out in Listing 5.90.

A derivative grammar can be used to re-arrange a syntax to better accommodate two or more optional syntax-level features (such as `weighted` and `coloured`). In Listing 5.90, this is achieved by the derivative grammar G3 by adapting edge statements to accept generic lists of key-value pairs as attribute lists (`AttrList` on lines 13 and 14). The attribute details provided by each DSL extension are then combined into a generic `Attr` rule (see line 15). The transforms on lines 20–23 remove the original (and effectively conflicting) edge-statement rules from the two

---

[56]The notion of derivative grammar expresses the nature of this intermediate grammar as being actually derived from the extension grammars by importing and manipulating their rules to resolve unwanted interactions Liu et al. [31].

```
1  # 1) G1: weighted extension
2  Grammar create WeightedExtGrm \
3      -start EdgeStmt $weightedGrmStr
4
5  # 2) G2: coloured extension
6  Grammar create ColouredExtGrm \
7      -start EdgeStmt $colouredGrmStr
8
9  # 3) G3: derivative grammar
10 Grammar create ColouredWeightedDerivGrm \
11     -start EdgeStmt -merges [list [WeightedExtGrm] [ColouredExtGrm]] {
12         # receiving rules
13     EdgeStmt    <-  Edge  CoreEdge AttrList;
14     AttrList    <-  OSQBRACKET Attr (SCOLON Attr)* CSQBRACKET;
15     Attr        <-  COLOUR EQ colour:Colour / WEIGHT EQ weight:Weight;
16 void: SCOLON    <-  WS ';' WS;
17 void: CoreEdge  <-  '';
18     } {
19     # transforms
20     WeightedExtGrm::EdgeStmt ==>;
21     ColouredExtGrm::EdgeStmt ==>;
22     WeightAttr <*> WeightedExtGrm::WeightAttr;
23     ColourAttr <*> ColouredExtGrm::ColourAttr;
24 }
25
26 # 4) G4: base + derivative extension
27 Grammar create FinalGrm2 \
28     -start G \
29     -merges [list [ColouredWeightedDerivGrm resulting] $dotGrammar] {} {
30     ColouredWeightedDerivGrm::WS ==>
31     ColouredWeightedDerivGrm::CoreEdge ==>
32     CoreEdge <-> Dot::EdgeStmt
33     EdgeStmt <*> ColouredWeightedDerivGrm::EdgeStmt
34     G <*> Dot::G
35     }
```

Lst. 5.90 An implementation of a DSL extension composition using a derivative grammar (ColouredWeightedDerivGrm, G3). First, two Grammar instances embody the extension grammars: WeightedExtGrm, ColouredExtGrm. Second, a derivative grammar combines the two extension grammars and resolves a syntax-level conflicts between them using extra rules and tranforms. Third, the product grammar FinalGrm2 becomes composed from the derivative grammar and the original DOT grammar (G0, whose definition is not shown here). See Fig. 5.89 for the corresponding overview

extensions ($\Rightarrow$, lines 20 and 21) and drag the definitional dependencies for colour and weight attributes into the derivative grammar ($\overset{*}{\Longleftrightarrow}$, lines 22–23). At the last stage of composition, to form the product grammar G4, deferred definitions are cleared (WS and CoreEdge, lines 30 and 31) and actual definitions are provided (EdgeStmt and the remainder for G on lines 32–34). These closing transforms, on the resulting product grammar, are identical to the unification implementation shown in Listing 5.86.

The derivative implementation presented above not only allows for a graph-definition syntax with attributes as expected by developers (i.e., writing attributed DOT statements as shown in Listing 5.91, lines 7–9), but has also other benefits.

First, the derivative is maintained in a distinct unit of definition and composition. This definition is only responsible for resolving unwanted interactions between two or more features for a given scope. Alternative derivatives could be provided. This yields a proper separation of concerns. As a distinct unit, second, it may enter compositions selectively, only in presence of these dependent features. At the same time, third, the dependent feature implementations (grammars) remain unmodified and operative as is. Any modifications in the original definitions will be tracked automatically. In addition, fourth, the derivative opens up the DOT syntax for further DSL extensions because it implants a generic extension point (attribute lists). A downside of distinct derivative grammars is their potential number. In cases of many (unwanted) interactions due to many different combinations of features (higher-order interactions, different composition scopes), DSL developers must maintain derivative grammars and track changes between them.

5.3 Related Work

DjDSL draws from related work on patterns for designing and implementing software languages (in particular, internal DSL), on grammar-composition techniques, and from designing parse representations (see Fig. 5.92).

On Internal DSL
As highlighted throughout this chapter (e.g., by thumbnail descriptions plus references), a number of pattern collections and pattern languages have influenced the design and the implementation of djdsl::dada. These include architectural design patterns [5], patterns on software-language design and implementation [19, 43], language integration [69], and general OO design patterns [20].

```
1    graph {
2        // node definitions
3        "1st Edition";
4        "2nd Edition";
5        "3rd Edition";
6        // edge definitions
7        "1st Edition" -- "2nd Edition" [weight = 5; colour = #eee];
8        "2nd Edition" -- "3rd Edition" [colour = #000];
9        "1st Edition" -- "3rd Edition" ;
10    }
```

Lst. 5.91 A definition of an undirected graph with weight or colour attributes using DOT notation

Fig. 5.92 Related work on
variable textual syntaxes

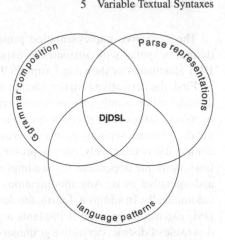

Fowler Fowler [19] hints at the use of *multiple* and connected builders (i.e.,
EXPRESSION BUILDER) from two related perspectives, briefly. On the one hand,
Fowler raises the question on whether to provide exactly one or several builders
as a construction facade in front of one language model (SEMANTIC MODEL; [19,
Sections 32.1 and 32.4]). This concern extends to having one or several builders for
a language-model fragment (e.g., a collaboration in DjDSL). On the other hand, the
motivation of (internal) DSL composition is glimpsed at in Fowler [Section 6.9 19].
To avoid bloating an internal DSL up (in terms of additional expressiveness sought),
composing two or more otherwise independent SEMANTIC MODELS is hinted at. At
the syntax-level, mixing (distinct builders) is only compared to composing with
the host language. This chapter adds to this very coarse-grained discussion a more
refined distinction based on Erdweg et al. [16]'s language-composition scenarios
(e.g., extension vs. unification) and corresponding design patterns (e.g., CHAIN OF
RESPONSIBILITY) to guide implementation.

On External DSL

The relevant context on variable external DSL, as realized by DjDSL, is set by
approaches to composable grammars, the particular type of parsing technique
supported (parsing expression grammars, PEG), and the way parse representations
are devised. Fowler [19, Section 31.2] gives a short excursus on the grammar-
based composition of DSL. This is approached mainly from the trade-off between
succinctness and (extended) expressiveness in the design of a solitary DSL. Rather
than bloating the language model and syntax of a single DSL, composing a
derived one from language-model fragments is proposed. Grammar (definition)
reuse without modification [16] is referred to, but mainly with respect to the
limitations perceived at the time. These include conflicting lexers (token scanners)
vs. scannerless parsing and parser generators being limited to single and closed
grammar definitions.

DjDSL builds on a rich body of approaches to transforming grammar definitions, originally developed for a variety of tasks in studying, analyzing, and rewriting the corresponding program sources, as well as the grammar sources themselves [8, 10, 67]. Landmark contributions regarding grammar composition as one type of grammar transformation include *syntax modules* of the series of Syntax Definition Formalisms (SDF, SDF2, SDF3; [66]), the grammar-inclusion mechanism by TXL [8], grammar-transformation operator suites [29, 30], and grammar imports by ANTLR [44, p. 257]. These approaches turned grammars into open and programmable definitions.

SDF [66] starting with version 2 introduced parametrized syntax modules. Modules can import from each other. When an imported module exposes nonterminals or terminals as named module parameters, they can be bound under different names in the importing module. The same can be achieved in SDF using explicit renaming, without formal parameters. SDF is contained by a number of DSL development systems, including Spoofax and RascalMPL. SDF also addressed composability issue by operating on scannerless and generalized parsing (i.e., scannerless GLR). It is noteworthy that the support for parametrized modules has been discontinued starting from SDF3.

TXL [8] allows a developer to derive task-specific variants of a base grammar in order to generate task-specific variants of an code-analysis program, for instance. For deriving grammar variants, TXL provides for placing rules over different files, rooted under one start symbol. More importantly, TXL provides for a constructs to replace (override) a non-terminal or add a new alternate to a given rule [8, 10].

These approaches have led to documenting comprehensive suites of established grammar-transformation operators. These operator suites contain primitive operators (e.g., adding and removing rules) that can be combined to more complex ones (e.g., a refactoring). These suites are the foundations of grammar-transformation languages such as FST [29] and XBGF [30]. While the aim of these operator suites is to accommodate a great variety of transformation scenarios, and the six transformation operators devised by DjDSL apply to composing object parsing-expression grammars (OPEG) only, they can be defined as combined uses of the more atomic FST or XBGF operators. For example, OPEG's extract with rewrite maps to XBGF's define and redefine, respectively, plus a subsequent rename. However, the OPEG operators align to PEG rather than CFG semantics in order to maintain the property of a semantics-preserving transformation.

ANTLR applies a union-with-override technique, with particularities regarding different types of definition artifacts. As ANTLR serves as the parsing infrastructure for several DSL development systems, both general-purpose (Xtext [6]) and for variable DSL (MontiCore [27], MetaDepth [36]), grammar imports have experienced some uptake (see also Sect. 2.4).

Parsing Expression Grammars

Recognition systems in the flavor of PEG have been applied successfully in the context of parsing for variable external DSL. In Sect. 2.4, the overview of the DSL development systems contains those driven by PEG: Helvetia's PetitParser [50] and APEG [49]. APEG is noteworthy because APEG is actually capable of re-defining syntax with the associated parser adapting dynamically based on new or changed rules. This corresponds closely to the notion of self-extension of an external DSL [16].

Throughout Sect. 5.2.2, the PEG-based system *Rats!* was referred to, mainly because *Rats!* provides for basic grammar composition on the basis of rules and alternates using dedicated transformations (add, delete, append). In addition, Grimm [22] highlights important barriers to composing PEG-based syntax definitions (e.g., ordering). Apart from composability of PEG, there are different implementation and generation techniques for a PEG-driven parser: classical recursive-descent parser [22, 45], virtual parsing machines, like in DjDSL and [33], parser combinators [50], and PEG interpreters.

Dejanović et al. Dejanović et al. [12] developed and maintained a PEG interpreter `Arpeggio`. As opposed to a parser generator based on PEG (like DjDSL's OPEG), a parser model is consumed by the `Arpeggio` parser along with processing the input in terms of a model walker that produces a parse tree. The parser model that effectively configures the `Arpeggio` parser for a parse can be defined using a native Python notation or two external PEG notations. The parse tree can then be processed using a conventional VISITOR approach.

Kuramitsu Kuramitsu [28] presents a PEG-based parser generator Nez that also operating on a virtual parsing machine, designed as an extension to the machine devised by Medeiros and Ierusalimschy [33]. Nez provides built-in support for context-sensitive recognition and tailorable AST construction. AST construction can be customized, e.g., by laying out a tree using regular expressions and by running built-in tree transformation (e.g., tagging and labeling for typing). This way, a DSL developer can produce parse representations suitable for a certain post-processing step. With this, Nez shares the ambition of DjDSL and Ensō, but at a different level of abstraction (parse trees rather than arbitrary object graphs). While Ensō and DjDSL connect parsed elements in terms of references, Nez allows for constructing parent-child relationships using a `connector` operator.

Parse Representations

In Sect. 5.2.2, the related work has been covered in detail. This includes Ensō's as a reference implementation of object grammars [64] based on a GLL parsing engine (as opposed to PEG in DjDSL). Ensō is also noteworthy because it allows, in principle, for different correspondence types between a primary abstract syntax (schemas in Ensō) and the syntax definition. Besides, Ensō provides round-tripping, from parsed to pretty-printed input.

`Xtext` [6] has also been covered already. It provides different tactics to process input into a high-level abstract syntax representation. This representation is provided by `Ecore` models and their instantiations. `Ecore` models take the role of DjDSL's language models. In summary, Xtext supports grammar-first, grammar-first plus post-processing, and model-first correspondences.

In the PEG arena, Dejanović et al. [13] build on the notion of Xtext's (meta) model inference in their DSL development system textX. Based on a single language-definition artifact (an textX grammar), a language model (metamodel) is generated and a packrat parser is configured. The parser will turn input into instantiations (Python objects graph) of the corresponding, previously generated language model (implemented by Python classes). In addition, predefined Python classes can be used as for instantiation, as opposed to the auto-generated ones, provided that these classes provide a constructor signature matching the corresponding rule attributes set. This is a lightweight variant of the model-first mode offered by Xtext. This variant is lightweight in the sense that a complete homologue of an Ecore model must not be provided and that, hence, custom and generated classes can be used side-by-side. In addition, post-processing can be applied to both the at class generation and instantiation time. textX builds on top of the PEG-based packrat parsing infrastructure Arpeggio [12].

5.4 Summary and Discussion

In this chapter, DjDSL approaches to developing variable internal DSL syntaxes (djdsl::dada) and variable external DSL syntaxes (djdsl::opeg) are presented. In both syntax styles (internal and external), different composition types at the syntactic level can be realized: DSL extension, DSL unification, and DSL extension composition. Even though other DSL development systems support the same range of composition types, DjDSL is original in that it provides a unified infrastructure to develop *more than one composable syntax*, internal or external, as alternatives for one DSL. At the same time, the way internal and external syntaxes are implemented using DjDSL allows for their *reuse without modification*. That is, new syntax variants of a DSL family can be implemented by reusing and leaving intact the existing syntax definitions. These benefits are highlighted again in Chap. 6.

The infrastructure for composable internal syntaxes (djdsl::dada; see Sect. 5.1) packages best practices and proven solutions on internal DSL development in terms of software patterns as a reusable development framework. Key contributions are support for developing internal DSL using BUILDERS and support for implementing internal DSL compositions by chaining BUILDERS as syntax processors [59]. In fact, it is established that using that one technique of *chaining*, all types of internal-syntax composition (extension, unification, and extension composition) can be implemented by a DSL developer. On top, a DSL developer DjDSL can define BUILDERS that act as derivative extensions to coordinate other syntax extensions under composition [31]. These language-implementation patterns are generic and can be implemented using different host languages (see [59] for Java examples).

The infrastructure for composable external syntaxes (djdsl::opeg; see Sect. 5.2) uses the foundations of advanced parsing expression grammars (PEG). DjDSL delivers *object parsing-expression grammars* (OPEG) to define—in one— an external syntax for a DSL *and* the syntax mapping to a DSL's primary abstract syntax (language model). The double aim is to avoid common abstraction mismatches of parse representations (e.g., decomposition mismatches) and to render the extended parsing grammars composable. The parsing grammars offered by DjDSL to DSL developers support different composition techniques. These include simple grammar unions and fine-grained grammar transformations. Grammar transformations are based on a number of well-defined transformation operators. These operators take as input the sets of parsing rules of two or more OPEG at different levels (e.g., rulewise, alternates) to form a valid OPEG as their output. This coverage of composition techniques is shown to be necessary to enable a DSL developer to implement the different, grammar-based DSL compositions: extensions, unification, and extension composition.

DSL Self-Extension

A fourth composition type discussed by current research is *self-extension* of a language. It turns out, however, that there are different views on this matter [11, 34]. Some read self-extension or self-extensibility as a property of the host language or of the language tooling in a DSL development system (e.g., an extensible host language or extensible compiler). This is a convenience view. Others consider self-extensibility a genuine property of DSL themselves. The former view includes the capacity of a host language (like Java or Tcl) to host internal DSL. The latter view requires that a DSL defined by a DSL development system like DjDSL can define extension for itself.

As for internal DSL developed using DjDSL and NX/Tcl, there is support for *actual* DSL self-extension. This is because the DSL can be extended by DSL scripts written using the very DSL under extension. For example, the expression language (BCEL) used throughout this chapter may extend itself to support new operators (on a given expression type) or new expression types.

In DjDSL, this example of self-extension can be tackled in two different ways: As a first option, a DSL syntax processor may provide more or less moderated access to the NX/Tcl host-language runtime and the DSL's language model (or a given instantiation) via pure embedding. In pure embedding, the DSL syntax can contain host-language scripts holding NX object API calls that can modify a language model or language-model instantiation.

Listing 5.93 exemplifies this, by showing a hash-prefixed annotation (line 1) that will cause a new operator-handling method to be added to the BUILDER on the fly. The BCEL expression on the subsequent line can already make use of this new comparison operator (>=). Any newly created BUILDER instance will be unaware

---

Lst. 5.93 A self-extensible
variant of the BCEL language

```
1   # {object forward >= %self %method}
2   or >= counter -1 = counter -1
```

of this operator. The BCEL annotation (#) provides direct access to the currently active BUILDER object.[57] This is used to set an instance-level forwarding method to handle the >= operator, when walking the input LITERAL LIST.

As a second option to provide for self-extensible internal DSL is to apply DSL unification. A DjDSL DSL may be composed with a DjDSL (hence, meta-level) DSL allowing for language-model modifications (including modifications to the variability model, the contracts, or the syntax processors). This option is closely related to the idea of a *meta DSL* whose scripts produce DSL definition artifacts for the shared DSL development system [16, Section 2.3].[58]

As for external, OPEG-based DSL in DjDSL, there is currently no support for self-extension in the strictest reading; that is, from within the grammar and parser definitions themselves. There are two paths worth exploring for DjDSL: First, related work on runtime-adaptive grammars such as APEG [49] will be reviewed. Second, the existing PEG framework and runtime is eligible to implement a minimal solution for *parser combinators* in DjDSL. With these, self-extension comes in reach because the parser combinators as host-language objects can be conveniently accessed and manipulated for the purpose of self-extension. In Chap. 6, a sophisticated example of both an internal and an external DSL syntax as part of one *mixed* DSL project is presented.

References

1. Aho AV, Ullman JD (1972) The theory of parsing, translation, and compiling: Parsing, vol I. Prentice Hall, Upper Saddle River
2. Aho AV, Ullman JD (1977) Principles of compiler design. Addison-Wesley, Boston
3. Aho AV, Lam MS, Sethi R, Ullman JD (2006) Compilers: Principles, techniques, and tools, 2nd edn. Addison-Wesley, Boston
4. Apel S, Batory D, Kästner C, Saake G (2013) Feature-oriented software product lines, 1st edn. Springer, Berlin, Heidelberg. https://doi.org/10.1007/978-3-642-37521-7
5. Avgeriou P, Zdun U (2005) Architectural patterns revisited: A pattern language. In: Proceedings of the 10th European Conference on Pattern Languages of Programs (EuroPlop'05), Irsec, pp 1–39
6. Bettini L (2013) Implementing domain-specific languages with Xtext and Xtend, 2nd edn. Packt Publishing, Birmingham
7. Buschmann F, Henney K, Schmidt DC (2007) Pattern-oriented software architecture – On patterns and pattern languages. Wiley, Hoboken

---

[57]Placing metaprogramming annotations (hooks) in a DSL (not the host language itself!) has been proposed before, e.g., for the Helvetia [51] DSL development system. Helvetia features hooks to access parser, validator, and transformations from within a DSL program.

[58]Self-extension is here a consequence of *self-application* [15]. In DjDSL, a number of definition languages (e.g., vle) are realized as DjDSL-based languages themselves. Similarly, alternative frontends to the language-model definition language (e.g., comparable to the XCore or EMFatic frontends to Ecore models) or a dedicated contract language like djdsl::ctx in DjDSL fall into this category.

8. Cordy JR (2006) The TXL source transformation language. Sci Comput Program 61(3):190–210. https://doi.org/10.1016/j.scico.2006.04.002
9. Czarnecki K, Eisenecker UW (2000) Generative programming — Methods, Tools, and Applications, 6th edn. Addison-Wesley, Boston
10. Dean TR, Cordy JR, Malton AJ, Schneider KA (2003) Agile parsing in TXL. Autom Softw Eng 10(4):311–336. https://doi.org/10.1023/A:1025801405075
11. Degueule T (2016) Composition and interoperability for external domain-specific language engineering. Theses, Université de Rennes 1 [UR1]. https://hal.inria.fr/tel-01427009
12. Dejanović I, Milosavljević G, Vaderna R (2016) Arpeggio: A flexible PEG parser for Python. Knowl-Based Syst 95:71–74. https://doi.org/10.1016/j.knosys.2015.12.004
13. Dejanović I, Vaderna R, Milosavljević G, Vuković Ž (2017) TextX: A Python tool for domain-specific languages implementation. Knowl-Based Syst 115:1–4. https://doi.org/10.1016/j.knosys.2016.10.023
14. Diekmann L, Tratt L (2014) Eco: A language composition editor. In: Proceedings of the 7th International Conference on Software Language Engineering (SLE'14). Lecture notes in computer science, vol 8706. Springer, New York, pp 82–101. https://doi.org/10.1007/978-3-319-11245-9_5
15. Erdweg S, Rendel T, Kästner C, Ostermann K (2011) SugarJ: Library-based syntactic language extensibility. In: Proceedings of the 2011 ACM International Conference on Object Oriented Programming Systems Languages and Applications (OOPSLA'11). ACM, New York, pp 391–406. https://doi.org/10.1145/2048066.2048099
16. Erdweg S, Giarrusso PG, Rendel T (2012) Language composition untangled. In: Proceedings of the Twelfth Workshop on Language Descriptions, Tools, and Applications (LDTA'12). ACM, New York, pp 7:1–7:8. https://doi.org/10.1145/2427048.2427055
17. Erdweg S, van der Storm T, Völter M, Tratt L, Bosman R, Cook WR, Gerritsen A, Hulshout A, Kelly S, Loh A, Konat G, Molina PJ, Palatnik M, Pohjonen R, Schindler E, Schindler K, Solmi R, Vergu V, Visser E, van der Vlist K, Wachsmuth G, van der Woning J (2015) Evaluating and comparing language workbenches: Existing results and benchmarks for the future. Comput Lang Syst Struct 44(Part A):24–47. https://doi.org/10.1016/j.cl.2015.08.007
18. Ford B (2004) Parsing expression grammars: A recognition-based syntactic foundation. In: Proceedings of the 31st ACM SIGPLAN-SIGACT Symposium on Principles of Programming Languages (POPL'04). ACM, New York, pp 111–122. https://doi.org/10.1145/964001.964011
19. Fowler M (2010) Domain specific languages, 1st edn. Addison-Wesley, Boston
20. Gamma E, Helm R, Johnson RE, Vlissides J (1995) Design Patterns – Elements of Reusable Object-Oriented Software. Addison Wesley professional computing series. Addison-Wesley, Boston
21. Ghosh D (2010) DSLs in action, 1st edn. Manning Publications Co., Shelter Island
22. Grimm R (2006) Better extensibility through modular syntax. In: Proceedings of the 27th ACM SIGPLAN Conference on Programming Language Design and Implementation (PLDI'06). ACM, New York, pp 38–51. https://doi.org/10.1145/1133981.1133987
23. Grune D, Jacobs CJ (2010) Parsing techniques: A practical guide, 2nd edn. Springer, New York
24. Johanson AN, Hasselbring W (2014) Hierarchical combination of internal and external domain-specific languages for scientific computing. In: Proceedings of the 2014 European Conference on Software Architecture Workshops (ECSAW'14). ACM, New York, pp 17:1–17:8. https://doi.org/10.1145/2642803.2642820
25. Johnstone A, Scott E, van den Brand M (2014) Modular grammar specification. Sci Comput Program 87:23–43. https://doi.org/10.1016/j.scico.2013.09.012
26. Kästner C, Apel S, ur Rahman SS, Rosenmüller M, Batory D, Saake G (2009) On the impact of the optional feature problem: Analysis and case studies. In: Proceedings of the 13th International Software Product Line Conference (SPLC'09), Carnegie Mellon University, pp 181–190
27. Krahn H, Rumpe B, Völkel S (2010) MontiCore: A framework for compositional development of domain-specific languages. Int J Softw Tools Technol Transfer 12(5):353–372. https://doi.org/10.1007/s10009-010-0142-1

28. Kuramitsu K (2016) Nez: Practical open grammar language. In: Proceedings of the 2016 ACM International Symposium on New Ideas, New Paradigms, and Reflections on Programming and Software (Onward!'16). ACM, New York, pp 29–42. https://doi.org/10.1145/2986012.2986019
29. Lämmel R, Wachsmuth G (2001) Transformation of SDF syntax definitions in the ASF+SDF meta-environment. Electron Notes Theor Comput Sci 44(2):9–33. https://doi.org/10.1016/S1571-0661(04)80918-6
30. Lämmel R, Zaytsev V (2011) Recovering grammar relationships for the Java Language Specification. Softw Qual J 19(2):333–378. https://doi.org/10.1007/s11219-010-9116-5
31. Liu J, Batory D, Lengauer C (2006) Feature oriented refactoring of legacy applications. In: Proceedings of the 28th International Conference on Software Engineering (ICSE'06). ACM, New York, pp 112–121. https://doi.org/10.1145/1134285.1134303
32. Mascarenhas F, Medeiros S, Ierusalimschy R (2014) On the relation between context-free grammars and parsing expression grammars. Sci Comput Program 89:235–250. https://doi.org/10.1016/j.scico.2014.01.012
33. Medeiros S, Ierusalimschy R (2008) A parsing machine for PEGs. In: Proceedings of the 2008 Symposium on Dynamic Languages (DLS'08). ACM, New York, pp 2:1–2:12. https://doi.org/10.1145/1408681.1408683
34. Mernik M (2013) An object-oriented approach to language compositions for software language engineering. J Syst Softw 86(9):2451–2464. https://doi.org/10.1016/j.jss.2013.04.087
35. Meyers B (2016) A multi-paradigm modelling approach to design and evolution of domain-specific modelling languages. PhD thesis, University of Antwerp
36. Meyers B, Cicchetti A, Guerra E, de Lara J (2012) Composing textual modelling languages in practice. In: Proceedings of the 6th International Workshop on Multi-paradigm Modeling (MPM'12). ACM, New York, pp 31–36. https://doi.org/10.1145/2508443.2508449
37. Nadkarni AP (2017) The Tcl programming language: A comprehensive guide. CreateSpace Independent Publishing Platform, Scotts Valley
38. Neumann G, Sobernig S (2009) XOTcl 2.0 – A ten-year retrospective and outlook. In: Flynt C, Fox R (eds) Proceedings of the Sixteenth Annual Tcl/Tk Conference. Tcl Association Publications, Portland, pp 179–204. http://nm.wu-wien.ac.at/research/publications/b806.pdf
39. Neumann G, Zdun U (1999) Enhancing object-based system composition through per-object mixins. In: Proceedings of the Asia-Pacific Software Engineering Conference (APSEC'99), IEEE CS, pp 522–530
40. Neumann G, Zdun U (1999) Filters as a language support for design patterns in object-oriented scripting languages. In: Proceedings of the 5th Conference on Object-Oriented Technologies and Systems (COOTS'99), USENIX
41. Nosál M, Porubän J, Sulír M (2017) Customizing host IDE for non-programming users of pure embedded DSLs: A case study. Comput Lang Syst Struct https://doi.org/10.1016/j.cl.2017.04.003
42. Ousterhout JK, Jones K (2009) Tcl and the Tk Toolkit, 2nd edn. Addison-Wesley, Boston
43. Parr T (2009) Language implementation patterns: Create your own domain-specific and general programming languages, 1st edn. Pragmatic Bookshelf, Raleigh
44. Parr T (2013) The definitive ANTLR 4 reference, 2nd edn. Pragmatic Bookshelf, Raleigh
45. Redziejowski RR (2008) Some aspects of parsing expression grammar. Fundamenta Informaticae 85(1–4):441–454
46. Redziejowski RR (2011) BITES instead of FIRST for parsing expression grammar. Fundamenta Informaticae 109(3):323–337
47. Redziejowski RR (2016) Cut points in PEG. Fundamenta Informaticae 143(1–2):141–149
48. Redziejowski RR (2018) Trying to understand PEG. Fundamenta Informaticae 157(4):463–475. https://doi.org/10.3233/FI-2018-1638
49. Reis LV, Iorio VOD, Bigonha RS (2015) An on-the-fly grammar modification mechanism for composing and defining extensible languages. Comput. Lang. Syst. Struct. 42:46–59. https://doi.org/10.1016/j.cl.2015.01.002
50. Renggli L, Ducasse S, Gîrba T, Nierstrasz O (2010) Practical dynamic grammars for dynamic languages. In: Proceedings of the 4th Workshop on Dynamic Languages and Applications (DYLA'10)

51. Renggli L, Gîrba T, Nierstrasz O (2010b) Embedding languages without breaking tools. In: Proceedings of the 24th European conference on Object-oriented Programming (ECOOP'10). Lecture notes in computer science, vol 6183. Springer, Heidelberg, pp 380–404. https://doi.org/10.1007/978-3-642-14107-2_19

52. Riehle D, Tilman M, Johnson R (2005) Dynamic object model. In: Pattern Languages of Program Design, Vol 5. Addison-Wesley, Boston, pp 3–24

53. Salomon DJ, Cormack GV (1989) Scannerless NSLR(1) parsing of programming languages. In: Proceedings of the 1989 Conference on Programming Language Design and Implementation (PLDI'89). ACM, New York, pp 170–178. https://doi.org/10.1145/73141.74833

54. Schmitz S (2006) Modular syntax demands verification. Technical Report I3S/RR-2006-32-FR, Laboratoire I3S, Université de Nice-Sophia Antipolis

55. Selic B (2012) What will it take? A view on adoption of model-based methods in practice. Softw Syst Model 11(4):513–526. https://doi.org/10.1007/s10270-012-0261-0

56. Servetto M, Mackay J, Potanin A, Noble J (2013) The billion-dollar fix. In: Proceedings of the 27th European Conference Object-oriented Programming (ECOOP'13). Lecture notes in computer science, vol 7920. Springer, New York, pp 205–229

57. Simons AJH (2003) The theory of classification, part 9: Inheritance and self reference. J Object Technol 2(6):25–34

58. Simons AJH (2004) The theory of classification, part 15: Mixins and the superclass interface. J Object Technol 3(10):7–18

59. Sobernig S (2019) Chain of builders: A pattern of variable syntax processing for internal DSLs. In: Proceedings of the 24th European Conference on Pattern Languages of Programs (EuroPLop'19). ACM, New York, pp 29:1–29:11. https://doi.org/10.1145/3361149.3361179

60. Sobernig S, Zdun U (2010) Inversion-of-control layer. In: Proceedings of the 15th Annual European Conference on Pattern Languages of Programming (EuroPLoP'10). ACM, New York. https://doi.org/10.1145/2328909.2328935

61. Spinellis D (2001) Notable design patterns for domain-specific languages. J Syst Softw 56(1):91–99. https://doi.org/10.1016/S0164-1212(00)00089-3

62. Stevens WP, Myers GJ, Constantine LL (1974) Structured design. IBM Syst J 13(2):115–139. https://doi.org/10.1147/sj.132.0115

63. van den Brand M, Sellink A, Verhoef C (1998) Current parsing techniques in software renovation considered harmful. In: Proceedings of the 6th International Workshop on Program Comprehension (IWPC'98), IEEE, pp 108–117. https://doi.org/10.1109/WPC.1998.693325

64. van der Storm T, Cook WR, Loh A (2014) The design and implementation of object grammars. Sci Comput Program 96:460–487. https://doi.org/10.1016/j.scico.2014.02.023

65. van Wyk ER, Schwerdfeger AC (2007) Context-aware scanning for parsing extensible languages. In: Proceedings of the 6th International Conference on Generative Programming and Component Engineering (GPCE'07). ACM, New York, pp 63–72. https://doi.org/10.1145/1289971.1289983

66. Visser E (1997) Syntax definition for language prototyping. PhD thesis, University of Amsterdam. http://eelcovisser.org/wiki/thesis

67. Wile DS (1997) Abstract syntax from concrete syntax. In: Proceedings of the 19th International Conference on Software Engineering (ICSE'97). ACM, New York, pp 472–480. https://doi.org/10.1145/253228.253388

68. Zdun U (2002) Language support for dynamic and evolving software architectures. Doctoral thesis, University of Essen

69. Zdun U (2006) Patterns of component and language integration. In: Manolescu D, Völter M, Noble J (eds) Pattern Languages of Program Design, Vol 5, Chap 14. Addison-Wesley, Boston, pp 357–400

70. Zdun U (2010) A DSL toolkit for deferring architectural decisions in DSL-based software design. Inf Softw Technol 52(7):733–748. https://doi.org/10.1016/j.infsof.2010.03.004

71. Zdun U, Strembeck M, Neumann G (2007) Object-based and class-based composition of transitive mixins. Inf Softw Technol 49(8):871–891. https://doi.org/10.1016/j.infsof.2006.10.001

Chapter 6
A Story of a DSL Family

The purpose of a *standard problem* is to allow for a qualitative and a quantitative benchmarking of suggested methods, techniques, and tools in software engineering. Benchmarking must be based on an agreed problem statement, previously established assessment and comparison criteria, and a shared artifact corpus.[1] The objective is to improve the common understanding of complementing or competing approaches based on their strengths and weaknesses that are observed when working on the standard problem. For software language engineering including domain-specific languages (DSLs), different standard problems are being applied. These include the problems defined for the series of Language-Workbench Competitions [2], relevant problem definitions from the modelware community,[2] and software-composition problem definitions (including the Graph-Product Line, GraphPL [8]).

A lack of standard problems or their application to one's approach is problematic for researchers and practitioners alike. From a researcher's perspective, regarding variable DSL, this hampers an analytical comparison making it difficult to answer questions, such as: To which extent does an approach allow for applying different DSL composition types? Does a given approach address abstraction mismatches under composition? For practitioners, the choice of a technique (implementation) so becomes determined by convenience, by uninformed selection, or by a premature technology choice (of a given DSL development system). Important characteristics of a standard problem on variable DSL are [2, 11]:

- The problem can be tackled by different composition types (i.a., extension and unification).

---

[1]Hence, Erdweg et al. [2] refer to them as *benchmark problems*.

[2]Please refer to Hoisl and Sobernig [4, Section 6] for an overview of standard problems in this area: model composition, model transformations, and model-based co-evolution.

© Springer Nature Switzerland AG 2020
S. Sobernig, *Variable Domain-specific Software Languages with DjDSL*,
https://doi.org/10.1007/978-3-030-42152-6_6

- The problem is capable of exposing abstraction mismatches (e.g., decomposition mismatches) specific to variability implementation techniques, if not mitigated as part of the approach.
- The problem allows for assessing a solution's fit based on agreed assessment criteria: openness to extension, preplanning effort, independence of extensions, etc.

On top, a standard problem must balance between being easy to understand and being non-trivial. The latter is a prerequisite to exhibit composition types and abstraction mismatches. Variable DSL development using DjDSL has been exercised a number of standard problems, including:

- *Pongo DSL*: A DSL family as part of the object-to-NoSQL mapping (ONM) framework Pongo. Pongo has been documented and applied as standard problem before by Hoisl and Sobernig [4].
- *Questionnaire DSL*: A DSL family as part of a web-application for authoring and deploying surveys. This is the frequently applied and reported standard problem of the 2013 instance of the Language-Workbench Competition (LWC'13) series [2].

They add to those used as running examples throughout this writing (e.g., EPL, GraphPL, and Miss Grant's). Both applications of DjDSL are fully documented and reported as supplemental tutorials available from the DjDSL repository [9]. The application on the Pongo DSL problem is elaborated on in what follows, to highlight important lessons learnt (see Sect. 6.6).

6.1 Object-to-NoSQL Mapping: Pongo DSL

6.1.1 Domain of Application

The captured domain of application is the one of object-to-NoSQL mappers (ONM; [10]). In the spirit of object-relational mappers, ONM abstract from specific NoSQL vendors (e.g., MongoDB, CouchDB, Redis) and from different types of NoSQL engines (e.g., document stores, key-value stores, column-family stores) to provide a uniform, cross-engine API for client applications to persist their object-oriented application data. The feature diagram in Fig. 6.1 models a variability selection of the ONM domain. ONM provide CRUD operations and, optionally, a cross-engine query language and runtime (i.e., generic read). The runtime is then responsible for transforming generic into native query statements (depending on the native querying capabilities of the mapped engine, in a given configuration). Generic queries render the ONM and their client applications independent from a specific engine and store type. Querying is typically offered as an SQL derivative and subset (e.g., Java Persistence Query Language, JPQL), which includes equivalents of SELECT, UPDATE, and DELETE statements. The latter relate to the support for single-valued and multi-valued properties and references.

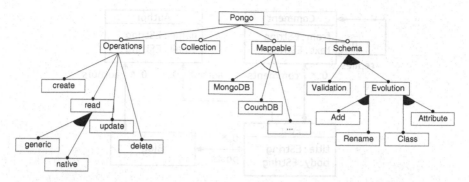

Fig. 6.1 An excerpt from a feature diagram representing the variability in the ONM domain, as described in full detail by Störl et al. [10, Section 3.3]. In addition, the following cross-tree constraint applies: Mappable ⇔ Operations. Optional ONM features excluded for the scope of this writing are visualization and different binding techniques (static, dynamic)

In a basic configuration, ONM are limited to single-valued properties and references. An optional feature is support for collections. UPDATE and DELETE statements then serve for batch updates and batch deletions of collections. ONM vary in their coverage of backend stores, from one specifically supported (e.g., the original Pongo or Morphia for MongoDB only to Kundera with support for five different stores). Moreover, ONM vary regarding their capabilities of *schema management*: schema validation and schema evolution. Generally, schemas in NoSQL stores are not maintained as data dictionaries, with built-in validation, but often implicit in the class structure of the mapped application data. At times, extrinsic validation based on a validation representation (JSON schema and JSON) can be used. The fit of stored data into valid instantiations of the class structure may be lost when application data evolves (e.g., renaming of entity classes or their attributes). An ONM may or not provide some guidance for adding, renaming, and removing different units (entities, attributes, relationships; see Fig. 6.1). Finally, some ONM include visualization support for application data (e.g., Pongo) and different binding times for mappings between application data and stores. Examples include binding at generation time in original Pongo or binding at load time using Java annotations in JPA-compatible ONM such as Morphia.[3]

6.1.2 Pongo

Pongo [6] describes itself as "a template-based Java POJO generator for MongoDB. Instead of using low-level DBObjects to interact with your MongoDB database, with Pongo you can define your data/domain model using EMFatic and then generate strongly typed Java classes you can then use to work with your database

---

[3]Note that for this standard problem, these two features (visualization and binding times) are out of scope.

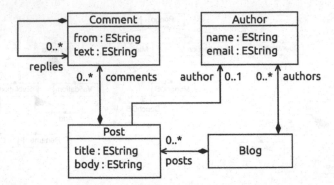

Fig. 6.2 Ecore model of the blogging system implemented using the Pongo DSL. This serves as a minimal viable and testable example of a DSL-based application in the chosen variability scenario

Lst. 6.3 A Pongo
data-model definition of the
blogging system using
EMFatic textual syntax

```
@db class Blog {
    val Post[*] posts;
    val Author[*] authors;
}
class Post {
    attr String title;
    attr String body;
    ref Author author;
}
class Author {
    attr String name;
    attr String email;
}
```

at a more convenient level of abstraction" [6]. The Pongo project fulfills the basic requirements: open source, publicly available, non-trivial model transformations for platform integration, and reusable assets (i.e., non-trivial applications using Pongo, model artifacts).

The problem assets are derived from material (domain model, test application) obtained from the Pongo tutorial (a blogging system) published on the project's website [5]. Figure 6.2 shows an Ecore model which defines four EClasses (Blog, Post, Comment, and Author) as well as corresponding attributes and references to represent the blogging domain. A corresponding domain model of the blogging system is specified using the EMFatic textual syntax in Listing 6.3.

In the original setup, M2T transformations are implemented in Epsilon. The transformations consist of EGL templates with EOL helper operations and EGX as coordination language for EGL templates [7] to generate Java source code from Ecore models. In the blogging-system example, by executing the transformations, Java compilation units are generated. These Java classes implement the domain model (see Fig. 6.2) and define helper methods (e.g., getter and setter) to conveniently work with the MongoDB database (e.g., for querying, reading, and writing blog data; see also Fig. 6.4).

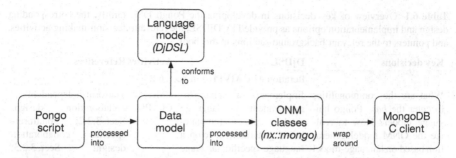

Fig. 6.4 An overview of the major transformation steps and artifact relationships in the Pongo ONM story

6.1.3   Problem Statement

A *reactive* trajectory is taken to develop a DSL family for a Pongo object-to-NoSQL mapper (Pongo ONM).[4] In a first step, a minimal viable Pongo ONM product line ("MVPL" in Table 6.1) is to be developed. The scope of this initial product line is a single supported DSL variant only. The objective of the initial, single-variant iteration is to develop an abstract syntax representation (language model plus context conditions) and one backend connector (MongoDB). The main CRUD operations should be supported, for single-valued properties only. Collections of elements (e.g., multi-valued attributes) are not supported. A client application to this Pongo DSL variant must handle collections, if required, at the application tier.

Each iteration (2–4) then adds an increment the DSL family. Depending on the development artifacts concerned, each iteration relates to different DSL development activities (see "Activities" column in Table 6.1). Note that two of the iterations directly correspond to the domain variability ("collection", "query support"), that is, they are consequences of the domain analysis and the reactive development of the DSL family.

In Sect. 6.6, important lessons learnt across the four iterations will be discussed according to the following quality attributes of the DjDSL-based solution [1, 2]:

- Unmodified reusability
- Preplanning effort
- Feature traceability ("feature mapping")
- Separation and composition of concerns ("abstraction mismatches")

---

[4]Based on one setup and a collection of assets, etc., different standard or benchmark problems can be defined. Erdweg et al. [2] list a number of relevant problem statements, e.g., language extension, language embedding, syntax migration, structure migration. The problem statement here aims at the *reactive* development style of a DSL family as overall problem, with each iteration focusing one key design decision. These design decisions reflect selected problems identified by Erdweg et al. [2].

Table 6.1 Overview of key decisions in developing the Pongo DSL family, the corresponding design and implementation options as provided by DjDSL, the relevant decision-making activities, and pointers to the relevant background sections in this book

Key decisions	DjDSL	Activities	References
	Iteration #1 ("MVPL") in Sect. 6.2		
What are the commonalities to enter the *base* Pongo language model? How to realize the ONM model generation based on language-model instantiations? How to realize basic platform integration with one backend (MongoDB) based on the language model?	Implement a platform-independent language model plus template-based generator, develop a language-specific language model plus native context conditions (e.g.,templating)	LM, CC, PI	Platform-independent collaboration design: Sect. 3.2.2; platform-specific collaboration design: Sect. 3.2.3; context conditions (trimming): Sect. 4.3
	Iteration #2 ("Frontend Syntax") in Sect. 6.3		
Should an internal or external syntax be provided to client applications?	Internal DSL using djdsl::dada builders, external DSL using djdsl::opeg parser, both	CS	See Sects. 5.1 and 5.2.4
	Iteration #3 ("Collections") in Sect. 6.4		
How to extend the base language-model to support multi-valued attributes and references. Can the previously chosen syntax type handle multi-valued declarations?	Internal DSL extension using djdsl::dada *chained* builders, external DSL composition using djdsl::opeg, both	LM, CC, PI, CS	Collaborations: see Sect. 3.2.3; builders: Sect. 5.1; grammar composition: Sect. 5.2.4; context conditions: Sect. 4.3
	Iteration #4 ("Mixed Syntax") in Sect. 6.5		
How to provide for robust syntax processing? How to develop different variants of an external DSL in DjDSL?	External DSL composition using djdsl::opeg: grammar union vs. explicit grammar transformations	CS	See Sect. 5.2.4

6.2 Iteration 1: MVLP

The first iteration in this problem setting is centered around the two key decisions related to the language-model design and definition using DjDSL. From these, the need for context conditions and a first integration with one backend (MongoDB) is planned for the first iteration. The expected output is a "minimum viable product line" (MVPL) that allows for defining the blogging application-data model and storing its instances with a given database hosted by one backend instance (i.e., MongoDB).

```
1   Asset create Base {
2     LanguageModel create Model {
3
4       Classifier create Element
5
6       Classifier create NamedElement -superclasses Element {
7         :property -accessor public name:required,alnum
8       }
9
10      Classifier create Class -superclasses NamedElement {
11        :property -accessor public {root:boolean false}
12        :property -accessor public attributes:0..*,object,type=Attribute
13        :property -accessor public references:0..*,object,type=Reference
14      }
15
16      Classifier create Attribute -superclasses NamedElement {
17        :property attributeType:object,type=DataType;
18      }
19
20      Classifier create Reference -superclasses NamedElement {
21        :property -accessor public {containment:boolean false}
22        :property referenceType
23      }
24
25      Classifier create DataType -superclasses NamedElement {
26        :create String -name "string"
27        :create Boolean -name "boolean"
28        :create Int -name "integer"
29        :create Float -name "float"
30      }
31    }; # Model
32  }; # Base
```

Lst. 6.5 A language-model implementation for the Pongo language using DjDSL

6.2.1 Language Model (LM)

The two guiding design decisions are: What are the means of expression for modeling application data required by client applications of the Pongo ONM? What are the commonalities to enter the base Pongo language model? See also Table 6.1. The language model must be capable of expressing application data as shown in Fig. 6.2. Pongo [5] itself is built on top of a subset of Ecore, with a single predefined annotation type to denote the root entity in a data model. More specifically, an initial prototype can be limited to single-value attributes and references (see the feature diagram in Fig. 6.1).

For this decision, DjDSL offers two paths: Designing the language model (and context conditions) in a platform-independent manner, using the UML profile plus OCL, or in a platform-specific manner defining djdsl::lm assets directly. The context conditions would then become defined as djdsl::ctx definitions on the assets. The platform-independent option is suited for situations in which the language model is developed from scratch, involving domain practitioners.[5] In the given case, the requirements on the language model have already been elicited by the relevant subset of Ecore and its Pongo extensions. There are even syntactic examples provided. Therefore, the platform-specific option is taken (djdsl::dada asset plus djdsl::ctx). The resulting language-model definition is shown in Listing 6.5.

6.2.2   Context Conditions (CC)

Based on the platform-specific DjDSL language model defined, only minor additional requirements are imposed on Pongo ONM models. The most importing being that, given an instance of Model, there must be exactly one Class instantiation being marked as the root entity. The root entity will be used to create a root collection in the backend store. This corresponds to the property root defined on line 11 of Listing 6.5. One possible implementation of a corresponding djdsl::ctx condition is given in Listing 6.6. The cond expression on line 5 makes use of a *model method*

```
1   context Base::Model {
2
3     cond {[llength [:info children]] >= 1}
4
5     cond {[:isRooted]}
6
7     # model method
8     op isRooted {} {
9       set childType ::djdsl::pongo::Base::Model::Class
10      set classes [:info children -type $childType]
11      set isRoot [lmap cl $classes {expr {[$cl root get] && 1}}]
12      return [expr {[tcl::mathop::+ {*}$isRoot]} == 1]
13    }
14  }
```

Lst. 6.6 Implementation of context conditions (featuring a model method) for the Pongo language using DjDSL

isRooted which implements the actual check by iterating the instantiations of Class and checks for exactly one of them being set to as the root entity. This allows for later, unanticipated refinements of the root condition by providing refinements to the model method. The cond on line 3 establishes the precondition for a model of having at least one defined model element. The two condition expressions are evaluated using a conjunction. The context conditions can be triggered by a Pongo

---

[5] Another driver for the platform-independent option was the requirement to model the application data as UML object diagrams and have them processed using M2T transformations (similar to the Pongo setup). This is, however, not the case.

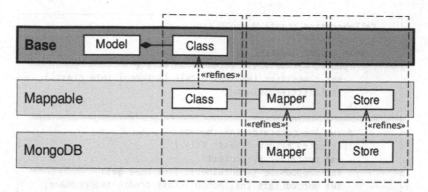

Fig. 6.7 An overview of the collaboration-based design as obtained during iteration 1. The implementation of the Base collaboration is shown in Listing 6.5 and corresponds to the root feature Pongo of the feature diagram in Fig. 6.1. The collaboration MongoDB implements the same-named feature and is depicted in Listing 6.8. The intermediate collaboration Mappable maps to the same-named decomposition feature in Fig. 6.1. It is fully reported in the accompanying tutorial. Its implementation is implied by the backend implementations and will be injected by DjDSL into any composition that contains a backend collaboration

client application directly or, in the next step, platform integration will execute them as a first step.

6.2.3 Platform Integration (PI)

Platform integration involves two steps: (a) generation of a native (NX) class structure based on a Pongo language-model instantiation (e.g., for the blog data); (b) having the application data handled by a client connector to a given backend (see also Fig. 6.4). In this iteration, the objective is to provide one backend connector to MongoDB. For this purpose, platform integration resorts to the built-in NX client library nx::mongo.

To perform an integration for a given Pongo model (e.g., the blog-system data in Fig. 6.2), a basic VISITOR structure is provided for Pongo language-model instantiations by the collaboration Mappable (see Fig. 6.7). In this collaboration, all classifiers (Class, Attribute, Reference) are extended to receive accept messages which, in turn, submit themselves to the VISITOR, called Mapper. For each backend, one specialized VISITOR can then be provided for generating the bindings for a given model (depending on the client library and backend). MongoDB integration is realized as a dedicated DjDSL collaboration (see Listing 6.8). This collaboration acts as the feature implementation for the corresponding feature MongoDB (see the feature diagram in Fig. 6.1). This collaboration implies and refines the Mappable collaboration. The VISITOR protocol is reused and the special Mapper is used to emit a particular class structure that binds to MongoDB via the nx::mongo

```
1    Collaboration create MongoDB {
2
3      Role create Mapper {
4        :public method visit {element:object} {
5          set classifier [namespace tail [$element info class]]
6          :$classifier $element
7        }
8
9        # runtime generator (nx::mongo)
10       :protected method "Class" {el} {
11         set container ${:context}
12         set mappedName ${container}::[$el name get]
13         set mappedClass [nx::mongo::Class create $mappedName]
14         set :currentClass $mappedClass
15       }
16     }
17
18     Role create Store {
19       :public method save {obj} {
20         $obj save
21       }
22       :public method delete {obj} {
23         $obj delete
24       }
25     }
26   }
```

Lst. 6.8 Integration of the Pongo language with the MongoDB ONM framework using a runtime code generator

```
1    Composition create MongoDBPongo \
2      -binds {Backends Base} \
3      -base [[Base]::Model] \
4      -features [list [[Backends]::Mappable] \
5                      [[Backends]::MongoDB]]
```

Lst. 6.9 Enabling the MongoDB integration by creating a language-model product

package.[6] As required by the variability model, a particular backend is, therefore, implemented in terms of an optional feature (i.e., it requires explicit composition). The commonality for all backends is captured in the Mappable collaboration.

In addition, the backend-specific collaborations introduce a helper classifier called Store. This classifier and its refinements enable a Pongo client developer to interact with the mapped data model (e.g., save, delete) in an cross-backend manner, abstracting from the underlying native API.

Listing 6.9 depicts how one possible feature configuration (for MongoDB) can now be defined as a DjDSL Composition, binding the previously defined

---

[6]The implementation details specific to nx::mongo, and hence the implementation of the VISITOR, are omitted here for the sake of clarity. Please consult the supplemental Pongo tutorial available from the DjDSL repository [9] for all these details.

assets (`Base`, `Mappable`).[7] Please note that one can also obtain a `Composition` without any backend support. Alternatively, a DSL developer can operate on the base `LanguageModel` only. This is not only permitted by the variability model (see Fig. 6.1), but also useful. For example, it may be sufficient for certain client applications requesting certain features only, e.g., visualization support.

6.3   Iteration 2: Frontend Syntax

The initial iteration provides in essence all prerequisites to define a mapping, to generate a mapped binding (at runtime), and to store application data conforming to the Pongo model (i.e., an instantiation of the language model) to a MongoDB database. At this point, this is achievable via *direct instantiation* only. This is because in the first iteration no dedicated syntax (neither internal nor external) has been implemented so far. For direct instantiation, NX host-language syntax is used to create instantiations of the Pongo language model. The instantiations model application data (e.g., blogs, posts).[8] Direct instantiation has downsides. These include the full exposure of the Pongo client developer to NX/Tcl as Pongo's host language. Besides, client developers already familiar with Pongo [6] or already having Pongo data models defined using the EMFatic syntax are not well supported. Therefore, the second iteration sets out to provide this frontend syntax. This amounts to providing a means of indirect instantiation.

6.3.1   Concrete Syntax (CS)

Pongo [6] suggests the textual notation depicted in Listing 6.3. To make this notation usable directly, a design decision must be taken: Should the frontend syntax be developed in an internal or external manner? See also Table 6.1. DjDSL offers the options of an internal DSL syntax using `djdsl::dada` builders or an external DSL syntax defined by an object parsing-expression grammar (`djdsl::dada`). A closer look reveals that the given syntax closely resembles Tcl's native one: curly braced blocks, semi-colon as statement delimiters, and command-like statements separated by whitespace. The decision is, therefore, to provide a `djdsl::dada` or internal syntax first.

This is achieved by defining a builder class `ModelBuilder` that implements OBJECT SCOPING [3].[9] In OBJECT SCOPING, DSL statements and their invocations

---

[7]Please refer to Sect. 3.2.3 for all the details on defining and managing compositions.

[8]Direct instantiation has been highlighted in Sect. 1.4.2 of the introductory tutorial (without collaborations) and in Sect. 3.2.3 on collaboration-based language models. See these sections for concrete examples. Direct instantiation has benefits, for example, a Pongo client developer can use NX/Tcl features to automate repeated construction details of an application-data model.

[9]Corresponding pattern descriptions are provided in Sect. 5.1.

```
1    # DSL invocation handler for "@db" annotation
2    :public method "<- @db" {args} {
3        set args [list {*}$args -root true]
4        :<- {*}$args
5    }
```

Lst. 6.10 Implementation of the @db internal-syntax handler

```
1    ModelBuilder create pongoBuilder \
2        -interp [EmptyInterp new] \
3        -output [MongoDBPongo new model]
4
5    set blogModel [pongoBuilder get $blogData]
```

Lst. 6.11 Implementation of a BUILDER object for the Pongo language

Lst. 6.12

```
@db class Blog {
    val Post[*] posts;
    val Author[*] authors;
}
class Post {
    attr String title;
    attr String body;
    ref Author author;
}
class Author {
    attr String name;
    attr String email;
}
```

(class, attr etc.) map to handler methods defined for the scope of a given builder. The DSL script as such is evaluated in a safe interpreter. Listing 6.10 highlights the handler method for the @db annotation. In essence, the handler injects a construction parameter (root) on the instantiation path for a Class object. See line 3 of Listing 6.10.

This builder implementation is capable of processing the Pongo frontend syntax as-is and returns—as a parse representation—a Pongo language-model instantiation. Listing 6.11 shows how a builder instance is created as part of the Pongo client application. Note that the builder is equipped with an EmptyInterp, a safe interpreter for evaluating the Pongo script, and a Pongo model as defined by the composition MongoDBPongo is requested as its output (see Listing 6.9 above).

The builder's get method is then handed over a Pongo script (see Listing 6.12) to produce the requested language-model instantiation. This model instantiation can then be used from a Pongo client application to manage its application data (i.e., blogs and their posts in the blog-system application).

A Store specific to the chosen MongoDB backend is obtained. This also covers connection management to a running MongoDB instance (see line 2 of Listing 6.13).

```
1    # 1) obtain a store (incl. MongoDB connection)
2    set store [$blogModel new store]
3
4    # 2) create and populate application data
5    set blog [${store}::Blog new]
6    set post [${store}::Post new -title "A post" -body "Some text"]
7    $blog posts set $post
8
9    # 3) persist application data
10   $store save $blog
```

Lst. 6.13 The newly supported @db annotation in action

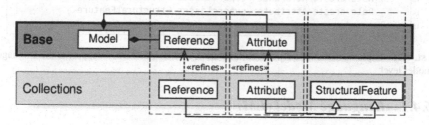

Fig. 6.14 The realization of the optional Collection feature as a DjDSL collaboration. The collaboration adds a classifier StructuralFeature to hold and to manage multiplicity ranges for Attribute and Reference instantiations

Then, blogs and posts plus authors can be created. Finally, these application data can be persisted using the previously obtained Store (see line 10 of Listing 6.13).

6.4   Iteration 3: Collections

The first two iterations yielded a Pongo ONM implementation accepting Pongo data-model scripts (in the established notation), generating a native (NX) class structure based on a Pongo language-model instantiation (as the primary abstraction for a client application), and providing for an abstraction to interact with different backends (Store). As captured by the feature diagram in Fig. 6.1, support for collections as required multi-valued attributes and references is optional. This is actually backed by the domain analysis. Certain ONM offer only the common subset of capabilities (excluding collections) by the abstracted NoSQL backends [10, Section 3]. The objective of this iteration is to add support for collections, conditional on backends supporting them (e.g., MongoDB). It turns out that this iteration touches on several artifacts at the same time (LM, CS, and PI). Key design decisions must be revisited. This is particularly the case of the concrete-syntax design.

```
1    # Collections::Model
2    Collaboration create Model {
3
4      Classifier create StructuralFeature {
5        :property -accessor public lowerBound:integer
6        :property -accessor public {upperBound:integer 1}
7
8        :public method isMultiValued {} {
9          return [expr {${:upperBound} == -1 || ${:upperBound} > 1}]
10       }
11     }
12
13     Role create Reference -superclasses StructuralFeature
14     Role create Attribute -superclasses StructuralFeature
15   }
```

Lst. 6.15 Implementation of a DjDSL collaboration realizing collection support at the language-model level

6.4.1   Language Model (LM)

A new Collaboration is implemented to enrich the base Pongo language model with multiplicities (see Fig. 6.14). The aim is to allow for Attribute and Reference elements to carry lowerBound and upperBound limits. These properties help discriminate between the single-valued and multi-valued case, as well as help impose arbitrary range restrictions on element collections. Listing 6.15 shows the corresponding implementation.

This collaboration highlights a particular characteristic of a collaboration-based design realized using DjDSL. In the base implementation, Attribute and Reference are not structurally related. The new Collaboration in Listing 6.15 introduces a common ancestor for the two classifiers, StructuralFeature, and modifies the superclass relationships accordingly. Note that these superclass relationships are only enacted when a composition has the feature Collection selected. When active, they can be used as defined from the very beginning. For example, the superclass can act as context element for context conditions to be enforced on Reference and Attribute alike; see the next paragraph.

6.4.2   Context Conditions (CC)

To enforce validity of the multiplicity ranges on references and attributes holding element collections, an additional triple of djdsl::ctx context conditions is necessary. This increment is given in Listing 6.16. The additional condition expression checks whether a given lowerBound is not below zero, whether a given upperBound is either −1 (for unbound), or whether greater than the lowerBound.

```
1  context Collections::Model::StructuralFeature {
2    cond {![info exists :lowerBound] || ${:lowerBound} >= 0}
3    cond {${:upperBound} >= -1}
4    cond {
5      ![info exists :lowerBound] ||
6      ${:upperBound} == -1 ||
7      ${:upperBound} >= ${:lowerBound}
8    }
9  }
```

Lst. 6.16 Implementation of additional context conditions using DjDSL

6.4.3 Platform Integration (PI)

Given the generic VISITOR structure already present in the base implementation, handling the extended generation of backend (nx::mongo) code is straightforward. The Collection feature implementation provides additionally a refinement of the MongoDB-specific Mapper that acts as the visitor participant. The refinement instruments the existing Mapper in a way that, for multi-valued references and attributes, multi-value aware nx::mongo properties are generated. For the single-value case, the existing generation logic is reused as-is. In addition, multi-valued properties receive incremental mutator and accessor operations (e.g., add, element-wise delete).

6.4.4 Concrete Syntax (CS)

The currently implemented internal DSL syntax (ModelBuilder) must be extended to handle multiplicity declarations (e.g., [*], [0..2]). At this point, they are silently dropped. To have them handled properly, while preserving the collection-unaware syntax, a syntaxwise internal DSL extension is needed. In DjDSL, for internal DSL, this is achieved using chained DjDSL builders.[10]

1. A new builder class CollectionBuilder is defined. This builder will act as predecessor (refinement) of the already provided base builder ModelBuilder.
2. The new builder implements DYNAMIC RECEPTION[11] to process the multiplicity declarations. This is because, the way the base builder is implemented, maps DSL syntax elements (e.g., attr) to method implementations of the builder.

---

[10]See Sect. 5.1 for the background on chaining builders for DSL extensions, and other DSL composition types (e.g., unification).

[11]Corresponding pattern descriptions are provided in Sect. 3.2.3.

```
1    # dynamic reception
2    :public method handleUnknown {range args} {
3      set :currentRange [string map {.. " "} $range]
4      if {[llength ${:currentRange}]==1} {
5        set :currentRange [list 0 {*}${:currentRange}]
6      }
7      if {[lindex ${:currentRange} end] eq "*"} {
8        lset :currentRange end -1
9      }
10     return
11   }
```

Lst. 6.17 The core of the BUILDER implementation to process multiplicity elements in Pongo definitions using an unknown handler

```
1    Composition create MongoDBPongo+ \
2      -binds {Collections Backends Base} \
3      -base [[Base]::Model] \
4      -features [list [[Collections]::Model] \
5                      [[Backends]::Mappable] \
6                      [[Collections]::MongoDB+] \
7                      [[Backends]::MongoDB]]
```

Lst. 6.18 Implementation of the language-model product having collection support enabled

Multiplicity declarations (especially those with custom lower and upper bounds) will be caught by an unknown handler and can so be processed accordingly.[12]

Listing 6.17 depicts the additional unknown handler as provided by djdsl:: dada builders. Multiplicity declarations are processed, mapped into a given value domain, and stored as a CONTEXT VARIABLE[3] currentRange. This CONTEXT VARIABLE is checked by refinements of the invocation handlers for attributes and references to set their lowerBound and upperBound properties accordingly.

The batch of refinements created in this iteration includes a collaboration at the level of the language model (LM), additional context conditions (CC), a special visitor implementation for platform integration with the backend (PI), and a chainable builder for an extended concrete syntax (CS). With this, a client developer of Pongo ONM can now create a collection-aware application data model and use it accordingly.

First, a corresponding Composition must be defined that incorporates the collection-specific collaborations (see Listing 6.18).

In a second step, the client developer creates a refined builder that is capable of producing collection-aware language-model instantiations (see Listing 6.19). Note

---

[12]Please note that this is just one of the design choices at this point. Alternatives would be variants of TEXTUAL POLISHING [3] to prefix multiplicity blocks by some invocation handler provided by the builder, right before evaluating DSL scripts, etc.

```
1  ModelBuilder create pongoBuilder+ \
2      -interp [EmptyInterp new] \
3      -predecessors [CollectionBuilder] \
4      -output [MongoDBPongo+ new model]
5
6  set blogModel [pongoBuilder+ get $blogData]
```

Lst. 6.19 Provide a syntax processor for the extended Pongo language

```
1  # 2) create and populate application data
2  set blog [${store}::Blog new]
3  set post1 [${store}::Post new -title "A post" -body "
   Some text"]
4  set post2 [${store}::Post new -title "Another post"
   -body "Some more text"]
5  $blog posts add $post1
6  $blog posts add $post2
```

Lst. 6.20 Use of the generated ONM structure to create blog posts

how the `CollectionBuilder` is set as a predecessor to the base `ModelBuilder` on line 3.

From this point onwards, the client developer can use the generated Pongo ONM structure to create application data including collections of posts (see Listing 6.20). Note the use of the elementwise addition on lines 5 and 6.

6.5 Iteration 4: Mixed Syntax

The addition of collections support in iteration three exposes some weaknesses of the design decision to provide for an internal DSL syntax.

1. The builder-based implementation of the internal syntax cannot properly enforce syntax restrictions on the placement of multiplicity blocks in a Pongo ONM script. Consider the following lines:

```
val Post[*] posts;
val[*] Post posts;
val Post posts[*];
```

Each of them, regardless of the placement of the multiplicity declaration [*], will be accepted by the internal-syntax processor, as implemented. This is troublesome, especially for those client-application developers that cannot use syntax-checked Pongo scripts. In such cases, the results of syntax processing are surprising and counterintuitive, at best.
2. In addition, an internal DSL syntax cannot accommodate (future) syntax extensions that violate the basic Tcl syntax.

```
1     P                ←  `Model` ClsStmt+;
2     ClsStmt          ←  `Class` root:(`true` DB / `false` !DB) CLASS name:ID
3                         OBRACKET StmtList CBRACKET;
4     StmtList         ←  (Stmt SCOLON)*;
5     Stmt             ←  attributes:AttrStmt / references:RefStmt;
6     RefStmt          ←  `Reference` containment:(`false` REF / `true` VAL)
7                         referenceType:(`$root` elements $0` ID) WS name:ID;
8     AttrStmt         ←  `Attribute` ATTR attributeType:(`$root` datatypes $0` ID)
9                         WS name:ID;
10    ID               ←  <alnum>+;
```

Lst. 6.21 This is an excerpt from the actual rules set defining the EMFatic syntax used by Pongo [6]. The auxiliary and scanner-level rules are omitted for brevity. The OPEG is based on the original EMFatic syntax definition for JavaCC. The complete OPEG is available from the accompanying tutorial

3. Existing Pongo scripts cannot be used as-is because, as a closer look reveals, the internal-syntax processor does not process correctly annotation elements (e.g., @db) when placed on separate lines.

To provide correct syntax handling for client applications and to prepare for future syntax extensions that are independent from Tcl's native syntax, a fourth and final iteration is scheduled. The aim is to implement an (optional) external DSL syntax on top of the existing implementation. This entails reusing the existing implementation, including the internal DSL, as is *without modification*. An additional objective is to provide two variants of the external DSL syntax, one with collections and one without collections. This is mandatory in order to support the same configuration space as the internal DSL currently does.

The resulting implementation makes use of DjDSL's object parsing-expression grammars (OPEG). This iteration is, therefore, only concerned with a concrete-syntax (CS) refinement.

6.5.1   Concrete Syntax (CS)

For this purpose, a first syntax variant w/o collection support is defined using an OPEG Grammar class. The Grammar class hosts the following parsing rules in OPEG's frontend syntax. This notation is inspired by E/BNF.[13] The OPEG in Listing 6.21 covers for the Pongo scripts relevant for the scope of this writing. This grammar exhibits some noteworthy OPEG highlights:

* Instantiation generators are used to bind match statements to language-model elements (e.g., ClsStmt to Class). This is the case for all major language-model elements, including Attribute and Reference.

---

[13]Please see Sect. 5.2.4 of this book for the details on *object parsing-expression grammars* (OPEG) as offered by DjDSL, including instantiation generator, assignment generator, and query generator.

```
1              ID ← <alnum>+ MP? ;
2              MP ← SQOBRACKET (lowerBound:(<digit>+) SEP)?
3                   upperBound:(`$root mapSymbol $0` '*' / <digit>+)
4                   SQCBRACKET ;
5 void:   SQOBRACKET ← WS '\[' WS;
6 void:   SQCBRACKET ← WS '\]' WS;
7 void:        SEP ← WS '..' WS;
```

Lst. 6.22 A grammar extension introducing multiplicity support

Lst. 6.23 Enabling the
grammar extension

```
1  Grammar create ExtPongoGrm \
2      -start P \
3      -merges [PongoGrm] $grm
```

- Assignment generators map matched sub-clauses of statement rules to properties of the language-model elements. For example, the Stmt rule on line 5 populates the attributes property with all attributes created by AttrStmt matches, as well as the references property with all references created by any RefStmt matches.
- Query generators are employed to lazily map identifiers (e.g., ID matches like "String" and "Author") to objects via helper methods (datatypes and elements, respectively) before assigning them to a property.
- Query generators can also be used to conveniently map syntactic toggles like @db to Boolean properties (root). See line 2 of Listing 6.21. A similar use of a query operator for the containment property is shown on line 6, based on distinction between a val and a ref match.

To implement a second variant, with syntactic collection support, a refining OPEG is provided that can enter a merge relationship with the base OPEG in Listing 6.21. This is an occurrence of an external DSL extension. The resulting OPEG extension is reproduced in Listing 6.22. It is built in a way that allows for a straightforward grammar union (i.e., union with override) between the receiving and the merged grammar. The extension point is the ID rule which is present in both grammars (see line 10 in Listing 6.21 and line 1 in Listing 6.22). The merged grammar substitutes the ID for an extended one which includes the parsing rule MP for recognizing multiplicity blocks. Upon recognition, the lowerBound and upperBound will be automatically added to the construction calls of the underlying references and attributes. This is achieved by the assignment generators as part of the MP rule (see lines 2–4 in Listing 6.22). The extended grammar is then defined as shown in Listing 6.23 by declaring the merges relationship between the corresponding Grammar classes: ExtPongoGrm and PongoGrm:

Having implemented two variants of an external syntax, client developers can now request and use two corresponding OPEG-based parsers, one with collection support and another without. Listing 6.24 contrasts the two usage variants. It is clearly visible that, from the perspective of a client developer, the differences are minuscule.

```
1  set lmf \                          set lmf \
2      [LanguageModelFactory new \        [LanguageModelFactory new \
3          -lm [MongoDBPongo]::Model]         -lm [MongoDBPongo+]::Model]
4  set pongoParser \                  set ePongoParser \
5      [PongoGrm new \                    [ExtPongoGrm new \
6          -factory $lmf]                     -factory $lmf]
7  set blogModel [$pongoParser parse {  set blogModel [$ePongoParser parse {
8    @db class Blog {                    @db class Blog {
9      val Post posts;                    val Post[*] posts;
10     val Author authors;                val Author[*] authors;
11   }                                  }
12   class Post {                       class Post {
13     attr String title;                 attr String title;
14     attr String body;                  attr String body;
15     ref Author author;                 ref Author author;
16   }                                  }
17   class Author {                     class Author {
18     attr String name;                  attr String name;
19     attr String email;                 attr String email;
20   }                                  }
21 }]                                  }]
```

Lst. 6.24 The client developer using the Pongo language can use the two Pongo syntax variants next to each other

On the left-hand side of Listing 6.24, a basic Pongo parser is requested from the `Grammar` class `PongoGrm`. The parser is associated with the corresponding language model without collection support (`MongoDBPongo::Model`; see line 2). On the right-hand side, a collection-aware Pongo parser is obtained from the refined `Grammar` class `ExtPongoGrm`. It is backed by the extended language model `MongoDBPongo+::Model` (see line 2). The resulting language-model instantiations (held by variable `blogModel` in Listing 6.24) can then be used directly as if they were created from the internal syntax (see iteration 3). Most importantly, they can be used to populate a data-model instance and to manage it via a `Store` object. Therefore, existing client applications of the Pongo ONM can switch to external syntax processing without major rewrite.

6.6   Lessons Learned

The Pongo ONM example shows the benefits of applying DjDSL in a reactive development approach to a DSL family. The first iteration resulted in a single-DSL product line which can be directly used to persist application data. This product line and the derivable DSL are directly useful to client developers. In addition, they allow for refining and for testing the language model; before adding features.

The subsequent iterations had different objectives. Iteration 3 followed the variability model by implementing a new feature (collection support). This way, new variants were added to the DSL family. Iterations 2 and 4 contributed DSL artifacts such as an internal, then an external syntax.

After having presented each iteration in isolation, the different design and implementation propositions offered by DjDSL can be revisited briefly to discuss how they performed with regard to the four quality attributes: feature traceability, separation and composition of concerns without mismatches, unmodified reusability, and minimal preplanning. Each iteration with increment could build on the results of previous iterations, without the need for modifying or even for rewriting prior results. This is a consequence of DjDSL contributing to realizing these four quality attributes.

6.6.1 Feature Traceability

DjDSL allows for maintaining a 1:1 correspondence between features defined by the variability model (see Fig. 6.1) and their implementations. Namely, features Pongo (the base feature), Collection, Mappable, and MongoDB mapped to four DjDSL collaborations in the code base. There is one exception, though. There is no corresponding collaboration for feature Operations. A distinction between backends (feature Mappable) and CRUD operations (feature Operations) had purpose during domain analysis. Implementationwise, they are equivalent (at least, for the scope of this application example). This is also indicated in the variability model by the cross-tree constraint Mappable ⇔ Operations.[14] Another point in favor of DjDSL is that both decomposition ("abstract") features and primary ("concrete") features can be mapped to DjDSL collaborations. This proved useful for Pongo ONM because the collaboration Mappable groups reusable items for all backend implementations.

6.6.2 Separation and Composition of Concerns

The collaboration-based design of the incrementally growing family of language-model variants precludes certain abstraction mismatches, to begin with (i.e., decomposition mismatches on the feature dimension). In addition, DjDSL mitigates decomposition mismatches at a lower level. Recall that iteration 3, adding collection support, introduced structure to represent multiplicity ranges on attributes and references (lowerBound and upperBound). The base language-model treats attributes and references as unrelated entities (classifiers). Typically, this would

---

[14]It can be discussed controversially whether the variability model should be refined, by merging these sub-features, or whether the implementation should be adopted to reflect the modeled variability more directly. The point to stress here is that DjDSL does *not* restrict these decision options.

require the DSL developer to define the structure twice (and related behavior); once for attributes, once for references. The result are code clones. DjDSL collaborations, however, are capable of introducing generalization relationships (superclasses). The collaboration Collection, therefore, introduced a common ancestor for attributes and references: StructuralFeature. Such superclasses are fully respected when computing the feature-resolution orders in DjDSL (see Sect. 3.2.1).

6.6.3 Unmodified Reuse

Regarding reuse of collaborations defined in early iterations by increments in later iterations, all increments (i.e., collaboration support, internal syntax, external syntax) could be implemented without touching on the code base of previous iterations.

6.6.4 Preplanning

Preplanning in a reactive setting means to anticipate future additions of feature implementations by providing more generic, more reusable structures and behaviors in the designs and implementations of the assets. The only occurrence of preplanning in the Pongo ONM example was the provision of a minimal and standard VISITOR, as a shared infrastructure for all backend implementations in iteration one. The alternative would have been that each backend implements traversals on the language-model instantiations independent from each other, resulting in redundancy.

To summarize, DjDSL offers dedicated abstractions and implementation techniques for growing a DSL family in an incremental manner. In case of unclear or ambiguous requirements, DjDSL allows for revisiting design and implementation decisions without incurring major modifications to an existing code base.

References

1. Apel S, Batory D, Kästner C, Saake G (2013) Feature-oriented software product lines, 1st edn. Springer, Berlin. https://doi.org/10.1007/978-3-642-37521-7
2. Erdweg S, van der Storm T, Völter M, Tratt L, Bosman R, Cook WR, Gerritsen A, Hulshout A, Kelly S, Loh A, Konat G, Molina PJ, Palatnik M, Pohjonen R, Schindler E, Schindler K, Solmi R, Vergu V, Visser E, van der Vlist K, Wachsmuth G, van der Woning J (2015) Evaluating and comparing language workbenches: Existing results and benchmarks for the future. Comput Lang Syst Struct 44(Part A):24–47. https://doi.org/10.1016/j.cl.2015.08.007
3. Fowler M (2010) Domain specific languages, 1st edn. Addison-Wesley, Reading
4. Hoisl B, Sobernig S (2015) Towards benchmarking evolution support in model-to-text transformation systems. In: Proceedings of the 4th Workshop on the Analysis of Model

Transformations (AMT@MoDELS 2015). CEUR-WS.org, CEUR workshop proceeding, vol 1500, pp 16–25. http://ceur-ws.org/Vol-1500/paper3.pdf

5. Kolovos D (2018) Pongo: 5 minute tutorial. Available at: https://github.com/kolovos/pongo/wiki/5-Minute-Tutorial

6. Kolovos D, Williams JR (2015) Pongo: Java POJO generator for MongoDB. Available at: https://github.com/kolovos/pongo/

7. Kolovos D, Rose L, García-Domínguez A, Paige R (2015) The Epsilon book. Available at: http://www.eclipse.org/epsilon/doc/book/

8. Lopez-Herrejon RE, Batory DS (2001) A standard problem for evaluating product-line methodologies. In: Proceeding of 3rd International Conference Generative and Component-based Software Engineering. Springer, Berlin, pp 10–24

9. Sobernig S (2019) DjDSL. Available at: https://github.com/mrcalvin/djdsl/

10. Störl U, Hauf T, Klettke M, Scherzinger S (2015) Schemaless NoSQL data stores—Object-NoSQL mappers to the rescue? In: Datenbanksysteme Für Business, Technologie und Web (BTW'15). Gesellschaft für Informatik e.V., pp 579–599

11. Zdun U (2010) A DSL toolkit for deferring architectural decisions in DSL-based software design. Inf Softw Technol 52(7):733–748. https://doi.org/10.1016/j.infsof.2010.03.004

Postface

Software systems are developed for frequently changing environments, heterogeneous groups of stakeholders and practitioners as end-users, and ever-varying use cases in mind [4, 11]. For this reason, many software systems target *variability* as a particular quality attribute. Variability denotes the ability to derive different variants of a software system systematically from a common set of design, implementation, and configuration assets. One technical approach to realizing variability in software systems is language-oriented software development. Developing a software system in a language-oriented manner follows the ambition to build an entire software-intensive information system (e.g., an energy-trading system, a software simulator for measurement devices, or an object-to-NoSQL mapper) around one or an integrated set of *domain-specific software languages* (DSL). In addition, for some domains (e.g., software gaming), stakeholders and practitioners are turned into *co-*developers of their language-based software systems.

As parts of variable software systems, DSL must also be able to vary in a systematic and efficient manner. Once in place, a DSL and its specific developer tooling (e.g., editor, code generator) will be confronted with new requirements emerging from the domain of application (e.g., support for new language constructs or optimizations). This has been referred to as *DSL evolution* [3, 8, 10]. As their application domains become related, two or more corresponding DSL will have to be integrated at different levels. This has been referred to as *domain globalization* [1]. Apart from drivers specific to the domains, DSL can be modularized to serve similar *niche domains* based on a common core of design, implementation, and tooling assets (*language kernels*; [5, 13]). Similarly, a DSL can be a vehicle to modernize a legacy software system. In this setting, the stepwise introduction of a growing DSL has been identified as critical [2].

In software language engineering, a variable DSL is implemented as a DSL product line (or DSL family). A *DSL product line* [6–9] can be used to derive different DSL as the variants (products) of the product line. The DSL product line can also be used to analyze static properties of the members of a language

© Springer Nature Switzerland AG 2020
S. Sobernig, *Variable Domain-specific Software Languages with DjDSL*,
https://doi.org/10.1007/978-3-030-42152-6

(DSL) family or to include variability into test plans. A DSL product line aims at realizing important properties of a variable DSL or DSL family. To begin with, base assets of a DSL family (abstract syntax, context conditions, concrete syntax etc.) can be reused when developing or deriving DSL variants without prior modification or adaptation (*unmodified reuse*). Second, the different features that characterize different DSL variants should be traceable across the levels of domain analysis, architecture, design, and implementation (*feature mapping* and *feature traceability*). Third, finally, a DSL product line should minimize the need for preplanning or anticipating the addition of new features and, therefore, new DSL variants to the family (*preplanning effort*).

Implementing DSL Families Using DjDSL

This book presents the *multi-DSL development system* DjDSL.[1] At the state of the art, DjDSL combines and extends techniques of modelware and grammarware approaches to facilitate the development of DSL product lines in a unique manner. DjDSL supports the integrated development of internal, external, and mixed DSL with one or several textual syntaxes. Internal DSL can be developed using an object-oriented framework (`djdsl::dada`) that provides support for a large variety of DSL design and implementation patterns. External DSL can be developed based on a parser framework (`djdsl::opeg`) driven by object parsing-expression grammars (OPEG). DSL variability can be modeled explicitly, using a built-in variability modeling and analysis environment (`djdsl::vle`). Whatever the DSL style adopted, core assets of DSL families in DjDSL such as the abstract syntax and the context conditions can be designed and implemented using canonical and composable language models (`djdsl::lm` and `djdsl::ctx`). In addition, core assets such as abstract syntax and context conditions can be developed in a platform-independent manner or in a platform-specific manner. For the former option, DjDSL provides UML extensions (profiles) and a battery of model-to-text transformations.

Equipped with these, DjDSL allows for feature mapping, feature traceability, unmodified reuse, and minimal preplanning (see Chap. 6). The features modeled by a DjDSL variability model are mapped to *collaborations* as the basic building block of DjDSL language models (collaboration-based designs). Based on a feature selection, a composition of collaborations forms a concrete language model of one specific DSL variant. Once mapped, a feature can be traced to all related implementation artifacts (language model, abstract syntax, and concrete syntax; whether internal or external); and vice versa. Unmodified reuse of abstract syntax (language models), context conditions, and concrete syntax is realized by a mix of composition techniques. As for language models, collaborations, refinement chains, and collaboration-aware linearization serve this common goal. Context conditions

---

[1]Documentation, tutorials, and distributions are available from the supplemental repository [12].

can be composed using an array of four different techniques (trimming, overriding, combining, and templating). Concrete-syntax definitions and the associated syntax processors can be combined by means of advanced object composition (i.e., decorator mixins) for internal DSL and by means of grammar composition (i.e., composable parsing expression grammars) for external DSL. Preplanning is minimized by providing advanced forms of composition. These include fine-grained grammar transformations and derivatives for parsing grammars.

To the best of my knowledge, DjDSL is original as a language-based compositional development system for DSL product lines. It is not only unique in that DjDSL embodies the above conceptual and technical contributions, but also with respect to its broader view on DSL variability. Developing variable DSL requires DSL development systems that support variable DSL development procedures (see Sect. 2.1) and variable design-decision making (see Sect. 2.2). DjDSL allows a DSL developer to postpone and to revise critical design decisions for an entire DSL family (e.g., internal vs. external DSL). At the design and at the implementation level, a DSL developer can even inject previously unanticipated variation points for a DSL family (e.g., to be matched by new variants or to consolidate the existing ones).

References

1. Deantoni J, Brun C, Caillaud B, France RB, Karsai G, Nierstrasz O, Syriani E (2015) Domain globalization: Using languages to support technical and social coordination. In: Proceedings of the International Dagstuhl Seminar on Globalizing Domain-specific Languages. Lecture notes in computer science, vol 9400. Springer, Berlin, pp 70–87. https://doi.org/10.1007/978-3-319-26172-0_5
2. Fehrenbach S, Erdweg S, Ostermann K (2013) Software evolution to domain-specific languages. In: Proceedings of the Sixth International Conference on Software Language Engineering (SLE'13). Lecture notes in computer science, vol 8225. Springer, Berlin, pp 96–116. https://doi.org/10.1007/978-3-319-02654-1_6
3. Fister IJ, Kosar T, Fister I, Mernik M (2013) Easytime++: A case study of incremental domain-specific language development. Inf Technol Control 42(1):77–85. https://doi.org/10.5755/j01.itc.42.1.1968
4. Galster M, Avgeriou P, Männistö T, Weyns D (2014) Variability in software architecture—State of the art. J Syst Softw 91:1–2. https://doi.org/10.1016/j.jss.2014.01.051
5. Hasu T (2017) Programming language techniques for niche platforms. PhD Thesis, University of Bergen
6. Jézéquel JM, Méndez-Acuña D, Degueule T, Combemale B, Barais O (2015) When systems engineering meets software language engineering. In: Proceedings of the Fifth International Conference on Complex Systems Design and Management (CSD&M'14). Springer, Berlin, pp 1–13. https://doi.org/10.1007/978-3-319-11617-4_1
7. Kühn T, Cazzola W, Olivares DM (2015) Choosy and picky: Configuration of language product lines. In: Proceedings of the 19th International Conference on Software Product Line (SPLC'15). ACM, New York, pp 71–80. https://doi.org/10.1145/2791060.2791092
8. Liebig J, Daniel R, Apel S (2013) Feature-oriented language families: A case study. In: Proceedings of the Seventh International Workshop on Variability Modelling of Software-Intensive Systems (VaMoS'13). ACM, New York, pp 11:1–11:8. https://doi.org/10.1145/2430502.2430518

9. Méndez-Acuña D, Galindo JA, Degueule T, Combemale B, Baudry B (2016) Leveraging software product lines engineering in the development of external DSLs: A systematic literature review. Comput Lang Syst Struct 46:206–235. https://doi.org/10.1016/j.cl.2016.09. 004
10. Meyers B (2016) A multi-paradigm modelling approach to design and evolution of domain-specific modelling languages. PhD Thesis, University of Antwerpen
11. Neumann G, Sobernig S, Aram M (2014) Evolutionary business information systems: Perspectives and challenges of an emerging class of information systems. Bus Inf Syst Eng 6(1):33–38. https://doi.org/10.1007/s12599-013-0305-1
12. Sobernig S (2019) DjDSL. https://github.com/mrcalvin/djdsl/
13. Völter M, Benz S, Dietrich C, Engelmann B, Helander M, Kats LCL, Visser E, Wachsmuth G (2013) DSL engineering: Designing, implementing and using domain-specific languages. dslbook.org, http://www.dslbook.org

Appendix A
A PEG for Object Parsing-Expression Grammars

This is the parsing-expression grammar (PEG, in E/BNF notational style) defining an extended PEG notation (again, in E/BNF notational style) to support DjDSL's object parsing expressions. The grammar snippets and parsing expressions presented throughout this book, in particular Chap. 5, are recognized by the packrat parser defined by and generated from this PEG.

```
PEG an_opeg_grammar (Grammar)
leaf: ALNUM          ← '<' 'a' 'l' 'n' 'u' 'm' '>' WHITESPACE ;
leaf: ALPHA          ← '<' 'a' 'l' 'p' 'h' 'a' '>' WHITESPACE ;
leaf: AND            ← '&' WHITESPACE ;
void: APOSTROPH      ← '\'' ;
leaf: ASCII          ← '<' 'a' 's' 'c' 'i' 'i' '>' WHITESPACE ;
Attribute            ← (VOID / LEAF) COLON ;
Char                 ← CharSpecial / CharOctalFull / CharOctalPart /
     CharUnicode / CharUnescaped ;
leaf: CharOctalFull  ← '\\' [0-2] [0-7] [0-7] ;
leaf: CharOctalPart  ← '\\' [0-7] [0-7]? ;
leaf: CharSpecial    ← '\\' ('n' / 'r' / 't' / '\'' / '\"' / '\[' /
     '\]' / '\\') ;
leaf: CharUnescaped  ← !'\\' . ;
leaf: CharUnicode    ← '\\' 'u' <xdigit> (<xdigit> (<xdigit> <xdigit
     >?)?)? ;
Class                ← OPENB (!CLOSEB Range)* CLOSEB WHITESPACE ;
Ctor                 ← OPENCB WHITESPACE Command WHITESPACE OPENCB
     WHITESPACE ;
void: CLOSE          ← ')' WHITESPACE ;
void: CLOSEB         ← '\]' ;
void: COLON          ← ':' WHITESPACE ;
void: COMMENT        ← '#' (!EOL .)* EOL ;
leaf: CONTROL        ← '<' 'c' 'o' 'n' 't' 'r' 'o' 'l' '>' WHITESPACE
     ;
leaf: Command        ← Word (WHITESPACE Word)*;
```

© Springer Nature Switzerland AG 2020
S. Sobernig, *Variable Domain-specific Software Languages with DjDSL*,
https://doi.org/10.1007/978-3-030-42152-6

```
void: DAPOSTROPH    ← '\"' ;
leaf: DDIGIT        ← '<' 'd' 'd' 'i' 'g' 'i' 't' '>' WHITESPACE ;
Definition          ← Attribute? Identifier IS Expression SEMICOLON
    ;
leaf: DIGIT         ← '<' 'd' 'i' 'g' 'i' 't' '>' WHITESPACE ;
leaf: DOT           ← '.' WHITESPACE ;
void: EOF           ← !. ;
void: EOL           ← '\n' / '\r' ;
Expression          ← Sequence (SLASH Sequence)* ;
void: Final         ← 'E' 'N' 'D' WHITESPACE SEMICOLON WHITESPACE ;
Grammar             ← WHITESPACE Header Definition* Final EOF ;
leaf: GRAPH         ← '<' 'g' 'r' 'a' 'p' 'h' '>' WHITESPACE ;
Header              ← PEG Identifier StartExpr ;
# leaf: Ident       ← ('_' / <alpha>) ('_' / <alnum>)* ;
leaf: Ident         ← '::' <alnum>+ ('::' / <alnum>+)* / ('_' / <
    alpha>) ('_' / <alnum>)* ;
Identifier          ← Ident WHITESPACE ;
Field               ← Ident WHITESPACE COLON WHITESPACE Suffix ;
void: IS            ← '<' '-' WHITESPACE ;
leaf: LEAF          ← 'l' 'e' 'a' 'f' WHITESPACE ;
Literal             ← APOSTROPH (!APOSTROPH Char)* APOSTROPH
    WHITESPACE / DAPOSTROPH (!DAPOSTROPH Char)* DAPOSTROPH
    WHITESPACE ;
leaf: LOWER         ← '<' 'l' 'o' 'w' 'e' 'r' '>' WHITESPACE ;
leaf: NOT           ← '!' WHITESPACE ;
void: OPEN          ← '(' WHITESPACE ;
void: OPENB         ← '\[' ;
void: OPENCB        ← ' ' ;
void: PEG           ← 'O' 'P' 'E' 'G' !('_' / ':' / <alnum>)
    WHITESPACE ;
leaf: PLUS          ← '+' WHITESPACE ;
    Prefix          ← (AND / NOT)? Suffix ;
    Primary         ← ALNUM / ALPHA / ASCII / CONTROL / DDIGIT /
        DIGIT / GRAPH / LOWER /
                    PRINTABLE / PUNCT / SPACE / UPPER / WORDCHAR /
                        XDIGIT / Identifier /
                    OPEN Expression CLOSE / Literal / Class / DOT
                        ;
leaf: PRINTABLE     ← '<' 'p' 'r' 'i' 'n' 't' '>' WHITESPACE ;
leaf: PUNCT         ← '<' 'p' 'u' 'n' 'c' 't' '>' WHITESPACE ;
leaf: QUESTION      ← '?' WHITESPACE ;
    Range           ← Char TO Char / Char ;
void: SEMICOLON     ← ';' WHITESPACE ;
    Sequence        ← Ctor? (Field / Prefix)+ ;
void: SLASH         ← '/' WHITESPACE ;
leaf: SPACE         ← '<' 's' 'p' 'a' 'c' 'e' '>' WHITESPACE ;
leaf: STAR          ← '*' WHITESPACE ;
    StartExpr       ← OPEN Expression CLOSE ;
    Suffix          ← Primary (QUESTION / STAR / PLUS)? ;
void: TO            ← '-' ;
leaf: UPPER         ← '<' 'u' 'p' 'p' 'e' 'r' '>' WHITESPACE ;
leaf: VOID          ← 'v' 'o' 'i' 'd' WHITESPACE ;
```

```
void: WHITESPACE      ← (<space> / COMMENT)* ;
leaf: WORDCHAR        ← '<' 'w' 'o' 'r' 'd' 'c' 'h' 'a' 'r' '>'
    WHITESPACE ;
leaf: Word            ← '$'? <wordchar>+ / '{' Command '}';
leaf: XDIGIT          ← '<' 'x' 'd' 'i' 'g' 'i' 't' '>' WHITESPACE ;
END;
```

Index

Printed in the United States
by Baker & Taylor Publisher Services

Printed in the United States
by Baker & Taylor Publisher Services